#MeToo and Literary Studies

Reading, Writing, and Teaching about Sexual Violence and Rape Culture

Edited by Mary K. Holland and Heather Hewett

BLOOMSBURY ACADEMIC
NEW YORK • LONDON • OXFORD • NEW DELHI • SYDNEY

BLOOMSBURY ACADEMIC
Bloomsbury Publishing Inc
1385 Broadway, New York, NY 10018, USA
50 Bedford Square, London, WC1B 3DP, UK
29 Earlsfort Terrace, Dublin 2, Ireland

BLOOMSBURY, BLOOMSBURY ACADEMIC and the Diana logo are trademarks
of Bloomsbury Publishing Plc

First published in the United States of America 2021

Copyright © Mary K. Holland and Heather Hewett, 2021
Each chapter Copyright © by the contributor, 2021

For legal purposes the Acknowledgments on pp. xii–xiii constitute an extension
of this copyright page.

Cover design by Alice Marwick

All rights reserved. No part of this publication may be reproduced or transmitted
in any form or by any means, electronic or mechanical, including photocopying,
recording, or any information storage or retrieval system, without prior
permission in writing from the publishers.

Bloomsbury Publishing Inc does not have any control over, or responsibility for,
any third-party websites referred to or in this book. All internet addresses given
in this book were correct at the time of going to press. The author and publisher
regret any inconvenience caused if addresses have changed or sites have ceased
to exist, but can accept no responsibility for any such changes.

Whilst every effort has been made to locate copyright holders the publishers
would be grateful to hear from any person(s) not here acknowledged.

A catalog record for this book is available from the Library of Congress.

	ISBN:	HB:	978-1-5013-7274-2
		PB:	978-1-5013-7273-5
		ePDF:	978-1-5013-7276-6
		eBook:	978-1-5013-7275-9

Typeset by Integra Software Services Pvt. Ltd.
Printed and bound in the United States of America

To find out more about our authors and books visit www.bloomsbury.com
and sign up for our newsletters.

PRAISE FOR #*METOO AND LITERARY STUDIES*

"Mary K. Holland and Heather Hewett's *#MeToo and Literary Studies* is a tour de force, a groundbreaking gathering of feminist scholars who have committed themselves to exposing, contextualizing, and challenging the ongoing trauma of sexual violence in popular culture and literature. Spanning antiquity to our current age, this book maps how artists, activists, and academics have both grappled with the devastating reality of sexual assault, while also imagining beyond the trauma and giving us a collective way forward. *#MeToo and Literary Studies* is an urgent, transformative, and mandatory read."

—SALAMISHAH TILLET, *Henry Rutgers Professor of African American Studies and Creative Writing, Rutgers University, Newark, USA, and author of* In Search of the Color Purple: The Story of an American Masterpiece

"The essays in this exciting collection by a diverse group of feminist scholars make the case that the study of literature is also a performance of activism. *#MeToo and Literary Studies* charts representations of rape culture across geographies both local and global, and wide-ranging texts from communities subjected to sexual violence. The book persuasively demonstrates how literature freshly analyzed through critically engaged writing and innovative pedagogies can lead to radical social change. A crucial anthology for our dark times."

—NANCY K. MILLER, *Distinguished Professor of English and Comparative Literature, The CUNY Graduate Center, USA, and author of* My Brilliant Friends: Our Lives in Feminism

"*#MeToo and Literary Studies* provides a crucial, fascinating, and truly comprehensive deep dive into the vexed relationship between rape culture and literary texts spanning over two thousand years, from Ovid to Jaquira Díaz. The breadth of perspectives canvassed—and interrogated—makes it a breathtaking feat, and a highly necessary volume, for any feminist thinker."

—KATE MANNE, *Associate Professor of Philosophy, Cornell University, USA, and author of* Entitled: How Male Privilege Hurts Women

"#MeToo is a powerful hashtag, rallying cry, and cudgel. But lasting change requires association, deep thinking, and nuance—and for that, we turn to literature. *#MeToo and Literary Studies* beautifully demonstrates how writers have been describing the realities of sexual violence for decades, and how literary analysis can help provoke meaningful transformation of rape culture."

—JENNIFER BAUMGARDNER, *writer, activist, editor, and publisher; director of* It Was Rape *and co-author of* Manifesta

"This collection of timely, wide-ranging, and diverse essays demonstrates the power of #MeToo to reframe prior debates *and* silences in literary studies. The editors make a compelling case for #MeToo storytelling as part of a long history of representing sexual violence in literature. The essays interweave literary studies, social activism, and pedagogy in generative new readings. *#MeToo and Literary Studies* is essential reading and invaluable equipment for scholars, teachers, and students engaging with rape culture, misogyny, and literature."

—LEIGH GILMORE, *Visiting Professor of English, The Ohio State University, USA, and author of* Tainted Witness: Why We Doubt What Women Say About Their Lives

"Fighting rape culture starts with making it visible. *#MeToo and Literary Studies* does that and so much more. It uses literature to expose the cultural normalization of sexual violence and finds in pedagogy the building blocks necessary to produce a viable alternative. It is scholarly activism at its best."

—CARINE MARDOROSSIAN, *Professor of English and Global Gender Studies, University at Buffalo, NY, USA and author of* Framing the Rape Victim: Gender and Agency Reconsidered

"*#MeToo and Literary Studies* belongs in every English department in middle schools, high schools, and in higher education. It should be read and discussed by English teachers in department meetings across the school year and every year. Wholly committed to intersectionality and dismantling systems of domination and power, each chapter offers starting points for addressing sexual violence, rape, and harassment in not only literature but also in our schools, universities, and communities. As a high school English teacher who has been in the classroom for nearly 25 years addressing sexual violence both pedagogically and institutionally, I wish I had had this book much sooner in my work as a feminist teacher-activist. I can keep fighting the good fight now that this book exists."

—ILEANA JIMÉNEZ, *founder of Feminist Teacher, @feministteacher*

*For survivors,
readers,
writers, and
teachers
everywhere*

CONTENTS

List of Figures xi
Acknowledgments xii

Introduction: Literary Studies as Literary Activism
Heather Hewett and Mary K. Holland 1

PART I: Critical Practices

1 "Dismissed, trivialized, misread": Re-examining the Reception of Women's Literature through the #MeToo Movement
   Janet Badia 31

2 Reading Survivor Narratives: Literary Criticism as Feminist Solidarity
   Tanya Serisier 43

3 Evoking the Specter of White Feminism in the #MeToo Movement: Publishing Memoirs and the Cultural Memory of American Feminism
   Amanda Spallacci 57

4 Pricing Black Girl Pain: The Cost of Black Girlhood in Street Lit
   Jacinta R. Saffold 71

5 From #MMIW to #NotInvisible: Indigenous Women in the #MeToo Era
   Kasey Jones-Matrona 83

6 Credibility and Doubt in the Age of #MeToo
   Namrata Mitra and Katherine Conner   99

7 Quite Possibly the Last Essay I Need to Write about David Foster Wallace
   Mary K. Holland   113

PART II: Re-readings

8 Philomela's Tapestry and #MeToo: Reading Ovid in an Indian Feminist Classroom
   Aditi Joshi, Anushka Srivastava, Katyayani, Mahwash Akhter, Prasanta Bani Ekka, Shivangi Tiwary, Shweta, and Zahanat   135

9 "Beware of the delusions of fancy!": Silencing and Rape Culture in Hannah Webster Foster's *The Coquette*
   Hannah Herndon   151

10 "Fearful of being pursued, yet determined to persevere": *Northanger Abbey* and the #MeToo Movement
   Douglas Murray   163

11 The Limits of #MeToo in India: Re-reading Bapsi Sidhwa's *Cracking India* and Deepa Mehta's *Earth*
   Nidhi Shrivastava   175

12 Intimate Violence and Sexual Assault in Kopano Matlwa's *Coconut:* Carving Spaces of Feminist Liberation in Post-Apartheid South African Literature
   Nafeesa T. Nichols   187

13 The Other Men of #MeToo: Male Rape in Hanya Yanagihara's *A Little Life*, Sapphire's *The Kid*, and Amber Tamblyn's *Any Man*
   Robin E. Field   199

14 Reading Junot Díaz after Me Too and #MeToo
Ann Marie Alfonso Short   211

PART III: Pedagogy: Practices and Methods

15 Beyond Safe Spaces: Working toward Access and Accountability Using Trauma-Informed Pedagogy
Maureen McDonnell   225

16 Trigger Warnings: An Ethics for Tutoring #MeToo Content and Rape Narratives in Writing Centers
Beth Walker   235

17 From Sympathy to Detoxification: Pedagogical Approaches for Dismantling Rape Culture
Jeremy Posadas   245

18 Theorizing "Toxic" Masculinity across Cultures and Nations: The Case of Achebe's *Things Fall Apart*
Heather Hewett   259

19 "I said nothing": Teaching *Corregidora* and Black Women's Relationship to Consent
Carlyn Ferrari   275

20 "Teach as if you aren't afraid of getting fired": A Queer Survivor's Use of Restorative Justice Circles to Embrace Vulnerability in the Classroom
Sarah Goldbort   287

21 Praxis of Empowerment: Latina Decolonial Feminist Pedagogy and Jaquira Díaz's *Ordinary Girls*
Roberta Hurtado   297

PART IV: Pedagogy: Classroom Contexts

22 Teaching the #MeToo Memoir: Creating Empathy in the First-Year College Classroom
Elif S. Armbruster   311

23 Teaching Courtly Love in the Medieval Literature Classroom: Desire, Consent, and the #MeToo Movement
Sara V. Torres and Rebecca F. McNamara 323

24 Centering Black Women in the Classroom: Teaching Harriet Jacobs's *Incidents in the Life of a Slave Girl* after #MeToo
Linda Chavers 339

25 Lessons in Credibility and Complicity in Two Modern Dramas
Amy B. Hagenrater-Gooding 351

26 An Impulse toward Agency: Teaching Scenes of Sexual Violence in Afro-Latina/o/x Literature
Ethan Madarieta 361

27 New Approaches to Short Fiction and Nonfiction in the Classroom: Challenging Violence from Queer and Straight Perspectives
Zoë Brigley Thompson 375

28 Recruiting Warriors: Using Literature in College Classrooms to Fight and Win "The Longest War"
Candice L. Pipes 389

Notes on Contributors 401
Index 408

FIGURES

5.1 #MMIW Twitter Post, late 2019   91

5.2 Native News Online Twitter Chat Announcement, October 8, 2019   92

5.3 MMIW USA Facebook Page, 2020   93

27.1 Triad of Contexts in Experiences of Violence. Created by Zoë Brigley Thompson, 2020   377

27.2 Strategies in Representing Violence. Created by Zoë Brigley Thompson, 2020   379

ACKNOWLEDGMENTS

(Mary) I thank the many women who bravely wrote and spoke about their experiences of sexual harassment, coercion, and assault in the initial outpouring of testimony when #MeToo reignited in 2017. I also thank the journalists who brought their stories to a wider audience, some of whom, like me, had so far failed to fully recognize—in their lived lives, rather than in theory—that this diversity of experience delineates a widely ranging spectrum of sexual violence and patriarchal oppression. Some of those stories kept me up all night, revolutionized my understanding of my past, transformed my research and teaching—and sparked the idea for this book. They also changed my life. Such transformations do not happen in isolation: I am deeply grateful for the people who continue to support me in working through what this understanding means for myself and my work, especially Shirl, who has been by my side from the beginning; Kirsten, with whom I work through everything; and my dear friend and co-editor Heather, from whom I have learned much over a decade of annual writing retreats and through this beautiful collaboration, and whose wise friendship helped me see and begin to say what I need to. I am enormously grateful for the unquestioning support and companionship of my boys—now young men—Evan and Camden, whose ability to dance between discussions of feminism and Star Wars lore at the dinner table delights me. As always, my deepest gratitude goes to Jeff, who showed me from the start what true acceptance is, and reminds me of it every day.

(Heather) Years ago, I read women's literature in a classroom taught by the brilliant Susan Stanford Friedman, who showed me how tracing the Woolfian spider threads connecting a text to its writer could engender a feminism rooted in both narrative and lived experience. Thank you to her and to the many writers who have courageously shared their stories, trusting that their words would change the world. They have. Thanks to my lifelong friends and writing partners Daphne Uviller and Deborah Siegel-Acevedo, who have believed in me for decades. Thanks to Alison Varianides for her astute counsel, to my students for teaching me, and to my departmental colleagues for enabling me to make collaboration a central part of my teaching and writing life. To my current collaborator extraordinaire and dear friend Mary, who has traveled with me on an amazing journey that took us from writing retreats to this book: I can still remember that first day we sat down to talk at Linwood. I am so grateful we kept on talking. I have learned so much from your perseverance, your indefatigable work ethic, and your intellectual courage. Thanks to my kids, who have supported me even when my work has demanded my full attention. Finally, to Matthew: your unwavering support, love, sense of humor, and wisdom undergird it all. I am grateful for our life together each and every day.

We are immensely grateful to Haaris and Bloomsbury for believing in this project and being willing to bring the whole huge thing into print at a time when publishers everywhere are struggling. Finally, thanks to our contributors, whose essays show us all the way forward as critics, teachers, and readers.

Introduction:
Literary Studies as Literary Activism

Heather Hewett and Mary K. Holland

#MeToo began in 2006 when Tarana Burke, crushed by how many middle-school girls in Selma, Alabama reported experiencing sexual violence, responded on MySpace with "Me Too."[1] It became a widespread phenomenon in 2017 when, after a *New York Times* investigation of sexual misconduct allegations against film executive Harvey Weinstein, a wave of celebrities followed Alyssa Milano in using the hashtag on Twitter to express their solidarity with Rose McGowan, Ashley Judd, and others publicly accusing Weinstein of sexual crimes ranging from harassment to rape.[2] Over the year following Milano's initial tweet, the #MeToo hashtag was used more than 19 million times on Twitter.[3] At the time of our writing, it remains a powerfully present cultural movement against rape culture and the misogyny that enables it, because of the tireless work of Burke and many other activists.

But #MeToo has by no means supported all victims of sexual violence equally. Within weeks of its stunning explosion in mid-October 2017, critics began to point out its limits, noting that it quickly became and remained centered on the experiences of privileged white cisgender women, while largely ignoring the suffering of women of color, Indigenous women, LGBTQ+ individuals, people with disabilities, and low-income populations.[4] Within months, lofty claims of its global effects were disproved by articles that documented its geographical limits and argued that it has failed to gain much ground in regions where women are denied legal protections and where complex legacies of patriarchy, colonialism, neoliberalism, authoritarianism, war, and a range of identity-based oppressions systematically thwart feminist social movements.[5] One year later, we began to hear from those who had bravely responded to its call for battle by reporting their own experiences of sexual harassment and assault, only to be cut down publicly "like front-line soldiers"—disbelieved and shamed in front of courtrooms (or, in the case of Dr. Blasey Ford, an entire country), threatened by lawyers and employers, fired, sickened by stress, even losing custody of their children.[6]

Meanwhile, real change has happened. #MeToo has spurred new activist movements, such as #TimesUp in the United States and the UK and the NOW campaign in Australia, and legal reform steps have been taken in France, China, Spain, Morocco, and elsewhere.[7] It has intersected with existing movements, such as #NiUnaMenos across Latin America, and has been reimagined as additional campaigns, such as #KuToo in Japan.[8] It has enabled journalists to undertake and publish investigative work, thus lending credibility to victim-survivors. Titans in the entertainment, news, politics, and media industries worldwide who used their power to sexually harass, assault, and rape have been imprisoned or driven out of their powerful positions (Harvey Weinstein, Roger Ailes, and Bill Cosby, to name but a few), and attorneys have had more success in prosecuting cases of sexual violence.[9] In the United States, thousands of rape kits that sat untested on shelves for decades are finally being processed.[10] Popular culture has begun to reflect on (and educate viewers about) aspects of misogyny and sexual abuse that had long been largely confined to activist spaces, academic journals, and select college classrooms, including testimonial injustice, gaslighting, and victim shaming, as in films and television shows such as *The Tale*, *Unbelievable*, and *Second Assault*.

And scholars and educators are addressing sexual assault, rape culture, and the power dynamics of misogyny and structural violence in publications, classrooms, and conferences with renewed energy and wider awareness. This book is a first attempt to collect individual literary scholars' and teachers' responses to #MeToo, understand the currents of thought and practice that unite and power them, and communicate those to the wider field of literary studies—to connect our individual efforts into a collective endeavor.

Before #MeToo: A (Brief) Genealogy of Sexual Violence and Literary Studies

Much of the power of #MeToo lies in the power of storytelling: the voicing of individual traumatic experience, shared with others who listen and support the victim; the creation of a community of individual victims who collectively bear witness to the larger problem of violence and in so doing dismantle silence, shame, and stigma; and the conviction that rape culture, while pervasive, is not acceptable, and that those who inflict harm and benefit from existing distributions of power must be held to account. It is testimony that Leigh Gilmore (2019) describes as providing a "vivid example of the autobiographical first-person interrupting dynamics of erasure and silencing" (162). While an example of hashtag activism fully borne of the digital era, #MeToo has its roots in over two centuries of activism, advocacy work, and writing about sexual violence.

The history of fighting against sexual violence—making it visible, seeking to end it, working to change culture—has multiple global origins and stretches back far beyond the twenty-first century. In the United States, Black women were the first to testify and organize against the use of rape and sexual violence as a means of intimidation and control of Black people during slavery and Jim Crow, continuing this fight into the Civil Rights Movement.[11] In the early to mid-1970s, local feminist activists established battered women's shelters, rape crisis centers, and speak-outs in the United States and across Europe.[12] Likewise, in the mid-to-late 1970s, local feminist activists turned their focus to violence across Latin America (particularly state violence against women) and Asia (particularly the issue of "comfort women" in Korea, and dowry death in India and Bangladesh).[13] The convergence of these movements helped to form transnational networks focused on violence against women in the early 1980s and in the following decades.[14]

In the mid-twentieth century, this activism converged with feminist theorizing and a new wave of writing committed to understand, document, and end sexual violence. Feminist work in literary studies during this period—producing literature; excavating, theorizing, and teaching the work of forgotten and overlooked writers; re-reading canonical texts—was affected by, and in turn affected, this activism. In the United States, feminist journalists such as Susan Brownmiller, author of *Against Our Will: Men, Women, and Rape* (1975), helped to bring "the ideas of the feminist anti-rape movement into the mainstream" (Cohen 2015); and a little over a decade later, Robin Warshaw exposed the prevalence of date and acquaintance rape on college campuses in *I Never Called It Rape* (1988). T. V. Reed (2016) reminds us that the writing of new literature, particularly poetry, was "a tool of social change" in the 1960s and 1970s as it enabled feminists to create a "new language" with which to "characterize the experiences of oppression and liberation" and to challenge "the separation of private and public spheres" (91, 93). Poets such as Adrienne Rich, Audre Lorde, Marge Piercy, June Jordan, Sonia Sanchez, Cherríe Moraga, and others wrote about formerly taboo topics, including rape and sexual violence, using poetry "as part of an ongoing dialogue about the nature(s) and purpose(s) of feminism(s)" (94). The scholarly examination of a range of literary genres central to cultural understandings of rape continues. For example, Robin Field (2020) traces the development of the twentieth-century "rape novel" in the United States during the 1970s and 1980s, a category that includes such authors as Toni Morrison, Gayl Jones, Maxine Hong Kingston, Marilyn French, Alice Walker, and Sandra Cisneros; and Tanya Serisier's (2018) examination of "speaking out" includes a chapter on the "boom" of "rape memoirs" published in the United States and the UK beginning in the mid-1990s.[15]

Feminist literary scholars' criticism on such writing, along with their theorizing more broadly, contributed to these shifts in cultural understanding. Some scholars reevaluated earlier writing, such as Jean Fagan Yellin's work beginning in the 1970s that helped to establish the authenticity and authorship of *Incidents in the Life of a Slave Girl* (1861), an autobiographical account documenting the sexual abuse Harriet Jacobs experienced as an enslaved Black woman.[16] Other scholars produced readings of rape and sexual violence in canonical literature, exposing them for the violent acts they were; Kate Millet's *Sexual Politics* (1970) is a paradigmatic example of such criticism. Over the next several decades, feminist critics explored representations of rape across literature, film, and media. For example, Lynn A. Higgins and Brenda R. Silver (1991) noted the existence of textual patterns of the "obsessive inscription—and an obsessive erasure—of sexual violence against women," calling for feminist modes of "reading rape" that demonstrate how "the politics and aesthetics of rape are one" (1). They argued that literary representations of rape must be understood literally, and that critics must return rape to the body; rather than read rape as a trope for something else, feminists must engage in a "critical act of reading the violence and the sexuality back into texts where it has been deflected, either by the text itself or by the critics" (4). Such re-literalizing would, they hoped, enable feminist critics to end sexual violence.[17]

Despite these feminist interventions, Carine M. Mardorossian claimed in 2002 that feminists needed to do more. In "Toward a New Feminist Theory of Rape," she argued that a decline of serious feminist theorizing about rape in the 1990s, combined with the publication of bestselling books by conservative authors including Katie Roiphe, Camille Paglia, and Christina Sommers, meant that political backlash now "set the tone and the parameters for the analysis of rape in the public sphere" (748). She further argued that postmodernism, with its profound skepticism about truth and language's ability to articulate it, brought to feminism a "wariness" about women's experience, so that "the practice of making the experience of victimization visible [was] immediately deemed suspect and undertheorized" (769). Mardorossian's intervention rejected these approaches, instead calling for a retheorizing of rape and its representation predicated on the understanding that "all violence is, in fact, sexual(ized) violence" and that gender is "always already constructed through multiple relations of class, race, and context" (3).

Mardorossian's theoretical approach is in conversation with many other scholars and writers, especially Black, women of color, Indigenous, postcolonial, and decolonial feminists who have long argued that rape is deeply racialized and produced by multiple forms of oppression and violent structures such as colonialism and slavery.[18] During the previous two decades, Black feminist scholars working in literary studies, such as Hazel Carby (1987) and Saidiya

Hartman (1997), had started to examine the function of rape in slavery and the impact of bodily violence on Black women's writing. The essays in the groundbreaking anthology *Transforming a Rape Culture* (Buchwald et al. 1993) provided structural, feminist analyses of sex and violence authored by a mix of activists, professors, theologians, writers, and survivors. The next decade saw additional interdisciplinary collaborations focused on particular groups of victims: *Color of Violence: The INCITE! Anthology* (2006), which brought attention to the violence experienced by women of color and trans people of color, and *Sharing Our Stories of Survival: Native Women Surviving Violence* (Deer et al. 2007).[19] Likewise, collections of survivor narratives centered the voices of marginalized groups, notably Charlotte Pierce-Baker's *Surviving the Silence: Black Women's Stories of Rape* (1998) and *Dangerous Families: Queer Writing on Surviving* (Sycamore 2004). Meanwhile, events such as the 1992–5 Bosnian war and the ensuing circulation of survivor narratives in journalistic work resulted in increased public awareness about the uses of rape as a weapon of war, as well as fictional and semi-fictional accounts about this war and others.[20]

More recent feminist literary and cultural criticism builds on these intersectional and structural understandings of rape. A collection by literary scholars Sorcha Gunne and Zoë Brigley Thompson (2009), for example, examines a diverse array of African, Caribbean, and South Asian texts and calls for nuanced intersectional analyses that move "beyond the victim/perpetrator binary" (9). Gunne (2014) finds that gendered violence in South African literature during and after apartheid extends beyond sexual violence to include many forms of violence.[21] The contributors to *African Women Under Fire: Literary Discourses in War and Conflict* (Uwakweh 2017) examine the impact of war and conflict on gender-based violence in African literary and testimonial narratives.[22]

Scholars have also called for an expanded understanding of what counts as sexual violation (Alcoff 2018), raising difficult questions about the limitations of testimony and the challenges faced by those who give it. Tanya Serisier (2018) further complicates our study of rape accounts by pointing out that sexual violence has not ended despite several decades of stories that "break the silence" of rape, asking us to consider both the strengths and the weaknesses of a "narrative-based politics" (210).[23] While Serisier identifies the problem as the way these accounts are "structured through discourses that see them reproduce gendered or neoliberal understandings of personal responsibility, carceral assumptions about criminality, and racist and class-based discourses about the identities of sexual predators and their victims" (213), Leigh Gilmore (2018) argues that these and other forces render women into "tainted witnesses" when they give testimony: they are "contaminate[d] by doubt, stigmatize[d] through association with gender and race, and dishonor[ed] through shame, such that not only the testimony but the person herself is smeared" (2).[24]

If #MeToo brings renewed focus to sexual violence and the hope that speaking out can create lasting change, it also repeats many of the shortcomings of the anti-rape activism that preceded it. In their book about #MeToo, Bianca Fileborn and Rachel Loney-Howes list some of these problems: the focus on cisgender, white, heterosexual women at the expense of marginalized groups of people; unequal access to "digital justice-seeking" (2019: 9); the question of whether even relatively privileged survivors, such as Dr. Blasey Ford, will be believed; and the challenge of translating the movement into structural and social change. Despite these critiques of the movement, its positive effects continue to be felt globally, as demonstrated by the numerous contributors to the collection *The Global #MeToo Movement* (Noel and Oppenheimer 2020). #MeToo has also "opened the way to longer, specific accounts of sexual violence" (Gilmore 2019: 163) such as Roxane Gay's edited collection *Not That Bad: Dispatches from Rape Culture* (2018) and memoirs such as Terese Marie Mailhot's *Heart Berries* (2018), Chanel Miller's *Know My Name* (2019), and Bri Lee's *Eggshell Skull* (2018).[25] Anthologies of survivor narratives have been published in Australia (Kon-yu et al. 2019), and poetry anthologies have been published in the UK (Alma 2018). The comics anthology *Drawing Power* demonstrates the power of graphic survivor narratives (Noomin 2019), and several collections continue the project of challenging heteronormative understandings of sexual violence, including *Written on the Body: Letters from Trans and Non-Binary Survivors of Sexual Assault and Domestic Violence* (Bean 2018).[26]

These and other texts (including many first-person narratives collected on activist, nonprofit, and media websites) are evidence of the ongoing "subversive work being done by modern and contemporary writers on the subject of sexual violence" (Gunne and Brigley Thompson 2009: 9). This outpouring of literature demands that we listen to victim-survivors' stories, even as we contemplate difficult questions about how they are rendered in character, narrative, language, and genre, and in relation to audiences, "testimonial networks," and possibilities for social change (Gilmore 2018: 3). Thus, this volume picks up and extends recent interdisciplinary feminist scholarship on sexual violence, focusing on the tools and capacities of literary studies—teaching and writing about literature—and proceeding with renewed inspiration from the victim-survivors who have shared their stories and demanded that change.

#MeToo and Literary Studies Today

The impact of #MeToo on popular culture is easily measured in terms of the sheer volume and relentlessness of essays and opinion pieces published since October 2017, in print newspapers and magazines and their websites (*The New York Times, The New Yorker, The Guardian, The Atlantic*, etc.) and on non-print websites (Vox, Bustle, Literary Hub, The Conversation, etc.). Scholarly print publications, always slow to react, have yet to register that impact to any significant degree, but those waves are coming: while at the time of our writing few journal articles or book chapters in literary studies directly address #MeToo, academia.edu (where academics post unpublished scholarly pieces) lists thousands of papers addressing #MeToo, over a thousand of those in literary studies alone. And our own call for papers for this project generated a response whose intensity—in terms of the number of submissions received and the passion expressed by their writers—is unlike anything we have seen before.

The texts examined here span over two thousand years, from Ovid to Jaquira Díaz; represent nearly every major genre and multiple sub-genres, including poetry, drama, short story, novel, personal narrative, memoir, social media, TV, film, and fantasy; and come from far-flung places, including South Africa, Nigeria, England, India, Puerto Rico, and ancient Rome, and multiple regions of the United States: literature everywhere is and always has been a site for exposing and resisting misogyny and cultures of sexual violence. How unsurprising it should be, then, to discover that #MeToo emerged in part out of literature itself, as Janet Badia details in our opening essay. And yet #MeToo is already making its mark on *how* we recognize, theorize, and respond to these themes and critiques, with the potential to, as Badia writes, "disrupt more than just male privilege"—to disrupt literary tradition and history, canon, narrative theory, pedagogical practices, notions of gender, race, ethnicity, and nationality, media studies, and even mainstays of interpretive practice such as the intentional fallacy. Meanwhile, it also adds new urgency—or wakes up academics not yet alert to that urgency—to literary studies' potential to do the kind of activist work that makes real change in the world.

In choosing their subject matter, the authors in this volume use literary studies to respond to many of the problems diagnosed in the #MeToo movement more broadly, not only by foregrounding sexual assault in literature by women of color and LGBTQ+ people, but also by examining the wider cultural movement from a variety of angles. Amanda Spallacci addresses accusations of racial bias head-on by linking the dismissal of work and writing by Burke and other women of color in the #MeToo movement to publishers' marketing of survivor memoirs in the context of second-wave feminism, perpetuating the exclusionary myth that "feminism" describes the work and concerns of only white cisgender women. Other essays take up the question of how we might use attention to traditional and social media not only to examine how survivors narrate and process the trauma of sexual violence, but also to dismantle the misogyny and rape culture that cause it. Namrata Mitra and Katherine Conner examine the politics of credibility on social media, in testimony, and in narrative, and consider how literature allows us to acknowledge the confusion and complexity of sexual desire that public campaigns for credibility force us to deny. Kasey Jones-Matrona demonstrates how literary and social media activism can enhance each other, by drawing attention to how Indigenous women writers link their literature to Indigenous women's social media campaigns, such as #MMIW and #NotInvisible.

Fiction and nonfiction narratives written by authors across the globe remind us that sexual violence, while ubiquitous, is also tied to histories of colonialism, imperialism, racism, and structural inequities, a reality often overlooked by #MeToo. Nafeesa Nichols acknowledges this reality by examining how intimate spaces become sites of sexual violence, and of resistance and agency, for women in post-apartheid South Africa in Kopano Matlwa's *Coconut*, while Roberta Hurtado proposes Latina decolonial feminist pedagogical approaches that make classrooms into spaces where students can identify colonialism and create subversive readings of texts. Linda Chavers proposes a pedagogy that explores the roots of contemporary sexual violence, and of resistance to it, in American slavery. Focusing on cis- and transgender sexual violence in Afro-Latinx literature, Ethan Madarieta offers a nuanced understanding of intersectionality and subjectivity that raises important questions about agency and consent.

Several of these essays address the ubiquity of sexual violence across literature and popular culture by examining rape culture and its thematic presence in both. Sara Torres and Rebecca McNamara propose re-reading Chaucer and other medieval writers to explore the complex ways in which female consent is constructed in relation to male desire as a coerciveness that women still find all too familiar. Similarly, Hannah Herndon and Douglas Murray read literature from the eighteenth and nineteenth centuries (Hannah Webster Foster and Jane Austen) as encoding the same dynamics of gaslighting and domination—women's forced submission masked as politeness—that women struggle against today. Other writers connect rape culture to larger systems of oppression. Eight students of the University of Delhi's Miranda House examine rape culture in Ovid's "Philomela" through a postcolonial lens, tracing it through retellings across the Western literary canon in which rape becomes simultaneously normalized and weaponized. Jacinta Saffold explores how street lit, in its representation of the lived experiences of Black girls and women, both normalizes the systemic exploitation of Black girls and profits from narratives about their pain. Acknowledging the often-ignored reality that rape culture also results in the rape of cis- and transgender men, Robin Field examines literature that confronts the rape of children and adults and the concomitant horror—that such rape can turn victims into perpetrators.

Other essays raise questions about reading, teaching, and writing about literature whose participation in or critique of rape culture remains difficult to discern, or frustratingly invisible to critics. Ann Marie Alfonso Short considers the spotlight thrown on Junot Díaz and his work after an essay in which he described his own experience of childhood rape was quickly followed by accusations against him of sexual assault; she asks how we can acknowledge Díaz's suffering as a survivor while criticizing his behavior as a perpetrator, and how productively to use his complicated history to reflect on constructs of masculine authority in his work. Mary K. Holland raises similar questions about the work of David Foster Wallace—once lionized, recently vilified because of accusations of sexual abuse, still the author of work that addresses in complex and often perceptive ways the suffering of women at the hands of misogynistic men. How must we read such authors differently in the wake of #MeToo? Should we read and teach them at all? What are the proper limits of biography in our teaching? What does it say about misogyny in the academy that the misogyny of these authors' works remained largely uncommented on until popular culture finally became concerned about sexual violence in general?

This relative silence around misogyny and sexual violence in academia reflects the pervasive silencing experienced by women everywhere. With its thousands of voices speaking out about sexual violence and the inevitable punishment of many for it, #MeToo is a stark reminder that patriarchal silencing continues to be the most pervasive and effective way of performing sexual violence and preventing victims from being heard or believed. Several essays in this collection explore how such silencing is enacted or resisted in literature through innovations in literary technique. Thus, they note how literary form records the effects of sexual violence and rape culture on women, and how these formal changes accumulate into new literary traditions. Carlyn Ferrari provides frameworks for students to read the silence of the main character in Gayl Jones's *Corregidora* (1975) in the context of slavery and contemporary Black womanhood, and to recognize the formal methods by which Jones connects the two; students' final personal reflection invites them to participate in breaking the silence whose legacy of suffering the novel has exposed. Nidhi Shrivastava examines representations of raped and abducted women in film and fiction (*Earth* and *Cracking India*) and the limits of bringing these narratives to the mainstream. In the context of teaching new college students, Elif Armbruster suggests methods for using survivor memoirs as opportunities to construct empathy and participate in their resistance to our culture of sexual violence and the silencing around it. Tanya Serisier provides a crucial theoretical framework for reading testimonial about sexual violence by considering the discursiveness of all experience, beginning to map out the tropes and conventions of the genre of the survivor narrative, and exploring how critical work can be an act of political solidarity aimed at breaking the silence around rape in a powerful and communal way.

The classroom is a powerful space in which to catalyze the kind of reflection that leads to individual and cultural change, which our pedagogical essays make clear by proposing a variety of methods for teaching about rape culture and sexual assault in transformative ways. Maureen McDonnell offers much-needed pointers for dealing with topics of sexual assault in any classroom; she considers the benefits and drawbacks of "trigger warnings," ways of supporting survivors as they encounter such topics in class, and how to assist universities in responding to the topic and to on-campus incidents of sexual assault. This essay provides a helpful general context for Armbruster's more specific essay about teaching empathy using survivor memoirs. Jeremy Posadas offers a clear lesson plan for teaching students not only what toxic masculinity is, but also how to begin to recognize and end their own participation in it. On the other hand, Heather Hewett charts how her *students'* accusations of "toxic masculinity" prompted her to rethink teaching *Things Fall Apart*, adding feminist pedagogy and contextual information about African masculinities to traditional postcolonial and antiracist approaches. Amy Hagenrater-Gooding's essay about using modern drama and contemporary TV shows to discuss agency and complicity in sexual relationships also grew out of a teaching dilemma, one that is faced eventually by any teacher who addresses such challenging topics in class: what do we do when students don't react as we expect them to, or as they "should," and how can we learn from past experiences in the classroom to make future approaches more productive?

Several of our essays, like Posadas's dismantling of toxic masculinity and Hurtado's decolonial feminist approach, offer pedagogical methods for using literature to make underlying structures of rape culture visible while enabling students to reflect on their own experiences of them productively and safely. Zoë Brigley Thompson suggests ways of teaching creative nonfiction and short fiction about sexual violence, from queer and straight perspectives, that reflect on the institutional responses and cultural narratives that seek to deny victims voice and agency. Focusing on the class dynamic rather than the texts themselves,

Sarah Goldbort describes her use of the restorative justice circle model to create a safe space in which students and teacher can reflect on their own experiences of sexual violence and, in a culture of patriarchal and heteronormative sexual violence, be transparent about their own identities as they examine theories about and depictions of the same in historical, fictional, and autobiographical accounts.

The contexts in which these writers contemplate effective teaching strategies for these topics likewise vary widely: while Posadas's lessons on toxic masculinity derive from his teaching at a conservative Christian college in rural Texas, Candice Pipes's emerge from her experience using literature to discuss sexual violence in classes at the United States Air Force Academy, while also drawing attention to the rampant sexual violence experienced by military members themselves. And Beth Walker's essay, which one might read in connection with those by McDonnell and Armbruster, gives excellent advice about tutoring, in university writing centers, to students who are writing about their own experiences of sexual violence.

Still, no one book, however wide-ranging, can address every facet of a movement and issue as complex as this one. While we were impressed and pleased by the diversity, in terms of topics, texts, and writers, of the excellent essays we received, we want to acknowledge that not all types of sexual violence or of people who experience it are represented here. Members of every racial, ethnic, income, and geographic group experience sexual violence—with members of some groups, including trans and non-binary people of color, Indigenous women, and prison inmates experiencing it at much higher rates—although we have not been able to acknowledge every possible type of abuse. This volume focuses on male violence against women in the context of misogyny and its attending rape culture in part because of the essays it attracted. But it is also fair to say that patriarchal sexual violence of men against women (both cis and trans) *is* by far the most pervasive form of sexual violence: 90 percent of rape victims identify as female, and 98 percent of perpetrators of rape against women identify as male (while 93 percent of perpetrators of rape against men identify as male, 93 percent of perpetrators of sexual violence other than rape against women identify as male).[27] Historically and still today, sexual violence is overwhelmingly a problem experienced by women and perpetrated by men in patriarchal culture, making it a core feminist issue that this volume aims to illuminate in new ways.

For nearly half a century, theorists and critics have been conceptualizing literary studies as integral to larger feminist projects. So far, feminist literary studies has been characterized by a diverse and at times conflicting set of methodologies and practices, including reading literature as reifying social ideology and power dynamics; "defensive rereadings"[28] in which critics make normalized misogyny visible and resist it; intersectional approaches to theorizing identity and power, accompanied by critiques of literary theorizing that does not attend to the multiple strands of identity (gender, race, class, sexuality, dis/ability, nationality, Indigeneity, location, etc.); establishing "counter-traditions" of literature by women writers reshaping technique, genre, and conventions in feminist narratives; recovering lost or ignored works; re-readings of male writers; attention to the power dynamics that govern access to publishing and reading publics; and the social, textual, and digital constructions of self. Remarkably, guided only by a loose call for papers, our contributors delivered a collection of essays aiming to do all these things—focused on the problem of sexual violence. Their responses—now this volume—suggest that #MeToo urges us collectively to sharpen our focus, as part of our larger, ongoing feminist project, on theorizing literary practice around rape culture and sexual violence.

What Remains To Be Done

At the time of our writing, #MeToo shows no signs of slowing or disappearing. Yet it will eventually do both: considering that the half-life of most media movements can be calculated in days, this one is enjoying a surprisingly robust, long life. The activist work against sexual violence that predated it, though, both inside and outside literary studies, must and will continue. It will be up to this and future generations of literary scholars and teachers to expand the work mapped out by contributors to this volume and by all the others working on these topics today.

We can continue that work by recognizing how #MeToo's cultural effects have changed the expectations of college students.

As many of our contributors demonstrate, professors must contend with these altered expectations in literary studies classrooms. Topics that might once have seemed to "belong" to classes focused on particular literatures (women's, LGBTQ+, African American and African Diaspora, postcolonial and transnational, etc.) or disciplines focused on the experiences and theoretical insights produced by marginalized and oppressed groups (women's and gender studies, Black studies, Latinx studies, Indigenous studies, etc.) should be raised across courses and disciplines. Doing so will in turn require teachers across disciplines to develop classroom and office-hour skills for dealing with what might feel like uncomfortable conversations about sexual violence, power, and pain.

We can also continue that work by staying attuned to the new directions in which the ongoing writing inspired by #MeToo takes conversations about rape and sexual assault, as several of our contributors have begun to do. #MeToo has inspired work not only in memoir but also in poetry, fiction, creative nonfiction, graphic narrative, and writing for stage and screen, requiring that literary critics working on all contemporary genres give renewed attention to writing that addresses sexual violence and trauma, and for professors to consider expanding the types of genres and narrative they teach.

Other issues and questions remain that are not directly addressed by this book; here we draw attention to a few, without offering an exhaustive list. Some of these are specifically literary. For example, how do we theorize the relationship between the stories of the #MeToo movement and the writing and performance of other, more traditionally "literary" genres? How might we rethink the possibilities and constraints of #MeToo in order to "tell different stories, individually and collectively" (Serisier 2018: 215)? How do we theorize testimony and life writing itself in a world characterized by technology, digital storytelling, and social media? How do we do so in relation to increasingly digital literature?

More pressingly, how do we encourage the genre blurring that enables so much contemporary writing—both wholly fictional and variously nonfictional[29]—to make meaning in newly productive ways, while maintaining a boundary between truth and nontruth? Having witnessed our own government displacing reality, in a terrifying enactment of Baudrillard's simulation theory, by replacing it with repeated statements of untruths,[30] rhetoric, and displays of anger and righteousness, reasserting the difference between fact and fantasy becomes more urgent than ever. If #MeToo and its reverberations in literary studies are going to dismantle our culture that disbelieves survivors and empowers perpetrators—though Kavanaugh of course leaps to mind here, we should also remember that former President Trump remains the most visible evidence of these aspects of misogyny in US culture[31]—academic studies across disciplines must conceive of truth in a way that survives poststructuralism while retaining real meaning. We must also find ways to communicate that understanding to the culture at large—a culture that, as Hardt and Negri (2000) argued twenty years ago, has absorbed concepts of postmodernism so thoroughly as to distort its every promise into the service of existing power structures.

Reconsidering constructive genre blurring entails explorations of the relationships among life writing, literature, and activism. One important effect that life writing and memoir might have on literary studies is in beginning to close the gap between theorized and lived experience. It is not at all uncommon for students and even professors of feminist theory and literature to be well trained in the facts and statistics of sexual abuse and yet shockingly unaware of the abuse happening in their own lives or in lives around them.[32] Professors may choose to participate in campus activities outside the classroom designed to raise awareness of the lived experience of sexual assault, such as Take Back the Night rallies, or to initiate their own in conjunction with their classes, a topic which merits consideration by future pedagogical essays or volumes. Meanwhile, incorporating life writing or memoir into syllabi offers a simple way to engage more directly with the kinds of lived experiences that inspire the fiction to which we devote much of our attention.

Likewise, we must strengthen the relationship between those who primarily do literary work and those who primarily do activism. Although many academics use not only their scholarship and teaching but also social media and embodied methods to draw attention to sexual violence and begin to change the conditions that enable it, in many contexts a gap remains, whether perceived or real, between academic and activist work. We literary scholars need to not only do the work, but also make it visible to the larger culture, and to build bridges to the activists outside literary studies whose own work would benefit from our participation in ways they might not yet fully see.³³

We hope that future work will take up these and other related issues on a truly global scale. While this collection includes work both produced and focused outside the North American academy, a need for transnational scholarship on #MeToo remains, particularly work that examines digital activism, writing, and performance that inform and/or emerge from engagements with rape culture, power, and violence in multiple geographical locations. In addition to looking at how #MeToo has crossed transnational borders, this scholarship must attend to local and regional specificities and examples of anti-violence activism that may not get named in English and North American-focused discussions of #MeToo, but which play significant roles in feminist movements; consider, for example, the #NiUnaMás and #NiUnaMenos movements across Latin America, and the "Un violador en tu camino" ("A rapist in your path") Chilean anthem.

We also hope to see future work that focuses specifically on academia and its attending institutions, where sexual violence, the silencing of survivors, and the empowerment of perpetrators continue largely unabated today. Memoirs and personal essays documenting the sexual harassment and violence experienced by women in English graduate departments (e.g., Terry Castle's *The Professor*, 2010; Nancy K. Miller's *My Brilliant Friends*, 2018; and Donna Freitas's *Consent*, 2019), in academia more broadly (Gray-Rosendale's edited collection *Me Too, Feminist Theory, and Surviving Sexual Violence in the Academy*, 2020), and in publishing (Adrienne Miller's *In the Land of Men*, 2020) are emerging; for perhaps obvious reasons, little exists by professors experiencing sexual harassment on campus or in other academic contexts, though such experiences are not uncommon. Academia will not be fully empowered to bring its tools to bear upon the cultural problem of rampant sexual violence and oppression until it recognizes and remedies the same within it.

Clearly, much work remains to be done, which we can expect to unfold in fits and starts along a long trajectory that we hope will lead to the eradication of rape culture and a massive reduction in instances of sexual violence. In the meantime, all of us have the tools we need to participate in that transformation. As critics, writers, and teachers, we have the power to decide what cultural artifacts we teach and write about and how we teach and write about them. We also have the power to critique and affect our culture by provoking individual reflection and change through public debate and classroom engagement. We hope this volume will be not only a valuable tool for critics and teachers looking to infuse their work with crucial contemporary issues and the energy surrounding them on social media and in the popular press, but also a tool for change in the world.

Notes

1   Burke (2019).
2   See Kantor and Twohey (2017).
3   Anderson and Toor (2018).
4   See White (2017), Michelson (2017), Wu (2018), and Alnes (2019).
5   See Ajayi (2018), Adam and Booth (2018), and Seales (2018).
6   Carmon and Schonbeck (2019).
7   See Stone and Vogelstein (2019), Fileborn and Loney-Howes (2019), and Noel and Oppenheimer (2020).
8   See Garibotti and Hopp (2019) and Rachelle (2019).
9   A year after #MeToo exploded on social media, *The New York Times* published an article titled "#MeToo Brought Down 201 Powerful Men. Nearly Half Were Replaced by Women" (Carlsen 2018). For a detailed history of accusations and consequences through January 2020, see *The Chicago Tribune*'s "#MeToo: A timeline of events" (2020).
10 See Hagerty (2019).
11 See Feimster (2009), McGuire (2011), Freedman (2013), Heldman and Brown (2014), Hobbs (2018), and Feinstein (2018).
12 See Bevacqua (2000), Heldman and Brown (2014), and Ake and Arnold (2017).
13 See Keck and Sikkink (1998).
14 Keck and Sikkink (1998). Also see Bradley (2020) for a more recent examination of global activism focused on violence against women.
15 Serisier (2018: 45–6). She observes that, with a few exceptions, this is "overwhelmingly a collection of white, heterosexual, educated women telling stories of stranger rape" (47).
16 The discovery of Jacobs's letters helped scholars to refute doubts about Jacobs's authorship and prove the "credibility" of her autobiography. See Yellin (1981: 480).

17 For a range of approaches to rape and representation, see Ferguson (1987), Tanner (1994), Sielke (2002), Horeck (2003), and Stockton (2006).
18 See, for example, Davis (1981, 1989), Lorde (1984), Kubitschek (1988), Gunning (1996), Crenshaw (1997), Richie (2012), Deer (2015), and Lugones (2016).
19 Also see West (2003) for a collection of essays focused on violence against Black women authored by therapists, researchers, activists, and survivors.
20 Consider, for example, Nora Okja Keller's *Comfort Woman* (1997), Slavenka Drakulić's *S. A Novel about the Balkans* (2000), and Lynn Nottage's *Ruined* (2009).
21 Also see Graham (2012) on rape in South African literature.
22 Also see Kalisa (2009).
23 Also see Alcoff (2018).
24 The most recent endeavor of this sort is *Believe Me: How Trusting Women Can Change the World* (Valenti and Friedman 2020), which collects not simply rape stories but essays contemplating an impressive variety of reasons why people continue to disbelieve women who speak out about rape, and possible ways of dismantling that knee-jerk disbelief.
25 While published right before #MeToo, it is worth mentioning the collection *We Believe You: Survivors of Campus Sexual Assault Speak Out* (Clark and Pino 2016) and Douglas's memoir *On Being Raped* (2016), which details the author's experience as a male survivor of rape.
26 Also see Patterson (2016).
27 See "The National Intimate Partner and Sexual Violence Survey" (Black et al. 2011) and "Victims of Sexual Violence: Statistics."
28 This term, and several other of the methodologies outlined in this paragraph, comes from Kolodny (1980).
29 Examples of recent genre blurring in nonfiction writing include Machado's memoir, *In the Dream House* (2019), and the many examples of "creative nonfiction" in *Indelible in the Hippocampus: Writings from the #MeToo Movement* (Oria 2019), among many others.
30 At the time of our writing—well before the 2020 election—*The Washington Post* had documented over 16,000 false or misleading claims made by Donald Trump since taking office. See "Fact Checker" (n.d.).
31 See Garber (2019).
32 The recent decapitation in New York of a woman trained in social work—and of her daughter—by her estranged husband

with a history of threatening them both is only one of many such devastating examples of how this gap between theory and lived experience impacts and even endangers the lives of women (Ray et al. 2019).

33 While the existence of academic practice that is ignorant of or even hostile to activism makes such a gap understandable, its persistence in spaces meant to unite us in fighting oppressions is troubling. One telling example comes from the September 2019 "Women and Power" seminar at the Omega Institute in Rhinebeck, NY (attended by Mary) where, over two and a half days of presentations, several speakers expressed anti-academicism ranging from skepticism to scorn.

Works Cited

Adam, Karla and William Booth (2018), "A Year after It Began, Has #MeToo Become a Global Movement?" *The Washington Post*, October 5. Available online: https://www.washingtonpost.com/world/a-year-after-it-began-has-metoo-become-a-global-movement/2018/10/05/1fc0929e-c71a-11e8-9c0f-2ffaf6d422aa_story.html (accessed October 29, 2019).

Ajayi, Titilope F. (2018), "#MeToo, Africa and the Politics of Transnational Activism," *Africa Is a Country*, July 6. Available online: https://africasacountry.com/2018/07/metoo-africa-and-the-politics-of-transnational-activism (accessed October 6, 2020).

Ake, Jami and Gretchen Arnold (2017), "A Brief History of Anti-Violence Against Women Movements in the United States," in Claire M. Renzetti, Jeffrey L. Edleson, and Raquel Kennedy Bergen (eds.), *Sourcebook on Violence against Women*, 3rd edn., 3–25, Los Angeles: SAGE Publications.

Alcoff, Linda Martín (2018), *Rape and Resistance*, Cambridge and Medford, MA: Polity Press.

Alma, Deborah, ed. (2018), *#MeToo: Rallying against Sexual Assault and Harassment—A Women's Poetry Anthology*, Oswestry, UK: Fair Acre Press.

Alnes, Jacqueline (2019), "Revisiting the #MeToo Movement: A Reading List," *Longreads*, January 17. Available online: https://longreads.com/2019/01/17/revisiting-the-metoo-movement-a-reading-list/(accessed June 4, 2019).

Anderson, Monica and Skye Toor (2018), "How Social Media Users Have Discussed Sexual Harassment Since #MeToo Went Viral,"

Pew Research Center, October 11. Available online: https://www. pewresearch.org/fact-tank/2018/10/11/how-social-media-users-have-discussed-sexual-harassment-since-metoo-went-viral/ (accessed November 6, 2020).

Bean, Lexie, ed. (2018), *Written on the Body*, London and Philadelphia: Jessica Kingsley Publishers.

Bevacqua, Maria (2000), *Rape on the Public Agenda: Feminism and the Politics of Sexual Assault*, Boston: Northeastern University Press.

Black, M.C., Basile, K.C., Breiding, M.J., Smith, S.G., Walters, M.L., Merrick, M.T., Chen, J., and Stevens, M.R. (2011), *The National Intimate Partner and Sexual Violence Survey (NISVS): 2010 Summary Report*, Atlanta: National Center for Injury Prevention and Control, Centers for Disease Control and Prevention. Available online: https://www.cdc.gov/violenceprevention/pdf/nisvs_report2010-a.pdf (accessed February 14, 2020).

Bradley, Tamsin (2020), *Global Perspectives on Violence against Women and Girls*, London: Zed Books.

Brownmiller, Susan ([1975] 1993), *Against Our Will: Men, Women, and Rape*, Reprinted edn., New York: Ballantine Books.

Buchwald, Emilie, Pamela Fletcher, and Martha Roth, eds. ([1993] 2005), *Transforming a Rape Culture*, 2nd edn, Minneapolis: Milkweed Editions.

Burke, Tarana (2019), [Keynote speech] Women and Power conference, Omega Institute, Rhinebeck, NY, September 27.

Carby, Hazel V. (1987), *Reconstructing Womanhood: The Emergence of the Afro-American Woman Novelist*, New York: Oxford University Press.

Carlsen, Audrey, et al. (2018), "#MeToo Brought Down 201 Powerful Men. Nearly Half Their Replacements Are Women," *The New York Times*, 29 October (updated). Available online: https://www.nytimes.com/interactive/2018/10/23/us/metoo-replacements.html (accessed February 14, 2020).

Carmon, Irin and Amelia Schonbeck (2019), "Was It Worth It?," *New York Magazine*, September, 30. Available online: https://www.thecut.com/2019/09/coming-forward-about-sexual-assault-and-what-comes-after.html (accessed September 30, 2019).

Castle, Terry (2010), *The Professor: A Sentimental Education*, New York: Harper Perennial.

Clark, Annie E. and Andrea L. Pino (2016), *We Believe You: Survivors of Campus Sexual Assault Speak Out*, New York: Holt Paperbacks.

Cohen, Sascha (2015), "How a Book Changed the Way We Talk about Rape." *Time*, October 7. Available online: https://time.com/4062637/against-our-will-40/ (accessed November 6, 2020).

Crenshaw, Kimberlé (1997), "Intersectionality and Identity Politics: Learning from Violence against Women of Color," in Mary Lyndon Shanley and Uma Narayan (eds.), *Reconstructing Political Theory: Feminist Perspectives*, 48–67, Cambridge: Polity.

Davis, Angela Y. (1981), "Rape, Racism, and the Myth of the Black Rapist," in *Women, Race, and Class*, 172–201, New York: Random House.

Davis, Angela Y. (1989), "We Do Not Consent: Violence against Women in a Racist Society," in *Women, Culture, and Politics*, 35–52, New York: Random House.

Deer, Sarah, Bonnie Clairmont, Carrie A. Martell, and Maureen L. White Eagle, eds. (2007), *Sharing Our Stories of Survival: Native Women Surviving Violence*, Lanham, MD: AltaMira Press.

Deer, Sarah (2015), *The Beginning and End of Rape: Confronting Sexual Violence in Native America*, 3rd edn., Minneapolis: University of Minnesota Press.

Douglas, Raymond M. (2016), *On Being Raped*, Boston: Beacon Press.

Drakulić, Slavenka (2000), *S. A Novel about the Balkans*, trans. Marko Ivić, New York: Viking Books.

"Fact Checker" (n.d.), *The Washington Post*. Available online: https://www.washingtonpost.com/news/fact-checker (accessed August 21, 2020).

Feimster, Crystal N. (2009), *Southern Horrors: Women and the Politics of Rape and Lynching*, Cambridge: Harvard University Press.

Feinstein, Rachel A. (2018), *When Rape Was Legal: The Untold History of Sexual Violence during Slavery*, New York and Abingdon: Routledge.

Ferguson, Frances (1987), "Rape and the Rise of the Novel," *Representations* 20: 88–112. Available online: https://doi.org/10.2307/2928503 (accessed 19 November 2020).

Field, Robin (2020), *Writing the Survivor: The Rape Novel in Late Twentieth-Century American Fiction*, Clemson, SC: Clemson University Press.

Fileborn, Bianca and Rachel Loney-Howes (2019), "Introduction: Mapping the Emergence of #MeToo," in Bianca Fileborn and Rachel Loney-Howes (eds.), *#MeToo and the Politics of Social Change*, 1–18, London: Palgrave Macmillan.

Freedman, Estelle B (2013), *Redefining Rape: Sexual Violence in the Era of Suffrage and Segregation*, Cambridge: Harvard University Press.

Freitas, Donna (2019), *Consent: A Memoir of Unwanted Attention*, New York: Little, Brown and Company.

Garber, Megan (2019), "A Reminder: Trump Has Been Credibly Accused of Rape," *The Atlantic*, November 21. Available online: https://www.

theatlantic.com/entertainment/archive/2019/11/trump-impeachment-hearings-rape/602428/(accessed November 21, 2019).

Garibotti, María Cecelia and Cecelia Marcela Hopp (2019), "Substitution Activism: The Impact of #MeToo in Argentina," in Bianca Fileborn and Rachel Loney-Howes (eds.), *#MeToo and the Politics of Social Change*, 185–99, London: Palgrave Macmillan.

Gay, Roxane, ed. (2018), *Not That Bad: Dispatches from Rape Culture*, New York: Harper Perennial.

Gilmore, Leigh (2018), *Tainted Witness: Why We Doubt What Women Say about Their Lives*, New York: Columbia University Press.

Gilmore, Leigh (2019), "#MeToo and the Memoir Boom: The Year in the US," *Biography*, 42 (1): 162–7. Available online: doi:10.1353/bio.2019.0024 (accessed June 28, 2019).

Graham, Lucy Valerie (2012), *State of Peril: Race and Rape in South African Literature*, Oxford: Oxford University Press.

Gray-Rosendale, Laura A., ed. (2020), *Me Too, Feminist Theory, and Surviving Sexual Violence in the Academy*, Lanham, MD: Lexington Books.

Gunne, Sorcha (2014) *Space, Place, and Gendered Violence in South African Writing*, New York: Palgrave Macmillan.

Gunne, Sorcha and Zoë Brigley Thompson, eds. (2009), *Feminism, Literature and Rape Narratives: Violence and Violation*, New York: Routledge.

Gunning, Sandra (1996), *Race, Rape, and Lynching: The Red Record of American Literature, 1890–1912*, Oxford: Oxford University Press.

Hagerty, Barbara Bradley (2019), "An Epidemic of Disbelief," *The Atlantic*, July 22. Available online: https://www.theatlantic.com/magazine/archive/2019/08/an-epidemic-of-disbelief/592807/ (accessed February 14, 2020).

Hardt, Michael and Antonio Negri (2000), *Empire*, Cambridge: Harvard University Press.

Hartman, Saidiya V. (1997), *Scenes of Subjection: Terror, Slavery, and Self-Making in Nineteenth-Century America*, Oxford and New York: Oxford University Press.

Heldman, Caroline and Baillee Brown (2014), "A Brief History of Sexual Violence Activism in the U.S.," *Ms. Magazine*, August 8. Available online: https://msmagazine.com/2014/08/08/a-brief-history-of-sexual-violence-activism-in-the-u-s/ (accessed November 6, 2020).

Higgins, Lynn A. and Brenda R. Silver, eds. (1991), *Rape and Representation*, New York: Columbia University Press.

Hobbs, Allyson (2018), "One Year of #MeToo: The Legacy of Black Women's Testimonies," *The New Yorker*, October 10. Available online: https://www.newyorker.com/culture/personal-history/one-year-of-metoo-the-legacy-of-black-womens-testimonies (accessed November 5, 2020).

Horeck, Tanya (2003), *Public Rape: Representing Violation in Fiction and Film*, London: Routledge.

INCITE! Women of Color Against Violence, ed. ([2006] 2016), *Color of Violence: The INCITE! Anthology*, Reprint edn., Durham: Duke University Press.

Jacobs, Harriet A. ([1861] 1987), *Incidents in the Life of a Slave Girl, Written by Herself*, ed. Jean Fagan Yellin, Cambridge, MA, and London: Harvard University Press.

Jones, Gayl (1975), *Corregidora*, New York: Penguin House.

Kalisa, Chantal (2009), *Violence in Francophone African and Caribbean Women's Literature*, Lincoln: University of Nebraska Press.

Kantor, Jodi and Megan Twohey (2017), "Harvey Weinstein Paid Off Sexual Harassment Accusers for Decades," *The New York Times*, October 5. Available online: https://www.nytimes.com/2017/10/05/us/harvey-weinstein-harassment-allegations.html (accessed November 6, 2020).

Keck, Margaret E. and Kathryn Sikkink (1998), *Activists beyond Borders: Advocacy Networks in International Politics*, Ithaca, NY: Cornell University Press.

Keller, Nora Okja (1997), *Comfort Woman*, New York: Viking Books.

Kolodny, Annette (1980), "Dancing through the Minefield: Some Observations on the Theory, Practice and Politics of a Feminist Literary Criticism," *Feminist Studies*, 6 (1): 1–25. Available online: doi:10.2307/3177648 (accessed November 5, 2020).

Kon-yu, Natalie, Christie Nieman, Maggie Scott, and Miriam Sved, eds. (2019), *#MeToo: Stories from the Australian Movement*, Sydney: Picador Australia.

Kubitschek, Missy Dehn (1988), "Subjugated Knowledge: Toward a Feminist Exploration of Rape in Afro-American Fiction," in Joe Weixlmann and Houston A. Baker (eds.), *Studies in Black American Literature, Vol. 3: Black Feminist Criticism and Critical Theory*, 43–56, Greenwood, FL: Penkevill.

Lee, Bri (2018), *Eggshell Skull*, Sydney: Allen & Unwin.

Lorde, Audre (1984), "Age, Race, Class and Sex: Women Redefining Difference," in *Sister Outsider: Essays and Speeches*, 114–23, Berkeley: Crossing Press.

Lugones, María (2016), "The Coloniality of Gender," in Wendy Harcourt (ed.), *The Palgrave Handbook of Gender and Development: Critical Engagements in Feminist Theory and Practice*, 13–33, London: Palgrave Macmillan UK.

Machado, Carmen Maria (2019), *In the Dream House: A Memoir*, Minneapolis: Graywolf Press.

Mailhot, Terese Marie (2018), *Heart Berries*, Berkeley: Counterpoint Press.

Mardorossian, Carine M. (2002), "Toward a New Feminist Theory of Rape," *Signs: Journal of Women in Culture and Society*, 27 (3): 743–75. Available online: https://www.jstor.org/stable/10.1086/337938.

McGuire, Danielle L. (2011), *At the Dark End of the Street: Black Women, Rape, and Resistance—A New History of the Civil Rights Movement from Rosa Parks to the Rise of Black Power*, New York: Vintage.

"MeToo: A Timeline of Events" (2020), *The Chicago Tribune*. Available online: https://www.chicagotribune.com/lifestyles/ct-me-too-timeline-20171208-htmlstory.html (accessed November 11, 2020).

Michelson, Noah (2017), "Me Too: The Difficult Truths about Gay Men and Sexual Assault," *Huffpost*, October 16. Available online: https://www.huffpost.com/entry/sexual-assault-gay-men_n_59e4badfe4b04d1d51834114 (accessed February 14,.2020).

Miller, Adrienne (2020), *In the Land of Men: A Memoir*, New York: Ecco.

Miller, Chanel (2019), *Know My Name*, New York: Viking.

Miller, Nancy K. (2018), *My Brilliant Friends: Our Lives in Feminism*, New York: Columbia University Press.

Millet, Kate ([1970] 2016), *Sexual Politics*, New York: Columbia University Press.

Noel, Ann M. and David B. Oppenheimer, eds. (2020), *The Global #MeToo Movement: How Social Media Propelled a Historic Movement and the Law Responded*, Washington, DC: Full Court Press.

Noomin, Diane, ed. (2019), *Drawing Power: Women's Stories of Sexual Violence, Harassment and Survival*, New York: Harry N. Abrams.

Nottage, Lynn (2009), *Ruined*, New York: Theatre Communications Group.

Oria, Shelly, ed. (2019), *Indelible in the Hippocampus: Writings from the #MeToo Movement*, San Francisco: McSweeney's.

Patterson, Jennifer, ed. (2016), *Queering Sexual Violence—Radical Voices from Within the Anti-Violence Movement*, Riverdale, NY: Riverdale Avenue Books.

Pierce-Baker, Charlotte (1998), *Surviving the Silence: Black Women's Stories of Rape*, New York: W. W. Norton & Company.

Rachelle, Vivian (2019), "What Is the #KuToo Movement?," *JSTOR Daily*, August 18. Available online: https://daily.jstor.org/what-is-the-kutoo-movement/(accessed April 13, 2020).

Ray, Eshra, Rocco Parascandola, Ginger Adams Otis, and Larry McShane (2019), "NYC Woman Decapitated by Estranged Husband, Who also Slit 5-Year-Old Daughter's Throat and Hanged Himself – On Day She Planned to File for Order of Protection," *New York Daily News*, 7 November. Available online: https://www.nydailynews.com/new-york/nyc-crime/ny-divorce-wife-daughter-killed-20191107-lfgsyqytfvfaflcpezfepawry4-story.html (accessed November.5, 2020).

Reed, T. V. (2016), "The Poetical Is Political: Feminist Poetry and the Poetics of Women's Rights," in Carole McCann and Seung-kyung Kim (eds.), *Feminist Theory Reader: Local and Global Perspectives*, 4th edn., 89–102, Oxfordshire and New York: Routledge.

Richie, Beth E. (2012), *Arrested Justice: Black Women, Violence, and America's Prison Nation*, New York: NYU Press.

Seales, Rebecca (2018), "What Has #MeToo Actually Changed?" *BBC News*, May 12. Available online: https://www.bbc.com/news/world-44045291 (accessed October 29, 2019).

Serisier, Tanya (2018), *Speaking Out: Feminism, Rape, and Narrative Politics*, London: Palgrave Macmillan.

Sielke, Sabine (2002), *Reading Rape: The Rhetoric of Sexual Violence in American Literature and Culture, 1790–1990*, Princeton: Princeton University Press.

Stockton, Sharon (2006), *The Economics of Fantasy: Rape in Twentieth-Century Literature*, Columbus: Ohio State University Press.

Stone, Meighan and Rachel Vogelstein (2019), "Celebrating #MeToo's Global Impact," *Foreign Policy*, March 7. Available online: https://foreignpolicy.com/2019/03/07/metooglobalimpactinternationalwomens-day/ (accessed February 14, 2020).

Sycamore, Matt Bernstein (2004), *Dangerous Families: Queer Writing on Surviving*, New York: Routledge.

Tanner, Laura E. (1994), *Intimate Violence: Reading Rape and Torture in Twentieth-Century Fiction*, Bloomington: Indiana University Press.

Uwakweh, Pauline Ada, ed. (2017), *African Women Under Fire: Literary Discourses in War and Conflict*, Lanham, MD: Lexington Books.

Valenti, Jessica and Jaclyn Friedman, eds. (2020), *Believe Me: How Trusting Women Can Change the World*, New York: Seal Press.

"Victims of Sexual Violence: Statistics," *RAINN.org*. Available online: https://www.rainn.org/statistics/victims-sexual-violence (accessed February 14, 2020).

Warshaw, Robin ([1988] 2019), *I Never Called It Rape: The Ms. Report on Recognizing, Fighting, and Surviving Date and Acquaintance Rape*, updated edn., New York: Harper Perennial.

West, Carolyn (2003), *Violence in the Lives of Black Women: Battered, Black, and Blue*, New York and Abingdon: Routledge.

White, Gillian B. (2017), "The Glaring Blind Spot of the 'Me Too' Movement," *The Atlantic*, November 22. Available online: https://www.theatlantic.com/entertainment/archive/2017/11/the-glaring-blind-spot-of-the-me-too-movement/546458/(accessed February 14, 2020).

Wu, Jay (2018), "Fighting for Survivors of Sexual Assault: A Trans Perspective," *Medium*, September 25. Available online: https://medium.com/transequalitynow/fighting-for-survivors-of-sexual-assault-a-trans-perspective-bc9ad328d36 (accessed February 14, 2020).

Yellin, Jean Fagan (1981), "Written by Herself: Harriet Jacobs' Slave Narrative," *American Literature*, 53 (3): 479–86. Available online: doi:10.2307/2926234 (accessed November 10, 2020).

PART I

Critical Practices

1

"Dismissed, trivialized, misread":

Re-examining the Reception of Women's Literature through the #MeToo Movement

Janet Badia

While the media continues to frame the hashtag "MeToo" through the now-famous viral moment of October 2017—a moment centered on actress Alyssa Milano, film executive Harvey Weinstein, and Hollywood more broadly—we know that the story of the MeToo Movement does not begin there. Rather, the MeToo Movement originated more than a decade before Milano's viral tweet when, in 2006, Tarana Burke, founder and director of the Just Be Inc. youth organization, developed the MeToo campaign on MySpace to help sexual assault survivors in underserved communities find resources and heal from their traumas (Ohlheiser 2017). On the website for Just Be Inc., Burke locates the roots of the campaign in one particular moment she experienced leading an all-girl bonding session at a youth camp (Burke 2013). The day following the session one of the girls, Heaven—who had "clung to" Burke throughout the camp and who had about her "a deep sadness and a yearning for confession"—asked to speak with her privately. Burke's description of her reaction to Heaven's revelation of sexual abuse is as honest as it is surprising:

> I was horrified by her words, the emotions welling inside of me ran the gamut, and I listened until I literally could not take it anymore ... which turned out to be less than 5 minutes. Then, right in the middle of her sharing her pain with me, I cut her off and immediately directed her to another female counselor who could "help her better."
>
> I will never forget the look on her face .... The shock of being rejected, the pain of opening a wound only to have it abruptly forced closed again .... I could not find the courage that she had found. I could not muster the energy to tell her that I understood, that I connected, that I could feel her pain .... I could not find the strength to say out loud the words that were ringing in my head over and over again as she tried to tell me what she had endured ... I watched her walk away from me as she tried to recapture her secrets and tuck them back into their hiding place. I watched her put her mask back on and go back into the world like she was all alone and I couldn't even bring myself to whisper ... **me too.**

I quote this context at length here, first, to underscore Burke's voice and place in the MeToo movement and, second, to tease out the complexities of this particular origin story. Burke's retelling of this crucial moment in the formation of the movement is, importantly, about both the invitation to witness and the inability to listen; it's about the sharing of pain and the retreat from what that sharing requires of its listeners; it's about the discovery of one's voice and about the repression of connection, of empathy, and of solidarity with that voice. In many ways, it is an unexpected origin story for a movement that is, above all, about connection and identification: me, too.

In fall 2018, I had the opportunity to hear Tarana Burke speak at Purdue University West Lafayette. Structured as a dialogue between Burke and an interviewer, the conversation on this occasion revealed yet another facet of the movement's origin story, one defined not by Burke's inability to whisper the words "me too" but by a suddenly materialized consciousness that Burke arrives at through her early experiences as a young reader. On the stage that day, Burke explained that her own MeToo moment of connection came when, as a young girl, she read the novel *The Bluest Eye* by Toni Morrison and the memoir *I Know Why the Caged Bird Sings* by Maya Angelou, two literary texts that place stories of childhood sexual abuse at their centers and that revolutionized literary culture when they were first published (Burke 2018a). As a scholar whose work has largely focused on women readers and the stories that are central to their reading experiences, I could not have scripted a better origin story myself. It highlights not only the "power of literature," as the two discussed that night on stage, but also the question of whose literature matters and deserves to be read.

Indeed, Tarana Burke's description of her own reading of Morrison and Angelou as a girl invites us to revisit the ways women's writing in general but especially women's writing about sexual assault and abuse has been understood or, as is often the case, misunderstood and devalued. In this essay, I explore this question of the politics of literary reception, focusing on how two women's literary stories of sexual assault from the late 1960s and early 1970s have been banned, marginalized, misread, and suppressed. In particular, I will examine the reception of *I Know Why the Caged Bird Sings* and *The Bluest Eye* in order to consider the politics of literary canons and curricular decisions (as evidenced in efforts to ban such books) and the relationship between institutions and systems of power and privilege. The #MeToo movement has disrupted more than just male privilege; it has disrupted syllabi and class discussions, and, as I hope to show in this essay, it has the potential to disrupt literary history, suggesting new ways to map out the constellation of issues that emerge from an examination of women's stories of sexual abuse and literary canons of male dominance.

It is perfectly fitting of course that Burke would single out *I Know Why the Caged Bird Sings* and *The Bluest Eye* in a conversation about #MeToo. Published just months apart in late 1969 and early 1970, each centers on the lives of Black girls coming of age in the middle decades of the twentieth century; both would eventually establish their authors as major new voices in a literary landscape undergoing significant upheavals in gender and racial politics; and both have vexing reception histories. In *A New Literary History of America*, Cheryl Wall provides important context for thinking about the significance of these two publications in the early 1970s, a period defined not only by the production of new texts by Black women writers but also by the recovery and republication of forgotten or subjugated texts from prior literary periods, by authors including Nella Larsen and Zora Neale Hurston. For Wall, the 1950s and 1960s were defined by the works of Richard Wright, James Baldwin, and Amiri Baraka, who produced a body of literature in which "female characters watched the action from the sidelines. Good women offered succor and encouragement, while bad ones got in the way." But in the 1970s, "Black women changed the script … Their plots, characters, and prose introduced something new to American literature," explains Wall. "Their protagonists were often females, who faced choices every bit as challenging as their male precursors, though their dilemmas were often more private than public" (Wall 2009: 968).

Bucking the tradition of autobiography as a genre about the lives of great men, *I Know Why the Caged Bird Sings* is certainly an example of one such game-changer. The autobiography opens with Angelou's early memories as a child living with her paternal grandmother in Stamps, Arkansas, and ends with the birth of her son when Maya, now relocated to California, is just sixteen. While the autobiography has been largely hailed as a work about personal perseverance, it's perhaps best known for the handful of pages that retell the trauma of eight-year-old Maya's sexual abuse and eventual rape by her mother's boyfriend, Mr. Freeman. It's an act of violence the young Maya is not equipped to understand but that propels her life forward, nonetheless. As if the trauma of the rape weren't brutalizing enough, Maya is also coerced into silence, as Mr. Freeman threatens to kill her beloved brother Bailey should she whisper a word to anyone about the abuse (Angelou 2015: 77). While Maya fully intends to heed Mr. Freeman's injunction against telling, her brother Bailey discovers evidence of the assault, and Mr. Freeman is tried in court and sentenced to one year and one day for the crime, but for reasons never made explicit in the text, he is "released that very afternoon" (2015: 84). Shortly thereafter, Maya learns that Mr. Freeman is found murdered, likely the victim of a beating delivered by her uncles; Maya's grandmother issues her own injunction when she realizes that the children had overheard the news of Mr. Freeman's death, telling them: "you didn't hear a thing. I never want to hear this situation nor that evil man's name mentioned in my house again" (2015: 85). Convinced that "evilness [was] flowing through my body and waiting, pent up, to rush off my tongue if I tried to open my mouth" (85), Maya mutes herself to everyone but her brother Bailey. When her muteness is mistaken for impudence and sullenness, she is sent (once again) to live with her father's mother in Stamps, Arkansas, where no one appears to acknowledge or even know of the violent assault, and where her silence is understood simply as a sign of how "tender-hearted" she is (91).

As Wall points out, "Relatively few autobiographies by black women had been published before Angelou wrote hers. None had delved as deeply into the writer's intimate life. In the process, the book helped break a long-standing public silence around the issue of sexual violence" (970). At times, *I Know Why the Caged Bird Sings* reads as if its author is fully aware of the mutinous nature of the narrative she unfolds, not only in terms of its treatment of taboo topics but also in its demonstration of the power of all kinds of literature in shaping consciousness. Indeed, it is literature, loaned to her by Mrs. Flowers, an acquaintance of her grandmother who invites Maya to her house and who encourages her to memorize and recite poems, that leads young Maya out of her silence (99). Although her time with Mrs. Flowers isn't Maya's first important experience with books, it remains a defining one and, one could argue, it initiates what one scholar has called Maya's "psychic reintegration" after the trauma of rape (Henke 2005: 28). Reading and the connections Maya forms with Mrs. Flowers through literature are central not only to the restoration of her voice and story but also to her recovery and her empowerment.

An obituary for Angelou that appeared in the *Guardian* in 2014 described the author as "one of the most admired and most banned authors in US literary history" (qtd. in Kich 2016: 80). To measure admiration, one need only point to the memoir's sales. Not only did the autobiography remain on the *New York Times* bestseller list for two years following its initial publication, but it has seen significant spikes in sales since then as well, including in the 1990s following Angelou's reading of her poem, "On the Pulse of Morning," at Bill Clinton's first inauguration. Reports collected by the American Library Association beginning in 1990 substantiate the second half of the *Guardian*'s claim, showing that *I Know Why the Caged Bird*

Sings was "the third most frequently challenged book of the previous twenty-five years" (2016: 80). Parents, school boards, politicians, and organizations with names such as "Parents Against Bad Books in School" have attempted to ban Angelou's autobiography. Martin Kich highlights a 2004 example in which parents in Niles, Indiana, objected to the "graphic depiction of Angelou's molestation as a child and other topics such as lesbianism and sexual activity of youths" (qtd. in Kich 2016: 83). This example is representative of challenges in other states, including Wisconsin, California, and Alabama, where the school superintendent reportedly argued that Angelou's "descriptions of being raped as a little girl are pornographic" (qtd. in Kich 2016: 82).

Interestingly, 2007 marked the last year *I Know Why the Caged Bird Sings* would crack the top ten list of the most challenged books (2016: 80). Kich appears to believe that this decrease in controversy illustrates the memoir's longevity and trajectory toward acceptance into the canon (2016: 80). But that conclusion seems less likely in light of the fact that over the past ten years, Toni Morrison's *The Bluest Eye* has become the target of the kinds of challenges that used to plague Angelou's memoir. In 2006, *The Bluest Eye* emerged as the new *I Know Why the Caged Bird Sings*, according to data collected by the American Library Association ("Top 10 Most Challenged Books Lists" 2013). Indeed, since 2013, Morrison's novel has been the second-most challenged book after Sherman Alexie's *The Absolutely True Diary of a Part-Time Indian*. Given that these challenges tend to come from parents and conservative groups objecting to books included in school curricula and school libraries, this information suggests that *The Bluest Eye* replaced *I Know Why the Caged Bird Sings* on the list because it also replaced it within curricula. Tellingly, in at least one case of complaining parents, *I Know Why the Caged Bird Sings* had just been added to the tenth-grade English curriculum to address complaints from the previous year that the curriculum lacked books by women and minority writers (Good 2002: 35). Apparently, there is room for *a* narrative about Black girls, provided, of course, that the content conforms to a single standard.

That *The Bluest Eye* has become central to debates about what stories are appropriate for and of value to teenagers is dismaying, if not surprising, given its obvious ability to impact young readers in positive ways about painful topics, as evidenced by Tarana Burke's own experience. That the novel has repeatedly faced questions about its potential to harm some audiences is also ironic, given that the issue of conventional children's stories and their potential for doing harm lies at the center of the novel. Built into the novel's very framework—indeed title—is Morrison's commentary on the harm white culture and white media do to Black girls as they come of age. Morrison makes this critique through retellings of the classic "See Dick and Jane run" stories from the readers that were used to teach children to read throughout the mid-twentieth century, while the title evokes white standards of beauty—from Shirley Temple films to blond, blue-eyed baby dolls—that surround the three Black girls at the heart of the story. These dominant cultural standards breed an internalized and intergenerational racial self-loathing that, in turn, leads a drunk Cholly Breedlove to rape his eleven-year-old daughter, Pecola.

Aware of the taboo she was breaking by telling Pecola's story, Morrison opens the novel with the phrase, "quiet as it's kept," which she explains in the afterword "had several attractions for [her]": "The words are conspiratorial. 'Shh, don't tell anyone else,' and 'No one is allowed to know this.' It is a secret between us, and a secret that is being kept from us. The conspiracy is both held and withheld, exposed and sustained .... Thus, the opening ('quiet as it's kept') provides the stroke that announces something more than a secret shared, but a silence broken, a void filled, an unspeakable thing spoken at last" (1994: 211–12). Whether the novel had an audience ready to encounter such an openly transgressive story is another question. Reception of the novel throughout the 1970s and 1980s was mixed. Mostly the subject of brief book notes and short reviews, *The Bluest Eye* did not sell copies the way *I Know Why the Caged Bird Sings* had. Morrison herself appeared to be disappointed in her first novel's reception. "With very few exceptions," she writes in 1993, "initial publication of *The Bluest Eye* was like Pecola's life: dismissed, trivialized, misread" (1994: 216). One wonders whether, when writing those words, Morrison had in mind a 1970 review of the novel that argued that her depiction of "the imaginary conversation of the now-maddened and schizoid child, delivered of a dead baby at 12, weakens the structure and adds little to the story" (Marvin 1970: 3806).

As Morrison's reputation as a writer grew with the publication of the novels that followed her debut, some reviewers returned to

The Bluest Eye to give context to her latest publication. In a 1988 "Books of the Year" feature for the *Times Educational Supplement*, writer James Berry notes that the novel only came onto his radar that summer, designating it, and *Song of Solomon*, as his books of the year, nearly twenty years after *The Bluest Eye* was first published (Evans 1988: 8). While it is not unusual for a writer's work to be reassessed and, as is often the case with Morrison, better appreciated in light of new work, this type of framing can sometimes be dangerous, as is evident in a *Newsweek* feature on Morrison from around this same time. Emphasizing Morrison's evolution in terms of subject matter, the piece relies on a troubling narrative of growth: "Unlike many successful authors who keep writing the same novel, Morrison has kept moving, taking risks, trying something larger with each new book. She wrote about little girls in 'The Bluest Eye,' older girls and young women in 'Sula' and a man in 'Song of Solomon'" (Strouse 1981: 57). Apparently, writing about the lives of little girls is something a writer outgrows on a path to less trivial subjects, notably men.

If the publication of *Song of Solomon* and, later, *Beloved* brought readers back to *The Bluest Eye*, Oprah Winfrey would reintroduce the novel to the world when she made it the selection of the Oprah Book Club in 2000. An example of what has been called "the Oprah effect," *The Bluest Eye* was more popular than ever thirty years after its publication. As a result, the novel began to be included not simply in neighborhood book clubs but also in high school curricula, including the Common Core State Standards list of text exemplars. Such inclusion can be a double-edged sword, of course, because it also subjects the novel to intense scrutiny by parents, education boards, and organizations created expressly to monitor what students are asked to read in schools. Already ranked thirty-four on the American Library Association's list of most frequently challenged books for 1990–9 ("100 Most Frequently Challenged Books: 1990–1999" 2013), *The Bluest Eye* would rise to the rank of fifteen on the list for 2000–9 ("100 Most Frequently Challenged Books: 2000–2009" 2013). In 2013, the novel would become the second most challenged book in the United States, the highest position it would reach ("Top 10 Most Challenged Books Lists" 2013).[1] As the ALA reports, challenges have happened across the United States, from Howell, Michigan, where the Livingston

Organization for Values in Education challenged the book, to Adams County, Colorado, where parents in one district demanded the book be withdrawn from classroom instruction because its "graphic" nature violated the "community standards of decency" governing policy on the use of media in the classroom ("Adams 12" 2013). Comments posted to a petition circulated by the group echoed accusations made against Angelou's memoir, deeming the novel "lewd to the point of pornographic," "trash literature" with "no educational value," and "a filthy book" that would "introduce our young people to pornography" ("Adams 12" 2013). In 2013, the president of the state school board in Ohio, Debe Terhar, made news when she repudiated the novel's inclusion in the Common Core for high school students, arguing the novel is "totally inappropriate" for any student before college. In its coverage of the meeting, the *Columbus Dispatch* reported that Terhar remarked, "I don't want my grandchildren reading it, and I don't want anyone else's children reading it. It should not be used in any school for any Ohio K-12 child" (Johnson 2013).

Pushing back on such narratives about the value of the novel, Shekema Silveri, a Milken National Educator of the year, defended the book in an interview for PBS's American Experience series: "Teaching novels like *The Bluest Eye* helps us break down barriers with students. After reading the book, I had a student who said that she is the product of incest. And I've had a student who said that she was molested by her uncle. Books allow us to help them heal in ways that we as educators couldn't help them heal on our own" (2017). Of course, Silveri's account of the novel's value challenges the very ways we traditionally understand what can be gained from reading a literary work within an educational setting. It asks us to revalue the experience as one designed to enhance empathy and opportunities for identification, instead of gaining a skill set focused merely on literacy, critical thinking, and analysis. We can argue about whether developing students' capacities for empathy or breaking down barriers to enable students to move out of positions of silence ought to be the goal of education. But if those arguments are taking place almost exclusively when the texts center the experiences of minorities, be they Black girls, LGBTQI+ youth, or those with disabilities, as the data tracked by the American Library Association suggest, then it seems reasonable to conclude that the problem is not valuing literature for teaching empathy and identification, but rather whom readers are asked to empathize and identify with.

One could characterize the #MeToo movement that has unfolded since the fall of 2017 in a number of ways. For many, it has been understood as an outsized example of twenty-first century "call-out culture." For others, it has been an example of our expanding understanding of trauma. And for others still—including both those sympathetic and unsympathetic to its cause—it has been an example of excess: it has gone too far, it has shared too much, it has been too unforgiving. Tarana Burke has expressed her fear that the scale and very public nature of the MeToo social media movement have actually overshadowed and even undermined the original intent of her Me Too campaign, which was to empower through empathy and to direct resources to those most vulnerable, specifically girls and women of color ("Me Too Is a Movement" 2018). While no one wants to direct effort away from those causes, Burke's own experience as a young reader of stories about two Black girls surviving in the wake of sexual trauma invites us to also pay attention to sites of cultural production, to the very institutions that are the vehicles for our stories and that decide which stories get to be told and, just as importantly, heard. Toni Morrison's complaint that Pecola's story is one that was too long "dismissed, trivialized, misread" reminds us that to be muffled, marginalized, and willfully misunderstood is the fate of too many stories centered on sexual violence—whether in the form of literary bestsellers or public testimonies. While the #MeToo movement must continue to center the experiences and empowerment of women and girls of color, the movement will not have gone far enough if it leaves unexamined the ways in which the stories we tell, and are allowed to tell and hear, are connected to systems of power and the institutions that uphold them.

Note

1 The last year the novel made the list of the top ten most challenged books was 2014, when it occupied the fourth slot ("Top 10 Most Challenged Books Lists" 2013).

Works Cited

"100 Most Frequently Challenged Books: 1990–1999" (2013), American Library Association. Available online: http://www.ala.org/advocacy/bbooks/100-most-frequently-challenged-books-1990-1999 (accessed March 10, 2019).

"100 Most Frequently Challenged Books: 2000–2009" (2013), American Library Association. Available online: http://www.ala.org/advocacy/bbooks/top-100-bannedchallenged-books-2000-2009 (accessed March 10, 2019).

"Adams 12 School District: Remove Developmentally Inappropriate & Graphic Content from the Instructional Reading List" (2013). Available online: https://www.change.org/p/adams-12-school-district-remove-developmentally-inappropriate-graphic-content-from-the-instructional-reading-list#supporters (accessed July 30, 2020).

Angelou, Maya (2015), *I Know Why the Caged Bird Sings*, New York: Random House.

"Banned: The Bluest Eye" (2017), PBS, September. https://www.pbs.org/wgbh/americanexperience/features/banned-bluest-eye/ (accessed July 28, 2020).

Burke, Tarana (2013), "The Inception," Just Be Inc. Available online: https://justbeinc.wixsite.com/justbeinc/the-me-too-movement-cmml (accessed March 1, 2019).

Burke, Tarana (2018a), *A Conversation with Tarana Burke*, Loeb Playhouse: Purdue University.

Burke, Tarana (2018b), "Me Too Is a Movement, Not a Moment," TEDWomen 2018. Available online: https://www.ted.com/talks/tarana_burke_me_too_is_a_movement_not_a_moment (accessed September 5, 2020).

Evans, Sarah Jane (1988), "Books of the Year," *The Times Educational Supplement*, December 23: 8–9.

Good, Howard (2002), "The Book Police." *Teacher Magazine*, 13 (4): 35.

Henke, Suzette (2005), "Maya Angelou's Caged Bird as Trauma Narrative," *The Langston Hughes Review*, 19: 22–35.

Johnson, Alan (2013), "State School-Board President Wants Toni Morrison Book Off Reading List," *The Columbus Dispatch*, September 12. Available online: https://www.dispatch.com/content/stories/local/2013/09/12/Debe-Terhar-questions-appropriateness-of-book.html (accessed July 30, 2020).

Kich, Martin (2016), "The Censorship of Maya Angelou's Work," in Mildred R. Mickle (ed.), *Maya Angelou: Critical Insights*, 79–92, Ipswich, MA: Salem Press.

Marvin, Patricia (1970), *Library Journal*, November 1: 3806.

Morrison, Toni (1994), *The Bluest Eye*, New York: Penguin.
Ohlheiser, Abby (2017), "The Woman behind 'Me Too' Knew the Power of the Phrase When She Created It—10 Years Ago," *Washington Post*, October 19. Available online: https://www.washingtonpost.com/news/the-intersect/wp/2017/10/19/the-woman-behind-me-too-knew-the-power-of-the-phrase-when-she-created-it-10-years-ago/ (accessed July 10, 2020).
Strouse, Jean (1981), "Toni Morrison's Black Magic," *Newsweek*, March 30: 52–7.
"Top 10 Most Challenged Books Lists" (2013), American Library Association. Available online: http://www.ala.org/advocacy/bbooks/frequentlychallengedbooks/top10 (accessed March 10, 2019).
Wall, Cheryl (2009), "1970: Maya Angelou, Toni Morrison, Alice Walker," in Greil Marcus and Werner Sollors (eds.), *A New Literary History of America*, 968–72, Cambridge, MA: Harvard University Press.

2

Reading Survivor Narratives:
Literary Criticism as Feminist Solidarity

Tanya Serisier

The outpouring of testimony around sexual harassment and violence in October 2017 was unprecedented in scale. The scope of the consequences and effects produced out of it are still being determined and contested. However, while the scale of #MeToo and its rapid dissemination on social media is hard to overstate, it arises out of long-standing feminist commitment to "speaking out" as a political practice in response to sexual violence. In my previous research, I argue that speaking out, the practice of telling personal stories of victimization and survival, is a form of "narrative politics," mobilizing the literary force of narrative in order to produce cultural and political change (Serisier 2018b). In other words, fighting sexual violence through personal testimony draws on long-standing feminist recognition of the cross-pollination of the literary and the political, and of the political significance of women's autobiographical narratives particularly.

#MeToo is a contemporary manifestation of a long-standing truism within feminism: that "breaking the silence" by harnessing the power of women's autobiographical narrative is key to ending sexual violence. This political practice is imagined as having at least three effects. Speaking out and reclaiming one's story transforms a silenced victim of violence into a heroic survivor. This individual empowerment then opens cultural space for other survivors to tell their stories, creating a collective practice and a genre of stories. Finally, this genre changes understandings of sexual violence, replacing long-standing myths with truths drawn from experience. When community activist Tarana Burke founded her "Me Too" campaign to share stories between and with young women of color to let them know that they weren't alone, she was taking part in this political tradition. Similarly, when Alyssa Milano composed her 2017 tweet, suggesting that if "all the women who have been sexually harassed or assaulted wrote 'Me too' as a status, we might give people a sense of the magnitude of the problem," she was participating in a long-standing feminist political practice based on the transformative power of narrative.

I suggest, following feminist critics such as Rita Felski (1989), that criticism itself can be a form of solidarity. Equally, my approach is guided by Wendy Brown's (1995) political argument that feminist critique can be a form of love and care. In relation to individual authors and texts, I argue that it is important to think in dialogue with rather than theorize about. I then suggest that such "theorizing with" must remain attentive to the gaps and absences in the feminist canon and the ways in which stories that remain untellable intersect with lines of structural marginality. Finally, I suggest that attentiveness to relations of vulnerability and solidarity between authors and their readers is crucial to a feminist politics. This chapter considers these aspects of feminist theorizing in relation to #MeToo, while placing it in a broader framework of survivor writing, drawing on the critical bibliography I have compiled of English-language rape memoirs, book-length personal narratives centered around an experience of rape (Serisier 2018b).

Survivor Narratives and the Politics of Making Meaning

Too often, the feminist response to survivor narratives reinforces experience as a category outside of politics, literature, and discourse, marking these texts as beyond criticism (Scott 1992). However, as the feminist historian Joan W. Scott (1992) reminds us, experience is not a transparent window to reality. Our experiences are shaped through the discursive conditions that surround them. The communication of experience similarly cannot be transparently "recounted" but must be narrativized through a process of, in the words of survivor and memoirist Patricia Weaver Francisco (1999a), "giving truth the shape of a story." Survivors who tell their stories author their experience rather than simply recounting it, and this is no less true for those who tweet or tell their stories orally than for those who turn them into books. Authoring a story rather than recounting an experience allows authors to see their "memories as material to be shaped" (Francisco 1999a). In her memoir, Francisco, for instance, writes that her "most deeply held belief" about her experience of sexual assault is "that, by talking, I saved my life" (Francisco 1999b: 17). During her rape, she decided that her only chance of survival was to engage her rapist in conversation. Reflecting on this decision later in the book, she concedes that it would be possible to interpret it as an error rather than as her salvation: "The conversation that I believed saved my life may also have given him confidence. He'd sized me up, too, found me desperate to live, willing to bargain" (28). What is clear to Francisco, however, is that the meaning is hers to author, not a pre-existing truth to uncover, noting that she chooses her version not because it is more plausible but because, "I like this part of the story. In fact, I have become committed to it. In this part, I look cagey and victorious and well worth saving" (28). In telling stories of rape, survivors take an experience of being subjected to the will of another person and remake it, so that they are able to ask, in the words of another survivor-memoirist, Martha Ramsey (1995: 202), "In my story, what did I want to say the rape had really meant?"

Reading these accounts as experience can lead literary critics to adopt one of two binary positions: celebrating survivors for their courage, or adopting what Felski (2003) describes as the role of the paranoid "detective," seeking to reveal that these narratives are not really what they claim to be. The dominant strand in feminist criticism is the former, whereby new stories or collective stories such as #MeToo are celebrated as powerful and their transgressive aspects are analyzed and elaborated (e.g., Alcoff and Gray 1993; Alcoff 2018). There is, however, also a strong strand of the second type.

Louise Armstrong (1978: 3), herself the author of a survivor memoir, came to decry what she described as "I-Stories" of sexual violence which, she said, reduced the "political to the merely personal" rather than politicizing the personal. Emphasizing the individualist aspects of autobiography, more suspicious forms of criticism describe these accounts as "neoliberal life narratives" (Gilmore 2017: 85) of individual overcoming in the face of structural violence, or "reverse conversion narratives where a perfectly good, intact life was destroyed, then painstakingly pieced back together again" (Brison 2002: 110). Rarely do theorists see these as complex texts that are shaped and constructed within dominant social and cultural discourses while retaining the possibility of contesting and exceeding them (Naples 2003).

Survivor accounts individually and collectively theorize or make meaning from experiences of rape—the relationship between sex and violence, the interaction between individual survival and recovery and social and cultural change, and the place of narrative in all of this. And they do so within discursive constraints so that they operate in a complex interplay with other types of feminist theorizing and writing. The meaning or moral of the story is not self-evident but constructed within available discourses, even as these discourses are shifted through the construction of new narratives. Much of feminist history references this process, including the famous "date rape" anthology, *I Never Called It Rape*, where survivors are able to rename an experience of "bad sex" by narrating it through newly available feminist discourses (Warshaw 1988). Narratives can exceed and bring into being new forms of cultural consciousness. Rebecca Solnit (2014) describes this process in the #YesAllWomen movement: "the term 'sexual entitlement' was suddenly everywhere, and blogs and commentary and conversations began to address it with brilliance and fury. I think that May 2014 marks the entry of the phrase into everyday speech. It will help people identify and discredit manifestations of this phenomenon. It will help change things." Many participants in #MeToo have recounted similar processes, including Monica Lewinsky (2018), who explicitly credits #MeToo with offering her a new narrative of her experience that allowed her to account for her own sexual agency while reconceptualizing the power relations between a president and an intern that make this far more than a story of a workplace affair.

These narratives also enable reflection on feminism itself, which may be experienced as liberating but may also be experienced as constricting and restrictive. The conflicts between feminism and individual authors draw attention to the discursive and political tensions in feminist responses to sexual violence and particularly between the goals of individual empowerment and collective liberation that are often assumed to be implicitly compatible. Author and survivor Alice Sebold (1999: 133), for instance, writes of her conflict with feminism in the form of Tricia, a representative of the rape crisis center who insisted on treating Sebold as "one of a group" when her sense of survival was dependent on her own exceptionality. The tension between Sebold and Tricia can be read in different ways: Tricia can be seen as representing collective politics impinging on Sebold's determination to construct a "neoliberal life narrative" or as Sebold representing a more authentic and embodied politics against what another survivor author calls "decades old" feminist rhetoric (Smith 2001: 190). Ultimately, the political point, I think, is in the tension itself, and its refusal of easy categorization or answers. As in individual survivor narratives, part of the ongoing narrative politics of feminism is to make meaning from these encounters rather than to uncover them, fully formed. To do this requires leaving behind the notion of experience as pure and authentic and the model of the critic as detective uncovering the ideological truth of the story.

Genre and the Collective Politics of Narrative

As Tanya Horeck (2004) argues in her book, *Public Rape*, feminist focus on the silences around sexual violence has resulted in neglecting the effects of the proliferation of discourse and speech about rape. In relation to survivor narratives, a focus on the silencing of survivors has led to a lack of attention to the history and effects of survivor narratives in the half century since the birth of the women's liberation movement of the 1960s and 1970s. This has also impacted understandings of outpourings of speech such as #MeToo where the public proliferation of survivor narratives is described as "unprecedented," despite the existence of prior cultural moments in which these accounts have achieved public significance (Gilmore 2017; Serisier 2018a). The recognition of a genre of texts and a history to that genre is important for several reasons. It works against a historical pattern of cyclical episodes of speech and silence by holding onto and insisting on a context and history, and allows for and enables critical attention to and engagement with a history that includes patterns of speech, change, silencing, and backlash through what Leigh Gilmore (2017) describes as the historical legacies of "publicly doubting" women who speak about sexual violence.

It also enables a more considered appreciation of the relationship between individual texts and the genres and intertextual relations that enable and shape them. The dual role of enabling and constraining stories is famously described by Derrida (1992) as the law of genre, which both opens narrative space and operates through "authoritarian summons to a law of 'do' or 'do not'" (224). To argue then that feminism has acted as a genre is to recognize the ways in which it enabled a new set of literary forms and social norms around sexual violence and survivor speech and to simultaneously recognize the constraining function of this speech. Equally, to argue that feminism sets limits on what stories can be told by women does not preclude acknowledging that feminism authorized the telling of these stories in the first place. There are no pure expressions of women's experiences that have been silenced or forced into a feminist mode. Instead, the authorization and the limiting of speech occur simultaneously as part of the same operations of power. The difficulties in overwriting these generic conventions can be seen in the most basic of narrative practices, such as naming the event. Susan Brison, an American philosopher raped and beaten by a stranger while on sabbatical in a French village, writes of her unease with the implications of naming her experience as rape:

> Using the word "rape" would have conventionalized what happened to me, denying the particularity of what I had experienced and invoking in others whatever rape scenario they had already constructed ... People would think they knew what had happened if they labelled the assault that way.
>
> (2002: 90–1)

There are already powerful narratives of rape that pre-exist any individual attempt to tell its story and frustrate attempts to use the narrative to assert an individual subjectivity. However, an experience must be named if it is to be narrated at all. And any successful narrative must rely on its audience's pre-existing understandings and socially established meanings. To refuse to label an experience as "rape" may deny the possibility of giving it any meaningful framework within the account of the author's life.

Being attentive to this collection of texts as a genre that both enables and constrains certain types of narrative, and which might both reinforce and contest dominant discourses around sexual violence, enables a more attentive and nuanced form of critical appreciation. The genre of memoirs is as notable for the exclusions and gaps, the spaces that they do not open, as for the spaces that they do. These gaps are most apparent in two areas: the types of stories told and who tells them. Survivor narratives are predominantly stories of stranger rape told by white, educated, heterosexual, able-bodied cis women. Reading the texts collectively thus illuminates an aspect of this politics about stories that remains untellable or more difficult to tell that reading any of the individual texts does not.

The predominance of narratives of stranger rape, told by white women, is central to understanding the genre and its political operation. It casts other traditions of storytelling around sexual violence as outside of the genre of rape autobiography and fails to acknowledge the variety of purposes that women's speech around rape may and has been used for. Stories of sexual violence were, for instance, key to foundational moments of the US civil rights movement and to the activism of women such as Rosa Parks (McGuire 2010). They have also played a role in regressive political movements and moments such as Islamophobia in countries including Australia and France in the early 2000s (Grewal 2016). The predominance of stories told by white women in defining the collective meaning of survivor narratives has produced what I have elsewhere described as a reliance on the "epistemological primacy of gender" in these accounts and a blindness to the ways in which this works to erase the stories of women of color and over-investments in racially biased criminal justice systems (Richie 2012; Serisier 2018b: 133). At its most extreme, it results in a generic boundary which is simultaneously a racialized boundary that constructs a genre of white women's writings.

Critics must both draw attention to these gaps and erasures and highlight the moments and movements that exceed and trouble these generic boundary-markings. Doing so requires recognizing the voices and stories of women of color particularly and finding ways to connect stories marked as feminist to, for instance, the production of stories of sexual violence within the civil rights movement, without simply seeking to incorporate these stories. Tarana Burke has spoken extensively about the danger that "acknowledgment" and "erasure" may exist at the same time. She is clear that simply noting her foundational role in the story of "Me Too" is insufficient if it does not engage with her leadership and the history of her efforts and other community efforts to center the narratives of Black and brown women and to make meaning from those narratives, rather than incorporating them within a genre of predominantly white stories while failing to complicate the overall meaning made from that genre (Serisier 2018b: 102). Leigh Gilmore's (2017) book *Tainted Witness*, which traces how women and their testimony become tainted socially and legally, similarly identifies and contests this tendency. Drawing throughout the book on narratives of Black women, Gilmore enacts the lessons of writers such as Kimberlé Crenshaw (1994) by centering the ways in which Black women's accounts are "tainted" in order to construct a general theory of how women's testimony is disbelieved. Doing this leads Gilmore to make "Black Lives Matter" her concluding example of testimony against sexual and sexualized violence, destabilizing both standard generic boundaries and the political meanings that are produced from them.

Audience, Vulnerability, and Solidarity

While much feminist work on speaking out has focused on the heroism of the speaking survivor and, in my case, her shaping of her story, perhaps the most fundamental contribution of feminism in constructing space for a genre of stories is in providing an audience willing to hear or read these stories and engage with them. The silencing of survivors is often represented in terms of force or the overt suppression of speech. A far more successful method of silencing is making the narrative itself unhearable, rendering the teller suspect and defining her speech automatically as lies or madness, a delegitimizing approach that has historically been used against survivors of sexual violence (Serisier 2018b). In his famous essay on storytelling, Walter Benjamin (2002: 149) also argues that modernity destroyed the figure of the storyteller by depriving him of a "community of listeners" able to offer time and attention to hear and respond to stories. Benjamin touches on the fact that listening is itself a form of work to enable storytelling; this work of listening and reading women's narratives has been central to feminist activism and criticism. In the realm of social media, both the benefits and harms of listening have become even more evident. In her memoir *Know My Name*, Chanel Miller (2019), previously known as "Emily Doe," attests to both forces. She writes of reading about her assault online and then of the effects of reading online comments minimizing her experience and defining her as the "nobody it happened to": "The rage that had crackled and roared in my chest all morning had been reduced to a few dying embers in my throat ... I wondered how in an instant my identity had been reduced to the blacked-out and raped woman" (45). In contrast, the response to her statement after it was published on *Buzzfeed* assisted her in constructing a new heroic version of herself: "I believe, out of the millions who knew I was brave and important, I was the last to know it" (250). Importantly, echoing Benjamin, Miller notes the significance of people "pausing" to read the statement. This is work that takes time.

> The work involved in listening means that it is not always simply hostility or indifference that impacts one's ability to fully listen. The story of surviving rape is a "hard story to hear" and harder to respond to, as survivor Migael Scherer (1992: 84) writes of her attempts to talk to friends and family about her experience. This difficulty exists even for those of us with feminist commitments, as Tarana Burke (2013) eloquently testifies to when she locates the "inception" of the "Me Too" movement that preceded the hashtag in her own inability to listen to a young woman of color who attempted to tell Burke her story of abuse.[1]

As Burke makes clear in her painful recounting of the day when "I could not find the strength to say out loud the words that were ringing in my head ... as she tried to tell me what she had endured," the ability to say "Me Too" is based in part on a willingness to speak but perhaps in larger part on an ability to hear, to take the time and do the work of listening and providing an audience that can engage with another's story.

Burke's vignette also illustrates that even without listening we can know, or think we know, another's story. The stories of survivors sit within a genre that has created not only cultural space and rules but also audience expectations. Narrative is, as Susan Brison (2002: 62) writes in her memoir and philosophical reflection on her experience of rape, a "social interaction" where "what gets told is shaped by the (perceived) interests of the listeners, by what the listeners want to know, and by what they cannot or will not hear." The effects of speaking out rely on this interaction, and on the efforts of the listener as well as of the speaker. And this interaction means that stories are never completely in the control of the one who tells them. As Alice Sebold (1999: 97) puts it in her memoir: "Magically I became story, not person, and story implies a kind of ownership by the storyteller." To tell one's story is to insist that the author has the right to say who she is and tell her own story, a project that, as I make clear, is more complicated than it first appears. But it is also to participate in the broader cultural narrative that societies tell of rape, its realities, its meaning, and its significance, for both the individuals who experience it and society. When the story is told by others, the victimized woman is placed solely in the position of character, trapped within the limitations of pre-existing narratives. As Sebold comments, this places the raped woman in a defensive position, attempting to counter the authority of others and their pre-existing stories. Writing of her struggle for control, Sebold (1999: 29) continues, "I was trying to prove to them and to myself that I was still who I had always been. I was beautiful, if fat. I was smart, if loud. I was good, if ruined." The power of audience is particularly pertinent to the efforts of feminist literary critics who must be aware of the potential harms as well as benefits of positioning oneself as a particularly authoritative audience member. It is in this context that I turn to consider ethical criticism in the context of the narrative politics of speaking out.

Intertextuality is an inherent part of narration, and Lacy M. Johnson (2014) notes that for rape narratives, which are so saturated with social significance and contestation, there can never be a definitive account:

There's the story I have, and the story he has, and there is a story the police have in Evidence. There's the story the journalist wrote for the paper. There's the story The Female Officer filed in her report; her story is not my story. There's the story he must have told his mother when he called her on the phone; there's the story she must have told herself. There's the story you'll have after you put down this book. It's an endless network of stories.

(177)

In telling her story, the survivor is uniquely vulnerable to other stories and to the rewriting or overwriting that is performed on her narrative. At the same time, the stakes of such narration are high: "This story tells me who I am. It gives me meaning. And I want to mean something so badly" (177). For survivors and for feminists, the narrative politics of speaking out does not come without risk. I argue that feminist politics cannot mitigate this risk by insisting on the purity or authenticity of women's narratives or acting as though they do not take place within generic rules and strictures. Rather, we must acknowledge that survivor narratives are not immune from literary tropes, intertextuality, and other rules of narrative.

Conclusion: Criticism as Narrative Political Solidarity

The narrative politics of speaking out recognizes that the experience of sexual violence can be used to generate knowledge and insight, which can be used to produce collective political analysis. As the feminist writer Susan Griffin (1979: 13) puts it:

> [O]ne of the untold burdens of the survivor of rape is what she has come to know. She has been left holding the truth .... For her the world has changed. And in this understanding she is isolated, because for us who have not been raped the world remains the same. We keep the fact of rape at the periphery of consciousness and do not let it bear on our vision.

To respect this insight means seeing the encounter between critic and author, both of whom may indeed share this "untold burden," as a dialogue. Neither reifying the author's narrated experience as an authentic artifact with assumed meaning nor seeking to uncover the potentially regressive discourses buried within it produces a dialogical encounter. As I have attempted to show here, these narratives, both singly and collectively, tell stories and engage in theoretical work, and as feminist politics has long acknowledged, at their best they may produce some of our most powerful conceptualizations of sexual violence and its relationship to the structures of gendered power. A criticism that engages with these stories and authors on the levels of both narrative and theory is in the end the most effective way of engaging in critical solidarity.

Note

1 See Janet Badia's chapter in this volume for more on Burke's description of this encounter.

Works Cited

Alcoff, Linda Martín (2018), *Rape and Resistance*, New York: Wiley.
Alcoff, Linda Martín and Laura Gray (1993), "Survivor Discourse: Transgression or Recuperation?" *Signs: Journal of Women in Culture and Society*, 18 (2): 260–90.
Armstrong, Louise (1978), *Kiss Daddy Goodnight: A Speak-Out on Incest*, New York: Hawthorn Books, Inc.
Benjamin, Walter (2002), "The Storyteller: Observations on the Works of Nikolai Leskov," in Howard Eiland and Michael W. Jennings (eds.), *Walter Benjamin: Selected Writings, Vol. 3, 1935–1938*, 143–66, Cambridge and London: The Belknap Press of Harvard University Press.
Brison, Susan J. (2002), *Aftermath: Violence and the Remaking of a Self*, Princeton and Oxford: Princeton University Press.
Brown, Wendy (1995), *States of Injury: Power and Freedom in Late Modernity*, Princeton: Princeton University Press.
Burke, Tarana (2013), "The Me Too Movement: The Inception," *JustBe Inc*. Available online: https://justbeinc.wixsite.com/justbeinc/the-me-too-movement-cmml (accessed August 31, 2020).
Crenshaw, Kimberlé (1994), "Mapping the Margins: Intersectionality, Identity Politics, and Violence against Women of Color," *Stanford Law Review*, 43 (6): 1241–99.

Derrida, Jacques (1992), "The Law of Genre," in Derek Attridge (ed.), *Acts of Literature*, 221–52, New York and London: Routledge.
Felski, Rita (1989), *Beyond Feminist Aesthetics: Feminist Literature and Social Change*, Cambridge: Harvard University Press.
Felski, Rita (2003), *Literature after Feminism*, Chicago: University of Chicago Press.
Francisco, Patricia Weaver (1999a), "Self Interview with Patricia Weaver Francisco," *Telling of Rape*. Available online: http://www.tellingofrape.com/tellingfiles/interviews.html#anchor14868517 (accessed August 31, 2020).
Francisco, Patricia Weaver (1999b), *Telling: A Memoir of Rape and Recovery*, New York: Harper Collins.
Gilmore, Leigh (2017), *Tainted Witness: Why We Doubt What Women Say about Their Lives*, New York: Columbia University Press.
Grewal, Kiran Kaur (2016), *Racialized Gang Rape and the Reinforcement of the Dominant Order: Discourses of Gender, Race and Nation*, New York: Routledge.
Griffin, Susan (1979), *Rape: The Power of Consciousness*, San Francisco: Harper & Row.
Horeck, Tanya (2004), *Public Rape: Representing Violation in Fiction and Film*, London and New York: Routledge.
Johnson, Lacey M. (2014), *The Other Side: A Memoir*, Portland: TinHouse Books.
Lewinsky, Monica (2018), "Emerging from 'The House of Gaslight' in the Age of #MeToo," *Vanity Fair*, February 25. Available online: https://www.vanityfair.com/news/2018/02/monica-lewinsky-in-the-age-of-metoo (accessed August 31, 2020).
McGuire, Danielle L. (2010), *At the Dark End of the Street: Black Women, Rape and Resistance—a New History of the Civil Rights Movement from Rosa Parks to the Rise of Black Power*, New York: Vintage Books.
Miller, Chanel (2019), *Know My Name: A Memoir*, New York: Penguin.
Naples, Nancy A. (2003), "Deconstructing and Locating Survivor Discourse: Dynamics of Narrative, Empowerment and Resistance for Survivors of Childhood Sexual Abuse", *Signs: Journal of Women in Culture and Society*, 28 (4): 1151–87.
Ramsey, Martha (1995), *Where I Stopped: Remembering an Adolescent Rape*, San Diego, New York, and London: Harcourt Brace & Company.
Richie, Beth E. (2012), *Arrested Justice: Black Women, Violence, and America's Prison Nation*, New York: NYU Press.
Scherer, Migael (1992), *Still Loved by the Sun: A Rape Survivor's Journal*, New York: Simon & Schuster.

Scott, Joan W. (1992), "Experience," in Judith Butler and Joan W. Scott (eds.), *Feminists Theorize the Political*, 22–40, New York and London: Routledge.
Sebold, Alice (1999), *Lucky*, New York and Boston: Black Bay Books.
Serisier, Tanya (2018a), "Speaking Out, and Beginning to Be Heard: Feminism, Survivor Narratives and Representations of Rape in the 1980s," *Continuum*, 32 (1): 52–61.
Serisier, Tanya (2018b), *Speaking Out: Feminism, Rape and Narrative Politics*, London: Palgrave Macmillan.
Smith, Charlene (2001), *Proud of Me: Speaking Out against Sexual Violence and HIV*, Sandton: Penguin Books.
Solnit, Rebecca (2014), "Our Words Are Our Weapons," TomDispatch, June 1. Available online: http://www.tomdispatch.com/blog/175850/ (accessed August 31, 2020).
Warshaw, Robin (1988), *I Never Called It Rape*, New York: HarperCollins.

3

Evoking the Specter of White Feminism in the #MeToo Movement:

Publishing Memoirs and the Cultural Memory of American Feminism

Amanda Spallacci

On December 6, 2017, *Time* magazine released its "Person of the Year" issue featuring a group of women—Ashley Judd, Taylor Swift, Adama Iwu, Isabel Pascual, and Susan Fowler—on the front cover, along with the title "The Silence Breakers: The Voices That Launched a Movement." Tarana Burke, who founded the #MeToo movement, and Alyssa Milano, who helped #MeToo go viral, appeared only in a photograph tucked away inside the issue, leading activists to express their outrage on social media. Not only was Burke, a Black woman, absent from the cover of the issue, but the article accompanying the cover failed to reference any of the anti-rape activism conducted by Black activists over the past century or acknowledge the ways online activism such as #MeToo builds on historical Black activist practices of collective enfranchisement and consciousness-raising (Crenshaw 2018; McGuire 2010; Thompson 2010). Instead, the authors of the *Time* article linked #MeToo to the work of white, second-wave feminist Betty Friedan and her 1963 book, *The Feminine Mystique*. Though *Time* put Burke on the cover the following year, this reference to Friedan—a highly regarded feminist icon from the Women's Liberation Movement— ensures that she remains central to discourse about anti-rape activism, including #MeToo, and to the broader cultural memory of feminism in the United States.

By looking closely at the promotion of feminist books that were published throughout the Women's Liberation Movement, Debbie Cameron (1999) argues that mainstream publishers often decided to publish these books based "on the strength of the author's name rather than the strength of the ideas inside them" (4). Moreover, according to June Arnold, publishers began to take an interest in publishing women's books at the beginning of the Women's Movement because feminism was "in style," and they often chose to publish feminist books by authors whom Arnold describes as the "least threatening, the most saleable, and the most easily controlled" (1976: 19). Both Cameron and Arnold assert that publishers are the gatekeepers who determine not only which feminist books they publish but also how these books circulate in the public, and both of these decisions are often tied to the author's image, including their position in society based on their race, sexuality, physical ability, gender, and ideological beliefs.

A similar trend appears in the publication history of contemporary memoirs about rape, including those studied in this essay: Lena Dunham's *Not That Kind of Girl* (2014), Sil Lai Abrams's *Black Lotus* (2016), Jessica Valenti's *Sex Object* (2016), and Roxane Gay's *Hunger* (2017). Gay's memoir, for example, is a deeply personal narrative about the intersections of trauma and identity; specifically, Gay documents being raped by a group of her peers when she was twelve years old, placing this event at the center of her narrative. While writing the memoir and circulating it in the public sphere are undoubtedly political acts, the promotional materials associated with the memoir tell a different story.[1] The Harper Collins website describes Gay's memoir as being "about food and bodies," reducing the memoir to a narrative about coping with body weight. Moreover, in an interview with Terry Gross from *NPR*, Gay stated that the public discourse about her memoir has been quite salacious because journalists tend to focus on her weight. This case demonstrates that promotional materials can sometimes publicly define memoirs more than does their content. Because all four of these memoirs are versions of anti-rape activism, their influential publication and promotional materials have political implications as well.

These memoirs respond directly to contemporary cultural antirape movements. In 2014, institutions and mainstream media began to investigate sexual assault on college campuses, and in 2017, the #MeToo movement went viral across various forms of social media. All four memoirs participate in this movement as consciousness-raising texts. Consciousness-raising is an activist technique that, according to Jaime Harker and Cecilia Konchar Farr, offers "firsthand accounts of individual transformation that discuss once-taboo subjects" and has the power to invite "millions of women" to experience a "vicarious 'aha' moment" (2016: 4). These memoirs are consciousness-raising documents in part because they challenge the imperative that survivors ought to prove that they were assaulted in a court of law for their testimony to be established as true.

Most of the memoirs make clear that survivors do not report that they were raped to the criminal justice system for a variety of reasons, all of which are linked to their worry that they will not be believed. Sexual assault trauma often impedes the survivor's ability to form a linear, coherent, and comprehensive testimony, and rape myths—popular misconceptions about rape that can displace the blame away from the perpetrator and onto the survivor, for example, by focusing on the survivor's clothing, substance use, and relationship to the perpetrator—can retraumatize and shame the survivor. Furthermore, systemic racism in the criminal justice system causes many survivors to receive discriminatory treatment by police due to intersecting identity signifiers such as race, class, gender identity, sexual orientation, ability, and cultural beliefs.

In *Hunger*, for instance, Gay acknowledges that survivors often avoid speaking publicly about their assaults due to "he said/she said" discourses in which "all too often, what 'he said' matters more" than what she says, and so women "just swallow the truth" (52).

Gay dispels misinformation about survivors' responses to rape, particularly the myth that anyone who was "truly" raped would immediately report it. Similarly, Dunham writes about being raped while a student at Oberlin College, and in her testimony, she refutes popular rape myths involving consent as well as alcohol and drug consumption. She describes consenting to sex with a man named Barry and repeatedly asking him to wear a condom, then noticing, while slipping in and out of consciousness, his continual refusal to use one (59). His refusal negates her consent and undermines her agency, especially considering that her intoxication level itself reduced her capacity to actively consent to any sexual act with him. In *Sex Object,* Valenti discloses that while she was unconscious at a party, she was raped by an acquaintance named Carl who later, at her request, ordered her a grilled cheese and paid for her taxi home the next morning (109). Valenti challenges the misconception that if someone was "truly" raped, they would immediately identify and respond to the event as traumatic and as rape. In *Black Lotus*, Abrams describes two rapes by different men that reveal how, while rape culture causes most women to blame themselves for their assaults, it disproportionately conditions Black women to do so. Cultural messages that "Black is dirty, coarse, violent, hypersexual, irresponsible, and ugly" (xii) not only normalize violent acts such as rape against Black women; they also cultivate an "acceptance on a social level of the idea that a [Black] woman's body can be violated in the most intimate way, and that it is usually 'her fault'" (206).

However clearly their contents identify these memoirs as pieces of anti-rape consciousness-raising, the books' promotion and marketing often tell a different story that powerfully influences the public discourses around the memoirs and authors. The paratext of a book, for Gerard Genette, includes titles, forewords, interviews, and authorial notes, and refers to "the means by which a text makes a book of itself and proposes itself as such to its readers, and more generally to the public" (1991: 261). Similarly, Gillian Whitlock uses "epitext" to describe "the elements outside of the bound volume" that include "interviews, correspondence, reviews, commentaries, and so on" (2006: 14). Though these elements play an important role in how feminist texts get published and circulate in the public sphere, Jennifer Gilley argues that they have not received critical attention because "the project of outlining the overall landscape of how feminist texts get published is in its infancy" (2012: 5). By accounting for the role of publishers and their marketing strategies, scholars can ascertain how certain stories about rape have circulated more widely than others in the United States, and why the contributions by middle-class white women have dominated the cultural understanding of mainstream feminism and anti-rape activism. In other words, the ways in which the news media and publishers talk about the memoirs and their authors determine not only whether or not people will read these texts, but also how the public—including those who will never even read the memoir— perceive the author and the memoir.

Kristen Hogan (2016) offers a framework to contextualize the circulation of feminist texts and their role, or lack thereof, in the cultural memory of anti-rape activism, called "feminist accountability." This framework requires scholars to acknowledge that representations of feminist activism, including narratives and images of women participating in and speaking about activism and others who were silent, are based on racialized histories. Thus, recognizing only the histories of women who have published feminist texts—those who constitute the official histories of mainstream advocacy—ignores the histories that are absent from the cultural memory of feminism, and "sacrifices feminist success" (184). A practice of queer, anti-racist feminist remembering for Hogan involves challenging official feminist histories: listening to the speech and silences of feminist history "holds us accountable to those histories of our allies across difference" (188) and can help us fill in the "missing pieces of feminist histories" (183) and end the invisibility of women of color and queer women in feminism. Furthermore, Susannah Radstone and Katharine Hodgkin advise feminists to consider collective memory as constructed and manufactured, since "what is understood as history and as memory is produced by historically specific contestable systems of knowledge and power that produce them" (2009: 11). According to Gilley, it is critical for scholars to analyze the "mechanisms by which feminist ideas get printed and distributed" (3); therefore, it is necessary to account for the publication history of selected memoirs about rape with a focus on the ways in which the memoirs are promoted by the publishers, news media, and the authors.

Promoting the Memoirs: Mainstream Publishers and News Media

Feminists looking to use memoir to do political work often wind up caught in a bind. The nonfiction genre, Cameron states, "is of most use to feminists" because the genre is "informative, decently researched, thought provoking and readable" (4). Yet Simone Murray claims that nonfiction texts by women, even more than fiction, risk "containment and political distortion" throughout the publication process with a mainstream publisher (2004: 168). Some feminists still choose to publish with mainstream publishers that have the promotional budget to afford to circulate their books to the large readership that nonfiction often attracts, but Cameron asks, "how much is really gained ... by feminists adopting the trappings, not of 'accessibility' (which I would define simply as writing in a way readers can understand) but of *popularity*, which is defined by the standards of the mass media?" (4). We can see evidence of publishers' "containment and political distortion" in the marketing materials of all four memoirs.

Harper Collins and Simon & Schuster use evasive language to allude to the rape narratives in Gay's and Abrams's memoirs. On its website, Harper Collins begins the description of *Hunger* by establishing Gay as a "*New York Times* bestselling author" who "has written with intimacy and sensitivity about food and bodies," omitting the brutal gang rape that shapes much of what she writes about food and bodies. Near the end of the description, the publisher alludes to Gay's rape, stating that "in *Hunger*, [Gay] casts an insightful and critical eye on her childhood, teens, and twenties—including the devasting act of violence that acted as a turning point in her young life." This simultaneous refusal to name the "act" as rape while loosely implying rape demonstrates the publisher's desire to appeal to both the readers who will understand the vague reference and be interested in the book's political content, and those who might be deterred by both rape content and anti-rape activism.

Similarly, though Abrams writes about being raped on two separate occasions, Simon & Schuster never directly refers to the rape in its description of the book; instead, like the description of Gay's memoir in which the publisher emphasizes her struggles with weight, this description focuses on Abrams's race, claiming that the memoir "will undoubtedly ignite conversations on race, racial identity, and the human experience." The publisher then repeats this pivot from specific race issues to the universal "human experience," ending in a general classification that may appeal to a wider demographic of consumers, as opposed to only those who are interested in race issues. Finally, the publisher vaguely alludes to Abrams's rape by claiming that her memoir is about "a quest for healing." But while the description notes that Abrams must heal from "overt racism" and "her own internalized racism," it adds that her healing also involves "depression, abuse, and an addiction," never naming rape per se. The publisher concludes this section by stating that the memoir demonstrates the "ability of the human spirit to triumph over tragedy." Again, the publisher opts to represent a universal memoir about the triumph of healing rather than a description about the intersections of racial identity and rape, among other serious subjects. Like the description of Gay's memoir, this description of Abrams's book seemingly presents a balance between the publisher's desire to reference the timely topic of rape testimony and its fear of alienating readers who are not interested in anti-rape activism.

Unlike the evasive language used to refer to the rape testimonies in Gay's and Abrams's memoirs, the publishers of Dunham's and Valenti's memoirs evoke the coming-of-age genre when they refer to the rape narratives. In its description of Dunham's memoir, Penguin Random House mentions three of Dunham's essays, about her disappointed expectations for sex, sexism in Hollywood, and death—all relatable and timely topics—but omits the essay about her sexual assault. When the description finally alludes to Dunham's essay about rape, it does so not with the vague language used to describe Gay's and Abrams's rapes, but using the tropes of the coming-of-age narrative, calling it "[e]xuberant, moving, and keenly observed" and stating that "*Not That Kind of Girl* is a series of dispatches from the frontlines of the struggle that is growing up." This "struggle that is growing up" assumes a shared experience of naivety and echoes the marketing campaign for Dunham's hit television show *Girls,* which Maša Grdešić claims presents a "dichotomy between girls and women" through taglines, including "one mistake at a time" and "mistakes that girls make" (2014: 356). This association transforms the trauma of rape into the comedy and light-heartedness of a popular coming-of-age story. At the end of the description, the publisher uses Dunham's own words to reference her rape:

> But if I can take what I've learned and make one menial job easier for you, or prevent you from having the kind of sex where you feel you must keep your sneakers on in case you want to run away during the act, then every misstep of mine will have been worthwhile.
>
> (n.p.)

This quotation, taken out of context, reads as a casual, humorous statement in which Dunham informs consumers that by reading her memoir, they might be able to learn from her mistakes and avoid the same "misstep." The coming-of-age conceit and trivializing language misrepresent the book as one about silly mistakes and progress or triumph, rather than about the life-long effects of rape, which is palatable rather than overtly political.

Harper Collins also presents Valenti's rape narrative as a coming-of-age memoir, promoting it as a "darkly funny" exploration of the "painful, funny, embarrassing, and sometimes illegal moments that shaped Valenti's adolescence and young adulthood in New York City." The publisher dilutes the gravity of the content by assuring readers that the book will make them laugh, just as the description implies that the "sometimes illegal moments" may refer to an experience as innocuous as moving into an illegal apartment in which "the building's superintendent had to build walls for bedrooms" (114), or as deeply disturbing as being raped while unconscious (109). This ambiguity, along with the humorous descriptive adjectives, depoliticizes the memoir's anti-rape activism.

Even more troubling, publishers seem to deploy these two different methods of depoliticizing rape memoirs—using evasive language and invoking the coming-of-age genre—according to the author's race. By analyzing the history of rape laws in the United States, Saidiya Hartman (1997) argues that the repression of legal recognition of the rape of Black women "was essential to the displacement of white culpability that characterized both the recognition of Black humanity in slave law and the designation of the Black subject as the originary locus of transgression" (79–80). The publishers' refusal directly to acknowledge Abrams's and

Gay's rape testimonies, therefore, participates in a long history of silencing Black women's rape testimonies as part of a larger culture of white supremacy. Publishers also choose, also according to an author's race, whether or not to promote a book or author as feminist. These decisions carry enormous power because, as Murray states, "the tendency within the industry is for feminism to be defined not by peer review, but by publisher press release" (2004: 209). Often this press release can take the form of a post on social media and involve promoting the feminist author as much as or even more than the text itself. The publisher's promotion of the author, therefore, is equally significant to the promotion of the book in constructing the public discourse of feminism.[2]

Mainstream publishers today seem to be continuing the pattern of excluding the vital work of women of color, lesbians, and radical feminists from contemporary discussions of feminism, just as they mainly published books by white feminists during the Women's Liberation Movement. A key difference of publishing in these two eras is that today, the exclusion of Black authors is more difficult to discern because Simon & Schuster and Harper Collins did publish Abrams's and Gay's memoirs, so, on the surface, it appears that mainstream publishers have progressed from their previously exclusionary and discriminatory publishing practices. However, Anne Anlin Cheng argues that, "while racism is mostly thought of as a kind of violent rejection, racist institutions in fact often do not want to fully expel the racial other; instead, they wish to maintain that other within existing structures" (2001: 34). Accordingly, mainstream publishers invite Abrams and Gay into the industry by offering them publishing contracts, but they do not promote these authors as feminists, as they do Dunham and Valenti.

Penguin Random House, for instance, promotes Dunham's memoir as a piece of feminism by featuring the memoir on its "Feminist Reading List" (2014) on its tumblr page, and by giving Dunham and her friend, Jenni Konner, their own publishing imprint, named after their digital feminist newsletter, also called *Lenny*. Similarly, Harper Collins used "#feminism" in its tweets promoting Valenti's memoir. Initially, it might seem unusual that while all of the memoirs are pieces of anti-rape activism, only some of the authors are marketed as feminists; however, as Cheng points out, this "national topography of centrality and marginality" manifests as a "profound ambivalence" around the racialized other that allows the nation to maintain "a dominant, standard, white national ideal" (2001: 30). Systemic racism inherent in public discourses of feminism, therefore, is sustained by the ambivalent promotion of Black authors, which excludes these women from public discourses or cultural memory of feminism and maintains the cultural memory of white, middle-class, liberal feminism.

Abrams and Gay are not passive victims of the publishing industry, though; they resist the racist promotional strategies of mainstream publishers by circulating their memoirs on their own terms. While Abrams and Gay tweeted about their own memoirs 42 and 131 times from January 2006 to July 2, 2019, Dunham and Valenti tweeted about theirs only 16 and 1 times. By promoting their memoirs considerably more than the other authors, Abrams and Gay use social media to exert some control over the marketing of their memoirs and circulation of their activist discourses. In so doing they demonstrate how, as Aisha Durham claims, "just as Black women have pushed feminism forward by theorizing power as it pertains to racialized gender and class, Black women have also demonstrated how mass communication ... could be used as a form of media activism" (2017: 208).

Whether promoting memoirs that are pieces of anti-rape activism or reporting on anti-rape movements, publishers and news media, like the #MeToo movement itself, must be more mindful of how their practices may participate in the ongoing silencing of Black women's rape testimonies and anti-rape activism. Linda Martín Alcoff and Laura Gray-Rosendale note that Black women who have been raped are far less likely to be believed than white women reporting rapes by men of oppressed races (1996: 216) because, as Valerie Smith writes, "a variety of cultural narratives that historically have linked sexual violence with racial oppression continue to determine the nature of public response" toward Black women who disclose that they were raped (1990: 274). Marketing strategies, ranging from the descriptions of the memoirs to promoting the white authors as feminists, illustrate how certain discourses and feminist icons can become feminist commodities in national consciousness, and remind us that, as Murray argues, scholars must "interrogate the media construction of supposed feminist success stories" (210). It is important, therefore, to not only analyze how the descriptions of the memoirs and feminist icons are represented, but also account for who is presented to the public as a survivor and a feminist.

Notes

1 The marketing and promotion teams housed at each publishing agency manage and produce the marketing content and descriptions for each memoir. For the sake of simplicity, the term "publisher," used throughout this essay, refers not only to the publishing company but also to the marketing and promotion divisions of the company.
2 Because it is not always possible to determine whether an author or publishing team wrote an author's biographical statement, I will focus on which authors the publishers choose to support and promote as feminist in other public mediums.

Works Cited

Abrams, Sil Lai (2016), *Black Lotus: A Woman's Search for Racial Identity*, New York: Gallery Books/Karen Hunter Publishing.
Arnold, June (1976), "Feminist Presses and Feminist Politics," *Quest*, 3 (1): 18–27.
"Black Lotus: A Woman's Search for Racial Identity," *Simon & Schuster*. Available online: https://www.simonandschuster.ca/books/Black-Lotus/Sil-Lai-Abrams/9781451688481 (accessed July 30, 2018).
Bradley, Patricia (2003), *Mass Media and the Shaping of American Feminism 1963–1975*, Mississippi: University Press of Mississippi.
Cameron, Debbie (1999), "The Price of Fame—I," *Trouble & Strife*, 39: 4–8.
Cheng, Anne Anlin (2001), *The Melancholy of Race*, New York: Oxford University Press.
Crenshaw, Kimberlé (2018), "We Still Haven't Learned from Anita Hill's Testimony: In the Great Awakening around Sexual Harassment, Race Was Politically Ushered Offstage. That Problem Persists," *The New Yorker*, September 27. Available online: https://www.nytimes.com/2018/09/27/opinion/anita-hill-clarence-thomas-brettkavanaugh-christine-ford.html (accessed May 2, 2020).
Dunham, Lena (2014), *Not That Kind of Girl: A Young Woman Tells You What She's "Learned,"* New York: Penguin Random House.
Durham, Aisha (2017), "Analog Girl in a Digital World: Hip Hop Feminism and Media Activism," in Victor Pickard and Goubin Yang (eds.), *Media Activism in the Digital Age*, 205–15, New York: Taylor & Francis Group.
Friedan, Betty (1963), *The Feminine Mystique*, New York: W. W. Norton & Company.

Gay, Roxane (2017), *Hunger: A Memoir of My Body*, New York: HarperCollins.

Genette, Gérard (1991), "Introduction to the Paratext," *New Literary History*, 22 (1): 261–71.

Gilley, Jennifer (2012), "This Book Is an Action: A Case for the Study of Feminist Publishing," *The International Journal of the Book*, 9 (1): 1–9.

Grdešić, Maša (2013), "'I'm Not the Ladies!': Metatextual Commentary in *Girls*," *Feminist Media Studies*, 13 (2): 355–8.

Harker, Jaime and Cecilia Konchar Farr (2016), "Introduction: Outrageous, Dangerous, and Unassimilable: Writing the Women's Movement," in *This Book Is an Action: Feminist Print Culture and Activist Aesthetics*, 1–19, Chicago: University of Illinois Press.

Hartman, Saidiya V. (1997), "Seduction and the Ruses of Power," in *Scenes of Subjection: Terror, Slavery, and Self Making in Nineteenth-Century America*, 79–114, Oxford and New York: Oxford University Press.

Hogan, Kristen (2016), *The Feminist Bookstore Movement: Lesbian Antiracism and Feminist Accountability*, Durham: Duke University Press.

"Hunger," *HarperCollinsPublishers*. Available Online: https://www.harpercollins.com/9780062362599/hunger/ (accessed May 24, 2020).

Martín Alcoff, Linda and Laura Gray-Rosendale (1996), "Survivor Discourse: Transgression or Recuperation?" in Sidonie Smith and Julia Watson (eds.), *Getting a Life: Everyday Uses of Autobiography*, 198–225, Minneapolis: University of Minnesota Press.

McGuire, Danielle (2010), *At the Dark End of the Street*, New York: Alfred A. Knopf.

Meagher, Michelle and Roxanne Loree Runyon (2009), "Backward Glances: Feminism, Nostalgia and Joan Braderman's *The Heretics* (2009)," *Feminist Theory*, 18 (3): 343–56.

Murray, Simone (2004), *Mixed Media: Feminist Presses and Publishing Politic*, London: Pluto Press.

"Not That Kind of Girl," *Penguin Random House*. Available online: https://www.penguinrandomhouse.com/books/227740/not-that-kind-of-girl-by-lena-dunham/ (accessed July 25, 2018).

Peterson, Valerie (2019), "Publishing and Book Marketing," *The Balance Careers*, June 25. Available online: https://www.thebalancecareers.com/about-book-marketing-2799981 (accessed June 2, 2019).

Radstone, Susannah and Katharine Hodgkin (2009), "Regimes of Memory: An Introduction," in Susannah Radstone and Katharine Hodgkin (eds.), *Memory Cultures: Memory, Subjectivity, and Recognition*, 1–22, New York: Transaction Publishers.

"Sex Object," *Harper Collins*. Available online: https://www.harpercollins.com/9780062435088/sex-object/ (accessed May 2, 2020).

Smith, Valerie (1990), "Split Affinities: The Case of Interracial Rape," in Marianne Hirsch and Evelyn Fox Keller (eds.), *Conflicts in Feminism*, 271–87, New York: Routledge.

Thompson, Becky (2010), "Multiracial Feminism: Recasting the Chronology of Second Wave Feminism," in Nancy Hewitt (eds.), *No Permanent Waves: Recasting Histories of U.S. Feminism*, 39–60, New Jersey: Rutgers University Press.

Valenti, Jessica (2016), *Sex Object*, New York: HarperCollins.

Whitlock, Gillian (2006), *Soft Weapons: Autobiography in Transit, Chicago*: University of Chicago Press.

Zacharek, Stephanie, Eliana Dockterman, and Haley Sweetland Edwards (2017), "The Silence Breakers," *Time*, December 6. Available online: https://time.com/time-person-of-the-year-2017-silence-breakers/ (accessed June 20, 2020).

4

Pricing Black Girl Pain:
The Cost of Black Girlhood in Street Lit

Jacinta R. Saffold

Walk into any used bookstore in an American metropolitan city, and you are likely to find a section of books dedicated to contemporary Black popular fiction. The section is home to novels like *Waiting to Exhale* by Terry McMillan, *The Coldest Winter Ever* by Sister Souljah (Lisa Williamson), and a host of others that rose to prominence through marketing networks like Oprah Winfrey's book club and African American book expos, fairs, and festivals. Black women, in particular, ensured that literature written for and about Black people was not only supported but also integrated into the cultural and capital tapestry of America. Nearly thirty years after McMillan's novel-turned-movie was published, *Waiting to Exhale* still registers in American cultural discourse, mainly because of its candid attentiveness to issues facing Black women. McMillan's successful film adaptation of her early novels such as *Disappearing Acts* and *How Stella Got Her Groove Back* created a cultural deluge of frank, often bordering on crass, stories about what it meant to be Black in America at the turn of a new millennium.

McMillan and her contemporaries used the technological advances in personal computing, microprinting, and the World Wide Web to publish and sell their stories directly to readers. Omar Tyree wrote *Flyy Girl* on his college laptop, paid classmates at Howard University to edit the novel and design the book cover, printed as many copies as he could afford at a local print and copy shop in Washington, D.C., then sold his work on street corners, at barbershops, and anywhere else he could catch Black folks congregating (Saffold 2019a: 13). Just as important as the creative approaches employed by Black authors to circumvent discriminatory gatekeeping practices in publishing was their determination to use their work to address impolite hip hop subjects like financial moralism and sexual violence, which helped illuminate just how difficult it was for Black girls to survive ordinary circumstances. Street lit novels such as *Flyy Girl, The Coldest Winter Ever*, and *G-Spot* by Noire address important issues endemic to Black girls and women that often sit in America's social blind spots.

Street lit was a contemporary Black fiction genre that intentionally gave voice to urban experiences in more graphic detail than Terry McMillan's early Black situation novels.[1] Though the genre is known by different names like "hip hop lit," "ghetto fiction," "sista lit"— just to name a few—its preoccupation with intentionally telling urban stories from the bottom and with using concrete cityscapes to ink out stories of Black people's real experiences defines the intimate relationship between the literature and the symbolic street that has come to represent urban America. While technological advances in publishing and a distinctly hip hop approach to storytelling marked street lit as a turn-of-the-twenty-first-century literary genre, it was also a continuation of the urban fiction genre that includes Donald Goines and Walter Mosley publishing hard-boiled stories about urban America, public figures like Malcolm X and Iceberg Slim sharing their autobiographies, and the rise of Blaxploitation films. Street lit was also transactional in nature; from its money-driven plots to the ways that texts were bought and sold, the genre fueled hip hop's obsession with hyper-consumerism.

Street lit was one of the only sites of hip hop cultural production that intentionally centered the lived experiences of Black girls and women. The most commercially successful street lit titles focused on the toll that drug abuse, sex work, and gang violence took on the lives of women in urban spaces. Street lit overwhelmingly focused on how young girls coming of age managed shifting cultural expectations that normalized linkages among female bodies, consumption, and sex. The exacting exchange of sensuality and sex for the comfort and security of money highlighted complex questions of morality and difficult choices. In particular, the financial arrangements between Black girls and men in these novels muddled and at times obliterated the line between being a girl and a woman.

Locating Black Girls on the Bookshelf

Hip hop was a youth expressive culture at the turn of the twenty-first century. And street lit's devotion to hip hop was best articulated in novels that were intentionally written to help Black and brown youth navigate the gray area between adolescence and adulthood. In its rapid permeation of American culture, hip hop became an ethos for many young people living and growing up in cities. Songs like "Brenda's Got a Baby" by Tupac, which depicts a twelve-year-old girl who becomes pregnant trying to survive by first selling drugs and then her body, and movies like *ATL*, which focuses on Southern teens using the communal practice of skating to find stable footing as they enter adulthood, highlight hip hop's preoccupation with telling coming-of-age narratives. The novel *Flyy Girl*, similar to "Brenda's Got a Baby," hinges on the difficulties a thirteen-year-old Black girl faces on her quest to be a young woman in the streets on the northside of Philadelphia.

Flyy Girl (1993) borrowed its title from other hip hop outputs like the sketch comedy television series *In Living Color*, which included the fly girls—young women who performed trendy dance routines in the transitions between skits. The Boogie Boys burst onto the hip hop scene in 1985 with their smash hit "A Fly Girl." Six years later, in 1991, Queen Latifah responded with her own depiction of what makes girls and women desirable with her song, "Fly Girl." In the chorus, Latifah emphatically declares, "I know you want me, thank you/but I'm not the type of girl that you think I am, I don't jump into the arms of every man/I don't need your money, you must be mad/easy lover is something that I ain't, besides I don't know you from a can of paint." Her attentiveness to safe sex practices, financial independence, and standards around intimacy directly refutes The Boogie Boys' ode to the money-hungry fly girls with "two gold teeth and cold cash money." By publishing *Flyy Girl* two years after Latifah's song was released, Tyree extended the cultural conversation on fly girls and illuminated some of the most complicated and conflicting gender expectations in hip hop.

Flyy Girl is dedicated to "all sisters and brothers, in memory of the glamourous and exciting '80s," a time when hip hop was emerging as a creative medium for youth to express their frustrations with the world (Tyree 1993). Tyree uses cultural landmarks like doorknocker earrings, the names of real streets on the northside of Philadelphia, and the African American vernacular English conversational cadence of hip hop to authentically situate the novel. In writing about the most alluring parts of the hip hop narrative arc—a rapid ascent to stardom (or in the case of *Flyy Girl,* neighborhood popularity), a preoccupation with material wealth as markers of status, and fast-moving girls who are willing to do anything to prove they are the flyest ones on the block—Tyree brings the moral imperatives plaguing hip hop to the forefront of the discourse on how to best guide young people through the tumultuous process of coming of age.

Tracy Ellison, the protagonist in *Flyy Girl*, is both an homage to earlier urban fiction writers like her namesake Ralph Ellison and a bold declaration of what it meant to be Black in America at the turn of the twenty-first century. In centering a young Black girl, Tyree is able to provide a different perspective on some of the most glamorous and exciting aspects of hip hop. Although the novel is a coming-of-age story, with a vibrant cover design that is clearly targeting young adult readers, it depicts Tracy losing her virginity at thirteen years old in sexually graphic language similar to McMillan's early novels about Black women's sex lives, marriages, and careers. Details like, "Victor was erect and throbbing against her, and Tracy quickly exhausted herself from the foreplay," frame this sexual encounter as something other than what it is: rape (175). Admittedly, Victor goes to considerable lengths to encourage Tracy to be ready before consenting. Undeterred, "Tracy undressed, piece by piece, as her heart raced, feeling trapped by young lust, confused for love" (174). Tracy recognizes that sex is the only way to maintain Victor's interest and believes that she can exchange her virginity for being his girlfriend. Her emotional immaturity around sex coupled with not being of legal consenting age shifts this scene from a sexual awakening to statutory rape. The text gestures toward the inappropriateness of the sexual encounter but stops short of acknowledging it as statutory rape. What the text does *not* say illuminates one of the ways street lit, and hip hop culture more generally, normalizes potentially harmful experiences for Black girls. Though *Flyy Girl* is intentionally allegorical, the casual, almost alluring, depiction of underage sexual experiences makes such unsafe behavior seem cool. *Flyy Girl* arguably resonated with McMillan's readers through asking controversial questions about appropriate sexual experiences, which resulted in more copies sold. But for Black girls, using sexually graphic words like "erect," "throbbing," and "foreplay" not only confuses rape with sex but also normalizes unsafe encounters. Moreover, selling a narrative about statutory rape on street corners for whatever price customers were willing to pay commodifies Black girls' experiences and sets a dangerous precedent in street lit.

The Coldest Winter Ever as a coming-of-age novel was further complicated by the presence of additional obstacles in the publishing industry. In the 1990s, writers like McMillan and Tyree struggled to secure publishing contracts with major presses because the industry preemptively decided there was no audience for Black situation novels. At the same time, publishers were only willing to pay Black authors to write about a narrow field of topics. The few authors who were able to sell enough independently published materials to prove publishers wrong saw the nuance of their work funneled into a catchall, generic "African American" category which, in effect, meant that Tyree's coming-of-age novel for teens was marketed to the same readers who bought *Waiting to Exhale* and *How Stella Got Her Groove Back*. Lumping together very different Black works of fiction confused librarians and booksellers who needed to categorize and market new books to their appropriate demographics.

These trends in contemporary African American literature were further exacerbated by the way that street lit novels intentionally blurred the lines between youth and sex. While the inclusion of erotic language in coming-of-age novels helped early Millennials feel like their literature more accurately depicted their lived experiences, it also further eroded the line between youth and adulthood for some of the most vulnerable young people in America. In particular, the graphic language used to describe young Black girls' bodies in contemporary Black fiction, especially within the street lit genre, implicitly encouraged the wider public to regard Black girls as already women. Street lit's overtly sexual language in telling Black girlhood stories acted as a new approach to a centuries-old tradition: the use of sex to control Black girls and women, which can be traced back to the period of enslavement (Wright 2016). The difference was the shift in terms of who was in control—from white men to Black men—which in turn altered the ways Black girls and women were able to navigate their relationships with men to assert agency in their lives.

Bad (Black) Bitches and Gender Control in Street Lit

Hip hop is overwhelmingly controlled by men, and the majority of its art is crafted from the male gaze. In writing about where and how Black girls and women enter the cultural tapestry of hip hop, street lit authors were able to make incisive commentary about misogynistic practices. Sister Souljah, in particular, used *The Coldest Winter Ever* to engage the myth of the "bad [Black] bitch." The novel's protagonist, Winter Santiaga, is instructed by her mother to be a bad bitch, which Mrs. Santiaga defines as a woman "who handle[d] her business without making it seem like business ... a bad bitch controlled without the man ever knowing that he was being dominated. A bad bitch was so slick that she made him think he was calling the shots while she planted the seeds and was the owner of all his thoughts" (Souljah 2004: 4–44). Mrs. Santiaga sees being a bad bitch as her daughter's best chance at having agency in life. Even so, being a bad bitch is multidirectional, bordering on hypocritical. First, the connotation of the word "bitch" when associated with women has come to be considered repulsive, wrong, and backwards in some contexts and a term of endearment or empowerment in others. Second, in *The Coldest Winter Ever*, "bad" really means "good" and thus can be understood as being good at being a bitch which, outside of the novel's context, is bad. Or, simply put, being a bad bitch is something women and girls like Winter Santiaga are expected to strive to be, despite its negative connotations.

The intertextuality between the *The Coldest Winter Ever* and Black feminist thinking concerning controlling images of Black women points to the myriad interpretations of the Black bitch figure and explains how harmful stereotypes are created. In *When Chickenheads Come Home to Roost: A Hip-Hop Feminist Breaks It Down*, Joan Morgan's definition recalls Mrs. Santiaga's explanation of a bad bitch. According to Morgan, a "STRONGBLACKWOMAN ... by the sole virtues of [her] race and gender [she] was supposed to be the consummate professional, handle any life crisis, [and] be the dependable rock for every soul who needed [her]" (Morgan 1999: 87).[2] Definitions of the bad Black bitch, like the conflicting interpretations of flyness in the early 1990s, were contested ground that served to further complicate narrow articulations of Black girlhood and womanhood. Patricia Hill Collins claims that "the controlling image of the 'bitch' constitutes one representation that depicts Black women as aggressive, loud, rude, and pushy" (Collins 2004: 123). Alternatively, Black bitches are also characterized as "super-tough, super-strong women who are often celebrated" (124). Collins concludes that "contemporary Black popular culture's willingness to embrace patriarchy has left the 'Black bitch' as a contested representation" (123–5). Souljah troubles the binary of a bad/Black bitch being loud, rude, and pushy and being able to handle any crisis by positioning Mrs. Santiaga as a tragic trophy wife. By the end of the novel, Mrs. Santiaga's "bad bitch" lifestyle results in multiple losses: her beautiful face to a stray bullet in one of her husband's drug wars, her husband to incarceration, and her children to the state of New York due to an inability to provide for them. Eventually, she crumples under the pressure of being a bad/Black bitch and succumbs to drug abuse.

The Coldest Winter Ever represents a subversive attempt to dismantle the bad bitch dominant cultural narrative. The text speaks to how and why some women choose to be bad bitches, while intentionally presenting alternative, more morally upright sexual and cultural representations of womanhood through messianic characters like Sister Souljah and Midnight.[3] Hypersexualization in *The Coldest Winter Ever* doubles down on old stereotypes of Black women as sexually insatiable and exotic. Mrs. Santiaga comes to represent entrenched social expectations of women who cater to the (hetero)sexual desires of men. As a part of her coming of age,

Winter is challenged to overcome her mother's expectations of her in order to reach an autonomous, empowered, and healthy ability to make decisions concerning sex and sexual self-representation. Ultimately, Winter is unable to achieve such autonomy, and the novel presents her failures as a narrative warning about the perils of street life.

And yet, Souljah's message of empowerment is undermined by the unconventional retail history of the novel: namely, its expedited trajectory from bestselling hardcover novel to cheap pulp fiction. *The Coldest Winter Ever* was easily one of the bestselling books in Black communities in the early 2000s. It appeared on the bestsellers' list for fiction published in *Essence Magazine* more often than any other book, a total of forty-three times (over nearly four years) and was listed for twenty-nine consecutive months (Saffold, forthcoming). The book was originally published in April 1999 with Pocket Books, a division of Simon & Schuster, retailed for $23, and reportedly sold over one million copies in that edition (Lawrence 2005). Despite the novel's staggering commercial success, Simon & Schuster released a pulp version eight months after the hardcover version was published, bypassing mass market versions that are typical of commercially successful books. The pulp Pocket Book edition originally retailed at $6.99, a 30 percent depreciation from the hardcover original. Arguably, this small shift in publishing catapulted *The Coldest Winter Ever* into popularity as it helped align the book with the larger hip hop cultural marketplace. The pulp edition's price was about the same as the average rap CD in the early 2000s and was "pocket" sized, ideal for the mobile lifestyle of hip hop fans. The relatively cheap price and the small size of the text helped encourage a wide circulation of the book among communities of readers. Often the book was passed from person to person with little expectation that the book would be returned to its original owner. It was, after all, about the same price as a Big Mac meal from McDonald's. *The Coldest Winter Ever*'s sustained success in mass-market publishing set the precedent for street lit titles to be cheaply bound and priced from the outset of publication, which has resulted in most titles being re-sold for pennies or for free through used bookstores and electronic book subscriptions twenty years later. This move also resulted in more copies of street lit titles sold, but at a considerably smaller profit margin per book for the author.

When considered together—the unconventional move from a well-performing hardcover edition to a rock-bottom priced pulp book and a distinctively hip hop ethos—*The Coldest Winter Ever* may have inadvertently contributed to the devaluation of Black girls' and women's stories. The novel demonstrated that stories about urban young girls like Winter Santiaga were more profitable for publishers when sold as cheap pulp books. At the same time, critical reception of the novel suggests differences in how stories about Black girl pain were told and received. *The Coldest Winter Ever* resonated with many who loved hip hop but not its misogyny, and it has been lauded as the quintessential hip hop feminist novel by African American Studies scholars who praise the novel for its commitment to interrogating the moral impact of hip hop culture on girls and women (Durham et al. 2013).[4] Along with *When Chickenheads Come Home to Roost*, *The Coldest Winter Ever* became a foundational text for the emerging framework of hip hop feminism. Despite these endorsements, Souljah herself has rejected feminist framings for their tendency to misconstrue her work or "shove it into a category heading that is false" (Saffold 2014). For street lit authors like Sister Souljah and Omar Tyree, school was not the antidote for the streets, and academic frameworks failed Black girls and women just as much as hip hop's misogyny.

Concrete Cityscapes, Financial Moralism, and Black Girlhood

By 2005, street lit novels were intentionally complicating distinctions of age-appropriate erotic scenes. *G-Spot* by Noire, for example, was marketed as *"The Coldest Winter Ever* meets *Addicted."* (*Addicted* was written by Zane [Kristina Lafrene Roberts], published in 2001, and is widely considered to be the first urban erotic novel, the precursor to *50 Shades of Grey* by E. L. James.) Combining young adult fiction and erotic romance literature to articulate Black girls' coming of age points to the ways that important rites of passage like a first sexual awakening become perverted extensions of the systemic sexual exploitation of Black girls and women. The "street" determines the options available to the protagonists, as the specific, yet ever changing, time and locational terrain of American city life presents geospatial fictive realities that ask young Black woman characters to grow up too fast. These characters embody the warring fragility and rigidity of being Black, female, and vulnerable. The opposing forces in these alternative fictive realities expect Black girls on the precipice of puberty to become extra-human simply to survive in everyday circumstances. Street lit presents narratives of Black girls negotiating the harsh realities of growing up in urban America by etching stories of Black girl pain onto the concrete cityscapes. The power dynamics in many street lit novels imply that girls are responsible for the sexual violence that happens to them, which echoes hip hop's deep-rooted abuse of Black girls and women. Street lit struggled with articulating healthy depictions of girls and women and refused feminist prescriptions to do away with hip hop culture completely. Without a clear moral imperative, the genre passively obscured problematic characterizations of Black women and girls. Between the publishing industry's profits based on the devaluation of Black books and street lit's repudiation of feminist remedies, telling contemporary stories about Black girls' pain came at a steep moral price.

During the peak period of street lit, 1990–2007, genre authors helped prove the existence of a robust African American reading public and carved out space to articulate the changing demands of Blackness and urbanity at the turn of a new millennium by packaging the pain associated with coming of age as a Black girl in urban space into neat pages and small books. As street lit infiltrated mainstream publishing with fantastically real narratives of urban girlhood, the people who profited from displays of Black girl pain further complicated themes of financial moralism within the texts. Street lit captured Black girl pain in sobering fictive narratives, then packaged and sold them for cheap, which begs the question: how much is Black girlhood worth?

Notes

1 Here Black situation novels are defined as realistic fiction devoted to articulating all facets of contemporary Black life.
2 See Stephane Dunn's "Hip Hop Ghetto Lit, Feminism, Afro-Womanism and Black Love in *The Coldest Winter Ever*" for more

3   *The Coldest Winter Ever* includes a character by the same name as the author.
4   For more on hip hop feminism and street lit, see "Literature Brave Enough to Fuck with the Grays: Hip-Hop, Black Feminism, and Street Lit" by Jacinta R. Saffold.

Works Cited

Boys, The Boogie (1985), "A Fly Girl" on *City Life*, Los Angeles: Capitol Records.

Collins, Patricia Hill (2004), *Black Sexual Politics: African Americans, Gender, and the New Racism*, New York: Routledge.

Dunn, Stephane (2012), "Hip Hop Ghetto Lit, Feminism, Afro-Womanism and Black Love in *The Coldest Winter Ever*," *FIRE!!!* 1 (1): 83–99.

Durham, Aisha, Brittney C. Cooper, and Susana M. Morris (2013), "The Stage Hip-Feminism Built: A New Directions Essay," *Signs: Journal of Women in Culture and Society*, 38 (3): 721–37.

Latifah, Queen (1991) "Fly Girl" on *Nature of a Sista'*, New York: Tommy Boy.

Lawrence, Arin M. (2005), "After a Season: The Book Credited with Igniting the Urban Genre, Sister Souljah's *The Coldest Winter Ever*, Is Back in a Collector's Edition," *The Free Library*. Available online: https://www.thefreelibrary.com/After+a+season%3A+the+book+credited+with+igniting+the+urban+genre%2C...-a0129811687 (accessed September 5, 2020).

Morgan, Joan (1999), *When Chickenheads Come Home to Roost: A Hip-Hop Feminist Breaks It Down*, New York: Touchstone.

Noire (2005), *G-Spot*, New York: Strivers Row, Ballantine Books.

Saffold, Jacinta (2014), "A Few Questions about No Disrespect and The Coldest Winter Ever: Email Correspondence with Sister Souljah," Email.

Saffold, Jacinta (2019a), "Always Been a Hustler: Legacies of Hip Hop and Urban Fiction: An Interview with Omar Tyree," *Words. Beats. Life: The Global Journal of Hip Hop*, 7 (2): 13–18.

Saffold, Jacinta (2019b), "Literature Brave Enough to Fuck with the Grays: Hip-Hop, Black Feminism, and Street Lit," *Words. Beats. Life: The Global Journal of Hip Hop Culture*, 7 (2): 45–53.

Saffold, Jacinta (forthcoming), *The Essence Book Project: An Archive of African American Literature & Culture*, New Orleans. http://jacintasaffold.com/the-essence-book-project/.

Souljah, Sister (2004), *The Coldest Winter Ever*, New York: Pocket Star Books.
Tyree, Omar (1993), *Flyy Girl*, New York: Simon & Schuster.
Wright, Nazera (2016), *Black Girlhood in the Nineteenth Century*, Champaign: University of Illinois Press.

5

From #MMIW to #NotInvisible:

Indigenous Women in the #MeToo Era

Kasey Jones-Matrona

On the Golden Globes red carpet in 2018, celebrities brought feminist activists including Tarana Burke and Calina Lawrence and applauded themselves for their efforts and for wearing black dresses as a symbol of resistance to sexual harassment and assault. While it is important for celebrities to use their influence to amplify activists' voices, these actions comprise a largely white feminist gesture that actually glosses over centuries of violence and harassment endured by women of color. As part of the activist backlash against the white-washing of #MeToo, North Dakota Senator Heidi Heitkamp coined the new hashtag #NotInvisible to expand the work being done by an existing hashtag to raise awareness about and address the legacy of missing and murdered Indigenous women (#MMIW). But how many hashtags will it take to make the United States and Canada address violence against Indigenous women?

I seek to honor Indigenous women in the #MeToo era by recognizing the activism of Indigenous women and communities who seek justice for their missing, murdered, and traumatized loved ones. Literary activism is an often-overlooked counterpart to the online activism of Indigenous voices in the #MeToo movement and the Indigenous-centric social media campaigns of #MMIW, #MMIWG (adding girls), and #NotInvisible. I argue that these more specific movements serve as useful vehicles for redirecting attention to issues faced by Indigenous women due to the history of settler colonialism. Both literary and digital forums create conversations and inspire and organize activism. A novel may lead a reader to research and explore Indigenous issues online, and encountering digital activism may lead a user to read literature by Indigenous authors and about Indigenous issues. Literary and digital activism function in similar and complementary ways to raise awareness about the plight of MMIW, seek justice for Indigenous women and their communities, and promote healing.

MMIW Background

Muscogee Creek lawyer and scholar Sarah Deer covers the history of violence against Native American women in her pivotal book, *The Beginning and End of Rape: Confronting Sexual Violence in Native America* (2015), in which she problematizes the data-collection methods used to document violence and sexual assault experienced by Native women. She notes, "In 2010 the Centers for Disease Control and Prevention issued a report on the results of the National Intimate Partner and Sexual Violence Survey, which found that 49 percent of Native women report a history of sexual violence" (4). But Deer believes, because of her own experience and research in Indian Country, that this percentage is actually much higher. Deer notes that the 1978 *Oliphant v. Suquamish Indian Tribe* Supreme Court decision "means that non-Native men who rape Native women on tribal lands completely escape tribal criminal sanctions" (7). Both non-Native and Native perpetrators contribute to widespread violence against Indigenous women.

Indian Country Today news reports that "Native women are 2.5 times more likely than any other ethnicity in America to be sexually assaulted" (2019). According to the Urban Indian Health Institute report,

The National Crime Information Center reports that, in 2016, there were 5,712 reports of missing American Indian and Alaska Native women and girls, though the US Department of Justice's federal missing persons database, NamUs, only logged 116 cases. The Center for Disease Control and Prevention has reported that murder is the third-leading cause of death among American Indian and Alaska Native women and that rates of violence on reservations can be up to ten times higher than the national average.

(2019)

Clearly, the US justice system continues to fail Indigenous women through false and negligent data reporting and lack of support for tribal communities and government legislation on this issue. In Canada, Highway 16 in Northwest British Columbia is referred to as the "Highway of Tears" because of the number of Indigenous women who have gone missing there. Billboards along the highway warn women about the dangers of hitchhiking for this reason. While this essay will focus on MMIW in North America, and the United States specifically, Indigenous women are killed and abducted at disproportionate rates across the globe.

The Trump Administration has recently tried to address MMIW, but their actions only demonstrate the desire to undo the work of the Obama Administration and to threaten the Violence Against Women Act (VAWA). On November 26, 2019, President Donald Trump signed an executive order creating a White House taskforce called "Operation Lady Justice" on missing and murdered Indigenous women. The *Guardian* reports that the order tasked the White House with "developing protocols to apply to new and unsolved cases and creating a multi-jurisdictional team to review cold cases" (Nagle 2019). This announcement seemed promising at first. But Cherry Nobiss points out that "[Trump's] administration has ... not been a true advocate of ending domestic violence nor been an ally to Indigenous Peoples as a whole with rollbacks to VAWA, reversing Obama era frameworks to uphold American treaty obligations to tribal nations and decreasing protections to Indigenous lands" (2020). Furthermore, Iowa senator Joni Ernst "introduced the Senate Republicans' version of the Violence Against Women Act (VAWA) reauthorization bill," which Rebecca Nagle claims "would give non-Native abusers who don't want to comply with tribal laws a way out" (2019). Many also note President Trump's history of racist comments about Indigenous peoples and his strong support of pipelines that threaten sovereign Indigenous lands. The naming of his taskforce alone is problematic since, as Nobiss argues, the name of the taskforce "is also a testament to his ignorance of this country's real history as Lady Justice is a personification of a colonially enforced judicial system" (2020).

On a legal level, sexual exploitation of Indigenous women is a human rights issue. Jessica Greer Griffith writes that "sexual violence against indigenous women is a violation of several human rights enumerated in a variety of international law treaties, conventions, and declarations, including the Convention Against Torture and Other Cruel, Inhuman or Degrading Treatment or Punishment's establishment of the right not to be tortured or ill-treated" (2015: 803). As Griffith notes, violence against Indigenous women circulates on local and global levels. This is why violence against Indigenous women is a humanitarian, community, legal, and cultural issue. Artists, nonprofits, and activists around the globe seek to draw attention to the plight of missing and murdered Indigenous women and girls and even help bring justice to their communities.

Literary Activism

Literature is less often recognized as activism than other art forms. Indigenous authors have composed poems, novels, short stories, graphic novels, and multimodal texts to share stories of harassment, assault, and murder that occur in Indian Country. Indigenous authors are always aware of multiple audiences even when they write literature specifically for Native audiences. This literature has the power to inform uninformed readers and inspire informed readers to enact sovereignty and participate in activism. Lisa Udel argues that "Native authors overtly seek to educate the non-Native reader uninformed of such history while also confirming experiences known to Native readers" (2007: 62). In her study of Native American literary activism, Udel names Winona LaDuke's novel *Last Standing Woman* and Linda Hogan's books, among others, as fitting into this category, especially through themes of environmental activism. Writing in Indigenous languages is another form of literary activism and linguistic sovereignty. Therefore, literature and all forms of storytelling, including oral traditions, are all acts of sovereignty that can inspire other forms of activism as well.

The majority of scholarship about Native American literary activism focuses on environmental activism, and Indigenous women are often linked to environmental activism through their roles as creators, water protectors, and matriarchs of their communities. Warren Cariou and Isabelle St-Amand note that "poetic, filmic, and scholarly narratives contribute to ongoing conversations on environmental ethics and social justice at times of climate crisis by exposing the planetary and the community implications of the state of relationships between the land and the people" (2017: 8). Environmental activism in Native American literature addresses issues such as climate change, fracking, and access to clean water. All of these issues pertain to Indigenous women specifically because environmental destruction is tied to violence against Native women. Constructing pipelines and fracking bring outsiders onto Native land in the United States and Canada for extended periods of time, in communities where rampant sexual assault of Native women often occurs. Therefore, exploitation of Indigenous lands and activism to combat it directly correspond with the problem of MMIW.

Louise Erdrich (Ojibwe) and other authors write about violence against Indigenous women and its link to threatening the sovereignty of Indigenous land. Erdrich's novel *The Round House* is one of the most widely read novels about the difficulties that tribes face with investigating and prosecuting crimes committed on tribal lands. Erdrich tells the story from the first-person perspective of a thirteen-year-old boy, Joe. Early in the novel, Joe's mother, Geraldine Coutts, is raped by a white man in the sacred round house. Geraldine's husband is a tribal judge and does his best to find justice, but is stifled by US law that does not allow tribal courts to prosecute white criminals. When Joe and his father find Geraldine after her attack, Joe describes her shocking state: "There was vomit down the front of her dress and, soaking her skirt and the gray cloth of the car seat, her dark blood" (Erdrich 2012: 7). Joe's description of his mother illustrates the brutality and violence of the assault on her body, while his description of the blood staining her dress and car demonstrates how this trauma seeps into the world around her. Joe is impacted by his mother's trauma, registering the trauma secondhand while dealing with the loss of the relationship he enjoyed with his mom before the assault. Later in the novel, when Geraldine is struggling to recover from the traumatic rape, Joe asks her, "Can't you eat? You'd feel better. Can't you get up? Can't you get back to life?". She simply replies, "No" (2012: 88). This heart-wrenching conversation reflects the toll that the assault of one woman has on the rest of her family and on her own spirit.

The Round House functions as activism because it draws awareness to violence committed by non-Natives on Native land and demonstrates the lasting impact the assault of a Native woman has on a tribal community. A review of Erdrich's novel states, "The round house thus becomes a metonymic feminine body. In violating Geraldine within the precincts of the round house, Lark simultaneously profanes the sacred feminized body representative of the Ojibway tribe and culture. This is a rape not only of one woman but of an entire community" (Bender and Maunze-Breese 2018: 145). Furthermore, Bender and Maunze-Breese write, "This novel is the tale not of one boy's pursuit of revenge but of an entire communal apparatus functioning together to neutralize a common threat represented by a single being" (2018: 148). That threat is white patriarchal violence. The mode of narration of the novel demonstrates how an assault on one woman impacts not only close family units but also the tribe's well-being as a whole. Maggie Ann Bowers writes, "It is clear from the Afterword of Erdrich's The Round House that her novel was also inspired by real-life events, and in particular a need to address gaps in the legal protection of Native American women from sexual violence" (2017: 51). Bowers also argues that "Erdrich carefully negotiates the space between her text as activist testimony and fiction" (2017: 51). This novel echoes the cries of all Indigenous communities whose women and girls have faced violence at the hands of sick predators.

While Erdrich calls attention to violence against Indigenous women through fiction that represents reality, poets such as Marilyn Dumont (Cree/Métis) write about specific Indigenous women who have been victimized. Dumont honors the life of an eponymous Cree woman in her poem, "Helen Betty Osborne." Osborne was abducted, assaulted, and brutally murdered by four white men in The Pas, Manitoba, on November 13, 1971 (Crawford 2017). She was only nineteen years old. Sixteen years after her murder, only one of the four men was convicted and sentenced to jail (Crawford 2017), offering late and incomplete justice to Osborne's family and loved ones. Dumont writes,

> Betty, if I set out to write this poem about you
> it might turn out instead
> to be about me
> or any one of
> my female relatives.
>
> (1–5)

In these beginning lines, Dumont argues that the abduction and murder of Indigenous women are so common that any and all Indigenous women are at risk. She also implies that most Indigenous women probably know someone close to them who has been a victim of this violence: these crimes create "'open season' on native women" (25). The poem also connects the normalizing of such violence to the hypersexualizing of Indigenous women, noting that in Canada, there were "townsfolk who 'believed native girls were easy' / and 'less likely to complain if a sexual proposition led to violence'" (31–2). But this poem is also an act of healing for the community of Helen Betty Osborne. Elizabeth Archuleta argues that "writing becomes a path to healing, and an Indigenous feminist ethos of responsibility compels women to share their stories and personal pain with one another to promote healing for everyone" (2006: 98). Whether Indigenous authors write about their own trauma or others', the act of sharing stories draws attention to societal issues that have long been ignored and encourages healing for individuals and communities.

Digital Activism

In 2008 and 2015, Sorouja Moll wrote the names of 1,000 MMIW on public walkways in Montreal, noting the lack of public awareness of Indigenous women's suffering. She called this act of public art and activism the "Writing Names Project." This project, and other public art projects like the REDress project which places red dresses in trees in public space to honor the memory of MMIW, raises awareness for MMIW by inserting names or symbols of MMIW into public spaces where passersby cannot ignore their presence. Just as Marilyn Dumont names Helen Betty Osborne in her poem, I am interested in how recognizing names in order to recognize larger systemic violence translates to digital forums.

It is important to first address the danger of the internet for Indigenous women before delving into its possibilities. Technology can create spaces in which violence and harassment occur, and the digital divide continues to disproportionately impact rural Indigenous communities. The internet can also serve as an additional space to stalk and harass women and even advertise and facilitate sexual trafficking. But Natanya Anna Pulley's article "Indigetechs" argues that even though online spaces can be unsafe for Indigenous peoples, it is a space worth claiming and using to politically mobilize:

> Native people acquire a political pulse online that in the past was sequestered on the reservation—and beaten down there, as was the American Indian Movement at Pine Ridge. Though surveillance of politically engaged Native gatherings continues even online, varying levels of involvement in Native American politics are at least guaranteed a voice through status updates, shared memes, and notices of events, petitions, and new movements.
>
> (Pulley 2014: 100)

Some notable online sources about MMIW include social media pages and online Indigenous news sources. *Indian Country Today* published a three-part series of articles on the #MeToo movement and violence against Indigenous women, written by Mary Annette Pember and published in May 2019. The staff spent nine months investigating the topic. Pember takes issue with the fact that mainstream media focuses on Native women as victims and ignores Native perpetrators. She also notes the inaccuracy of available statistics due to a lack of reporting that itself stems from centuries of silencing Native women. One of Pember's articles also shares a story of the assault of a young Native American woman graduate student, illustrating how individuals and organizations can carve out digital space for Native women to tell their stories when they are otherwise silenced.

I first encountered these articles while scrolling through Facebook, one of the main social media sites from which one in five Americans now get most of their news (Shearer 2018). I do not report that fact critically or feel nostalgia for the time when everyone read their news in the daily print paper. Young generations who are active on social media will come across news that they may not otherwise seek out. Ruth Page argues that "the storytelling that is proliferating in social media attests to the limitations of narrative linearity as a closed temporal sequence" and "combines new structural forms and co-production by multiple individuals, a networked narrative" (2013: 194). Stories are posted, shared, and commented on in online spaces that always entail collaboration in knowledge making and knowledge consumption.

Hashtags help to curate and organize these stories. Upon searching a social media platform for a specific hashtag, users can find a stream of posts by individuals and organizations conversing about that particular subject matter. Digital collections of stories are organized by the tags users attribute to their posts. In the era of the #MeToo movement, women share their own stories or simply post the hashtag #MeToo in solidarity to show that they, too, are survivors. Many survivors find these online communities to be sites of healing. The hashtags #MMIW or #MMIWG began to circulate more widely in the 2010s. These hashtags offer an intersectional approach to the #MeToo movement and demonstrate how Indigenous women in particular suffer violence from both outside and within their communities. Even simple posts such as this one from late 2019 on Twitter (Figure 5.1) increase online visibility of the suffering of and lack of justice for MMIW:

FIGURE 5.1 *#MMIW Twitter post, late 2019.*

FIGURE 5.2 *Native News Online Twitter Chat Announcement, October 8, 2019.*

And tweets like these continue their work for a long time: this tweet continues to generate trending posts today.

Nonprofit, activist, and news sites also use these hashtags to circulate information about their own work. Native News Online held a twitter chat on legislation related to MMIW on October 8, 2019 (Figure 5.2).

On Facebook, nonprofit groups organize community events and searches for MMIW. Missing and Murdered Indigenous Women USA (Figure 5.3) is a nonprofit organization that reports cases of missing Indigenous girls or women on a daily basis. It is often a sobering page to view. By circulating photographs and information such as the last known location of a missing girl or woman, this group has been able to help find missing girls and women. Their website and social media page also have a link where users can report cases so the nonprofit may quickly circulate that information. Missing and Murdered Indigenous Women USA also hosts events such as powwows, awareness events, and self-defense classes. The Facebook page is dedicated to Sherry Ann Wounded Foot, who was murdered on August 16, 2016. The National Indigenous Women's Resource Center is another nonprofit created specifically for providing Indigenous women with resources that are often unavailable to them, including technical assistance for those looking to escape domestic violence, links to advocacy and emergency hotlines, informative webinars, and policy development training for tribes. They have also launched multiple advocacy campaigns, including the StrongHearts Native Helpline, the VAWA Sovereignty Initiative, and the NativeLove project.

Many critics of online activism are quick to dismiss social media users as "slacktivists" or "clicktivists," but the power of posting online should not be underestimated. Slacktivism and clicktivism refer to modes of online activism that seemingly require "little time

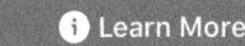

FIGURE 5.3 *MMIW USA Facebook Page, 2020.*

or involvement" and include reading, posting, sharing, and liking information and stories (Franklin 2014). M. I. Franklin argues that "there are good, bad, and indifferent forms of online political engagement just as there are in the offline world" (2014). Therefore, all online activism should not be considered lackluster or apathetic. Depending on their knowledge of their online audience, users can curate their feed and share news and posts that can help shift attitudes and actions, raise awareness, and enlist help from a range of communities. Social media activism should not be the only kind of activism we engage in, but it is a crucial element for creating conversations, mobilizing, and organizing.

Conclusion

I delivered a version of this essay in the 2020 MLA session "The Other Me-Too's." At the end of my presentation, I encouraged the audience to take a moment of silence in recognition of all of the Missing and Murdered Indigenous women and girls around the globe, but also to make it a moment of action. I now encourage readers to do the same. Here are a few ways to become more active in regards to MMIW: read books about violence against Indigenous women, like *The Round House* by Louise Erdrich and *The Beginning and End of Rape* by Sarah Deer; add books by Indigenous women to your reading list (Linda Hogan, Joy Harjo, Elissa Washuta, Terese Marie Mailhot, etc.); teach stories of MMIW and the legal, communal, human rights complexity of MMIW in your classroom; search #MMIW, #MMIWG, #NotInvisible, or #NoMoreStolenSisters on any social media platform and consider sharing a post; research community and public events on MMIW in your region and consider how you can aid in the efforts of preventing these abductions and assaults; write to your local representatives; "like" and "follow" Indigenous feminist organizations, such as the National Indigenous Women's Resource Center or Missing and Murdered Indigenous Women USA on social media; watch a YouTube video about MMIW. This list is far from exhaustive. But reading and teaching literature about MMIW and written by Indigenous women, along with participating in online activism, contribute meaningfully to activist movements whose ultimate goal is the elimination of violence against Indigenous women.

Works Cited

Archuleta, Elizabeth (2006), "'I Give You Back': Indigenous Women Writing to Survive," *Studies in American Indian Literatures*, 18 (4): 88–114.

Bender, Jacob and Lydia Maunze-Breese (2018), "Louise Erdrich's *The Round House*, the Wiindigoo, and *Star Trek: The Next Generation*," *American Indian Quarterly*, 42 (2): 142–61.

Bowers, Maggie Ann (2017), "Literary Activism and Violence against Native North American Women," *Wasafiri*, 32 (2): 48–53, doi: 10.1080/02690055.2017.1294364.

Cariou, Warren and Isabelle St-Amand (2017), "Introduction Environmental Ethics through Changing Landscapes: Indigenous Activism and Literary Arts," *Canadian Review of Comparative Literature*, 44 (1): 7–24.

Cernison, Matteo (2019), *Social Media Activism*. Amsterdam: Amsterdam University Press.

Crawford, Blair (2017), "15 Canadian Stories, Helen Betty Osbourne, A Murder That Resonates Nearly 50 Years Later," *Ottawa Citizen*, September 25. Available online: https://ottawacitizen.com/news/local-news/15-canadian-stories-helen-betty-osborne-a-murder-that-resonates-50-years-later (accessed July 22, 2020).

Deer, Sarah (2015), *The Beginning and End of Rape: Confronting Sexual Violence in Native America*, Minneapolis: University of Minnesota Press.

Dumont, Marilyn (2015), "Helen Betty Osborne," *Poetry Foundation*. Available online: https://www.poetryfoundation.org/poems/147310/helen-betty-osborne (accessed July 22, 2020).

Erdrich, Louise (2012), *The Round House*, New York: HarperCollins.

Franklin, M. I. (2014), "Slacktivism, Ckicktivism, and 'Real' Social Change," *OUP Blog*, November 19. Available online: https://blog.oup.com/2014/11/slacktivism-clicktivism-real-social-change/ (accessed August 7, 2020).

Griffith, Jessica Greer (2015), "Too Many Gaps, Too Many Fallen Victims: Protecting American Indian Women from Violence on Tribal Lands," *University of Pennsylvania Journal of International Law*, 36 (3): 785–819.

MMIW USA. *Facebook*. Available online: https://www.facebook.com/mmiwusa/ (accessed August 7, 2020).

Moll, Sorouja (2016), "The Writing Names Project: UnSilencing the Number of Missing and Murdered Indigenous Women and Girls," *Canadian Theatre Review*, 168: 94–7.

Nagle, Rebecca (2019), "Trump Issues Order to Create Taskforce on Violence against Indigenous Women," *The Guardian*, November 26. Available online: https://www.theguardian.com/world/2019/nov/26/trump-executive-order-taskforce-violence-against-indigenous-women (accessed January 2, 2020).

Nobiss, Christine (2020), "President Trump's Operation Lady Justice: The Truth about Violence to Indigenous Womxn, Girls, and LGBTQIA+/2S," *Seeding Sovereignty*, May 5. Available online: https://seedingsovereignty.org/blog/2020/1/4/trumps-operation-lady-justice-and-the-truth-about-violence-against-native-women (accessed July 20, 2020).

Page, Ruth (2013), "From Small Stories to Networked Narrative: The Evolution of Personal Narratives in Facebook Status Updates," *Narrative Inquiry*, 23 (1): 192–213.

Pember, Mary Annette (2019), "#MeToo in Indian Country; 'We Don't Talk about This Enough'," *Indian Country Today*, May 28. Available online: https://newsmaven.io/indiancountrytoday/news/metoo-in-indian-country-we-don-t-talk-about-this-enough-oXkstdPmDk2-zSXoDXZSZQ (accessed December 30, 2019).

Pember, Mary Annette (2019), "#MeToo. Toxic Masculinity: Addressing a Terrible Truth," *Indian Country Today*, May 30. Available online: https://newsmaven.io/indiancountrytoday/news/metoo-toxic-masculinity-addressing-a-terrible-truth-RuptdDeOa0atVczu7G-WCA (accessed December 30, 2019).

Pember, Mary Annette (2019), "#MeToo What Happens When Native Women Come Forward with Harassment Complaints," *Indian Country Today*, May 29. Available online: https://newsmaven.io/indiancountrytoday/news/metoo-what-happens-when-native-women-come-forward-with-harassment-complaints-6W2mE2aNgE6bJw4m84nHTg (accessed December 30, 2019).

Press Pool (2019), "Dancing IN Justice—A Missing and Murdered Indigenous Women Public Service Announcement," *Indian Country News*, September 6. Available online: https://newsmaven.io/indiancountrytoday/the-press-pool/dancing-in-justice-a-missing-and-murdered-indigenous-women-public-service-announcement-PL9VfOm9lEenkDWVEs6gvg (accessed December 30, 2019).

Pulley, Natanya Anne (2014), "Indigetechs: The Original Time-Space Traveling Native Americans and Our Modern World Hyper-Pow-Wow," *Western Humanities Review*: 95–101.

Shearer, Elisa (2018), "Social Media Outpaces Print Newspapers in the U.S. as a News Source," *Pew Research Center*, December 10. Available online: https://www.pewresearch.org/fact-tank/2018/12/10/social-media-outpaces-print-newspapers-in-the-u-s-as-a-news-source/ (accessed January 6, 2020).

Smiley, Cherry (2016), "A Long Road Behind Us, a Long Road Ahead: Towards an Indigenous Feminist National Inquiry," *Canadian Journal of Women and the Law*, 28: 309–13.

Udel, Lisa (2007), "Revising Strategies: The Intersection of Literature and Activism in Contemporary Native Women's Writing," *Studies in American Indian Literatures*, 19 (2): 62–82.

6

Credibility and Doubt in the Age of #MeToo

Namrata Mitra and Katherine Conner

How do teaching and studying in the age of #MeToo shape how we think about credibility and doubt in narratives of sexual violence and desire? In this essay, we—Namrata Mitra, a professor of English, and Katherine Conner, recent graduate in Media Studies and English, both at a small liberal arts college in New York—take up a conversation that began in our course on contemporary feminist literature in Fall 2018. In October of that semester, the Senate hearings of Supreme Court nominee Brett Kavanaugh aired on every television, radio, and streaming service, making it imperative that we unpack the public reception of the testimonies by Kavanaugh and Dr. Christine Blasey Ford as part of the coursework. Taking her cues from those discussions, Mitra, in the first section of this essay, argues that #MeToo has dismantled common myths about credibility as a virtue or source of truth in our society to show that it is instead a currency of power that is a necessary tool of both sexual oppression and resistance. In the second section, Conner, whose undergraduate years were saturated with media coverage of decades-long sexual assaults committed by Harvey Weinstein and other high-ranking figures in media, politics, and corporate industry, examines the complicated role of doubt in politics and in desire.

Unpacking Credibility

The #MeToo movement has exposed some of the ways in which credibility and doubt are central to maintaining structural power hierarchies. One of its main political contributions is its contesting of the unequal distribution of credibility in our society. I set this in discussion with Miranda Fricker's influential work on "testimonial injustice," which explores how a speaker is epistemically wronged when she is unjustly denied credibility by a hearer. She asks, what is the injustice done to someone's status as an agent of knowledge, or one's epistemic capacity, when one is not assigned credibility in proportion to the evidence? I then draw on her discussion of "hermeneutic injustice," which she argues is experienced by marginalized groups in a culture that denies them the shared resources to interpret their experiences.

#MeToo has helped expose a long-standing norm in our society: one who accuses someone more powerful of sexual assault will not be believed. Catharine MacKinnon, a law professor who helped shape sexual harassment laws in the United States, argues that #MeToo has been finally able to assign survivors credibility that institutional practices have historically denied:

> Many survivors realistically judged reporting pointless. Complaints were routinely passed off with some version of "she wasn't credible" or "she wanted it." I kept track of this in cases of campus sexual abuse over decades; it typically took three to four women testifying that they had been violated by the same man in the same way to even begin to make a dent in his denial. That made a woman, for credibility purposes, one-fourth of a person.
> (MacKinnon 2018)

Western liberal democracies have perpetuated the myth that sexual assault claims are easily and falsely made, harming the reputation of the accused whom the law is meant to guard (Edelstein 1998). Underlying this popular myth are the twin beliefs that everyone in society enjoys more or less the same level of credibility, and that accusers of sexual assault frequently abuse this default credibility. However, #MeToo and writings on the movement have repeatedly repudiated this myth by exposing three intertwined aspects of credibility distribution in our society. First, survivors of sexual assault are immediately denied credibility when they accuse someone in a position of greater power. In this case, the accused is usually believed and the harm understood to be his (or her) loss of reputation, as we saw in the cases of Anita Hill and Clarence Thomas (1991), Christine Blasey Ford and Brett Kavanaugh (2018), the many accusers of Bill Clinton and Donald Trump, and more recently Tara Reade and Joe Biden (2020). Second, if the power relationship is reversed, the accuser will be readily believed without any substantive demand for evidence while the less powerful accused will be subject to public wrath and violence. In the United States, this power discrepancy and its consequences have historically fallen along color lines as a way to ensure white supremacy, where unsubstantiated stories of white women assaulted by Black men have fueled a long history of lynching, most famously in the case of Emmett Till. Third, credibility is a currency of power and operates much like money; it can be acquired forcefully from another and used to influence others. While credibility has been historically weaponized as a tool of oppression, the #MeToo movement seeks to claim it as a means of resistance.

Jodi Kantor and Megan Twohey, in *She Said* (2019), reveal the obstacles they faced while reporting on Harvey Weinstein for *The New York Times*. In addition to the threat of lawsuit, they encountered the well-oiled legal machine designed to erase survivors' credibility while increasing the credibility of powerful men who routinely assaulted women. That Weinstein routinely assaulted women in lesser positions of power was common knowledge among long-time Hollywood actors and agents (Kantor and Twohey 2019: 27–48). However, following its existing policy, the Equal Employment Opportunity Commission (EEOC) removed the survivors' complaints from public record, and settled whenever possible. In almost all other cases, Weinstein and his lawyers silenced the survivors through legal intimidation and non-disclosure agreements (NDAs) (Kantor and Twohey 2019: 49). Excerpts of one of the NDAs located by Kantor and Twohey revealed extremely stringent rules imposed upon one of Weinstein's victims, Zelda Perkins. She was forbidden even from informing her accountant about the source of the settlement funds, and any medical practitioner to whom she disclosed the assault would have to sign their own NDA. Perhaps most outrageously, the NDA stipulated that if any information were to leak, Perkins would need to corroborate Weinstein's denial in order "to prevent any further disclosure or as the case may be to mitigate such effect" (Kantor and Twohey 2019: 66).

Should a survivor not want to sign an NDA or decide to break with its terms, she can still be silenced by an attack on her credibility. Ronan Farrow, who had also investigated allegations against Weinstein, uncovered a common media practice, called "catch and kill," in which a news outlet approaches someone who wants to share their testimony of assault, pays them for exclusive rights, then does not publish it. Run by powerful men who are friends with other powerful men, tabloids most commonly use this technique, disempowering accusers further by publishing salacious stories that depict survivors as manipulative and prone to lying, before they can go public with their account (Farrow 2019: 56–62). Farrow's own reporting on #MeToo was "killed" by his former employers at NBC, before *The New Yorker* agreed to publish his story.

In this context, credibility cannot be conceptualized as a virtue, like honesty, as though it were based on repeated acts of truth telling. Instead, credibility emerges as a currency of power that can be acquired, and weaponized against the weak. Credibility in the context of #MeToo operates as a zero-sum game: the more we believe the accused, the less we believe the accuser. Like money, credibility is not equally distributed in our society. Dominant groups hoard it to shape the story of our collective past and present, while subordinated groups claiming a different account are discredited as liars, delusional, and dangerous. Worse, the use of power to seize and deny credibility operates in a feedback loop, in which the dominant keep their power by controlling public narratives of their own and others' experience in order to maintain their excessive credibility, which in turn is the basis of their power.

The #MeToo movement has long recognized this relationship between power and credibility and seeks to redress power inequality maintained by the cycle of oppression in which a powerful person commits sexual violence and then controls the narratives of the event, thus garnering impunity from negative consequence for future sexual violence. The declaration "#MeToo" on social media, in person, and via email exchange, which roughly translates to "It happened to me too, so I believe you," is a means of attributing credibility to the speaker while expressing solidarity. #MeToo teaches us that to grant credibility to the accuser is to contest the power of the accused. Campaigns such as "#ibelieveher" (which emerged during Christine Blasey Ford's testimony against Kavanaugh) sought to do exactly this.

Sexual assault accusations at the intersection of #MeToo and Black Lives Matter movements illustrate that this power-credibility relationship works to maintain dominant power structures even when the positions of power of accuser and accused are reversed. In a recent example, a white woman responded to a Black man's request that she observe park rules and leash her dog by calling the police and claiming that "there is an African American man recording me, threatening me and my dog" (Closson 2020; Nir 2020). While Amy Cooper may not have expected Christian Cooper's recording of her threats to be viewed over 50 million times on Twitter, or the ensuing backlash, it seems she was counting on the long-standing credibility excess assigned to white women who call the police on Black men in lesser positions of power and portray them as dangerous figures. Social media users dubbed her "Central Park Karen" or the "Queen of Karens," employing a figure whose roots stretch back to the Antebellum "Miss Ann" (Bates 2020; Goldblatt 2020). These tropes illustrate the credibility excess assigned to middle-class white women when they summon the forces of state and patriarchy to inflict physical harm on Black men, even though the same women are denied credibility when they accuse more powerful white men. Meanwhile, routine sexual violence against Black women by white men, which has been historically normalized and rendered invisible in the public sphere, has long relied on a culture of silencing and denying credibility to Black women's testimonies of harm (Hammonds 1997; Threadcraft 2016). Thus, the intersection of #MeToo and Black Lives Matter reveals that credibility is fixed not to specific identities so much as it is to power relations: to have power over another relies on having credibility excess in relation to another who is assigned lesser credibility.

The unequal distribution of power is sustained by an unequal distribution of credibility. Yet, Miranda Fricker, in her landmark work *Epistemic Injustice*, conceptualizes credibility differently and so arrives at a very different conclusion about the effects of credibility excess. According to Fricker, the two main forms of epistemic injustice are testimonial injustice and hermeneutic injustice. Testimonial injustice occurs when one is assigned "a deflated level of credibility" (Fricker 2010: 5) based on the hearer's prejudice and implicit bias. Here, the harm of being denied credibility is epistemic, that is, "someone is wronged specifically in her capacity as a knower" (2010: 20, original italics). One of the many things we value in ourselves and in others is our shared capacity for knowledge and the soundness of judgment on the basis of which we understand what is real, unreal, true, a lie, or a misconception; to be denied the status of a knower is to be deemed a person of lesser worth. However, Fricker reasons that since testimonial injustice is an act of assigning credibility that is deficient to the evidence, a person cannot be wronged by being assigned excess credibility. So, for example, when a patient thinks their generalist doctor has the knowledge of a specialist doctor, that assumption does not harm the generalist. While framing credibility in epistemic terms, as Fricker does, exposes credibility excess as unjust only in specific circumstances, framing it in political terms, as asserted in this essay, exposes credibility excess as always unjust. As #MeToo shows, credibility is a finite good, like wealth, and it operates as a zero-sum game; the powerless have less of it because the powerful have so much more of it. Credibility distribution in our society has little to do with the evidential basis of our claims and much more to do with having the political and cultural power to control the narrative of events. By contrast, Fricker's epistemic approach to credibility, which only examines what is owed to the speaker on the basis of evidence, views credibility as an infinite good, unlike wealth or health care (2010: 19). Therefore, for Fricker, neither credibility excess nor unequal distribution of credibility is a condition of injustice (2010: 19).

However, Jennifer Lackey, who also draws on an epistemic approach to credibility, finds clear ways in which credibility excess harms the speaker in the context of the law and courtroom practices. She examines cases of police detainees who are assigned a credibility deficit when they deny the police's account of a charge, but then are granted credibility excess when they make a false confession, even though the evidence is insufficient in both instances. That is, the level of credibility granted to someone making a confession exceeds the level of evidence available and thus harms them (Lackey 2018).

Hermeneutic injustice, on the other hand, is a systemic epistemic condition whereby socially shared knowledge, such as in education curriculum, literature, film, laws, and social norms, is shaped by the experiences and perspectives of dominant groups (Fricker 2010: 148). We might think of it as a form of mass gaslighting of subordinated groups, who are denied the epistemic resources to fully make sense of their experiences. Fricker gives the example of someone who was sexually harassed at her workplace for years, blamed herself, and left her job. Only many years later did she come to understand her experience as sexual harassment. Similarly, rape survivors often blame themselves and feel confused for years until they encounter socially shared epistemic resources such as testimonies of other survivors, therapy, and feminist writings, which help them understand their experience and its effects more fully. The harm of hermeneutic injustice, as Fricker explains, is that "it tends to knock your faith in your own ability to make sense of the world, or at least the relevant region of the world" (Fricker 2010: 163).

Hermeneutic injustice is structural; it is caused not by an agent but by an unequal system that marginalizes certain groups (2010: 159). In this respect, Fricker's framework of hermeneutic injustice, unlike that of epistemic injustice, supports this essay's political analysis of unequal credibility distribution as a form of unequal power distribution. Such a framework carries significant implications for teachers and students of literature: in what ways do cultural representations contribute to hermeneutic injustice, and in what ways do they disrupt it?

Unpacking Doubt and Desire in Politics and Kristen Roupenian's "Cat Person"

The 2020 election poses a political "trolley problem" for feminist voters. In the famous philosophical thought problem, a trolley is barreling down a track that forks. One track has five people stuck on it; the other has one. By pulling a switch that changes the trolley's path, you can choose to kill one person and save five, or you can do nothing and allow five to die while saving one. In our current political situation, the track containing five is labeled "Trump," and those five being threatened are our society's most vulnerable: detained children, sexual violence survivors, DACA recipients, police brutality victims, and other marginalized communities targeted by Trump's policies. The track with one person reads "Biden." That person is Tara Reade, Anita Hill, and other survivors of workplace sexual violence. In 2016, I was a college freshman and first-time voter who was disgusted with Trump's stances toward the marginalized. #MeToo's 2017 social media revival resonated with my concerns as a woman entering the media workforce and a student of literature. Having graduated from college in 2020, I now find myself facing the choice between two nominees with sexual assault allegations. What is a feminist standing behind the switch, or at the voting booth, to do? Unwavering support for Biden says one of two things to Tara Reade and Anita Hill: either, "I don't believe you," or worse, "I believe you, but what happened to you doesn't matter enough."

As intense as this election may be for the feminist voter, the stakes have been as high for Biden's potential vice-presidential picks. In "The Biden Trap," Rebecca Traister noted that any woman selected as Biden's VP would be drinking from "a poisoned chalice" because "the promise to choose a woman ensures that whoever she is, she will be forced to answer—over and over again—for Biden's treatment of other women" (Traister 2020). Women are repeatedly asked to defend powerful men to the detriment of other women. In order to remain politically strong, Stacey Abrams and Kirsten Gillibrand were forced to answer that they support Biden, or to stay silent (Ehrlich and Barrett 2020; LeBlanc 2020). It is as though there is no room for women politicians supporting Biden to articulate any doubt aloud. Thus, women vice-presidential hopefuls became necessary and useful to Biden because the greatest blow to a survivor's credibility is a blow from someone of a shared marginalized identity. Since a woman is claiming she was abused by Biden, his campaign needed women to vouch for him against Reade's word. In politics, this is how credibility is acquired by the abuser at the cost of the survivor.

Of course, this issue cuts across party lines. Following the release of the infamous Access Hollywood tape, Anderson Cooper opened his interview of Melania Trump by asking, "Did you ever expect that all this stuff would come out, that allegations would be made, that you would be here defending him?" (Bradner 2016). By defending Trump publicly, as she was expected to, and calling other women's allegations lies, Melania used a traditionally doubted, gendered voice to deny credibility to accusers while adding credibility to the powerful accused. In this act, Melania drank from the same poisoned chalice that has been recently handed to Kamala Harris. As demonstrated here, doubted voices acquire credibility when mobilized in the interest of powerful figures.

As we see in the cases of Christine Blasey Ford, Tara Reade, and Anita Hill, any minor expression of doubt made by a marginalized survivor places their narrative at risk of being discredited altogether. Therefore, certainty of one's desire is strategically necessary to the #MeToo movement. Yet, our cultural scripts of desire that are predominantly written by rich, white, straight, cisgender men have been internalized by most people, even if they are at odds with their own desires. The gap between one's learned scripts of desire and experiences of desire can produce doubt in one's own understanding of desire. Published in *The New Yorker* in December 2017, Kristen Roupenian's "Cat Person" addresses this tension between the expectation that women be absolutely certain of whom, when, and how they desire while being immersed in a culture that has already told them whom to desire and how and when to desire and be desired. The story demonstrates the limitations of consent as a gatekeeper of positive sexual encounters, as the protagonist wills herself into a sexual encounter that she doesn't desire, in service of her internalized cultural expectations. Roupenian uses limited third-person point of view to tell the story of Margot, a college student who briefly dates the older Robert, allowing access only to her thoughts about the relationship.

"Romantic" images from popular novels, films, and television shows shape how Margot wants to be seen by Robert. When the twenty-year-old Margot feels like an "idiot" for crying after being denied entry to a bar, she soothes herself by rewriting the scene as something out of a romantic film: Robert was "gazing at her; in his eyes, she could see how pretty she looked, smiling through her tears in the chalky glow of the streetlight, with a few flakes of snow coming down" (Roupenian 2017). Margot follows a typical script in imagining how she desires to be desired by him: "Smiling through her tears" indicates a certain delicacy to the moment and eroticizes her vulnerability. The image of a heterosexual couple kissing in the snow is the basis for an entire genre of romantic comedies, including Hallmark films and Hollywood's *Love Actually*, both of which feature kisses or confessions of love in the snow.

Later that evening, Margot's learned scripts of desire come into direct conflict with her sense of her own desire during her visit to Robert's place. As Margot watches Robert undress clumsily, she feels nauseous, yet convinces herself to engage in sex with him:

> Margot recoiled. But the thought of what it would take to stop what she had set in motion was overwhelming; it would require an amount of tact and gentleness that she felt was impossible to summon [...] insisting to stop now, after everything she'd done to push this forward, would make her seem spoiled and capricious, as if she'd ordered something at a restaurant and then, once the food had arrived, had changed her mind and sent it back.
>
> (Roupenian 2017)

While Margot seems to no longer desire Robert, the cultural scripts of romance that have informed her understanding of desire, in which a woman who interrupts a man's sexual expectations is "spoiled" or "capricious," prevent her from leaving. Her fear of being seen through these sexist tropes is not unfounded. When she later rejects Robert from pursuing a relationship with her, he calls her a "whore" (Roupenian 2017).[1]

The story illustrates Margot's confusion and uncertainty when her ideas about how she should desire and her perceptions of her lack of desire conflict with each other. I read this story in two different classroom settings. In both scenarios, there was overwhelming agreement from the women in the room: many had been there and had done this.

The conflict between learned desire and experiences of desire faced by marginalized groups poses an issue for #MeToo. The movement relies on the expression of certainty in marginalized narratives of desire, to avoid risk of being discredited. Women are raised in a culture that affords little to no sex education and rarely cultivates sex-positive conversations, yet they are expected to claim absolute certainty about whom, what, and how they desire and want to be desired. So #MeToo cannot strategically afford to foster doubt in statements and claims of desire. Literature can therefore be a productive hermeneutic resource, as it can nurture the necessary ambiguity that is missing from wider cultural conversations about desire. The absence of such resources creates the conditions for hermeneutic injustice. Readers of "Cat Person" may feel an impulse to resolve Margot's felt contradictions between desire in representation and desire in experience, and the paradox of necessity yet unaffordability of doubt in #MeToo. However, any resolution to these tensions would force a loss of uncertainty, which denies the experiences of many, or a loss of certainty, which movements like #MeToo require in order to assign credibility to those who have been historically denied it.

By disseminating the accounts of sexual violence from the perspectives of marginalized and silenced people, #MeToo begins to expose and resist the testimonial injustice produced by our economy of credibility that benefits powerful accusers while discrediting the less powerful accused. Moreover, literature can be a valuable resource for challenging discussions within #MeToo as it recognizes that sexual relationships are full of ambiguities. As such, it invites us to consider the complexity of desire, a complexity that a mere performance of consent cannot fully capture.

Note

1   For an examination of "Cat Person" in relation to institutional causes and strategies for representing sexual violence, see Zoë Brigley Thompson's essay in this volume.

Works Cited

Bates, Karen Grigsby (2020), "What's in a Karen?" *Codeswitch: National Public Radio*, July 15. Available online: https://www.npr.org/2020/07/14/891177904/whats-in-a-karen (accessed July 16, 2020).

Bradner, Eric (2016), "Melania Trump: Donald Trump Was 'Egged On' into 'Boy Talk,'" *CNN*, October 18. Available online: https://www.cnn.com/2016/10/17/politics/melania-trump-interview/index.html.

Closson, Troy (2020), "Amy Cooper's 911 Call, and What's Happened Since," *New York Times*, July 8. Available online: https://www.nytimes.com/2020/07/08/nyregion/amy-cooper-false-report-charge.html?auth=login-email&login=email.

Edelstein, Laurie (1998), "An Accusation Easily to Be Made? Rape and Malicious Prosecution in the Eighteenth-Century England," *American Journal of Legal History*, 42 (4): 351–90.

Ehrlich, Jamie and Ted Barrett (2020), "Kirsten Gillibrand on Tara Reade Allegation: 'I Support Vice President Biden,'" *CNN*, April 29. Available online: https://www.cnn.com/2020/04/29/politics/kirsten-gillibrand-joe-biden-support/index.html.

Farrow, Ronan (2019), *Catch and Kill*, New York: Little, Brown and Company.

Fricker, Miranda ([2007] 2010), *Epistemic Injustice: Power & Ethics of Knowing*, New York: Oxford University Press.

Goldbatt, Henry (2020), "A Brief History of 'Karen,'" *The New York Times*, August 3. Available online: https://www.nytimes.com/2020/07/31/style/karen-name-meme-history.html (accessed August 5, 2020).

Hammonds, Evelynn (1997), "Toward a Genealogy of Black Female Sexuality: The Problematic of Silence," in M. Jacqui Alexander and Chandra Talpade Mohanty (eds.), *Feminist Genealogies, Colonial Legacies, Democratic Futures*, 170–82, New York: Routledge.

Kantor, Jodi and Megan Twohey (2019), *She Said: Breaking the Sexual Harassment Story That Helped Ignite a Movement*, New York: Penguin Press.

Lacky, Jennifer (2018), "Credibility and the Distribution of Epistemic Goods," in Kevin McCain (ed.), *Believing in Accordance with Evidence: New Essays on Evidentialism*, 145–65, Cham, Switzerland: Synthese Library.

LeBlanc, Paul (2020), "Stacey Abrams on Sexual Assault Allegation against Former VP: 'I Believe Joe Biden,'" *CNN*, April 29. Available online: https://www.cnn.com/2020/04/29/politics/stacey-abrams-joe-biden-tara-reade-cnntv/index.html.

MacKinnon, Catharine A. (2018), "#MeToo Has Done What the Law Could Not," *The New York Times*, February 4. Available online: https://www.nytimes.com/2018/02/04/opinion/metoo-law-legal-system.html (accessed October 2018).

Nir, Sarah Maslin (2020), "How 2 Lives Collided in Central Park, Rattling the Nation," *The New York Times*, June 14, Updated July 7. Available online: https://www.nytimes.com/2020/06/14/nyregion/central-park-amy-cooper-christian-racism.html (accessed July 15, 2020).

Roupenian, Kristen (2017), "Cat Person," *The New Yorker*, December 4. Available online: https://www.newyorker.com/magazine/2017/12/11/cat-person.

Threadcraft, Shatema (2016), *Intimate Justice: The Black Female Body and Body Politic*, New York: Oxford University Press.

Traister, Rebecca (2020), "The Biden Trap," *The Cut*, April 27. Available online: https://www.thecut.com/2020/04/the-biden-trap-woman-vice-president.html.

7

Quite Possibly the Last Essay I Need to Write about David Foster Wallace

Mary K. Holland

David Foster Wallace's work has long been celebrated for audaciously reorienting fiction toward empathy, sincerity, and human connection after decades of (supposedly) bleak postmodern assertions that all had become nearly impossible. Linguistically rich and structurally innovative, his work is also thematically compelling, mounting brilliant critiques of liberal humanism's masked oppressions, the soul-killing dangers of technology and American narcissism, and the increasing impotence of our culture of irony. Wallace spoke and wrote movingly about our need to cultivate self-awareness in order to more fully see and respect others, and created formal methods that construct the reader-writer relationship with such piercing intimacy that his fans and critics feel they know and love him.[1] A year after his death by suicide, as popular and critical attention to him and his work began to build into the industry of Wallace studies that exists today, he was first outed as a misogynist who stalked, manipulated, and physically attacked women.

In her 2009 memoir, *Lit*, Mary Karr spends less than four pages narrating the several years in which Wallace pursued her, leading to a brief romantic relationship that ended in vicious arguments and "his pitching my coffee table at me" (321). Unlike her accounts of the relationship nearly a decade later, Karr's tone here notably remains clever and humorous throughout. She also follows each disclosure of Wallace's ferocity with a confession of her own regrettable behavior: regarding his "temper fits" she admits to "sentences I had to apologize for" and assures us—twice—that "no doubt he was richly provoked" (320, and in an appended interview). After describing the coffee-table incident, she notes parenthetically that "years later, we'll accept each other's longhand apologies for the whole debacle," as if having a piece of furniture thrown at you makes you as guilty as having thrown it.

Three years later D. T. Max published his biography of Wallace, in which he divulged more shocking details about the relationship with Karr—that Wallace tried to buy a gun to kill her husband, that he tried to push her from a moving car (2012: 163, 175)—while also dropping enough details about Wallace's sex life and professed attitudes toward women to make him sound like one of his own hideous men. Wallace called female fans at his readings "audience pussy"; wondered to Jonathan Franzen whether "his only purpose on earth was 'to put my penis in as many vaginas as possible'"; picked up vulnerable women in his recovery groups; admitted to a "fetish for conquering young mothers," like Orin in *Infinite Jest*; and "affected not to care that some of the women were his students" (232, 233). In a 2016 anthology dedicated to the late author, one of those students, Suzanne Scanlon, published a short story about a student having a manipulative, emotionally abusive sexual affair with her professor (called "D-," "Author," and "a self-identified Misogynist"), using characteristic formal elements of "Octet" and "Brief Interviews" and dominated by the narrative voice popularized by David Foster Wallace.[2]

None of these accounts had any visible impact on fans' or readers' love of Wallace's writing or on critics' readings and opinions of his work. Rather, one blogger confessed in 2013 that Max's record of (some of) Wallace's misogynistic acts and statements could not shake her "faith in [his] fundamental goodness, intelligence, and likeability" because his "work seemed more real to me than his behavior did" (Rothfeld). Critic Amy Hungerford took the opposite stance in 2016, proclaiming her decision to stop reading and teaching Wallace's work, but without mentioning his abusive treatment of women or the question of how that behavior presses us to re-read the same in his work. Another blogger explained her discomfort at reading Wallace not in terms of the author's own behavior—which she gives no sign of being aware of—but because of sexual and misogynistic violence perpetrated on her by men she sees as very much like Wallace ("Small liberal arts colleges are breeding grounds for these guys") and in terms of patriarchy in general ("It's hard to distinguish my reaction to Wallace from my reaction to patriarchy"; Coyle 2017). Any woman who has been violated, talked over, and condescended to by this kind of man, the kind who thinks his pseudo-feminism allows him to enlighten her about her own experiences of male oppression and sexual violation, cannot help but sympathize with Coyle. But in rejecting Wallace because of other men's sexual violence and misogyny in general, she shifts the argument away from questions about how these function in the fiction and how Wallace's biography might force us to re-read that fiction, and allows for the kind of circular rebuttal that a (male) Wallace critic offered a year later: not all male readers of Wallace are misogynists; therefore, women should listen to the good ones and read more Wallace; let me tell you why (Hering 2018).

These pre-#MeToo reactions to Karr's and Max's reports of Wallace's abuse of women clarify what is at stake as readers, critics, and teachers consider this biographical information in the context of Wallace's work. For, while Wimsatt and Beardsley's argument against the intentional fallacy is compelling and important, its goal is to protect the sanctity of the *text* against the undue influence of our assumptions about the person who wrote it. Arguments defending the importance of Wallace's beautiful empathizing fiction in spite of his abuse of women threaten to do the opposite. Like Rothfeld, whose admiration for Wallace's fiction renders his own misogynistic acts less "real," David Hering argues that "the biographical revelation of unsavoury details about Wallace's own relationships" leads to an equation between Wallace and misogyny that "does a fundamental disservice to the kind of urgent questions Wallace asks in his work about communication, empathy, and power"—as if Wallace's real abuse of real women is not worth contemplating in comparison with his writing about how fictional men treat fictional women. Hering's use of the euphemism "unsavoury" to describe behavior ranging from exploitation to physical attacks, like his description of Wallace's work regarding gender as "troublesome," illustrates another widespread problem with nearly all critical treatments of this topic so far[3]: an unwillingness to say, or perhaps even see, that what we are talking about in the fiction and in the author's life is gender-motivated violence, stalking, physical abuse, even, in the case of Karr's husband, plotting to murder.

In the wake of the October 2017 resurgence of Burke's #MeToo movement, we see a curious split between Wallace-studies critics and others in their reactions to these allegations. Not only does Hering's response downplay the severity of Wallace's behavior and its relevance to his work; it also asserts Hering's "belief" that Wallace's work "dramatize[s]" misogyny, rather than expressing it—without offering a text-based argument or pointing to the critical work that had already done this analysis and found exactly the opposite to be true (see Himmelheber 2014; Holland 2016). He also relies on a technique used by memoirists, bloggers, and critics alike in their attempts to save Wallace from his own biography: he converts an example of male domination of women into a universal human dilemma, erasing the elements of gender and power entirely, by reading Wallace's silencing of his female interviewer's voice in *Brief Interviews* as "embody[ing] the richness of Wallace's work— its focus on the difficulty and importance of communication and empathy, and its illustration of the poisonous things that happen when dialogue breaks down" (Hering 2018). Such a reading ignores the fact that when dialogue breaks down between an entitled *man* and a pressured *woman*, the things that can happen go beyond metaphorically poisonous to physically sickening and injurious—as so many of the stories in that collection illustrate.

Given the same platform and the same task—celebrating Wallace around what would have been his fifty-sixth birthday—critic Clare Hayes-Brady offered "Reading David Foster Wallace in 2018," mere months after the social media flood of women's testimonies about sexual violence had begun. It does not mention #MeToo or the public allegations that had been made about Wallace, raising the question of what "in 2018" refers to. When asked several months later "what's changed?" in Wallace studies, after the public (but not critical) backlash had begun, Hayes-Brady falls back on the same generalizing technique used by Hering. She reframes accusations of misogyny as an entirely academic development, beneficial to Wallace studies and unrelated to #MeToo outcry against perpetrators of sexual violence ("a coincidence of timing"). She equates "flaws in his writing both technical and also moral and ethical," as if women had been up in arms across Twitter over Wallace's exhausting sentence structures. When directly asked if Wallace was a misogynist, she replies "yes, but in the way everyone is, including me," as if we neither have nor need a separate word for men who do not just live unavoidably in our misogynistic culture but also willfully perpetrate selfish, cruel, and violent acts of misogyny against women. That is, rather than responding humanely to indisputable evidence that our beloved writer was not the saint he would have liked us to think he was (and that we would have liked to believe him to be), Wallace critics—including me, in my silence at that time—refused to allow #MeToo to force the reckoning that was so clearly required. We did so by denying the relevance of his personal behavior to his fiction and to our work, or—worse—by participating in that age-old rape culture enabler: refusing to believe women's testimony.

Those outside literary studies reacted quite differently to the renewed attention #MeToo brought to these accusations. After Junot Díaz was publicly accused on May 4, 2018, of sexually abusing women, causing immediate public protest, Mary Karr responded by reminding us on Twitter of the abuse she had reported nearly a decade earlier, prompting a series of blog articles and interviews that supported Karr by recounting the allegations made by Karr and Max. They also began to reveal the misogyny that had shaped and stifled public reception of those allegations. Whitney Kimball (2018) pointed out that Max described Wallace's violent treatment of Karr as beneficial to his creative output and part of what made him "fascinating"; that in praising the "quite remarkable" "craftsmanship" of one of Wallace's letters, Max notes only in passing that the letter is Wallace's apology for planning to buy a gun to kill Karr's husband. Megan Garber (2018) noted the misogyny of an interviewer asking Max why "his feelings for [Karr] created such trouble for Wallace"—an example of what Kate Manne (2018) calls "himpathy," or empathizing with a male perpetrator of sexual violence rather than the victim.

#MeToo also began to make the misogyny of Wallace's work more visible to his readers. Devon Price describes how reading about Wallace's abuses against women caused her to revisit his work and see its gender violence for the first time. Tellingly, she also realizes that one of the reasons she was depressed when she fell in love with Wallace's work is that she was then in a physically, emotionally, and sexually abusive relationship. Price's realization points to another common reason why readers are blind to or defensive about the misogyny in Wallace's work and behavior, and to a key way in which the #MeToo movement can allow reading and literary studies to illuminate misogyny in synergistic ways: we are often blind to misogyny and sexual abuse, in fiction and in others' behavior, because we are living in it unaware. And the awareness of the spectrum of sexual abuse brought by #MeToo testimonies reveals misogyny not just in the fiction that we read, but in our own lives—one revelation causing the other.

To date, no new criticism has emerged that directly considers the implications to his work of Wallace's now widely reported misogyny and violence toward women.[4] But the recent publication of Adrienne Miller's memoir *In the Land of Men* (2020), which describes her years-long relationship with Wallace while she was literary editor at *Esquire*, makes a compelling, if unwitting, argument for the necessity of such biographically informed criticism. Miller documents the connection between Wallace's life and work in excruciating detail, recounting extended scenes between them in which Wallace speaks and acts nearly identically to the misogynists of *Brief Interviews*, an identification he encourages by telling her that "some of the interviews were 'actual conversations I had when I had to break up with people'" (247). But though Miller lays out the "sexism" of Wallace's fiction, especially *Jest* and *Brief Interviews*, more baldly than any of us Wallace scholars has so far (212, 234, 246, etc.), she remains, even from the vantage point of twenty years later and post-#MeToo, unable or unwilling to identify Wallace's treatment of her as abusive or misogynistic. In fact, most shocking about the memoir is not its record of Wallace's behavior but its methodical and steadfast refusal to acknowledge the gender violence of that behavior, and Miller's disturbing pattern of normalizing, apologizing for, and denying it (262, 265, 321–2, 303, 310, etc.).

Ultimately, she attempts to redirect us from the question of whether her relationship with Wallace qualifies as abuse or sexual harassment by asking, "Who looks to the artist's life for moral guidance anyway?" and "What are we to do with the art of profoundly compromised men?" (323). But rather than neatly pivoting from Wallace's culpability, these questions reveal important reasons why we must consider the lives of such men in conversation with their art. For these men are not merely passively "compromised" but aggressively compromis*ing*, in ways that our misogynistic culture obscures, and which savvy investigation of their art and lives can illuminate. And "moral" investigation is particularly indicated by the work of Wallace, who declared himself a maverick writer willing to return literature to earnestness and "love" ("Interview with David Foster Wallace" 1993), who wrote fiction that quizzes us on ethics and human value ("Octet" 1999), and who delivered a beloved commencement speech arguing the importance of recognizing one's inherent narcissism in order to extend care to others (2005).

What does it mean that *this* artist could not produce in his life the mutually respecting empathy he all but preached in his work (or, most clearly, in his statements about it)? What does it mean that a man and a body of work that claimed feminism in theory primarily produced a stream of abusive relationships between men and women in life and art? What can we learn about the blindness of both men and women to their participation in misogyny and rape culture, despite their professions of awareness of both? How might reading Wallace's fiction in the contexts of biographical information about him and women's narratives about their experiences of sexual violence enable us to better understand—and interrupt—the powerful hold misogyny and rape culture have on our society, our art, and our critical practices?

Misogyny in Wallace Studies

The short history of Wallace studies is a history of blindness to and silencing about the misogyny that pervades Wallace's work— and Wallace studies itself. In two dozen books devoted solely to his work and over two hundred articles and book chapters about it,[5] only a handful focuses on gender at all, and only one article—by Rachel Himmelheber, who tellingly is not a "Wallace scholar," with no other published work on him—accurately and directly describes what so much of his fiction considers or reproduces: rape culture. Every other critical piece that takes up the subject—including my own to this point—misreads, erases, obscures, or even enacts the fiction's misogyny and rape culture without fully naming them. The first article to focus on the dynamics of heterosexual relationships in *Brief Interviews* is the most offensive, going so far as to read "Brief

Interview #20" exactly as the manipulative and misogynistic narrator wants us to—as a love story, in which a (silenced) woman's brutal rape and near death at the hands of a mentally ill stranger (another rape culture myth about the "typical" rapist, as Himmelheber will later point out) become the narrator's opportunity to empathize and demonstrate his noble growth (while also attempting to seduce his female interviewer; Diakoulakis 2010).

While my own reading three years later goes to great pains to point out "the fraught interplay between language, desire, and power" in that story and throughout the collection, and offers readings of moments in which men commit rape, threaten rape, and manipulate women into "consenting" to rape, I never describe the stories as portraying or interrogating rape culture. Instead, I maintain tight focus on core ideas in Wallace studies at the time—language and empathy—noting "the linguistic contortions men undergo to make [sexual acts] happen" and that "men's sexual desire for women taints and often prevents any attempts by men to extend empathy ... to women" (2013: 107, 108). Of "Brief Interview #20" I offer my own evasive conclusion about "the impossibility of ... transcending either the narcissistic self or language" (121). Even while proceeding thus blindly, my reading leads me to declare that "many of [the interviews] consist of men manipulating a woman, their interviewer, into doing their sexual and/or emotional bidding, and/or further forgiving them for their objectifying behavior," and that "the entire body of interviews implies the woman's dawning understanding that the objectification she suffers is part of a larger hideousness of gender relations whose spectrum spans from quotidian to pathological" (117, 118–19). I could hardly have produced a better description of rape culture if I had tried, and yet at the time I had no word for it, so I did not.

Another chapter in the same critical volume aims to consider Wallace's misogyny head on, but produces equally unhelpful, if not damaging, results. "Language, Gender, and Modes of Power" uses dangerously false definitions of "misogyny" and inherently misogynistic arguments to argue against the misogyny of Wallace's writing. It blames the absence of fully drawn and voiced female characters on Wallace's "awareness of the inviolable strangeness of the female to the male" (Hayes-Brady 2013: 131) and "the alterity of the feminine" (134), as if these are objective things and not misogynistic fantasies. It denies male domination of women, sexual and otherwise, by arguing that brutalized women are empowered by men's desire of them (131) and that total submission, like the woman's in "Brief Interview #20," is a feminine form of power (143–5, 148). It asserts that what Franzen suggests might be misogyny is really male fear of solipsism and need of woman as stabilizing Other (133–4), and attributes the "absence of the feminine" to "mystery" rather than "dislike," then claims that "the term 'misogyny' in its strict sense is both too negative for Wallace's approach to women, and too positive, in the sense that the passion that informs misogyny implies sufficient subjectivity in the Other as to inspire fear, where Wallace's women are beyond the human Other" (134). That is to say, merely viewing women as unknowable, mysterious, Other, and inhuman does not constitute misogyny—*contra* Simone de Beauvoir's entire argument in *The Second Sex*. One must view them as human and passionately dislike them. Ultimately the chapter flees the subject altogether by pivoting to general frameworks that hide their misogyny, by enlisting a Hegelian framework of Self/Other rather than male/female, calling "Wallace's attitude to femininity ... not a matter of simple chauvinism or misogyny, but rather of balance and delicacy" (132), and concluding about "Brief Interview #20" that "the complexity of the narrator's attitude to the girl" (the character is a woman in her twenties) "maps on to Wallace's expression of the attitude of a writer to his readers" (146). Once again, the story was about Wallace all along, not a culture that allows men to violate and silence women and then coopt their stories.[6]

My own essay on "Gender and Communication" across Wallace's work, published in 2016, makes the opposite case, but again without directly confronting that work's participation in misogyny and rape culture. The essay uses readings of his work from *The Broom of the System* to *The Pale King* to argue that Wallace consistently constructed women for the use of men, and men as seeking to dominate women, often sexually, by "physical or linguistic force"; that the fiction imagines no way out or clear critique of its misogyny; and that Wallace saw himself as complicit in it. Yet I rarely use the word "misogyny," instead citing "heterosexual male assertions of power against women in physical and linguistic male acts of self-definition" (6). I turn similar verbal somersaults to demonstrate the pervasive misogyny in his work without directly accusing him of putting it there, just as—a firm believer in Wimsatt and Beardsley—I am scrupulous about proving his complicity with his characters' misogyny using only his essay "The Empty Plenum" and his own words as cited by Lipsky—even though at the time I had read both *Lit* and Max's biography. Not unlike Hayes-Brady in her attribution of Wallace's misogyny to the frameworks he employed, I even seem to imply that Wallace's men are misogynist because they exhibit a Lacanian structure of self, rather than seeing that his notions of male self can helpfully be explained by Lacan because they (like Lacan's notions of self, other, and gender) are misogynist (2).[7]

I can explain the evasive title of my essay and its refusal to speak directly to misogyny by my not-irrational fear that an essay accusing Wallace of misogyny in his fiction and life in 2016 would never be published.[8] I still think that was probably true then but is not today, which only proves how powerfully #MeToo has already affected literary studies. But in redirecting culpability for that misogyny; not seeing the sexual violence perpetrated by his characters as stemming from that misogyny or as part of a spectrum of methods of dominating women that comprises our rape culture; and not viewing Wallace's own acts of violence toward women as even more telling and relevant to his work than the intellectual complicity he confessed to in his essay, I demonstrated my own blindness to what should have been one of my essay's key arguments, and produced a reading that was powerless to help a reader like Price make the crucial connection between Wallace's fiction and the abuse she had endured in her own life.

The Wallace criticism that has emerged since #MeToo exacerbates this problematic record rather than remedying it.[9] Edward Jackson's *David Foster Wallace's Toxic Masculinity* (2020), whose title suggests it will address these issues directly, surprisingly ignores the real-world accounts one would expect it to grapple with. Though admitting to the "conservatism" on gender and sexuality of Wallace's work (179), the book consistently reads male sexuality in the framework of "neoliberal logics" and as "a form of capital" (3, 14) and converts sexual toxicity into "anti-futurist negativity" and sexual violence into "an unrepresentable 'real'" (10), containing the argument in the realm of gender-neutrality, impersonal systems, and theory. It thus erases the feminist question of men's attitudes toward women (misogyny) and male treatment of and sexual violence toward women (rape and rape culture) as thoroughly as it erases the many reports of Wallace's own abusive treatment of women, and the question of how that reality must inform our reading of the fiction. Such a direct translation of gendered sexual violence into intellectual abstraction is an alarming example of academic silencing and denial of the issue and real-life experiences of women's domination and suffering at the hands of men.

Earlier the same year, Mary Shapiro used her impressive examination of dialect across Wallace's work to demonstrate that his protagonists are "hypermasculine" and prone to "himpathy." But when she obliquely refers to the "less admirable" qualities of Wallace-the-man, she never mentions misogyny or gender violence, then apologizes for bringing the biography up at all, again pivoting from the question of gender to ask "who among us can live up to the image we'd rather project to the world?" (2020: 190, 192). Her only mention of #MeToo and the spotlight it trained on Wallace's violence against women is her "guess" that, if alive, "he would have produced the world's most gut-wrenching, self-excoriating, beautifully poetic apology" (193)—which feels rather a lot like Max praising the "remarkable craftsmanship" of Wallace's letter about plotting to kill Karr's husband.

This tendency of Wallace studies not simply to passively omit the misogyny it should be examining but to actively deny, misrepresent, and even contribute to it clarifies why it is crucial for literary studies to purposely consider sexual violence and misogyny across fields and authors, and suggests the work individual academics need to do to make that happen. First, critics require sufficient understanding and vocabulary to diagnose rape culture and misogyny in literary works, and thus to enable literature and criticism to interrupt these damaging cultural forces. Critics for whom the systemic misogyny of our culture—and thus of our own assumptions about gender, power, and sex—remains invisible will be likelier to enlist and perpetuate elements of misogyny in our arguments than to critique them. Second, we need such work to be done in every literary field, especially on authors whose works do not invite such readings (and may even repel feminist-oriented readers). The feminist re-readings called for by second-wave literary feminism have barely begun on the subject of sexual violence and rape culture. The failure of Wallace studies—and of the insularity it promotes—to face these issues head-on over decades of prolific criticism underscores this need.

At stake is not only the health and cultural relevance of literary studies, or the power of individual academics to do their most meaningful and courageous work, but also the well-being of thousands of survivors, especially women. We recognize the need to write and teach about misogyny and rape culture in order to educate young people about their many invisible dangers. But we seldom acknowledge academics' need to examine misogyny and rape culture in order to more fully recognize the patterns of abuse in our own lives. When Devon Price realizes that the depression she was in when she fell in love with Wallace's work was largely caused by her emotionally, physically, and sexually abusive relationship at the time, she is also realizing that she was able to fall in love with Wallace's work because she was as blind to the abusiveness in it as she was to that in her own life. I can say the same about what my former love of Wallace's work says about my blindness to the misogyny and rape culture at work in my own life, a blindness I incorporated into and passed on with my work about his fiction. Reading women's accounts of rape, coerced sex, and other forms of misogynistic violence—catalyzed by #MeToo—made plain for me what studying and teaching feminist theory for years could never do.

Using Biography and Testimony in Criticism and Teaching

Mary Karr, whose feminist credentials are much more impressive than mine, described a similar revelatory experience as a result of #MeToo: "I'm in my 60s, and ... I've been a feminist since I was 8 years old, but ... I feel like all my life I have pandered to men in a way that I wasn't aware of" (2018). She also acknowledges the power of #MeToo to make more widely visible the damaging complicity between patriarchy and rape that should have been visible all along: "When people used to tell me there was a rape culture, it's not a new idea that it's bad to rape people, but you know what, it's kind of a new idea that it's bad to rape people. It kind of is" (2018). #MeToo continues to demonstrate the power of sharing personal narratives, testimony, and survivor stories to reveal systemic and particular injustices that no amount of intellectual or individual work could make plain. One lesson academics must take from #MeToo, then, is that we must find ways to incorporate these narratives into our literary criticism and teaching,[10] even as we allow our own encounters with survivors' stories to change how we think about our lives and our work. Meanwhile, we also need to consider how most productively to use in our criticism and teaching the biographical information about authors that is being unearthed (or paid attention to) because of #MeToo.

Without regressing to the subjectivism of nineteenth-century criticism, we can bring biographical information to bear on literary criticism around the topic of sexual violence and rape culture in several productive ways. Given the invisible pervasiveness of both in our patriarchal culture, the kind of information we have about Wallace's life should make us approach the fiction with more skepticism, less ready or eager to read sympathetically and more insistent on establishing the presence (or absence) of critique in the text, rather than being content to assume or invent it, as the critics examined above have been. Such biographical information can also press us to connect the issues being raised in the fiction with real-world problems and consequences, reminding us that fiction is continuous with our lived experience, an artifact of culture that requires our careful consideration as well as an important site for changing that culture. That Wallace struggled with his own misogyny at least as much as do his characters is significant to me as a critic not solely because of what it says about Wallace but because it underscores the fiction's own struggles and helps us see how it can open up a necessary conversation about these problems: our critical readings can construct the critiques of misogyny and rape culture that the fiction cannot fully mount. And given the enduring popularity of Wallace's work, especially among young male readers—in particular with dissertating graduate students and so with future assistant professors—it's crucial that we continue to do so.[11] So while this essay may be the last I choose to write about Wallace's work, having invested a significant portion of my career so far in it, and now wanting to take my writing in new directions, I continue to view Wallace's work as requiring (a new kind of) critical attention.

Deciding when to include information about Wallace's misogyny in our teaching and whether to assign his work depicting sexual violence raises thornier questions. In this context, Shapiro's claim that Wallace's work is not "*toxically* masculine" because "those who choose to keep reading *invite* Wallace to continue" (192, original italics), which I don't find altogether convincing as a critic, becomes quite relevant to me as a teacher. How do we decide under what circumstances, and to what ends, to assign fiction that dramatizes sexual assault as required reading for students, some of whom might be survivors?

In a course focused on period or form, in which I typically do not spend much time on authors' biographies, I can imagine continuing to use "Octet" or "Good Old Neon" to discuss how Wallace influenced the transition out of postmodernism, without taking what would feel like a prurient rather than relevant detour through Wallace's catalog of misogyny. But in the wake of #MeToo, with the rawness of so many women's stories of sexual abuse fresh in my mind and the new clarity and pain of my own understanding, I could never again teach *Brief Interviews* as a whole (or its individual "interviews") as anything other than a complicated and failed interrogation of misogyny and rape culture. I would also not teach it outside the wider context of sexual violence as perpetrated by Wallace in his life, reported but largely ignored by multiple women, misogynistically inflected by his biographer, denied by critics, and mostly left uncommented upon in his own fiction. I would assign excerpts by Karr, Miller, Max, Hering, Hayes-Brady, Price, and myself to illustrate how blind women can be to misogyny and sexual abuse in our own lives, how blind "self-aware" men can be to the misogyny and violence they commit, how blind well-meaning critics can be about the authors we admire. I would use this constellation of fiction, biography, criticism, blog, and memoir to consider the contradiction of an intellectually feminist man producing fiction that can't find its way out of its misogyny, alongside the contradiction that the same mind that produced this misogyny also produced fiction whose commitment to nonjudgment and mutual respect is at times stunning and beautiful. I would admit that I have taught *Brief Interviews* many times before without mitigating its brilliance with its misogyny, and I would describe the power of #MeToo to profoundly change how I see my own life, and thus how I read fiction, write criticism, and teach. I would place myself in the good company of Karr, Miller, Price, and Hayes-Brady, feminists all, who require other women's testimony and reflection to comprehend in our real lives—and so to apply in our life's work—what we have been trained to understand intellectually for years, even decades.

Reading Wallace's fiction in this context would not prioritize biography at the expense of his work. Instead, it would add another dimension to the many ways in which the fiction famously reflects upon itself and forces readers into infinite acts of self-reflection. Such an all-encompassing approach—barring nothing and attempting to swallow all contradiction—makes perfect sense for the work of a fundamentally deconstructive writer. But I would suggest that we take this approach to the work of all authors who have been so accused, neither denying the abuse nor jettisoning the intellectual and cultural work that their literature can still enact. In so doing, we can make these works do things their authors never dreamt of. Wimsatt and Beardsley would approve.

Notes

1 Cory Hudson argued against such an approach in 2018, calling on Wallace critics—namely me—to stop using what Wallace said about his fiction in interviews as a basis for reading the fiction. Without agreeing with all the readings in Hudson's essay, I do agree with that corrective. We might go so far as to ask whether, in the wake of information about Wallace's consistently manipulative treatment of women, the serious skepticism with which we must view his claims of sincerity likewise forces us to reconsider the validity of the "new sincerity" lens through which scholars often read his fiction (see Adam Kelly 2010).
2 Charles Harris, who edited the volume and was Wallace's close friend and the father of a woman with whom Wallace had a long relationship, claims in the Introduction that "none of the contributions is *about* David in a strict biographical or autobiographical sense" and that characters resembling him are "wholly imagined" (2016: xxxiii, original italics). In light of reports of Wallace's behavior, this disavowal is wholly unconvincing, and instead evidence of how tempting it is to remain blind to misogyny and sexual harassment when perpetrated by our friends and colleagues. Scanlon's 2015 story "The Rape Essay (or Mutilated Pages)" depicts a student's ambivalence about her sexual affair with a professor (easily identifiable as Wallace) who insists she read an essay that explores the murky gradations between rape and consent.
3 Rachel Himmelheber's 2014 "'I Believed She Could Save Me'" is the notable exception.

4   One article (Sheldon 2020) appears to aim to do so, but winds up co-opting Karr's story of suffering and silencing for its own larger argument about the persistence of Wallace's public image—another version of the "himpathy" enacted by "Brief Interview #20" (Wallace 1999).
5   As documented by the David Foster Wallace Research Group out of the University of Glasgow (https://davidfosterwallaceresearch.wordpress.com/).
6   Hayes-Brady repeats and expands on these arguments about Wallace and gender in *The Unspeakable Failures of David Foster Wallace* (Bloomsbury 2016).
7   Hamilton Carroll's "Desire, Self, and Other" does (and does not do) in 2019 for teaching Wallace what my 2016 essay did: it suggests ways of teaching Wallace's work that interrogate his constructions of gender and power, and points out the limits of his attempts to escape patriarchy, without going so far as to illustrate the ways in which that work (much less the author's life) participates in rape culture.
8   Indeed, though I had published numerous chapters and essays on Wallace by then, the piece was rejected by multiple journals known for publishing essays on Wallace—one of which has asked me several times (before and since) to evaluate others' Wallace essays and recommend for or against publication.
9   Daniela Joffe's "No Man's Land" (2018) echoes several main arguments of "'By Hirsute Author.'"
10 See chapters by Tanya Serisier, Elif Armbruster, Sarah Goldbort, Roberta Hurtado, and Zoë Brigley Thompson in this volume.
11 The importance of continuing to work with graduate students who are determined to write on Wallace became painfully clear to me recently when I served as the external reviewer for a dissertation that not only significantly misread Wallace as a whole but entirely subscribed to Diakoulakis's misogynistic reading of "Brief Interview #20" (2010). When I explained why this reading was not just mistaken but offensive, the committee decided to have the student cut the section rather than rewriting it, thus in no way making this student aware of the misogyny of the story or of her reading.

Works Cited

Carroll, Hamilton (2019), "Desire, Self, and Other: Wallace and Gender," in Stephen J. Burn and Mary K. Holland (eds.), *Approaches to Teaching the Works of David Foster Wallace*, 169–81, New York: MLA.

Coyle, Dierdre (2017), "Men Recommend David Foster Wallace to Me," *Electricliterature.com*, 17 April. Available online: https://electricliterature.com/men-recommend-david-foster-wallace-to-me/ (accessed June 3, 2020).

Diakoulakis, Christoforos (2010), "'Quote Unquote Love ... a Type of Scotopia': David Foster Wallace's *Brief Interviews with Hideous Men*," in David Hering (ed.), *Consider David Foster Wallace: Critical Essays*, 147–55, Los Angeles: Sideshow Media.

Garber, Megan (2018), "David Foster Wallace and the Dangerous Romance of Male Genius," *The Atlantic*, May 9. Available online: https://www.theatlantic.com/entertainment/archive/2018/05/the-world-still-spins-around-male-genius/559925/ (accessed December 9, 2019).

Harris, Charles, ed. and Introduction (2016), *Proofread or Die!: Writings by Former Students & Colleagues of David Foster Wallace*, xxvii–xxxiii, Gillson, IL: Lit Fest Press.

Hayes-Brady, Clare (2013), "'...': Language, Gender, and Modes of Power in the Work of David Foster Wallace," in Stephen J. Burn and Marshall Boswell (eds.), *A Companion to David Foster Wallace Studies*, 131–50, New York: Palgrave.

Hayes-Brady, Clare (2018), "Belatedness: Reading David Foster Wallace in 2018," *Bloomsbury Literary Studies Blog*, February 20. Available online: http://bloomsburyliterarystudiesblog.com/continuum-literary-studie/2018/02/belatedness-reading-david-foster-wallace-2018.html (accessed December 9, 2019).

Hering, David (2018), "Thinking about David Foster Wallace, Misogyny and Scholarship," *Bloomsbury Literary Studies Blog*, February 19. Available online: http://bloomsburyliterarystudiesblog.com/continuum-literary-studie/2018/02/thinking-david-foster-wallace-misogyny-scholarship.html (accessed December 9, 2019).

Himmelheber, Rachel Haley (2014), "'I Believed She Could Save Me': Rape Culture in David Foster Wallace's 'Brief Interviews with Hideous Men #20'," *Critique: Studies in Contemporary Fiction*, 55 (5): 522–35.

Holland, Mary K. (2013), "Mediated Immediacy in *Brief Interviews with Hideous Men*," in Stephen J. Burn and Marshall Boswell (eds.), *A Companion to David Foster Wallace Studies*, 107–30, New York: Palgrave.

Holland, Mary K. (2016), "'By Hirsute Author': Gender and Communication in the Work and Study of David Foster Wallace," *Critique: Studies in Contemporary Fiction*, 58 (1): 65–78.

Hudson, Cory (2018), "David Foster Wallace Is Not Your Friend: The Fraudulence of Empathy in David Foster Wallace Studies and 'Good Old Neon'," *Critique: Studies in Contemporary Fiction*, 59 (3): 295–306.

Hungerford, Amy (2016), "On Not Reading," *The Chronicle of Higher Education*, September 11. Available online: https://www.chronicle.com/article/On-Refusing-to-Read/237717 (accessed June 4, 2020).

Jackson, Edward (2020), *David Foster Wallace's Toxic Sexuality: Hideousness, Neoliberalism, Spermatics*, New York: Bloomsbury.

Joffe, Daniela Franca (2018), "No Man's Land: David Foster Wallace and Feminist America," *The Journal of David Foster Wallace Studies*, 1 (1): 2–21.

Karr, Mary (2009), *Lit*, New York: Harper Perennial.

Karr, Mary (2018), "Memoirist Mary Karr on God, #MeToo and Speaking Up about David Foster Wallace," *WBUR.org*, May 15. Available online: https://www.wbur.org/hereandnow/2018/05/15/mary-karr-tropic-squalor (accessed December 9, 2019).

Kelly, Adam (2010), "David Foster Wallace and the New Sincerity in American Fiction," in David Hering (ed.), *Consider David Foster Wallace: Critical Essays*, 131–46, Seattle: Sideshow Media.

Kimball, Whitney (2018), "Mary Karr Reminds the World That David Foster Wallace Abused and Stalked Her, and Nobody Cared," *Jezebel*, May 15. Available online: https://jezebel.com/mary-karr-reminds-the-world-that-david-foster-wallace-a-1825799769 (accessed May 29, 2020).

Manne, Kate (2018), *Down Girl: The Logic of Misogyny*, London: Oxford University Press.

Max, D. T. (2012), *Every Love Story Is a Ghost Story*, New York: Viking.

McCaffery, Larry ([1993] 2012), "An Interview with David Foster Wallace," in Stephen J. Burn (ed.), *Conversations with David Foster Wallace*, 21–52, Jackson: University Press of Mississippi.

Miller, Adrienne (2020), *In the Land of Men*, New York: HarperCollins.

Paulson, Steve (2018), "David Foster Wallace in the #MeToo Era: A Conversation with Clare Hayes-Brady," *The Los Angeles Review of Books*, September 10. Available online: https://lareviewofbooks.org/article/david-foster-wallace-in-the-metoo-era-a-conversation-with-clare-hayes-brady/(accessed December 9, 2019).

Price, Devon (2018), "A Brief on Hideous Things about David Foster Wallace," *Medium*, May 6. Available online: https://medium.com/@devonprice/a-brief-on-hideous-things-about-david-foster-wallace-72034b20de94 (accessed December 9, 2019).

Rothfeld, Rebecca (2013), "The Misogyny of David Foster Wallace," *New York Daily News*, May 15. Available online: https://www.nydailynews.com/blogs/pageviews/misogyny-david-foster-wallace-blog-entry-1.1640569 (accessed June 4, 2020).

Scanlon, Suzanne (2015), "The Rape Essay (Or Mutilated Pages)," in Belinda McKeon (ed.), *A Kind of Compass: Stories on Distance*, Dublin: Tramp Press.

Scanlon, Suzanne (2016), "Final Exam," in Charles Harris (ed.), *Proofread or Die!: Writings by Former Students & Colleagues of David Foster Wallace*, 115–26, Gillson, IL: Lit Fest Press.
Shapiro, Mary (2020), *Wallace's Dialects*, New York: Bloomsbury.
Sheldon, Zachary (2020), "Public Memory and Popular Culture: Biopics, #MeToo, and David Foster Wallace," *Atlantic Journal of Communication*. doi:10.1080/15456870.2020.1712603.
Wallace, David Foster (1999), *Brief Interviews with Hideous Men*, Boston: Back Bay Books.
Wimsatt, William K., Jr. and Monroe C. Beardsley ([1946] 2010). "The Intentional Fallacy," in Vincent B. Leitch (ed.), *Norton Anthology of Literary Criticism*, 2nd edn., 1232–46, New York: W. W. Norton & Company.

PART II

Re-readings

8

Philomela's Tapestry and #MeToo:

Reading Ovid in an Indian Feminist Classroom

Aditi Joshi, Anushka Srivastava, Katyayani, Mahwash Akhter, Prasanta Bani Ekka, Shivangi Tiwary, Shweta, and Zahanat[1]

In early May 2020, in the midst of the pandemic lockdown in India, news about an online chat group run by teenage boys at elite schools in Delhi, the "Bois Locker Room," made headlines for its casual conversations about vivid descriptions and photographs of slut-shaming and sexual objectification of girl students (Gupta 2020). Even while the incident was strongly condemned and the matter was handed over to the police, a disquieting phrase recurred in the media regarding the "normalization" of rape and misogyny in everyday culture ("*Bois Locker Room*" 2020). We, college-going women students who have learned to critique rape narratives in literary texts and the endemic rape culture in social texts in the age of #MeToo, take issue with the term "normalization." It suggests acquiescence to, if not justification of, the misogyny and violence inherent in social structures, stereotypes, and myths, a "normalization" that regulates and sanctions social identities within biological categories and rejects the wider register of gender rights. As postcolonial feminist critics, we mediate our feminist-materialist approach to deconstructing literary myths of rape cultures with our locations as women in multiple and contested social histories in contemporary India. In this chapter, through an examination of Ovid's "Philomela," a prescribed text in our curriculum, we address the issue of female solidarity and justice as it has emerged in the wake of the global #MeToo campaigns that began in the United States in October 2017.

While reading the Ovidian story of rape and justice, we were struck not just by the sexual and physical violence perpetrated by the Thracian king, Tereus, on his sister-in-law Philomela, but also by the retributive justice dealt by Tereus's wife Procne and by Philomela. While the violence implicit in the acts of filicide and cannibalism remains unparalleled, we found a ready reception of the myth in subsequent retellings in Western literary texts in the medieval and modern periods. Simultaneously, we found disconcerting similarities between Ovid's myth and our present-day rape culture insofar as both authorize a cycle of coercion, rape, and silencing of the survivor aided by social and institutional power structures. The etymological moorings of the Latin term *rapare* and the Hindi-Sanskrit word *balatkar* are suspiciously close in their emphasis on the use of force. Are rape cultures universal? We probed further.

Our heuristic intentions prompted us to analyze the myth's competing claims of motherhood and misogyny—Procne's murder of her son and Tereus's rape of Philomela. We further examined the rape tapestry woven by Philomela, an act which produces the sisterly solidarity between Procne and Philomela. The tapestry functions as a metaphor for female solidarity and resistance by asserting the female voice against the structural silencing of rape survivors. Contextualizing the text in our times, we found a powerful resonance in the shared sisterhood of the #MeToo movement, in the woven tapestries created out of social networking platforms that empower women survivors to publicly name predatory men in high places, in universities, and in the entertainment and media industries. Since September 2018, the Indian #MeToo movement has named and shamed several celebrities, politicians, and academics. While the possibility of using the movement to access the legal justice system is still limited, the Harvey Weinstein conviction does instill hope.

However, the price of #MeToo has been heavy, as survivors also face the threat of defamation, and given the evidentiary weaknesses inherent in the accusations, most perpetrators in India have gone scot-free. So, even while the #MeToo movement animated our classroom discussions of the complexities of consent and forced consent—a recurring problem in rape myths and trials—our attention was drawn to the heavily skewed justice system that punishes the survivor while exonerating the accused. We seek to explain the lack of justice in silenced rape narratives that are excluded from the urbane worlds of social media and news portals. Our critical imperative was to connect our feminist literary texts with the silent worlds of these women survivors.

Drawing inspiration from Philomela's loom, this chapter weaves a tapestry out of our personal, political, and scholarly identities and commitments. In the first section, we draw attention to the issue of retributive justice in Ovid's "Philomela" and examine its reception in specific Western texts that revise the myth through a patriarchal lens. Mapping this journey as critical practitioners who seek to connect the "academic lit speak" with the "lay discourses of culture" (Pathak 1992: 427), we trace the disembodiment of Philomela's tongue in the silenced rape narrative from two strikingly different contexts: the politically restless and heavily militarized region in Kashmir, and the deeply underdeveloped, poverty-driven, tribal majority district in the state of Chhattisgarh. Our objective is to study the ways in which established socio-political structures repress and silence rape survivors, deny justice, and attempt to delegitimize the tapestries of solidarity. We conclude by reiterating that as readers and critics, we believe that the literary and social struggle for meaning "enables us to live our lives more critically" (Pathak 1992: 426)— challenging our assumptions about others, and empowering us to build solidarity against oppression.

Philomela's Tapestry and the Canon

Written in 8 CE, Ovid's "Philomela" is based on the Greek myth of the Athenian sisters Procne and Philomela. Tereus, king of Thrace and husband of Procne, rapes the captive "virgin" princess Philomela and slices off her tongue (*Metamorphoses,* bk 6, lines 486–548). Procne receives Philomela's tapestry, which narrates the story of Tereus's deceit and predatory power. In an act of "retributive-justice," the two sisters kill Itys, Procne and Tereus's son, and trick Tereus into eating the boy. At the end of the story, the three are metamorphosed into birds, with Tereus eternally chasing the sisters. This *deus ex machina*, the metamorphosis into birds, spares the reader from further brutalities, but at the same time leaves the question of justice unanswered. That maternal filicide appears to be the sisters' only mode for attaining retribution suggests that justice requires Tereus to lose his heir, symbol of the virility and paternity that legitimize his kingship and power.[2] Thus, the myth suggests that for the sisters, Tereus's heir symbolizes all that absolves him from the culpability of his crime: his virility and his paternity which legitimize his kingship and power. Therefore, to punish Tereus for a crime for which he thinks he is not answerable to anyone, Procne and Philomela transgress social and natural laws.

The infanticide, considered in ancient myth "as a woman's crime … a woman's way of marking the dissolution of her marriage," offers retributive justice as "the elimination of the shared offspring, [and] becomes a perverse but logically consistent mechanism for a woman to punish her husband" (McAuley 2015: 218–19). While the visual text of Philomela's weaving remains undisclosed and has been a subject of scholarly debate, it is the foundation of female subversive potential as it is through this creative agency that she reclaims her voice and unites with her sister. Procne believes Philomela's truth without hesitation. Female solidarity is thus intrinsic to Procne and Philomela's resistance to male aggression and patriarchal power, making Ovid's tale a challenging and rewarding text to read through the contemporary lens of female justice. The reception of the Ovidian myth in the Western canon, however, illustrates authors recasting the tale of sisterly solidarity as one of patriarchal ascendancy. Geoffrey Chaucer's "The Legend of Philomela," a fourteenth-century text, begins with a lament that the Gods allowed the birth of a man like Tereus. While the poem follows Ovid, it abruptly halts at the sisters' reunion. Chaucer insists that the story ends there and that the "remenant is no charge for to telle" (*The Legend of Good Women* 7.155–6). The erasure of the revenge episode preserves the notion of "good women" who are virtuous, chaste, and nurturing. This literary silencing of Philomela is further pursued in Renaissance tragedy, albeit through a "craftier" modus operandi. In Shakespeare's *The Tragedy of Titus Andronicus* (1594), in which the titular character's daughter, Lavinia, recalls Philomela, Shakespeare's two Tereuses employ the Ovidian barbaric tactics while adding another: cutting off Lavinia's hands, a clever ploy that prevents any possibility of weaving a tapestry. It is Titus who murders his daughter's rapists and, following Procne's example, feeds them to their mother. However, unlike her Ovidian predecessor, Lavinia is a passive spectator. Moved around like a pawn, her character functions solely to establish the "rights" of the male characters—her father, her betrothed, and her rapists—over the female body. Her only moment of active agency occurs when she writes down the names of her attackers on the ground by holding a stick between her "stumps" and her mouth. Yet this moment is short-lived: Titus soon kills his daughter, for "the girl should not survive her shame, And by her presence still renew his sorrows" (*Titus Andronicus* 5.3.40). Quite clearly, the powerful Ovidian tale of crime and punishment becomes a precedent for Lavinia's increased suffering as a passive victim of rape and honor killing.

While the myth of Philomela occurs in many contemporary texts, its reshaping in Margaret Atwood's short story "Nightingale" is most fascinating. Published in 2007, the story departs from the Ovidian narrative and, instead, employs Robert Graves's version of the myth "Tereus."[3] Recast as a Freudian dream narrative, Atwood's story introduces an "afterlife" led by the sisters after their metamorphoses, dominated by their conversations about blame, anger, and jealousy. The recriminations are directed against each other such that Tereus's crimes slip into the background and Procne's mutilation is represented through a disconcerting Freudian slip: "Maybe he had his reasons" (Atwood 2007: 76). Such a psychoanalytic retelling disquietingly introduces elements not in the tale (suspicion and hostility between the sisters) while evading what was in it (Tereus's deceit and violation of the sisters). Atwood's narrative undercuts the myth by obfuscating the sisters' solidarity, which is central to Ovid's tale. In Atwood's tale, Philomela places the onus on Procne for *choosing* not to speak. Itys's murder is presented as a "mistake" committed by Procne in a fit of rage and passion. Their story of solidarity and resistance is reduced to a requiem of "grief" that Philomela seems to be tired of singing. What is common to both the female voices is trauma and passivity. The myth of Philomela is "never too old," but how it is remembered has changed over time. One could say that the successive retellings show how the tale undergoes a patriarchal metamorphosis, a turnaround from the original premise of the Ovidian myth.

Katy Waldman's "Reading Ovid in the Age of #MeToo," an article that inspired this chapter, reminds us that Philomela's grotesque mutilation as well as deft creation of her tapestry in Ovid presages conditions of our own social reality: "Ovid had the power to illuminate disturbing aspects of our contemporary culture … something close to home" (Waldman 2018). In India, the campaign solidarity of #MeToo has not been able to rein in powerful perpetrators such as M. J. Akbar, a politician with over ten cases of sexual harassment leveled against him. In February 2020, he told a city court in New Delhi that the main allegations made by a female journalist in 2018 were a "figment of her imagination" and that he cannot be expected to remember what happened over twenty-five years ago (*Press Trust of India*, February 27, 2020). In 2019, the Mumbai police gave a "clean chit" to accused Bollywood actor, Nana Patekar, over the sexual harassment allegations leveled by fellow actor, Tanushree Dutta, primarily because, as stated by Dutta's lawyers, credible witnesses were excluded from testifying during the trial (*India Today Web Desk*, June 13, 2019).

Metaphorically speaking, we find that the narratives of rape and sexual assault and the routine silencing of latter-day Philomelas continue, as the solidarity tapestries are hard to weave. Women's lives are under constant surveillance by the many powerful "Tereuses" who have emerged in our rape culture, accentuating the obvious toxic masculinity, evident in the Bois locker room syndrome. In the next section, we trace, through actual rape narratives, a pattern of shamed survivors and absolved perpetrators. We examine the overt and covert state control in matters of sexual violence, the colluding nature of the family and community in denying women's autonomy, and the role that the corporatized media plays in discreetly erasing non-urban and non-metropolitan cases of sexual violence, after the initial news reports.

Philomela's Travails in Times of Impunity

Traveling with Philomela to Kashmir is not just an exercise in time and culture; it is also an experience of the endemic historical silences that shroud Philomela's tapestry and prevent her and it from speaking. In geopolitical terms, Kashmir is internationally known as a politically restive place that the Indian state has been trying to control for at least three decades. However, what is less known is how women lead their lives in this embattled militarized zone where, like in all political conflicts, the female body is an intense battleground for "militarized violence and also resistance" (Kanth 2018: 44) and female agency is extremely restricted. We present one case in which an "everyday" action became a trigger for violation and violence, an account popularized on social media as #HandwaraGirl.

The incident took place in Handwara, a heavily garrisoned town in the northwestern part of the Kashmir valley. On the afternoon of April 12, 2016, a sixteen-year-old schoolgirl had gone to use a public washroom—overlooked by a military watch post and used mainly by the soldiers—on her way home from school. Nearby shopkeepers saw a soldier enter the washroom, and the girl soon emerged crying and screaming. As she came to the road, a group of schoolboys asked her why she had gone to the washroom and physically assaulted her. Soon a crowd collected, and she was taken to the police station by her relative and neighbor, also a policeman. For several hours, the girl did not return. Her father went to the station and was detained as well. In the meantime, the protesting crowd began attacking the military bunker. The army fired tear gas shells at the crowd. Violent protests continued and the public washroom, the site of the alleged molestation, was burnt down. That night, the army authenticated a video that had gone viral in the town and reported that she had been assaulted by the local boys. For the next three days, entry into the town was restricted, and as the protests kept growing, the internet was shut down and several districts were placed under cordon and search instructions. Five Kashmiri civilians were killed by the security forces. The girl and her father's whereabouts remained unknown. Only after the mother filed a habeas corpus petition was the girl brought from an undisclosed location to the Magistrate's office where she repeated what she had said in the video authenticated by the army—that she had been assaulted by local boys.

Almost a month after the incident, on May 12, 2016, the girl was released from police protection after court orders. In a press conference held by the girl and her family on May 16, she claimed that the police, while recording the video, had assured her that it wouldn't be made public. She further stated that the police advised her against mentioning the matter of the soldier for her and her family's sake, in terms of safety and stigma. She also said that she and her father were taken to the house of a relative on the night of the incident and that they were not allowed to leave. The mother was able to meet her after hectic negotiation with the army, four days later. Many local boys were arrested on charges of molestation, rioting, and inciting rumors.

The many excesses of the Handwara episode—including the illegal detention in the name of protective custody of a minor girl and her father, the use of repressive force, and deliberate manipulation of facts—seem to prove the cliché that "truth is stranger than fiction." But don't they instead illustrate how very similar truth and fiction can be? Isn't excess built into the fabric of rape culture, exactly as it structures Ovid's text? Excesses help camouflage the routine violence that structures sexual conduct and women's lives. In the Handwara episode, several issues remain opaque. In her article about the incident, Shrimoyee Nandini Ghosh states, "there is a lot we don't know about what happened … And sometimes what we just don't know gets in the way of what we do know" (Ghosh 2016). First, it is not clear what happened inside the washroom, and the incident, like all others, raises the perennial doubt and suspicion that cling to every female complainant of sexual harassment. Did she consent or not? Second, why was she assaulted by the group of schoolboys? Did they think that she had deliberately brought dishonor to the community by seeking out a soldier in the washroom? Three, why was she detained in the police station? Is it because her actions had provoked the crowd? Four, why did she consent to the video in which she blamed the boys for the assault? Is it because she was scared and forced to agree? In keeping with the fundamental tropes of rape culture where accountability is demanded from the survivor and not the aggressor, the soldier was never asked to explain his actions. Shortly after the incident, the survivor dropped out of school, and she and her family were eventually forced to leave their home.

But there is more than the ordinary rape culture at work here. Since the soldier is protected by the special powers of a draconian act called the Armed Forces Special Powers Act (AFSPA), he has legal immunity and can only be prosecuted by a military court. This unnamed soldier—a bizarre inversion of anonymity where the soldier's life is protected from prying eyes while the survivor's is not—knows that he can never be made accountable by the existing criminal justice system that gives him extra rights, extra privileges, extra power over people's lives. While the justification for the soldier's presence has been sought on the grounds of militancy, a ruthless and militarized state has been created that has clamped down on the freedoms of the people, their lives, their lands, their rights, and their fights, for nearly thirty years. Meanwhile, women in Kashmir have been fighting their own war against the soldiers. The mass rape committed by the personnel of an army regiment during a search operation on February 23, 1991, in the twin villages of Kunan and Pushpora located in Kupwara district of Kashmir is a prominent example of this systemic repression and denial of human rights. Like the soldier's missing account in the Handwara case, those guilty of these rapes were never identified, and worse, the highest journalist body of the country, the Press Trust of India, deeply doubted the medical evidence and claimed the whole incident to be a "hoax" contrived to ignite hatred against the Indian army. Such is the power of the army in Kashmir.

Fortunately, survivor statements were recorded in a book evocatively called *Do You Remember Kunan Poshpora?* in which the survivors narrate how they were raped in the presence of their husbands, fathers, brothers, and children. In fact, in 2013 many of these women, along with the authors, filed a joint petition to reopen the mass rape case. As a result, the Jammu and Kashmir High Court ordered the state to compensate the victims. The compensation was first agreed upon but later denied. The verdict was challenged in the Supreme Court. Unsurprisingly, the case is still pending since no resolution was reached due to the protection that the state promises to the men in uniform ("Kashmir 'mass rape' survivors", *BBC Asia*, October 7, 2017).

Panchayats and the Plight of Rural Philomelas

In many rural outposts of India, Philomela's loom cannot contend against the powerful and endemic rape culture fashioned by coercive institutions and by patriarchal customs of dominant communities. Jashpur is a remote, underdeveloped *adivasi*[4] majority district in the Central Indian state of Chhattisgarh, infamously known for trafficking women. Consequently, women of Jashpur are often treated as battlegrounds in matters related to community honor, "honor" that the *khap*—customary, extra-constitutional bodies comprising community elders—seeks to protect (Baxi et al. 2006: 1244). Even *panchayats*, the village-level elected bodies, sometimes assume "*khap*" power to intervene in sexual assault cases and inhibit the functioning of the duly constituted criminal justice system. This deprives rural impoverished women from finding institutional support and media coverage in matters of sexual assault. When reported, the reports focus not on the survivor's trauma but on the arbitrary *khap* verdicts for "disciplining" transgressors. Through a few instances from Jashpur, we analyze how the *panchayats* punish female survivors and shield perpetrators for money and "honor."

In July 2016, when a nineteen-year-old woman was gang-raped during her "routine visit" to the fields to defecate, the *panchayat* fined the four accused, as well as the male acquaintance who had tried to rescue her, one thousand rupees each. Yet only two local newspapers reported the case, and with evident discrepancies wherein one "confirmed rape" (Kashyap 2016), whilst the other reduced the crime to an "attempt to rape" (*Nai Dunia*, July 28, 2016). In July 2018, another *panchayat* slammed a penalty of ten thousand rupees on each of three men accused after they gang-raped three minor *adivasi* girls. It then used the money to arrange a grand feast, distributed the leftover money amongst forty-five community members, and promptly set the accused men free. Later in November 2019, when a 23-year-old woman was raped by male acquaintances at a construction site where they had promised her a part-time menial job, her attempt to seek justice from the local police infuriated the *panchayat*. While the accused were fined a sum of five thousand rupees by the mercenary *panchayat*, the survivor was ordered to pay the same amount by the *panchayat* for maligning her community by choosing "the police over the *panchayat*"! (*The Times of India*, November 19, 2019). Such mercenary *khap* verdicts, in which payments are made to the *panchayats*, and not as compensation to the victims, foreground how female suffering is instrumentalized to siphon money for the community.

In March 2020, a *panchayat* in Jashpur decided to profit from a molestation case. After the police refused to register a survivor's complaint, since the perpetrator was related to a political representative, the *khap* punished the accused with two slaps and made the perpetrator touch her feet, enacting the ritualized practice of marking hierarchy as atonement. Worse, the survivor's spouse as the head of the *khap* took hush money from the accused! Given the refusal by the police to record survivor testimonies and the reluctance of local political representatives to oppose *khap* verdicts, "the spectacle of public violence" then becomes the reinforcement of the customary norms "despite their conflict with state law and constitutional mechanisms" (Baxi et al. 2006: 1243). *Khaps*, as bulwarks of oppressive caste-norms, frequently not only protect perpetrators of rape but actually inflict it as punishment in other regions similar to Jashpur, adding to the misery of rural women. In Baghpat, Uttar Pradesh, the *khap* ordered two *Dalit*[5] sisters to be raped and paraded naked following their brother's elopement with an "upper caste" woman in August 2015. Fortunately, the matter made it to the Supreme Court, which ordered a police investigation into the incident (*Express News Service*, September 17, 2015). Nonetheless, the predatory power dynamics of class and caste alongside institutions such as the police, *panchayats*, or even the family under the patriarchy continue to perpetrate layers of subjugation and stifle tapestries of numerous unheard Philomelas.

In Ovid's "Philomela," when Tereus cuts off Philomela's tongue it quivers, calling "for the '*nomen patris*,' the name of the father." This serves as an "invocation of the patriarchal law" (Marder 1992: 160). The above cases of Jashpur mirror the Ovidian representation of rape as a disruption of social order besides being a violation of the female body. Female solidarity, integral to the text, manifests itself in rare instances of community support for survivors. Yet, the consequences of such solidarity acts remain unpredictable as they can, paradoxically, exacerbate the public attention surrounding the stigma of rape and compel the survivor to "hide in shame." The media, in this context, acts as a double-edged sword enabling elite women to register their rebellion through campaigns like #MeToo while voices of marginalized women in places such as Jashpur remain silenced in the margins, their narratives awaiting attention beyond such absurd *panchayat* pronouncements.

Conclusion

Our analytical praxis shows the patriarchal continuity between the mutilation (and silencing) in Ovid and other texts' interpretations of "mutilation." The patriarchal restructuring of the myth effectively silences and undermines the subversive potential of Philomela's tapestry. We encounter a similar silencing of rape survivors in contemporary times, as evident in the select rape cases of Kashmir and Jashpur, which share one thing—a deliberate exclusion of the rape narrative from public memory. This visible disappearance is secured by institutions such as the military or the *panchayats* along with manipulative media. But our reading of Ovid also reminds us of the power of the tapestry, a metaphor for female solidarity. Significantly, we find that the women of Kashmir have been weaving their tapestries of hope and resistance, an intimate world of affect that Uzma Falak describes as a "critical female alliance" (Falak 2018: 77). Falak examines *Vyestoan*—a Kashmiri practice of togetherness, of collective mourning and of seeking voice that state forces seek to mutilate. By singing of a silenced past, the women of Kashmir reclaim their autonomy of speech while weaving tapestries of trauma. In addition, with the collation of testimonies of survivors in texts such as *Do You Remember Kunan Pushpora?*, we can hope this female solidarity will find a new dimension beyond kinship ties.

A similar hope has been ushered in by the #MeToo campaign, which has woven a tapestry of solidarity from the shared trauma of survivors across countries and cultures. Undoubtedly, this culture of solidarity exists in constant struggle against hegemonic control in places like Kashmir where social media, though accessible, is suspended at the will of the state while the national media continues to appropriate narratives. It has yet to find its voice in many regions like Jashpur, where women still struggle for basic necessities, far removed from the elite world of social media. However, we believe in the power of Philomela's tapestry to forge solidarity and make the numerous survivor testimonies heard.

Notes

1 The authors are students of English Honours in Miranda House at the University of Delhi, India. Under the guidance of Professor Sharmila Purkayastha (Department of English), they came together as a collective to examine their felt experiences of patriarchy and of the #MeToo movement through a re-reading of Ovid's *Philomela* for a student seminar in 2018. While working on this chapter, they deconstructed the binaries between literary and social texts and shared individual experiences to arrive at a common postcolonial feminist understanding of the endemic and local natures of sexual assault.
2 The patriarchal "oikos" (city-state) and "polis" (household) in ancient Athens were instrumental in the exclusion of women from the public sphere. Women's lives were infused with "Patriarchy and Misogyny," as suggested by Marilyn Katz (1992). The Ovidian myth asserts Itys's murder and female solidarity against such patriarchal control.
3 In Robert Graves's "Tereus," the title character convinces Philomela of Procne's apparent death and proceeds to rape and marry her. In this version, instead of Philomela it is Procne whose tongue gets cut off and who subsequently gets confined to the slaves' quarters. She weaves a message into the pattern of a bridal robe for Philomela which reads, "Procne is among the slaves" (Graves 1990: 169, eBook file).
4 *Adivasis* are indigenous communities of India listed as Scheduled Tribes under the Indian Constitution.
5 "Dalit" is a term of resistance that people, classified as Scheduled Castes under the Indian Constitution, use for fighting caste discrimination.

Works Cited

Atwood, Margaret (2007), "The Nightingale," in *The Tent*, 1st edn., 76–8, New York: Anchor Books.

Baxi, Pratiksha, Shirin M. Rai, and Shaheen Sardar Ali (2006), "Legacies of Common Law: 'Crimes of Honour' in India and Pakistan," *Third World Quarterly*, 27 (7): 1239–53.

"Bois Locker Room: It Exposes That the Normalization of Rape Starts Young," (2020), *The Times of India*, May 5. Available online: https://timesofindia.indiatimes.com/blogs/toi-editorials/bois-locker-room-it-exposes-that-the-normalization-of-rape-starts-young (accessed July 2, 2020).

Chaucer, Geoffrey (1894), *The Complete Poetical Works*, ed. W. W. Skeat, Oxford: Clarendon Press.

Drolia, Rashmi (2019), "Chhattisgarh: Panchayat Fines Gang Rape Survivor Rs 5000 for Going to Police," *The Times of India*, November 19. Available online: https://m.timesofindia.com/city/raipur/chhattisgarh-panchayat-fines-gang-rape-survivor-rs-5000-for-going-to-police/articleshow/72119037.cms (accessed June 27, 2020).

Express News Service (2015), "Baghpat 'khap diktat': UP Police Can Probe Rape Case," *The Indian Express*, September 17. Available online: https://indianexpress.com/article/india/india-others/baghpat-khap-diktat-up-police-can-probe-rape-case/lite/ (accessed August 2, 2020).

Falak, Uzma (2018), "The Intimate World of *Vyestoan*: Affective Female Alliance and Companionships of Resistance in Kashmir," *Economics and Political Weekly*, 53 (47): 77–9.

Ghosh, Shrimoyee Nandini (2016), "How a Kashmiri Girl's Search for a Bathroom Became Truth vs. Lie, Us vs. Them and Patriot vs. Traitor," *The Ladies Finger*, July 12. Available online: http://theladiesfinger.com/handwara/ (accessed April 25, 2020).

Graves, Robert (1990), *The Greek Myths: Vol. 1*, London: Penguin. eBook file. Google Books.

Gupta, Nistha (2020), "Bois Locker Room: Delhi Schoolboys Create Groups to Share Lewd Photos, Chats on Classmates," *India Today*, May 4. Available online: https://www.indiatoday.in/india/story/bois-locker-room-delhi-schoolboys-create-group-to-share-lewd-photos-chats-on-classmates-1674303-2020-05-04 (accessed July 2, 2020).

India Today Web Desk (2019), "Tanushree Dutta: Nana Patekar Bought Himself Clean Chit to Continue Bullying Hapless Young Women," *India Today*, June 13. Available online: https://www.indiatoday.in/movies/celebrities/story/-tanushree-dutta-nana-patekar-bought-himself-clean-chit-to-continue-bullying-hapless-young-women-1548127-2019-06-13 (accessed August 2, 2020).

Kanth, Fatima Mir (2018), "Women in Resistance: Narratives of Kashmiri Women's Protests," *Economic and Political Weekly*, 53 (47): 42–6.

"Kashmir 'Mass Rape' Survivors Fight for Justice," (2017), *BBC Asia*, October 7. mise: http://www.bbc.com/news/world-asia-41268906 (accessed April 1, 2020).

Kashyap, Kajal Kiran (2016), "Panchayat Decides 1000 Rupees as Punishment for Gang Rape," *Patrika*, July 28. Available online: https://m.patrika.com/jashpur-nagar-news/panchayat-decided-onethaousend-rs-rape-sentence-1360761/ (accessed June 27, 2020).

Katz, Marilyn (1992), "Ideology and 'The Status of Women' in Ancient Greece," *History and Theory*, 21 (4): 70–97.

Marder, Elissa (1992), "Disarticulated Voices: Feminism and Philomela," *Hypatia*, 7 (2): 148–66.

McAuley, Mairéad (2015), *Reproducing Rome: Motherhood in Virgil, Ovid, Seneca, and Statius*, Oxford: Oxford University Press.

Ovid (2000), "*Ovid's Metamorphoses*," trans. Anthony S. Kline, University of Virginia Library. Available online: https://ovid.lib.virginia.edu/trans/Metamorph6.htm#480077267 (accessed July 18, 2020).

"Panchayat Takes 1000 Rupees and Frees Four Accused of Rape Attempt" (2016), *Nai Dunia*, July 28. Available online: https://www.naidunia.com/chhattisgarh/jashpurpanchayat-take-one-thousand-rupee-and-free-four-accused-of-rape-attempt-787335 (accessed June 27, 2020).

Pathak, Zakia (1992), "A Pedagogy for Postcolonial Feminists," in Judith Butler and Joan W. Scott (eds.), *Feminists Theorize the Political*, 426–41, New York: Routledge.

Press Trust of India (2020), "#MeToo: Ramani's Allegations of Sexual Misconduct Figment of Her Imagination, MJ Akbar Tells Court," *The New Indian Express*, February 7. Available online: www.newindianexpress.com/nation/2020/feb/07/metoo-ramanis-allegations-of-sexual-misconduct-figment-of-her-imagination-mj-akbar-tells-court-2100380.html (accessed July 3, 2020).

Shakespeare, William (2009), *Titus Andronicus. The Cambridge Dover Wilson Shakespeare*, ed. John Dover Wilson, New York: Cambridge University Press.

Waldman, Katy (2018), "Reading Ovid in the Age of #MeToo," *The New Yorker*, February 12. Available online: www.newyorker.com/books/page-turner/reading-ovid-in-the-age-of-metoo (accessed July 3, 2020).

9

"Beware of the delusions of fancy!":

Silencing and Rape Culture in Hannah Webster Foster's *The Coquette*

Hannah Herndon

About halfway through *The Coquette; or, The History of Eliza Wharton*, Reverend Boyer, the man who supposes himself to be engaged to Eliza Wharton, discovers her in the garden with Major Sanford, a notorious libertine. Confirmed in his suspicions that Eliza is a coquette, Boyer refuses to listen to her side of the story, explaining, "Your conduct ... cannot be vindicated; your motives need no explanation; they are too apparent!" (Foster [1797] 2012: 64). Despite the fact that Eliza meets with Sanford only to put an end to his attentions and that Boyer finds the pair only because he ignored Eliza's explicit request that "no person might intrude on her retirement" (63), Eliza listens to Boyer without retort. She laments, "My excuses would be deemed utterly insufficient, and truth would not befriend and justify me" (74). Eliza knows that as a woman, she does not get to claim "truth." Boyer's words will be believed over hers, which points to the "long and brutal tradition of asserting that men are credible but women are incredible" (Solnit 2019). This routine discrediting of women's words and emotions is a tenacious feature of rape culture—one that the #MeToo movement has criticized and that its detractors have demonstrated. By re-reading *The Coquette* in light of activists' demand to "believe women," I call into question readings of early American literature that consider silencing women and requiring their affective labor "'natural' and inevitable" (Higgins and Silver 1991: 3). For over two hundred years, these learned behaviors have been fundamental to reproducing rape culture in the United States.

Reading Foster's novel of "seduction" through the lens of rape culture acknowledges that acts that are not rape—such as sexual microaggressions or misogynistic verbal abuse—are nevertheless deeply entrenched in and crucial to sustaining a system that encourages sexual violence. For that reason, I move away from the question of whether Sanford's "seduction" of Eliza is actually rape by contemporary standards and focus on the more pressing question of how, specifically, the new republic established rape culture. I pay particular attention to Boyer's invalidation of Eliza's voice, arguing that this verbal assault resembles a sexual assault not because it *symbolizes* rape but because it is *connected to* rape. When Boyer refuses to listen to Eliza, he asserts power over her in the same way that rapists deny their victims' agency. Because sexual violence is motivated by perpetrators' desire not for sex but for power, both silencing and rape are mechanisms of control. It is neither metaphorical nor hyperbolic to say that Eliza *experiences* Boyer's verbal assault in line with sexual assault even though it is Sanford who "seduces" her.

Critical conversation in the late twentieth century explores Foster's protofeminist commentary on what sociologists described, in the 1970s, as rape culture. Cathy Davidson distinguishes *The Coquette* from more conservative accounts of Elizabeth Whitman's story, arguing that the novel "does not openly challenge the basic structure of patriarchal culture but, instead, exposes its fundamental injustices through the details and disasters of the plot" (Davidson [1986] 2004: 226). Taking up this focus on gender politics, Sharon M. Harris reads *The Coquette* as a "political novel" that centers early America's "double standard for men and for women" (1995: 4). Donna R. Bontatibus argues that Foster appropriates the seduction genre for female audiences, eschewing its didactic function and "dismantling the traditional ways of viewing 'fallen' women" (1999: 15). This criticism's implicit and, in the case of Bontatibus, explicit acknowledgment of rape culture in *The Coquette* sets the precedent for considering gendered verbal norms in a continuum with sexual violence.

More recently, however, critics have been less inclined to consider *The Coquette* radical on the basis of gender politics. Laura Korobkin claims that Eliza's behavior signifies not a legitimate political protest but an appetite for aristocratic vices. Korobkin counters readings of Eliza as a "protofeminist rebel" (2006: 79) by arguing that Eliza desires not "political freedom and self sufficiency but ... sensuality, self-absorption, and social caresses" (90). It is true that Eliza is no political heroine: she represents white, middle-class women with a proclivity for parties, not activism. But Korobkin's interpretation of "what Eliza *wants*" (80) is problematic because it enacts the very issue of presuming women's unreliability that I am arguing supports rape culture. Analyzing Eliza's "course of conduct," Korobkin concludes that Eliza "avoids commitment [to Boyer] hoping that Sanford will yet propose" (95), fulfilling her "dream of material gratification" (91). This interpretation of Eliza's desires dismisses her clear and repeated statements that she intends to delay marriage, which suggests that Eliza cannot be taken at her word—that she is inherently deceitful and untrustworthy. Like any other character, Eliza exhibits moral imperfections and, of course, is as capable of lying as any other narrator. But there is no particular reason to consider her behavior, which is ambiguous, more telling than her words, which are not. Because the tendency to discredit women automatically—especially regarding their desires and intentions—has become so normalized, it is imperative that critics take into account the inevitability of rape culture and its verbal manifestations in novels of "seduction."

Readers may assume that the central conflict of *The Coquette* is Eliza's looming decision between two suitors, but if they listen to Eliza's words, they will hear her clearly announce her intention *not* to choose for the time being. In the first half of the novel, Eliza states this conviction to many people, repeatedly, but no one takes her seriously. She pointedly declares, "marriage is the tomb of friendship" (Foster [1797] 2012: 19–20) in response to Mrs. Richman's praise of Boyer. Similarly, Eliza corrects Boyer as soon as he confesses romance, insisting that he must substitute the term "affection" for "some more indifferent epithet" (20); and when he proposes marriage, she thoroughly declines:

> I recoil at the thought of immediately forming a connection, which must confine me to the duties of domestic life, and make me dependent for happiness, perhaps too, for subsistence, upon a class of people, who will claim the right of scrutinizing every part of my conduct; and by censuring those foibles, which I am conscious of not having prudence to avoid, may render me completely miserable.
>
> (24)

Eliza's reasons for avoiding marriage remain consistent no matter whom she tells. When Sanford asks her if she plans to marry Boyer, she explains, "I do not intend to give my hand to any man at present. I have but lately entered society; and wish, for a while, to enjoy my freedom, in the participation of pleasures, suited to my age and sex" (40). Eliza's protestations against marriage could be read as feminine demureness in the face of Boyer and Sanford's brazen expressions of love, but her feelings are the same when she speaks with platonic friends. Reiterating her resolution to Mrs. Richman, she states, "I am not sufficiently acquainted with either [Boyer or Sanford] yet, to determine which to take. At present, I shall not confine myself in any way" (41). Despite Eliza's constant objection to marriage, fictional and scholarly readers of her letters alike tend to hear her words as deceitful or forget them altogether.

One reason that women's perspectives were so readily ignored in early America was that, legally, women had little to no voice. When a woman married, she gave up her legal rights to her husband through the doctrine of coverture. A "feme covert," as the law called a married woman, "had no individual legal identity": she could neither inherit nor bequeath property, and her signature on documents had no legal meaning (Davidson [1986] 2004: 194–5). Under coverture, a woman "was to be protected by her husband, and she was protected, so far as the law was concerned, because her rights were subsumed in his" (194). Protection in name, ownership in practice, coverture revealed the reality of women's sexual obligation and financial dependence. Marylynn Salmon explains, "Women could not enter into any agreements that might result in court actions against them, for if women could be imprisoned their husbands would be denied sexual and household services" ([1986] 2004: 42). Remaining single, then, might seem a favorable alternative, but despite the legal independence it would afford, "spinsterhood hardly embodied a respectable option in the society of the time. On the contrary, the spinster was an object of pervasive cultural ridicule" (Davidson [1986] 2004: 198). And, as *The Coquette* shows, women's attempts to remain single while still enjoying society were interpreted as coquetry.

Another contributing factor to women's inaudibility was the stereotype that they were irrational. As Sharon Block explains, Revolutionary-era ideology promoted the belief that "the control of the passions" was "increasingly necessary to a well-ordered society" (2006: 35), and women, who were assumed to be deficient in reason, were seen as a threat to this order. As such, elite white women were encouraged to develop their sense of reason through education. This duty of moral improvement, often associated with the "republican wife," took on "a political role of no little significance" (Kelley 2015: 250) as privileged women cultivated their intellect in accordance with manuals written by men (249), with the expectation that they "place their learning at the service of [their] families" (252). Ultimately, any claim these women had to the masculine domain of reason was predicated on their duty to men, and any deviance from reason they exhibited became an excuse to ignore their perspectives.

This dismissal occurred not only at the hands of men but also between women. In *The Coquette*, Eliza's friends are more inclined to correct her than to consider her words seriously. When Eliza rejoices in the "pleasure" she feels upon leaving her "paternal roof," her friend Lucy responds with a "moral lecture" that calls Eliza "coquettish" (Foster [1797] 2012: 6). Rather than engage in dialogue, Lucy flattens Eliza's complex emotional and intellectual life into the stereotype of a coquette, a label that haunts Eliza whenever she dares to suggest that marriage restricts women. Appearing, in some form, sixteen times in the novel, the word "coquette" becomes a convenient shortcut for Eliza's correspondents to dismiss her words, followed by various forms of "deluded," which appear eleven times. When Eliza's disposition shifts from lively to dejected, her friends still fail to listen. Lucy accuses her of being overly emotional after Boyer verbally assaults her. She mocks, "your truly romantic letter came safe to hand. Indeed, my dear, it would make a very pretty figure in a novel. A bleeding heart, slighted love, and all the et ceteras of romance, enter into the composition!" (84). Writing Eliza off as irrational, Lucy asks, "[W]here is that fund of sense" (84). Women's words were also ignored due to the stereotype that they were untrustworthy, especially regarding matters of sex. Block excerpts Revolutionary-era ditties, comics, almanacs, and poems that depict women as "ruled by the impulses of their own passions" (2006: 50) while simultaneously portraying heterosexual relations as antagonistic: "men pursued, and women resisted" (39). Noting the implications of the desiring but resisting woman, Block concludes, "[t]his dual construction of women's sexual role—always resisting, therefore never really resisting—had a powerful result: women could not be trusted to judge or represent their own consent" (40). Women allegedly "could not admit their true desires" (40), so men's judgment superseded women's on matters of sexual desire and consent.

If it was up to women to say whether or not a sexual encounter was consensual, yet women could not be trusted to know or articulate what they wanted or to report truthfully, then their actual ability to define nonconsensual sex as rape was extremely limited. As is the case today, the number of rape cases that ever came before a judge in early America was disproportionately small compared to the number of nonconsensual sexual encounters estimated to have occurred (Block 2006: 89). By constricting the definition of sexual violence and discrediting survivors, early American rape culture began to normalize silencing women in a variety of situations, setting the precedent for rape apologists today to doubt, suspect, and minimize women when they speak about their own experiences.

A closely related and equally tenacious feature of rape culture is its demand for women's affective labor. Political philosopher Michael Hardt, building on feminist concepts such as "kin work" and "caring labor," defines affective labor as a social "production of affects" (1999: 89) that is "intangible: a feeling of ease, well-being, satisfaction, excitement, passion—even a sense of connectedness or community" (96). This labor is uncompensated and expected of women even outside of marital or familial contexts. As Emanuelle Wessels puts it, "putting one's empathy and charm to work ... become[s] essentialized ... as part of a woman's innate nature. Consequently, this surplus of feeling generated by feminized affective labor is implicitly coded as non-work" (2016: 513). Where women's affective labor exists, women's sexual labor follows close behind. Silvia Federici explains that "giving pleasure to [*sic*] man is an essential part of what is expected of every woman," arguing that for women in capitalist patriarchy, "sex is work" (2012: 25). Linking women's "duty to please" (2012: 24), a blend of affective and sexual labor, to the underlying problem of women's "economic dependence" (2012: 25), Federici shows how the expectation of women's affective labor undergirds rape culture. Notably, the way affective laborers feel "depleted" (Gutiérrez Rodríguez 2010: 6) and "alienat[ed] ... a disconnection from the feeling self" (Wessels 2016: 513) parallels some common emotional responses of survivors of sexual violence: depression and disassociation.

The Coquette illuminates this connection between affective labor and rape culture in Eliza's interactions with Boyer, who attempts to pressure Eliza into marital commitment by appealing to the belief that she owes him gratification. When Boyer finds Eliza's response to his declaration of love unsatisfying, he pleads, "Take what time you think proper, only relieve my suspense, as soon as may be. Shall I visit you again tomorrow?" (Foster [1797] 2012: 21). At first, Boyer seems to respect Eliza's need for time and space, but he quickly puts the onus on her to "relieve [his] suspense" and almost comically requests that she do so the very next day. As time goes on and Eliza refuses to respond to his marriage proposal, Boyer becomes increasingly impatient, feeling his "temper rise" when he finds "the same indecision ... [and] previous excuses," and warns that he "was not thus to be trifled with" (61). Boyer considers her statement that she cannot "bear the idea of confinement to the cares of a married life at present" an "excuse" (61) rather than a legitimate concern. He makes it clear that Eliza owes him a response lest she be a coquette and, upon deciding that she is, casts himself as an "injured man" who was "enslaved" by her "artifice and dissimulation, of which [she] strove to render [him] the dupe" (81). His anger reveals a man who is used to women prioritizing his emotions, and the fact that he feels "injured" indicates his perceived entitlement to the affective labor of women.

When Boyer labels Eliza a coquette without letting her speak, her reaction typifies that of someone who has experienced sexual violence: she falls silent, begins to doubt herself, and feels worthless. Though usually loquacious, Eliza is unable to defend herself against Boyer's allegations:

> He accused me of treating him ill, of rendering him the dupe of coquetting artifice, of having an intrigue with Major Sanford, and declared his determination to leave me forever, as unworthy of his regard, and incapable of love, gratitude, or honor!—There was too much reason in support of his accusations for me to gainsay them, had his impetuosity suffered me to attempt it. But in truth I had no inclination to self defence. My natural vivacity had forsaken me; and I listened without interrupting him to the fluency of reproachful language, which his resentment inspired.
>
> (Foster [1797] 2012: 73)

The way that Boyer's "reproachful language" kills Eliza's "inclination to self defence" and "natural vivacity" shows his verbal domination. Aware that his position as not only male but also a minister authorizes him to pass judgment, Eliza plunges into a deeper silence. She soon finds it difficult to "compose [her]self" to write to her friends (83) and eventually concedes, "writing is not so agreeable to me as it used to be" (100). After Boyer so easily denies her voice, she loses faith in her words.

Following Boyer's verbal assault, Eliza's thoughts begin morphing to fit his narrative that she is untrustworthy. Distressed, she writes Lucy, "he has penetrated the cause of my proceedings" (Foster [1797] 2012: 74) and in a more composed letter to Boyer, "I frankly confess [my misconduct] …. Casting off the veil of dissimulation, I shall write with frankness" (80). Yet until this point, Eliza has not given a "cause of [her] proceedings" to "penetrate." In her earlier letters, Eliza's only "cause" is her campaign not to marry any time soon, and there is no need to "penetrate" it because she states it explicitly to several people. Thus, when Eliza "confess[es]" her "misconduct," she is confessing to an offense she never committed. The authority of Boyer's words overshadows her own conviction of her "innocent heart" (6) and right to "enjoy [her] freedom" (41). By the time Boyer renders Eliza silent, it is as if she never voiced her reluctance to marry.

To express this erasure of her words, Eliza uses the phrase, "I am undone!" (82), which, as Davidson notes, is "the precise word that in seduction novels typically signals a woman's fall" ([1986] 2004: 228). Eliza utters this phrase not after she "falls more conventionally into the affair with Sanford" (Davidson [1986] 2004: 228) but after Boyer has asserted his "power" by "triumphing in [her] distress" and condemning her behavior (Foster [1797] 2012: 83). While she had previously "escaped the censure of [her] own heart" (58), she now feels "self-condemnation" and "inward torture," even stating that she is not "worthy" of Boyer (83). Eliza's "fall" does not denote simply her wounded pride but also, and more importantly, rape culture's silencing of her voice.

As Eliza's mental decline reveals, the only thing as disheartening as not having a voice is having one that can so easily be disrespected, overpowered, and sabotaged. Boyer deprecates Eliza even though, and perhaps because, she confessed to him her fear of censure when she refused his proposal (Foster [1797] 2012: 24). Exercising his power as a male figure of authority, Boyer denies her any means of defending herself against his condemnation: he relies on the convenient formulation of male credibility and female incredibility set in place by rape culture to rob Eliza of voice and agency. Misrepresented and exploited, Eliza is haunted by Boyer's reprimand until her death. She writes, "Having incurred so much censure by the indulgence of a gay disposition, I am now trying what a recluse and solitary mode of life will produce" (106). When she speaks romantically of death, she imagines herself free of the judgment of others: "soon shall I be insensible to censure and reproach!" (112). Boyer's capitalization on Eliza's fear of criticism triggers her obsession with "censure" and descent into isolation.

Eliza's mental and emotional collapse arises, as well, from the impossibility of aligning her society's promise of marital happiness with the reality of her lived experience. Foster takes pains to emphasize that marrying Boyer, the supposedly rational choice, scarcely offers Eliza more opportunity for happiness than any of her other options. Hesitant to commit to Boyer, Eliza muses, "His worth I acknowledge; nay, I esteem him very highly. But can there be happiness with such a disparity of dispositions?" (Foster [1797] 2012: 58). Despite the logic of Eliza's query, her friends warn her to "beware the delusions of fancy!" and declare that "reason must be our guide, if we would expect durable happiness" (41). The republican ideals of early America mislead Eliza into believing that she might possess the rights of an individual—that, "life, liberty, and the pursuit of happiness" (Declaration of Independence, US 1776) could be achievable through rational decision-making— when, in actuality, a "woman's function was to be possessed or dispossessed" (Davidson [1986] 2004: 185). Eliza's "fall" occurs in the gap between her experience of subjectivity and rape culture's denial of it.

The invalidating responses of Eliza's friends, on top of Boyer's verbal assault, illustrate the destructive power of not believing women and anticipate the troubling underside of the #MeToo movement. Women have used personal stories to foster political consciousness and solidarity through multiple feminist movements. But it is crucial to note, especially given the #MeToo movement's public forum, that the voices of survivors are ignored, distorted, and silenced with alarming regularity. While *The Coquette* does not offer solutions, it does highlight the verbal dynamics of rape culture with remarkable clarity, and articulating the problem is a prerequisite to solving it. By showing how gendered verbal norms devalue women's thoughts, feelings, and experiences and justify sexual violence, *The Coquette* portrays the dire effects of a rape culture that normalizes not listening to women. Jennifer Airey notes, "it is all the more important," as literary critics, "that we promote women's voices and that we take women seriously as narrators of their own experiences" (2018: 10). If we are to disrupt the reproduction of centuries-old rape culture in our readings of literature, the #MeToo movement's imperative to "believe women" must include women of the past, even if we must listen harder to hear them. By reconsidering *The Coquette*'s classification as a novel of "seduction" and questioning the inclination to consider Eliza untrustworthy, we begin to counteract centuries of silencing and amplify the perspective of a woman in early American rape culture.

Works Cited

Airey, Jennifer L. (2018), "#MeToo," *Tulsa Studies in Women's Literature*, 37 (3): 7–13.

Block, Sharon (2006), *Rape and Sexual Power in Early America*, Chapel Hill: University of North Carolina Press.

Bontatibus, Donna R. (1999), *The Seduction Novel of the Early Nation: A Call for Socio-Political Reform*, East Lansing: Michigan State University Press.

Davidson, Cathy N. ([1986] 2004), *Revolution and the Word: The Rise of the Novel in America*, Expanded edn., Oxford: Oxford University Press.

Federici, Silvia (2012), *Revolution at Point Zero: Housework, Reproduction, and Feminist Struggle*, Oakland: PM Press.

Foster, Hannah Webster ([1797] 2012), *The Coquette and the Boarding School*, ed. Jennifer Harris and Bryan Waterman, New York: W. W. Norton & Company.

Gutiérrez Rodríguez, Encarnación (2010), *Migration, Domestic Work and Affect: A Decolonial Approach on Value and the Feminization of Labor*, New York: Routledge.

Hardt, Michael (1999), "Affective Labor," *Boundary*, 26 (2): 89–100.

Harris, Sharon M. (1995), *Redefining the Political Novel: American Women Writers, 1797–1901*, Knoxville: University of Tennessee Press.

Higgins, Lynn A. and Brenda R. Silver (1991), *Rape and Representation*, New York: Columbia University Press.

Kelley, Mary C. (2015), "'The Need of Their Genius': A Women's Revolution in Early America," in T.A. Foster (ed.), *Women in Early America*, 246–69, New York: New York University Press.

Korobkin, Laura H. (2006), "'Can Your Volatile Daughter Ever Acquire Your Wisdom?' Luxury and False Ideals in *The Coquette*," *Early American Literature*, 41 (1): 79–107.

Salmon, Marylynn (1986), *Women and the Law of Property in Early America*, Chapel Hill: The University of North Carolina Press.

Solnit, Rebecca (2019), "The Fall of Men Has Been Greatly Exaggerated," *Literary Hub*, April 2. Available online: lithub.com/the-fall-of-men-has-been-greatly-exaggerated/ (accessed September 15, 2019).

Wessels, Emanuelle (2016), "Homeland and Neoliberalism: Text, Paratexts and Treatment of Affective Labor," *Feminist Media Studies*, 16 (3): 511–26.

10

"Fearful of being pursued, yet determined to persevere":
Northanger Abbey and the #MeToo Movement

Douglas Murray

Northanger Abbey is Jane Austen's most patronized novel, often dismissed as a silly parody of the Gothic, as not really about very much—certainly not about sexual predation. This critical interpretation extends back to Marvin Mudrick's 1952 *Jane Austen: Irony as Defense and Discovery*, which argues that the novel's young heroine Catherine Morland "finds no iniquity in Bath" (46) and that the character John Thorpe is merely annoying and "unwelcome": "but there is nothing sinister about him" (46). However, I propose that if we systematically apply terms and concepts of the #MeToo movement to *Northanger*, a different novel emerges: an unsettling fiction dramatizing the dangers—both physical and psychological—of growing up female in a patriarchal society. In *Northanger Abbey*, Austen and the #MeToo movement embrace each other. The social movement provides conceptual tools that allow us to read Austen more astutely; at the same time, Austen affirms the validity of #MeToo concepts, allowing readers to understand them more fully and perhaps spot them in their own lives. Thus, this analysis of *Northanger Abbey* allows a new reading—and pedagogical approaches implied by that reading—to emerge from a familiar text.

Willful Misinformation

In the experience of many contemporary women and of many characters in *Northanger Abbey*, men communicate misinformation in order to impress, destabilize, or manipulate their (female) audience. This misinformation can take three forms, perhaps not always distinguishable from each other: braggadocio, deliberate untruth (which I will call "fake news"), and gaslighting. These last two terms—borrowed from political discourse and popular psychology—might at first seem irrelevant to #MeToo, but both fake news and gaslighting undermine female agency and self-confidence, ultimately undermining women's abilities to report sexual assault and to be believed.

In *Northanger Abbey*, men exaggerate to impress women. They brag to disempower women, to transform them into passive admirers, malleable witnesses to male possession and power. John Thorpe, the novel's most notorious self-promoter, begins by trumpeting his mastery of two male signifiers: speed and modes of transportation. In every comment, he substantially exaggerates and misinforms. During Thorpe's first meeting with Catherine, he misstates or misremembers his hour of departure from Tetbury for Bath so that his trip can seem to have transpired at record pace (40). He asserts that his sense of distance trumps "the authority of road-books, innkeepers and milestones" (39).[1] He brags about his horses, telling Catherine that his horse is incapable of traveling "less than ten miles per hour" (40). Thorpe does not just brag about horseflesh, speed, and carriages: he tells Catherine that he had read Lewis's *The Monk* in a single day (43)—a remarkable feat since the first edition, in three volumes, contains 750 pages. Thorpe later brags about how much he and his friends drank in an evening—"upon an average we cleared about five pints a head" (60)—and about the quality of his alcohol: "*Mine* is famous good stuff" (60). And Thorpe is not the novel's only braggart: General Tilney is only a more refined show-off, pointing out that his country house Northanger Abbey boasts new wings, the newest stoves (165) and china (179), the most advantageous situation (180), a kitchen replete with "every modern invention" (189), the best-stocked kitchen garden, and, in the General's words, "a village of hot-houses," producing a minimum of one hundred pineapples per year (182).

Often in both real life and in *Northanger Abbey*, lying extends beyond exaggeration to the fictional, justifying the use of the term "fake news," or as Axel Gelfert defines it, "deliberate presentation of … false or misleading claims as news" (84). Fake news is always "misleading *by design*" (Gelfert's emphasis, 108), and it succeeds largely because its creators understand what Gelfert has called its "*systemic* dimension" (Gelfert's emphasis, 109). In other words, the manufacturers of fake news understand how it operates within an ideological system, how the "news" will affect and "infect" the person who hears it. It is abundantly clear that John Thorpe has mastered this variety of miscommunication. When he wishes to impress—and control—Catherine, for example, he fabricates a description of Blaize Castle, which functions as "news" for the Gothic-mad Catherine. In reality, Blaize was a medium-sized, pseudo-Gothic garden folly, containing only one small room; it was barely thirty years old, having been constructed in 1766. But Thorpe invents an alternate identity for the place: in his account, Blaize is truly medieval, "The finest place in England … The oldest in the kingdom," with "dozens" of rooms that can be explored by the Gothic-besotted tourist (Austen [1817] 2006: 83). Thorpe's fakery insidiously takes advantage of the Castle's "*systemic* dimension." He knows that such a "doctored" travel description will appeal to Catherine's naïve infatuation with Gothic literature. Thorpe's fake news admirably succeeds: Catherine is captivated, asking him if Blaize is "like what one reads of," if it contains "towers and long galleries" (83). Thorpe's well-crafted fakery has caught his prey.

Given Thorpe's success with his Blaize Castle ploy, he again uses blatant misinformation. Later in the same scene, he fabricates a story to discredit and undermine the Tilneys, who have arranged a walk with Catherine. Thorpe fabricates a report that the Tilneys have not waited for Catherine: "I saw them [in a carriage] as we turned into Broad-street" (83). Then he reiterates his claim: "I saw [Henry Tilney] at that moment turn up the Lansdown Road,—

driving a smart-looking girl" (84). Thorpe next embellishes his narrative with plausible detail, carefully chosen to enhance his own credibility as observer: Thorpe "heard Tilney hallooing to a man who was just passing by on horseback, that they were going as far as Wick Rocks" (84). What is particularly sinister about Thorpe's procedure here is his understanding of how such a fabrication will appeal to Catherine's social insecurity. He instinctively knows that if he can make Catherine doubt the Tilneys' word, he will reduce her independence as a member of the community of visitors to Bath and her connection with the Tilneys. She will become more subject to his power—and physically present in his gig, giving him more control over her body. Again, as in the Blaize Castle ploy, Austen shows him isolating and demoralizing Catherine: she sadly says, "I suppose [the Tilneys] thought it would be too dirty for a walk" (84) and to herself reflects, "To feel herself slighted by them was very painful" (85). Thorpe's fake news has reduced Catherine to a state of sad self-doubt.

Another species of misinformation to which Catherine is vulnerable is gaslighting, a series of fabrications during which the practitioner prevaricates so repeatedly and confidently as to make the victim doubt their perception and even sanity. As Paige L. Sweet (2019) has argued, gaslighting is "rooted in social inequalities, including gender" (851); it damages "victims' sense of reality, autonomy, mobility, identity and social supports" (852). The above scene can be interpreted as an example of gaslighting, as Thorpe's fabrication increases Catherine's sense of insecurity—and her dependence upon him. But this is not the novel's first instance of gaslighting. Thorpe first gaslighted Catherine at a ball, attempting to convince her that they were already engaged to dance. As in the later Tilney episode, he uses gaslighting to wrest her body and her attentions away from another man. He also again accompanies misinformation with detailed recollections that are completely manufactured:

> Scarcely had they [Catherine and Henry Tilney] worked themselves into [the line of couples waiting to join the country dance, when Catherine's] attention was claimed by John Thorpe .... "Heyday, Miss Morland!" said he, "what is the meaning of this?—I thought you and I were to dance together."
> I wonder you should think so, for you never asked me.

"That is a good one, by Jove!—I asked you as soon as I came into the room, and I was just going to ask you again, but when I turned round, you were gone!—this is a cursed shabby trick! ... Yes; I remember, I asked you while you were waiting in the lobby for your cloak."

(Austen [1817] 2006: 73)

Read alone, this scene could merely suggest Thorpe's comic boorishness—but as part of a pattern, his gaslighting becomes a more sinister technology for masculine control. Such careful planning and targeted "grooming" place these behaviors on a spectrum of sexual assault.

Thorpe feels that it is his right and responsibility to explain the world to Catherine—a tendency that we might now identify as "mansplaining." We have already noted how he feels it is his function to make his views known on stereotypically masculine subjects: physical distance, maps, horses, carriages, and prime tourist sites. But he also assumes that Catherine will benefit from his views on novels (*Tom Jones* and *The Monk* are the only two worth reading; Burney's *Camilla* is "unnatural stuff" [43]) and on female beauty: early in their acquaintance, he provides "a short decisive sentence of praise or condemnation on the face of every woman they met" (42). He clearly thinks that it's a man's right to judge women—and to judge them on physical appearance. Catherine has been acculturated to accept such masculine opinions: as Austen's narrator tells us, Catherine listened and agreed "as long as she could, with all the civility and deference of the youthful female mind, fearful of hazarding an opinion of its own in opposition to that of a self-assured man" (42).

Thorpe is not the only male character who believes he has the right to pronounce judgment. The hero Henry Tilney issues rulings on language use, current events, the value of novel reading, the importance of history, and the picturesque (107–16). Though the naïve Catherine might need some instruction, Henry's mansplaining can take a more ominous, controlling tone, as in a critically debated sequence later in the novel. When Henry learns that Catherine suspects his father, General Tilney, of having hastened or caused his mother's death—in short, of having been a Gothic villain—Henry mansplains. In the process, he invokes English history and institutions to censor Catherine's speculation, to limit her exploration of the family mansion, and to stifle questions about family history and possible domestic abuse:

> Dear Miss Morland [he tells Catherine in real or pretended indignation], consider the dreadful nature of the suspicions you have entertained. What have you been judging from? Remember the country and age in which we live. Remember that we are English, that we are Christians. Consider your own understanding, your own sense of the probable, your own observation of what is passing around you—Does our education prepare us for such atrocities? Do our laws connive at them? Could they be perpetrated without being known, in a country like this ... ? Dearest Miss Morland, what ideas have you been admitting?
>
> (203)

Four generations of readers, since C. S. Lewis's influential "A Note on Jane Austen" (1954), have been urged to read this scene as the turning point of the novel, the moment when Catherine gives up the Gothic, and when, according to Lewis, the innocent Catherine awakens from disillusionment (25–7). It is true that, after this impassioned speech from Henry, Austen's narrator tells us that Catherine "thoroughly opened her eyes to the extravagance of her late fancies" (Austen [1817] 2006: 204). However, Austen focalizes this passage through Catherine, who is at this moment cowed by enculturated submissiveness and by a rich and powerful man who disciplines her, making her run away crying "tears of shame" (203). Here Austen provides no objective or critical commentary from a heterodiegetic narrator who might convey authorial truth from outside the narrative, and so we must not interpret this scene separately from the novel's broader atmosphere of gendered violence. In fact, the narrator tells us later in the novel that Catherine's suspicions of General Tilney had been, in the main, correct: Catherine had "heard enough to feel, that in suspecting General Tilney of either murdering or shutting up his wife, she had scarcely sinned against his character or magnified his cruelty" (256).

Considering these patterns of misinformation and mansplaining, we must interpret Catherine's "epiphany" (she "thoroughly opened her eyes") in this scene not as Catherine's palinode to the Gothic, but rather as Austen's clear-eyed acknowledgment of the effective power of mansplaining to shame women and stifle investigations into the misogynistic behavior of men, particularly when the subject of those investigations is "respectable." Already trained to defer to men in the name of "civility and deference" (42), Catherine is here cowed by social forces and patriarchal ideologies that urge silence and compliance. At times she might escape their power, as when she breaks the physical hold of Isabella Thorpe or when she refuses to corroborate Thorpe's lies about having secured her as a dance partner. But sometimes—as here—the forces against Catherine are so strong that she can only bow her head in ideological servitude.

Rape Culture: Community Complicity

John Thorpe could not gaslight or so successfully create fake news without assistance, both active and tacit, from his community. When he enlists multiple individuals to maintain patriarchal power structures—specifically to gain access to Catherine's body—*Northanger Abbey* demonstrates the pervasiveness of rape culture. In several scenes of the novel, the social group that condones and enforces Thorpe's masculine power consists of two powerful forces in Catherine's world: her best friend Isabella Thorpe, representing the power of the heroine's peer group, and her own brother James Morland, representing the power of her family. It is undoubtedly Thorpe's sister Isabella who, behind the scenes, has revealed Catherine's fascinations with the Gothic and with the Tilneys, thus allowing Thorpe the information he requires to exploit and manipulate Catherine's vulnerabilities. But Isabella does not exert power only behind the scenes. In Book I, chapter 13, she and her community also work more directly and even physically to get an unwilling Catherine into a carriage alone with Thorpe. In this scene, Austen uses free indirect discourse to relate the episode from Catherine's point of view and thus replicates Catherine's feeling of receiving inexorable, escalating demands of friends and family; the cumulative effect is suffocating. First, Isabella, in urging her brother's plan, wheedles and simpers: "Isabella became only more and more urgent; calling on her in the most affectionate manner, addressing her by the most endearing names. She was sure her dearest, sweetest Catherine would not seriously refuse such a trifling request to a friend who loved her so dearly" (98). When this insinuating technique fails, Isabella becomes direct and confrontational: "She reproached [Catherine] with having more affection for Miss Tilney, though she had known her so little a while" (98). Next, Isabella tries tears: she, "in the meanwhile, had applied her handkerchief to her eyes" (99). Then Catherine's brother James joins the attack, significantly escalating the pressure upon Catherine and manifesting pressure from the heroine's patriarchal family—an added social force whose importance Austen clearly signals: "This," the narrator tells us, "was the first time of her brother's openly siding against her" (99). Finally, in a passage of extraordinary power, Catherine's community surrounds her, imprisoning and impinging on her body: Isabella and James are "walking in a most uncomfortable manner" (99); Isabella's "arm was still linked" with Catherine's (100). Here, Austen's use of free indirect discourse communicates Catherine's confusion and panic, as her community coalesces to threaten her bodily freedom and agency.

Against such cultural forces, Catherine struggles to assert her will. Building on a tradition of unheeded women in Richardson's *Clarissa* and other eighteenth-century novels, *Northanger Abbey* depicts her repeatedly saying "No"—and being ignored. The scene in which Thorpe uses Blaize Castle to entice Catherine is only one of many such examples. Here, the heroine says "No" at least four times. Catherine's first denial is polite and delicate, justifying her refusal in practicality and a vague reference to a previous social commitment: "To Bristol!" Catherine says. "Is not that a great way off?—But, however, I cannot go with you to-day, because I am engaged; I expect some friends every moment" (82). In her next denial, Catherine escalates the tone by repeating "cannot" three times and providing information about her previous social commitment: "I should like to see it [Blaize Castle, but] I cannot—I cannot go ... I cannot go [because] I expect Miss Tilney and her brother to call on me to take a country walk" (83). Then, after Thorpe has lured her into his gig—and thus established physical control over her—Catherine's tone expresses panic, indicated by short, imperative phrases: "'Stop, stop, Mr. Thorpe,' she impatiently cried; 'it is Miss Tilney; it is indeed.—How could you tell me they were gone?—Stop, stop, I will get out this moment and go to them'" (85). Here, Catherine expresses her anger ("How could you tell me ... ?") and envisions escape, even if escape might be the spectacle of a disheveled girl running panicked through the streets of Bath. But

Thorpe's control is unabated and Catherine understands her nearly complete powerlessness. Her next denial begins in subservience but then rises in volume toward resistance: "In another moment she was herself whisked into the Market-place. Still, however, and during the length of another street, she entreated him to stop .... Pray, pray stop, Mr. Thorpe.—I cannot go on.—I will not go on.—I must go back to Miss Tilney" (85–6). This scene demonstrates a pattern of escalating refusals accompanied by ever-increasing denials of agency—a pattern common in sexual assault scenarios.

Two chapters later, Austen carries the violence against Catherine one step further as Thorpe works to seize her power to speak on her own behalf. When he suddenly announces a jaunt to Clifton, Catherine again repeatedly withholds consent: "She had that moment settled with Miss Tilney to take their proposed walk tomorrow; it was quite determined, and she would not, upon any account, retract" (97). Upon hearing this refusal, Thorpe goes to the Tilneys' lodgings and lies in Catherine's name, saying that she had "recollected a prior engagement of going to Clifton" (100). Here, in another form of gendered violence, Thorpe takes away Catherine's will and voice. He attempts to treat her as the mythical Apollo treats Daphne, turning a fleeing wood nymph into an instrument that plays only his own tune.

By this point in the novel, the assaults against Catherine seem to have had a pedagogical effect, strengthening her resolve. In this particular scene, she effects a decisive objection:

> "Let me go, Mr. Thorpe; Isabella, do not hold me." ... Away walked Catherine in great agitation, as fast as the crowd would permit her, fearful of being pursued, yet determined to persevere. As she walked, she reflected on what had passed. It was painful to her to disappoint and displease them, particularly to displease her brother; but she could not repent her resistance.
>
> (101–2)

It would be tempting to read Catherine's escape here as evidence that she has "learned" how to keep safe in a world of dangerous misinformation and gendered violence. But as the beginning of the final sentence demonstrates, her community still exerts mental power over her: she still feels pained "to disappoint and displease them" (101–2). Despite Catherine's resolve, patriarchal and tribal forces have not relinquished their power—she has been socialized to be nice and submissive. This reminds us that Catherine's success rate in countering misinformation has been spotty. Indeed, Austen has illustrated all along that Catherine's progress in recognizing and resisting patriarchy and rape culture is decidedly not linear. Even after her confident rejoinder to Thorpe's attempt to gaslight her on the dance floor, she believes his fake news about Blaize Castle and the Tilneys. Instead, the lesson Austen suggests is women's need for eternal vigilance against ever-evolving threats.

Spectacles of Male Power

Throughout the novel, Austen never lets us forget the power of these threats. We have seen the barrage of braggadocio, misinformation, complicity, denial, and silencing that women face. They also face what I label "spectacles of male power": staged spectacles of male power intended to intimidate their (often female) witnesses. John Thorpe repeatedly implies his ability and willingness to control Catherine by demonstrating for her his aggressive control of horses. On setting off for their first ride, he tells Catherine, "You will not be frightened, Miss Morland ... if my horse should dance about a little at first setting off. He will, most likely, give a plunge or two ... but he will soon know his master" (43). Austen repeats the analogy later in the same chapter but moves Catherine from witness to participant in the demonstration: when she demands to be set down from Thorpe's gig, he "only lashed his horse into a brisker trot" (85). When Catherine then tells him that she cannot "go on"—this is the second time she withdraws consent—he responds with a sinister spectacle that forces her to submit to his power: "Mr. Thorpe only laughed, smacked his whip, encouraged his horse, made odd noises, and drove on; and Catherine, angry and vexed as she was, having no power of getting away, was obliged to give up the point and submit" (86).

Conclusion

Today, it is clear that the forces threatening Catherine Morland are very real. We now know that, at her most terrorized moments,

Catherine stands in danger, recalling nothing so much as a Gothic heroine or hero. Late in the novel we learn that both John Thorpe and General Tilney have gotten hold of some "fake news" that Catherine is an heiress—both want her supposed fortune; even Isabella Thorpe is in on the plot.[2] In an unsettling but real sense, the Tilneys' invitation to Northanger is merely a more polite and socially acceptable form of kidnapping than the one clumsily practiced by John Thorpe. At the very moment when Catherine escapes *from* the Thorpes' power in Book I, Chapter xiii, when she runs to the Tilneys' lodgings, she is in fact running *into* danger—like a heroine in many a thriller. The novel's supposed hero, the Rev. Henry Tilney, despite all his charms, defends his controlling father, limits Catherine's physical exploration of Northanger, and preempts her legitimate investigation of the family's history of gendered violence.

Northanger Abbey illustrates that fear and danger are to be found not only in a crumbling castle in Medieval Italy but also in the here and now, in Bath and in the English country house, in the moments in which women find themselves resisting male power and aggression and an enabling rape culture. It is far from a light and comforting novel. Reading the novel in the age of #MeToo reveals that, despite its occasional lighthearted tone, it is a cautionary tale in which the world turns threatening, even Gothic. Catherine's—and Jane Austen's—resistance to this world was always there, in the pages of *Northanger*'s text. But sometimes it takes new terms and new social movements to reveal just how dystopian a novel has always been.[3]

Notes

1   References from *Northanger Abbey* are taken from *The Cambridge Edition of the Works of Jane Austen*, ed. Barbara M. Benedict and Deirdre Le Faye.
2   Janine Barchas's "Mapping *Northanger Abbey*" has revealed the intricate financial plotting in the novel.
3   A longer version of this essay appeared in *Nineteenth-Century Gender Studies*, 16 (2): 2020. http://ncgsjournal.com/issue162/PDFs/murray.pdf.

Works Cited

Austen, Jane ([1817] 2006), *Northanger Abbey*, ed. Barbara Benedict and Deirdre Le Faye, Cambridge and New York: Cambridge University Press.

Barchas, Janine (2009), "Mapping *Northanger Abbey*: Or, Why Austen's Bath of 1803 Resembles Joyce's Dublin of 1904," *The Review of English Studies*, New Series, 60 (245): 431–59.

Gelfert, Axel (2018), "Fake News: A Definition," *Informal Logic*, 38 (1): 84–117.

Lewis, C. S. (1963), "A Note on Jane Austen," in Ian Watt (ed.), *Jane Austen: A Collection of Critical Essays*, 25–34, Englewood Cliffs, NJ: Prentice-Hall.

Lewis, M. G. (1796), *The Monk. A Romance in Three Volumes*, Waterford: Printed for J Saunders. Available online: http://find.galegroup.com/ecco/infomark.do?contentSet=ECCOArticles&docType=ECCOArticles&bookId=1164400301&type=getFullCitation&t

Mudrick, Marvin (1952), *Jane Austen: Irony as Defense and Discovery*, Princeton: Princeton University Press.

Sweet, Paige L. (2019), "The Sociology of Gaslighting," *American Sociological Review*, 84 (5): 851–75.

11

The Limits of #MeToo in India:

Re-reading Bapsi Sidhwa's *Cracking India* and Deepa Mehta's *Earth*

Nidhi Shrivastava

Does speaking up, as the #MeToo movement celebrates, give a subject agency and empower the rape survivor? The answer to this question is complicated: while the movement received global recognition in 2017, the turning point for women's rights in India occurred five years earlier, after the heinous 2012 Delhi gang-rape case that drew widespread outrage against sexual violence. Since 2012, there have been ongoing digital movements such as #PinjraTod and #WhyLoiter, launched online in December 2014, to coincide with the anniversary of the Delhi gang-rape case. Yet existing power structures continue to silence rape victims who assert themselves in public: in 2019, for example, a Unnao gang-rape victim was burned alive by her perpetrators after she called them out (BBC 2019a). As popular Indian actress Nandita Das puts it, the culture of silence reinforces and perpetuates the culture of fear (Bordoloi 2017). India's current climate does not encourage rape survivors to express themselves.

In this chapter, I explore how women's experiences of violence have been silenced in India by examining Indo-Canadian filmmaker Deepa Mehta's *Earth* (1999), a film adaptation of Pakistani-American author Bapsi Sidhwa's novel *Cracking India* (1991). By comparing the treatment of Ayah/Shanta, a raped and abducted woman, in the novel and film, I argue that the film fails to bring the experiences of victims and survivors into mainstream media discussions. Indeed, the failures and limitations of this film continue a longer pattern of silencing and making invisible the pervasive sexual violence in India that has its roots in 1947, during Partition.

Although estimates vary, Urvashi Butalia (2000) reports that during the genocidal violence of Partition, at least a million people lost their lives and 75,000 women were abducted (3). Yet a long silence followed this cataclysmic event. It was not until 1984 that pioneering feminist historians Urvashi Butalia, Ritu Menon, and Kamla Bhasin began their research on the gendered violence that happened during Partition.[1] These scholars initiated the reclamation of narratives of sexual violence.[2] Yet despite the efforts of cultural critics, historians, and activists, many people—and the mainstream media—continue to overlook the experiences of women during Partition. For example, in the aftermath of the Delhi rape case, Indian news channels only reported cases of sexual violence as early as the 1970s, as if the rapes and abductions of Partition had never taken place (BBC 2013; Newsable 2018). Likewise, since 1949, relatively few films that address this period have been released in Hindi cinema, and only five of them truly focus on the plight of raped and abducted women. In this chapter, I argue that in order to better understand India's rape culture, we need to reclaim the voices of raped and abducted women from Partition. After all, if we cannot see them or hear them, then their lives are made *unreal* to us, as if they never existed.

Partition: Sexual Violence and Public Memory

Partition revealed the patriarchal and misogynistic attitudes of families, communities, and the newly minted governments of India and Pakistan that continue to exist today, especially in conversations about honor and shame. As Pavitra Sundar (2010) notes, Partition discourse is usually "framed in the terms of *izzat*, familial, and communal honor" (278). "Honor" continues to frame the value placed on women; one example can be seen in the aftermath of the Delhi rape case, when Leslee Udwin's controversial documentary, *India's Daughter* (2015), included the comment made by defense lawyer A. P. Singh that "if my daughter or my sister were involved in pre-marital relationships or disgraces to her character, then I would take her to my farmhouse and in front of my entire family, douse petrol on her, and set her alight" (translations mine, Udwin 52:22–52:42). Such disturbing yet traditional views that are based on "honor" problematically legitimize gender-based violence.

As the cataclysmic events of the Partition unfolded, many communities feared that their women would be abducted, raped, and much worse, converted to their enemy's religion. Butalia observes that there was an assumed belief that while men could fight, women were vulnerable to rape and could get impregnated, thus humiliating the entire community. To prevent such shame, men would often resort to violence, either encouraging women to jump into wells or killing them. Butalia writes that although rapes, abductions, and physical mutilations are acknowledged publicly, no "mention was made of family violence by anyone—neither the families, nor the State, nor indeed by historians. And yet, its scale was not small. Virtually every village had similar stories" (2000: 162). If a woman did survive and was recovered during Operation Recovery Program (1948–56), the joint agreement between India and Pakistan to repatriate abducted women to their original homes, they were seen as polluted and often their own families did not accept them for being tainted after being sexually involved with men from other religious communities. In fact, as Ritu Menon and Kamla Bhasin were conducting research, they found that many people with whom they spoke said that "it's too late—they're all dead" (1998: 13). The lives of these women were not even considered worthy of their memories because they had not committed suicide to protect the "honor" of their families and communities. Despite this communal rejection, Menon and Bhasin found that some of the women who survived continued to live in *ashrams* (communities for widows or single women) for the rest of their live as refugees.

The film industry was also complicit with India's cultural silence about Partition. During the 1990s, *Earth* was one of only two films that centered on the gendered experiences of the Partition.[3] Several sociopolitical and cultural conditions contributed to the dearth of films. India witnessed a surge of sectarian violence throughout the 1990s, including the Babri mosque's demolition and subsequent communal rioting in 1992–3. The Hindu nationalist party, Bhartiya Janta Party (BJP), also rose to electoral power in 1996 (BBC 2019b). These conditions led to the emergence of identity politics that affected the film industry and led to certain types of censorship. The power dynamics that influenced censorship laws shifted as Shiv Sena (Hindi: Army of Shiva), a right-wing regional Hindu nationalist party (with the BJP), competed with the Central Board of Film Censorship (CBFC), the government's censorship body, for power and control to suppress films that did not align with their point of view. The BJP's election manifesto makes visible their vested interest in cinema: "*Sex and violence on the screen is beginning to gnaw at the moorings of our cultural ethos. The BJP is committed to checking this abuse of popular cinema*" (BJP Manifesto 1998: 232). Thus, this era saw a notable shift in the film industry's media landscape because the CBFC was no longer the only entity imposing draconian censorship laws by allowing right-wing organizations to have the authority to control film content. Hindu fundamentalists did *more* than act as proxy censors upon the release of films that they considered offensive to their beliefs. They *weaponized* the culture through violent methods, threats, and destruction of public property to terrorize filmmakers such as Deepa Mehta, whom they found made films that opposed their view of Hinduism.

Deepa Mehta's *Earth*, Censorship, and the Rise of Hindu Fundamentalism

Mehta's films, known to disrupt the traditional status quo of Hindi commercial films with their thought-provoking themes, have often led to mass protests and violence. After the release of *Fire* (1996) and *Water* (2005), Hindu extremists questioned Mehta's relationship with India as a transnational filmmaker and protested against her films because they explored issues such as lesbianism and Hindu widow remarriages. For them, anyone who challenged their view of Hinduism was considered anti-Indian and, in Mehta's case, an outsider because of her hybrid identity as Indo-Canadian. In response to her films, Hindu extremists brought identity politics to the forefront. Elisabeth Bumiller (2006) reports that Mehta cancelled *Water*'s film shoot after Hindu fundamentalists protested that it was "anti-Hindu." There were "some 500 demonstrators [who] took to the streets, ransacked the set and burned Ms. Mehta in effigy. She appealed to the State government for help, but fearing more violence, local officials asked the film crew to leave" (Bumiller 2006). Not only did Mehta receive death threats, but Hindu fundamentalists also damaged her net worth by $650,000 (ICFI 2000). Although Mehta's Elements trilogy focuses on female sexuality, *Fire* and *Water* have faced the most scrutiny from the Hindu fringe groups who merely "denounced" *Earth* (Phillips 2000). Given the strict state censorship laws and moral policing of Hindu fundamentalists, it is remarkable that *Earth* (1999) did *not* face the same volume of scandals and controversy as *Fire*. The Shiv Sena-BJP only retaliated when her films questioned traditional Hindu norms of female sexuality but were not concerned with the depictions of Muslims as rapists and abductors, as is the case in *Earth*. Thus, the 1999 film did not create an opportunity for audiences to reflect on the experiences of women during Partition, even though Mehta's position as an Indo-Canadian filmmaker could have enabled her to take risks that many mainstream filmmakers could not have taken due to Indian censorship laws.

Set in Lahore, the film recounts the events leading to the Partition and its aftermath. Lenny Sethi (Maia Sethna), an eight-year-old polio-stricken girl from an affluent Parsi family, narrates the plot as an adult (Shabana Azmi), recalling the memories of her nanny, a Hindu woman, Shanta/Ayah (Nandita Das) and her two suitors. The first, Dil Nawaz (Aamir Khan), is a prudent, tender, and kind-hearted man who undergoes a radical transformation after the brutal massacre of his sisters, coupled with Shanta's rejection during the climax of the film. The second is Hassan (Rahul Khanna), known as the Masseur in Sidhwa's novel; he is a gentle, charming Muslim man willing to convert his religion and migrate to India for Shanta. As the Partition's genocidal violence unfolds, Lenny experiences firsthand the savagery that transpires as Lahore's streets are swarmed with rioters looting, burning, and destroying the city. Lenny's parents are unable to sustain the veneers of neutrality, making Shanta vulnerable amidst the chaos. On the fateful day when Hassan and Shanta plan to escape Amritsar, Lenny and Hari discover Hassan's body and hear the mob charging toward Lenny's home. Meanwhile, Shanta hides in the room. As Imam Din (Kulbushan Kharbanda) attempts to diffuse the angry mob, Dil tricks Lenny into giving away Shanta's hiding place; as soon as she reveals the truth, Dil tells the mob, and they forcefully pull Shanta into a horse cart and take her away. The film ends on an ambiguous note, unlike the novel, but pans to the adult Sidhwa as she speculates on Shanta's ill fate.

Hindu fundamentalists did not hold protests against Shanta as they had for *Fire*'s Sita and Radha. Nor did Shanta's rape and abduction provoke a response from them, perhaps because they would have considered Shanta damaged goods (she is sexually involved with a Muslim suitor). More broadly, though, Shanta's story is reduced and minimized in Mehta's film. *Earth* abruptly ends after Shanta's capture—an omission that, as Kavita Daiya (2008) notes, "mark[s] her [Shanta's] death as a social subject, a citizen, and an agent" (62). By not exploring the aftermath of Shanta's trauma, and by focusing on the spectacle of her death, *Earth* echoes retrogressive views of women that celebrate women who sacrifice themselves to protect their honor—a school of thought shared by the Hindu nationalist narrative.

Earth's sudden ending left scholars critical of the film. Daiya argues that "Ayah [Shanta] as the raped woman disappears from the horizon of national history in the film after sexual violence" (2008: 62). Jill Didur also states that Shanta's body is "sexually exploited, policed, and made emblematic of the national imagination" (1998: 44). Furthermore, Uraizee affirms that the "gaze is used to render [Shanta] as a passive victim or an erotic spectacle in need of our sympathy and compassion" (2010: 26). While Mehta creates awareness about the bodily atrocities afflicted on women for global audiences, her film fails to explore Shanta's social, psychological, and emotional trauma: we witness the moment when the Muslim mob apprehends her onscreen, but we cannot access her ultimate fate. Shanta's abduction is nothing more than "a visual spectacle" (Daiya 2008: 62). Its power lies in its shock value: the scene is meant to evoke strong emotions like anger, disgust, and horror. Beyond creating that initial shock, however, the film does not explore her destiny. The ending, while memorable and abrupt, dilutes the event's complexity.

Mehta's focus on the abduction scene, therefore, leaves more to be desired. Filmmakers have an opportunity to use techniques to make movies impactful in the short term and memorable in the long term. Audiences experience a wide variety of emotions—thrill, excitement, disgust, outrage, tears—and in the short term, strong emotion and affect can make a film compelling (Platinga 2009: 3). However, Carl Platinga argues that filmmakers who use these techniques correctly will achieve a longer-term effect, as "experiences may burn themselves into the memories of audiences and may become templates for thinking and behavior" (6). By contrast, although *Earth*'s ending leaves an impression for the short term, it *does not* achieve a lasting impact. Mehta's inadequate representation of Shanta's rape and abduction follows the trend of certain techniques used in Hollywood films and television series such as *13 Reasons Why* (2017). Amanda Spallacci contends that these film techniques construct the rape scene so that it "foreground[s] the protagonist's emotional responses during the rape through close-up shots of the protagonist's face, which may invite empathy from the audience" (2019: 3). Thus, the traumatic event of rape is the main focus rather than an exploration of the rape victim's memory of the event. Shanta's abduction in the film follows a similar stylistic technique: the tension is palpable as her body is dragged from the Sethi house as she screams and shouts, calling for Lenny's mother. Indeed, this scene elicits disgust and perhaps empathy from the audience, but that is all it does.

By contrast, in the novel, Sidhwa represents Ayah's identity in a complex and nuanced way: Lenny's Godmother helps her family locate Ayah in Lahore's red-light district only to find her married and forcibly converted. As readers, we have access to her when she meets with Lenny's Godmother. Despite having a "harsh, gruff" voice, Ayah asserts: "I want to go to my family" (Sidhwa 1991: 273). She exclaims, "I cannot forget what happened" (273), recalling her violent abduction and discloses to Lenny's Godmother that "I am past that. *I am not alive*" (274; emphasis added). When Godmother reminds her that her family might not accept her, Ayah says: "Whether they want me or not, I will go" (274). With the Sethi family's help, she is emancipated and returns to India. Rajan (1994) proposes the notion of "life after rape" in which she notes that in alternative feminist texts, the "development of the female subject's 'self' begins *after* the rape and occupies the entire length of the narrative" (72; author's emphasis). Sidhwa's novel can arguably be considered feminist because it allows us as readers access to Ayah's "life after rape" narrative.

Toward the end of the novel, we hear about Ayah's marriage through the Ice Candy Man when Godmother confronts him about his licentious actions (Sidhwa 1991: 262). Sidhwa demonstrates that Ayah at least has a voice. Ayah can convey that she is unhappy, feels trapped, and wants to escape. Because she communicates her feelings to the Godmother, she returns to Amritsar. The novel thus offers closure. In *Earth*, by contrast, we do not hear the rape victim speak. Mehta reduces Shanta to a member of collective violence. While the film suggests that innumerable women encountered rape and abduction, Mehta takes away any individuality from Shanta's rape experience. Shanta's rape, abduction, and subsequent social death define her subjectivity. On the cinematic screen, where speech demonstrates one's subjectivity, Shanta is denied any opportunity to speak, thus precluding any opportunity for her trauma to become "real" for the audiences. By contrast, in the novel, her words are a source of agency: they enable her to return to her family in Amritsar.

Pedagogically, the film's lack of emphasis on Shanta's agency affects its reception among students. I have taught *Cracking India* and *Earth* since 2015, primarily to non-South Asian first-year students at North American universities. While I have seen empathy for Shanta from my students, they are unable to grasp the gravity of the women's experiences until I show them key scenes from *Pinjar* (2003) and *Khamosh Pani* (2003). Both explore life after rape and the abduction of the female protagonists and give us access to them as complex, agential characters rather than merely as characters emblematic of collective violence (Hai 2000: 405). This teaching experience underscores how Shanta, as a subject on the silver screen, is *"read"* differently than in the novel.[4] Because she is denied the ability to speak, she is primarily defined by her presence on the screen. If we cannot hear her speak, then we cannot truly understand the trauma that she is experiencing, and her subjectivity—in many ways a symbol for other raped women—is diminished.

Mehta's editorial choices reduce the severity of Shanta's abduction to a singular event creating mere shock value for audiences, and as a result, Shanta suffers a social and physical death into the abyss: audiences cannot access her future, so she is made *unreal* to them. It is striking that the representation of Shanta's rape and abduction did not cause a similar commotion from Mehta's *Fire*. One could argue that this was perhaps because Shanta was "a passive victim" (Uraizee 2010: 26) and her fate was sealed whether she married Dil or remained in a brothel. In the end, her rape and abduction, as well as her trauma, did not seem to have the same value as the other women's stories in *Fire* and *Water*.

Conclusion

Mehta's problematic framing of Shanta silences her characterization in the film and in so doing reinforces the silencing of rape survivors. This silencing is emblematic of larger issues within India, where speaking up as a rape survivor continues to carry risk. Women still face backlash for speaking up, and in some instances, court cases are still pending years after they were filed (Goel et al. 2018). These are among the many reasons why the #MeToo movement has not gained as much traction in India as elsewhere. Despite ongoing activism, women's speech faces formidable obstacles that result in silence.

By not acknowledging the gendered violence that occurred during Partition and the implications of the trauma that followed, we have limited understanding of India's contemporary rape culture. This has implications for understanding the possibilities and limitations of digital movements such as #MeToo in India. We need to rethink digital activism by acknowledging the voices that are seldom heard and by ensuring that these voices get a presence in mainstream discourse, as Jha (2018) and Guha (2015) have pointed out; but we also need to better understand the many ways that women's voices and experiences continue to be silenced even when they gain access to these conversations. By understanding, learning, and acknowledging the gendered violence that occurred to women's bodies during Partition, we can better reflect on these attitudes and perhaps engage in a broader conversation to understand why the culture of fear still continues to exist, making rape survivors feel afraid to speak up or file reports in police stations.

Notes

1. They were influenced by the 1984 anti-Sikh riots that enveloped parts of India.
2. Many other scholars and activists spearheaded the work of research and preservation, which resulted in important research and organizations such as the Partition archive (established in 2010), the citizenship archive of Pakistan, and the first Partition museum (founded in 2017).
3. Prior years included one film, *Garam Hawa* (1973), and a television series, *Tamas* (Hindi: *Darkness*; 1989), which focused on Partition but were not concerned with the depictions of women's experiences.
4. Carl Plantinga (2009) calls for a rethinking of the literary metaphor—reading—to describe a viewer's experience with a film. This use of terminology, according to him, in effect denies audiences the fundamental differences between "viewing images" (2) and "reading words" (2). We have a different experience seeing the subjectivity of a character on the screen versus reading them as characters in a novel.

Works Cited

13 Reasons Why (2017), [Television Show] Dir. Jessica Yu, USA: July Moon Productions.

BBC (2013), "The Rapes That India Forgot," January 5. Available online: https://www.bbc.com/news/world-asia-india-20907755 (accessed August 28, 2020).

BBC (2019a), "Unnao Rape Case: Indian Woman Set on Fire on Way to Hearing Dies," December 7. Available online: https://www.bbc.com/news/world-asia-india-50697139 (accessed June 26, 2020).

BBC (2019b), "India Profile-Timeline," March 4. Available online: https://www.bbc.com/news/world-south-asia-12641776 (accessed July 25 2020).

BJP Election Manifesto (1998), "Our Policy on Media, Cinema, Arts." Available online: http://www.bjp.org/manifes/chap17.htm (accessed June 5, 2019).

Bordoloi, Satyen K. (2017), [Video] "Culture of Silence Is Manifestation of Culture of Fear: Nandita Das," *YouTube*, 15:17. December 20, 2017. Available online: https://www.youtube.com/watch?v=4iAs3dBSH8A.

Butalia, Urvashi (2000), *The Other Side of Silence: Voices from the Partition of India*, Durham: Duke University Press.

Bumiller, Elizabeth (2006), "Film Ignites the Wrath of Hindu Fundamentalists," *New York Times*, May 3. Available online: www.nytimes.com/2006/05/03/movies/03wate.html (accessed January 15, 2018).

Daiya, Kavita (2008), *Violent Belongings: Partition, Gender, and National Culture in Postcolonial India*, Philadelphia: Temple University Press.

Didur, Jill (1998), "Cracking the Nation: Gender, Minorities, and Agency in Bapsi Sidhwa's *Cracking India*," *ARIEL: A Review of International English Literature*, 29 (3): 43–64.

Earth (1999), [Film] Dir. Deepa Mehta, Canada: Hamilton Mehta Productions.

Fire (1996), [Film] Dir Deepa Mehta, Canada: Kaleidoscope Entertainment.

Goel, Vindu, et al. (2018), "After a Long Wait, India's #MeToo Movement Suddenly Takes Off," *New York Times*, October 9. Available online: https://nyti.ms/2A0ZtqF (accessed October 25, 2020).

Guha, Pallavi (2015), "Hash Tagging but Not Trending: The Success and Failure of the News Media to Engage with Online Feminist Activism in India," *Feminist Media Studies* 15 (1): 155–7.

Hai, Ambreen (2000), "Border Work, Border Trouble: Postcolonial Feminism and the Ayah in Bapsi Sidhwa's *Cracking India*," *MFS Modern Fiction Studies*, 4 (2): 379–426.

India's Daughter (2015), [Film] Dir. Leslee Udwin, London: Assassin Films.

International Committee of the Fourth International (ICFI) (2000), "Letters in Support of Indian Filmmaker Deepa Mehta," *World Socialist Website*. Available online: https://www.wsws.org/en/articles/2000/05/corr-m11.html (accessed January 28, 2018).

Jha, Sonora (2018), "Gathering Online, Loitering Offline: Hashtag Activism and the Claim for Public Space by Women in India through the #whyloiter Campaign," in Alka Kurian and Sonora Jha (eds.), *New Feminisms in South Asia: Disrupting the Discourse through Media, Film, and Literature*, 15–42, London and New York: Routledge.

Khamosh Pani (2003), [Film] Dir. Sabiha Sumar, India: Srinagar Films.

Menon, Ritu and Kamla Bhasin (1998). *Borders & Boundaries: Women in India's Partition*, Delhi: Kali For Women.

Newsable (2018), "Ten Rape Cases That India Will Never Forget," March 31. Available online: https://newsable.asianetnews.com/india/ten-rapes-cases-that-india-will-never-forget (accessed August 2, 2020).

Pinjar (2003), [Film] Dir. C. P. Dwivedi, India: 20th Century Fox.

Plantinga, Carl (2009), *Moving Viewers: American Film and the Spectator's Experience*, Los Angeles: University of California Press.

Phillips, Richard (2000), "Deepa Mehta Speaks Out against Hindu Extremist Campaign to Stop Her Film," *World Socialist Website*, February 15. Available online: https://www.wsws.org/en/articles/2000/02/meht-f15.html (accessed June 26, 2020).

Rajan, Rajeshwari S. (1994), "Life after Rape: Narrative, Theory, and Feminism," in Margaret R. Higonnet (ed.), *Borderwork: Feminist Engagements with Comparative Literature*, 61–78, Ithaca: Cornell University Press.

Sidhwa, Bapsi (1991), *Cracking India*, Minneapolis: Milkweed Editions.

Spallacci, Amanda (2019), "Representing Rape Trauma in Film: Moving beyond the Event," *Arts (Basel)* 8 (8). doi: 10.3390/arts801000.

Sundar, Pavitra (2010), "Silence and the Uncanny: Partition in the Soundtrack of *Khamosh Pani*," *South Asian Popular Culture*, 8 (3): 277–90.

Uraizee, Joya (2010), "Gazing at the Beast: Describing Mass Murder in Deepa Mehta's *Earth* and Terry George's *Hotel Rwanda*," *Shofar: An Interdisciplinary Study Journal of Jewish Studies*, 28 (4): 10–27.

Water (2005), [Film] Dir. by Deepa Mehta, Canada: David Hamilton Productions.

12

Intimate Violence and Sexual Assault in Kopano Matlwa's *Coconut:*

Carving Spaces of Feminist Liberation in Post-Apartheid South African Literature

Nafeesa T. Nichols

Sexual assault has a long and complex history of representation within South African literature. In the middle of the twentieth century, sexual violence appeared frequently in the short fiction of *Staffrider* magazine (Gqola 2015: 23), and Black South African author Miriam Tlali often wrote about sexual assault and rape survivors with what Pumla Gqola calls "gentleness and empathy for her woman characters" (2015: 25). More recently, sexual assault, rape, molestation, and the predominance of violent masculinities in South African gender politics are increasingly thematized in the work of South African novelists ranging from J. M. Coetzee's *Disgrace* (1999) to Redi Tlhabi's *Khwezi: The Remarkable Story of Fezekile Ntsukela Kuzwayo* (2017).

Kopano Matlwa's award-winning debut novel *Coconut* (2007) weaves intersecting themes of identity, space, race, and gender in a novel about the promise and betrayals of the "new South Africa" and the contradictions between the promise of freedom and the realities of post-apartheid life. While several texts engage these themes, *Coconut* is unique in that these contradictions converge powerfully in Matlwa's depiction of sexual assault. Moreover, few South African texts capture the particular dynamics of race, gender, space, and sexual abuse through the voice and perspective of a child survivor. This essay explores these intersections in an effort to unpack creative attempts to deconstruct and address rape culture in post-apartheid South Africa. It also contributes to a broader set of questions about how contemporary South African authors document the racialized and gendered nature of space in contemporary South Africa. I am particularly interested in how Matlwa's project exposes various geographies of sexual violence and fosters new insights into the ways that Black women navigate and create resistance within and around these geographies.

Feminist scholarship from a variety of disciplines successfully argues that space is both racialized and gendered.[1] Not only do racial and gender oppressions manifest themselves in materialist spatial terms, such as land theft, urban planning, plantation layout, South African township placement, and the like, but dominant geographies and existing cartographies also discursively naturalize hierarchy among human populations and throughout various locations.[2] Indeed, codes of sexual stereotypes and sexual violence that plague post-apartheid South Africa are based in the colonial-era over-sexualization of Black women and men. Rationalizations for this violence are rooted in a general belief in an innate proclivity toward sexual deviance in both men and women. This discourse of sexual deviance directly links to assumptions of sexual ownership of Black women's bodies (Baderoon 2014: 85–6), which informed the various ways that slave owners and colonial authorities worked to limit physical and mental mobility. In this way, enslaved people were both literally and metaphorically "kept in their place." Thus, as Gqola argues, the foundations for contemporary rape culture were laid not only in South Africa but also as part of the dynamics of any slavocracy throughout the world (2015: 44–6).

Gqola further suggests that Black women are rendered rhetorically "unrapable" because of how they are oversexualized in white supremacist patriarchal discourse: "black women are most likely to be raped because of these combined histories about who matters least ... rapists rape the women long burdened with assumptions of rapability" (53).

In contemporary South Africa, the legalities and political rhetoric of gender progressivism and freedom brought about by a change in regime have often been undercut by continued heteropatriarchal control, the perpetuation of heteronormative sexist constructions and stereotypes, and gender-based violence. Moreover, what Gqola calls the "female fear factory," or the fear associated with the threat of rape, reveals the spatialized nature of sexual violence:

> The threat of rape is an effective way to remind women that they are not safe and that their bodies are not entirely theirs. It is an exercise in power that communicates that the man creating fear has power over the woman who is the target of his attention; it also teaches women who witness it about their vulnerability either through reminding them of their own previous fear or showing them that it could happen to them next. It is an effective way to keep women in check and often results in women curtailing their movement in a physical and psychological manner.
>
> (2015: 79)

Gqola makes a significant point here with regard to the connections between spatiality and sexual violence, noting how heteropatriarchal control enforced through sexual violence or its threat curtails women's mobility on multiple levels. It is within this framework that Matlwa's novel *Coconut* allows several important insights into rape culture and gender politics in post-apartheid South Africa.

Coconut is a novel about two young Black women growing up within two different social classes, both struggling to navigate their racial and gender identity in post-apartheid South Africa. The novel is divided physically and textually into two different halves. In each half, one of the protagonists, Ofilwe Tlou and Fikile Twala, provides a first-person narrative of a single day in her life. The novel is richly interspersed with memories from their childhoods and recent events. Both experience various forms of racist and sexist violence, psychological and physical, and their growth and development diverge and converge on the axis of their class differences and their individual lived realities. These realities frequently unfold in the space of home.

In literature set during apartheid, home often means transience, exile, lack of ownership, and a perilous existence. Indeed, for many Black South Africans, home (and nation) signified homelessness. Thus, the concept requires revisiting after the 1994 transition of power. Njabulo Ndebele, in his own attempts to imagine the post-apartheid nation, interrogated the concept of home just two years after the 1994 elections: what does home mean in a post-apartheid context when so many lost their homes under the former regime? If by implication the newly established nation anchors the notion of home in nation, he asks, how can there be space for intimacy (1996: 1)? Indeed, the protagonist of the second half of *Coconut*, Fikile Twala, sees home as a "hole" where one dares not even sleep because "you lose all control and are vulnerable to the many monsters of the night" (Matlwa 2007: 109). Home, for Fikile, is a dangerous masculinist space where one's safety is never guaranteed. Intimacy does not have a place in such a home.

Fikile's experience of domestic space is reminiscent of other novels published around the same time in which home has become an overly Black masculinist space—an attempt, one might surmise, to reflect a Black masculinist nation.[3] However, in contrast to these, *Coconut* represents the perils of a space entrenched in white supremacist heteropatriarchy. Although the connection between domestic space and the nation is not made completely clear, there are significant moments in *Coconut* suggesting that the homes represented in the novel are symbolic of the South African nation-state. A focus on the doorway or border between the exterior and interior of Ofilwe's and Fikile's homes (Matlwa 2007: 71, 111) and the significance of that border is one example of Matlwa's interest in questioning long-held assumptions about home and nation. In Fikile's case, the entrance to her and her uncle's shack acts as the border between a relatively safe exterior world and the dangers of the interior (111). Meanwhile, for Ofilwe, it is the blurring of the border between the white upper-middle class exterior world and her Blackness that further raises questions with regard to home and nation (75). In neither case does entering into the interior of the home signify safety and comfort.

In interrogating home and nation, Matlwa also suggests new ways of thinking about intimacy. Taking my cue from Ndebele's interest in home and intimacy, I draw on the concept of intimacy as a tool with which to interrogate domestic space. Building on the geopolitical work of Rachel Pain and Lynn Staeheli (2014), I focus on a "politicized understanding of intimacy" (344). As such, I am interested in the "ambivalence of intimacy," "intimate violence," and intimacy as a "set of spatial relations ... a mode of interaction, and a set of practices" (344–5).

Intimacy in *Coconut* is closely linked to the past. Here, intimacy results from lack of personal space and overcrowding which, Sam Raditlhalo reminds us, "have been the bane of black South Africa for years, in single sex hostels and roughly constructed two-room township houses" (2008: 95). This is evidenced in Fikile's offhand comments that she sleeps on a cement floor without proper space for her belongings (Matlwa 2007: 117). Furthermore, the two narrator-protagonists invite the reader into the novel with their frequent deviations from the linear narrative through memories rendered in epistolary-style entries. Marked by italics, these journal entries invite the reader into the characters' thoughts, suggesting how intimacy in the text also refers to "exposure" (Bystrom 2013: 339). Exposure in this case has to do with what Bystrom calls "hospitality," a sort of invitation into the novel, or into the characters' narratives (340). However, with Matlwa's project the meaning of exposure shifts, unmasking the hidden or silenced truths of intimacy: intimate violence, sexualized violence, fear, and control.

In this vein, *Coconut* "exposes" oft-silenced patterns of patriarchal domination, gender-based violence, sexual molestation, and other realities for Black South African women and girls. The concept of "exposure" takes on a political tenor reminiscent of Carol Hanisch's now well-known feminist argument that the "personal is political" (Hanisch 1969). Matlwa significantly argues that domestic spaces need not be overtly masculinist in order for the violence of white heteropatriarchy to ensue or to characterize that space. In Ofilwe Tlou's more conventional home, for example, her mother, Gemina, seems to dominate the domestic space with her voice reverberating throughout the house (Matlwa 2007: 75–8) while Ofilwe's father is symbolically most at home outside of the house:

> Through the window I see Daddy in the garden ... Standing in the heart of it in his Sunday suit, where all the mazes lead and where a clay boy wees into a stream of stones and pebbles below ... Oh, but how picturesque it looks, Daddy, at home in the garden, framed by the window's silk curtains that are draped like ball gowns over the wrought iron rods.
>
> (79)

The symbolism of this image is twofold. Because it directly follows Gemina's dominance of the inside space, it establishes the dynamic of the father's place outside the home. However, by creating the image of a stereotypical upper-class English garden, complete with the statue of the boy peeing and the maze, which are framed by the ballgown curtains, Matlwa suggests that it is Ofilwe's father who is complicit in and subscribes to the aspirations of white heteropatriarchy. Matlwa juxtaposes this characterization with Ofilwe's grandmother's censure of her daughter Gemina's grief and anger at her husband's infidelity: "*Without him, my girl, you is nothing*" (13). This comment illustrates how patriarchal violence intersects with white supremacy. These kinds of overlaps underpin Black patriarchal aspirations to assume hierarchical places in society as well as the societal structures that both silence and oppress Black women, reflected in Gemina's mother's reality check to her daughter.

The representation of white heteropatriarchy in the Tlou's home lays the foundation for the second half of *Coconut*, where the reader is exposed to the intensity of the violence found in male-dominated spaces. For Fikile, living with her discontented Uncle has meant that she, similar to Pecola Breedlove in Toni Morrison's *The Bluest Eye* (1970), is the body upon which shame, racial oppression, and self-hatred are deposited. Fikile's character embodies several intertextual references to Pecola Breedlove, a well-known symbol of "internalized racism" (Roye 2012: 215). Matlwa's reference to Morrison's novel is likewise seen in the two characters' similarity in their circumstances: their subjection to incestuous sexual abuse, and the shame and self-loathing that accompany it. In addition, Matlwa alludes to Morrison's use of blue eyes as a symbol of whiteness through Fikile's use of "the dainty little emerald-green coloured lenses [and] lemon-light skin lightener cream" (2007: 117), both of which contribute to her transformation from the "naïve orphan child" to "the charming young waitress with pretty green eyes and soft, blow-in-the-wind, caramel-blond hair (pinned in perfectly to make it look real)" (117). Matlwa's reference to Morrison's novel emphasizes the intimacy of violence in domestic space and the shame that accompanies it. In other words, this kind of violence is entangled with trust and confidence, and it is executed by those closest to its victims physically and emotionally. Moreover, it is ironically carried out in the most intimate space that is supposed to signify safety and comfort.

Home is a space of peril for Fikile's character and has contributed to her alienation from her identity as a Black woman. Consider a few excerpts, written in the above-mentioned italics, from her description of her molestation at the hands of her uncle:

I'd be sitting on the kitchen floor still in my uniform writing out my mathematics or practicing my English readings when I would hear him dragging his feet through the dirt past the Tshabalala's house to our one-bedroom hovel at the end of the Tshabalala's garden ... [...] so I would ... stand facing the front door so I could see what kind of expression he had on his face when he walked in. And if it was that sorry look ... that sorry, pathetic 'Oh, woe is me' look, then I would know ...

I would try to cheer him up with all my might ... I would stretch my little arms up and onto his back and then march him around the room, away from the bedroom door, singing ... I would push at his back, marching and stomping my little feet with all the stompingness that they had in them, throwing my tiny voice up into the heavens ...

It was only a single bed, so when Uncle would turn his massive form to face me, I'd be stripped of the thin covers that were my only protection.

(111–13; italics in original)

Through spatial orientation, the reader is apprised of the shifting geographies of safety, fear, and uncertainty in the domestic space. In this passage, the dynamic of space changes so that the kitchen, normally a public space, is Fikile's only opportunity for privacy whereas the bedroom, ostensibly a space of safety, is dangerous and to be avoided. Frequently, Fikile tells us that she sits in the kitchen when alone in the house and later that she dresses in the kitchen (118). Conversely, when describing her desperate attempts to avoid her Uncle's sexual attention, she purposely "*marches him away from the bedroom door*" and later avoids the bedroom as long as she can in the hopes that her Uncle will fall asleep before she climbs into the bed they share. The comment that only "*thin covers*" (113) were her protection speaks to the perilousness of the bed and the absence of any recourse or protection from sexual violence.

The spatial details also illustrate the complexity with which spaces are produced by and reflect the psychological violence enacted by heteropatriarchy and white supremacy. This is further clarified in Matlwa's use of language, which connects the spatial dynamics of the interior/exterior spatiality of the shack to Fikile's rising tension and fear. The connection is illustrated in the description of the young character's hyper-awareness of the sound of "*him dragging his feet through the dirt*" and the tension of "*wait[ing] in front of the door*" (112) for her Uncle to come in and, once in the house, the emphasis on movement and space are indications of heightened danger and fear (112).

Matlwa repeats phrases and formulations to draw readers' attention to layers of violence in this scene. Repetition reminds the reader that this is a memory from childhood—"*all the stompingness,*" "*my little arms,*" "*I would try to cheer him up. I would try to cheer him up with all my might*" (112)—thus emphasizing the child's innocence, fear, and confusion. The wording reflects the size difference between Fikile and her uncle and signals age and gender as intersecting sites of vulnerability. It also highlights the psychological impact of child molestation at the hands of a trusted family member. Simultaneously, the repetition of the phrase "*that sorry look … that sorry pathetic look*" implies, similar to *The Bluest Eye*, a connection between sexual molestation and colonization and/or racial oppression. Fikile's uncle himself is a product of apartheid-era structures of oppression and white condescension. The "look" on his face reflects his failure to succeed at university and disappointments of his unrealized potential (127). In this sense, one might read sexual violence against women as a reaction to colonial and apartheid-era emasculation and infantilization of Black men.

However, while Matlwa's text may fall in line with a long legacy of using the trope of gender-based violence as a means of implicating colonial/apartheid violence,[4] I would also argue that Matlwa, similar to Grace Musila's work, dismantles the problematic rhetoric of Black emasculation. The "emasculation thesis ... reduc[es] colonial subjugation to a masculine castration anxiety" and links general freedom to the "restoration of African manhood" (Musila 2002: 153). This particular line of thinking permeates not only *Coconut* but also other contemporary novels such as Kgebetli Moele's *Room 207*, justifying violence against women and disregarding Black women's experiences and subjectivities. Matlwa's choice of phrasing (*"I hated that Uncle was such a sorry and pathetic and weak man and hated even more that I was the only one who was able to comfort him"* [2007: 114]) establishes an important link between castration anxiety and larger intersectional constructions of Black women and girls as available receptacles of Black male frustration, shame, and anger along with white supremacist and misogynistic discourses. These discourses equate Black skin and especially Black women with dirt, hypersexuality, and moral degeneracy. The notion of comfort, as Fikile imagines it, implies, among other things, an ease or alleviation of personal feelings of grief or distress, and suggests that Fikile is a means of finding relief. Through the rationalization provided by these discourses, she is made the vessel of everyone else's shame and the "victim of her [Black] femaleness" (Nfah-Abbenyi 1997: 68).

Nonetheless, I caution against oversimplifying Fikile's character as simply the embodiment of internalized racism (Goodman 2012). It is true that she disassociates from her identity as a Black woman, insisting that in the future she will not be "black, dirty and poor" but "white, rich and happy" (Matlwa 2007: 118). It is also true that Fikile's assumption that she is "dirty" directly correlates with common feelings of shame that follow sexual violence. However, choosing to live in a kind of exile in her own home, she moves from the bed shared with her uncle to the cement floor in order put a stop to the sexual abuse (115). While her narrative reinforces the sense that home for Black women is often one of pain, exile, and alienation, it also sees home as about agency, choice, and refusing to be a victim. Enough emphasis cannot be placed on the significance of that one act of defiance on the part of Fikile.

More importantly, if we think about Fikile's character with more nuance, then we can also see how Matlwa's novel invites us to reconsider Desiree Lewis's point that, in the context of the national space, "women's citizenship is mediated by their subordination to men and their symbolic roles" (1999: 38). Fikile's character adds to the growing number of women's voices that critique national space when it comes to gender, gender-based violence, and the subsequent links between emasculation and Black male sovereignty. Because pre-1994 conversations about oppression were often reduced to racial oppression and "required" racial solidarity in order to successfully defeat the apartheid regime, gender-based violence and other forms of gendered oppressions were both silenced and erased from the national narrative (Gunne 2014). Moreover, as Lewis eloquently states, "the extent to which masculine 'dignity' (as power and control) may be predicated on women's indignity and silence continues to be a disturbing element in South African gender politics" (1999: 43). Consequently, Matlwa's text adds to a growing feminist project of not only exposing violence and refusing silence, but also rejecting the rhetoric of Black emasculation and the mobilization of violent masculinities as a necessary avenue to freedom: "yes, five years since that night I decided it was not my responsibility to lull Uncle to sleep by rubbing his dick" (Matlwa 2007: 116). This is a game-changing line because the disavowal of responsibility and refusal suddenly transforms the text. *Coconut* is not a South African version of Morrison's work, as rich as the intertextuality is, but is rather a new and important position taken by Matlwa that speaks directly and defiantly to the increasing associations of dominant manhood with national sovereignty. In *Coconut*, Matlwa imagines different kinds of feminist geographies within which Black women and girls can carve out spaces of agency and liberation within white supremacist patriarchal spaces.

Notes

1 See Mamphela Ramphele (1993), Stephanie Camp (2004), and Katherine McKittrick (2006).
2 I am thinking specifically of laws like the Squatters Act of 1895 that regulated Black residence on white "owned" land and the Natives Land Act of 1913. See Plaatje (1982).
3 For example, see Kgebetli Moele's *Room 207* (2006) and Niq Mhlongo's *After Tears* (2007).
4 See Lynn Orilla Scott (2006), Emy Koopman (2013), and Sorcha Gunne (2014).

Works Cited

Baderoon, Gabeba (2014), *Regarding Muslims: From Slavery to Post-apartheid*, Johannesburg: Wits University Press.

Bystrom, Kerry (2013), "Johannesburg Interiors," *Cultural Studies*, 27 (3): 333–56.

Camp, Stephanie M.H. (2004), *Closer to Freedom: Enslaved Women and Everyday Resistance in the Plantation South*, Chapel Hill: University of North Carolina Press.

Coeztee, J. M. (2000), *Disgrace*, London: Secker and Warburg.

Goodman, Ralph (2012), "Kopano Matlwa's *Coconut*: Identity Issues in Our Faces," *Current Writing: Text and Reception in Southern Africa*, 24 (1): 109–19.

Gqola, Pumla Dineo (2015), *Rape: A South African Nightmare*, Johannesburg: Jacana Media.

Gunne, Sorcha (2014), *Space, Place, and Gendered Violence in South African Writing*, New York: Palgrave Macmillan.

Hanisch, Carol (1969), www.carolhanisch.org/CHwritings/PIP.html, October 2018.

Koopman, Emy (2013), "Incestuous Rape, Abjection, and the Colonization of Psychic Space in Toni Morrison's *The Bluest Eye*," *Journal of Postcolonial Writing*, 49 (3): 303–15.

Lewis, Desiree, Ellen Kuzwayo, and Mamphela Ramphele (1999), "Gender Myths and Citizenship in Two Autobiographies by South African Women," *Agenda*, 40: 38–44.

Matlwa, Kopano (2007), *Coconut*, Johannesburg: Jacana Media.

McKittrick, Katherine (2006), *Demonic Grounds: Black Women and the Cartographies of Struggle*, Minneapolis: University of Minnesota Press.

Mhlongo, Niq (2007), *After Tears*, Capetown: Kwela Books.

Moele, Kgebetli (2006), *Room 207*, Capetown: Kwela Books.

Morrison, Toni (1970), *The Bluest Eye*, Austin: Holt McDougal.

Musila, Grace (2002), "Violent Masculinities and the Phallocentric Aesthetics of Power in Kenya," in Samson Opondo and Michael J. Shapira (eds.), *The New Violent Cartography: Geo-Analysis after the Aesthetic Turn*, 151–70, New York: Routledge.

Ndebele, Njabulo (1996), "A Home for Intimacy," *Mail & Guardian*, April 26. Available online: https://mg.co.za/article/1996-04-26-a-home-for-intimacy (accessed December 15, 2017).

Nfah-Abbenyi, Juliana Makuchi (1997), *Gender in African Women's Writing: Identity, Sexuality and Difference*, Bloomington: Indiana University Press.

Pain, Rachel and Lynn Staeheli (2014), "Introduction: Intimacy-geopolitics and Violence," *Area*, 46 (4): 344–7.

Plaatje, Sol (1982), *Native Life in South Africa*, Johannesburg: Raven Press.
Raditlhalo, Sam (2008), "A Proletarian Novel of the City Streets," *Journal of Postcolonial Writing*, 44 (1): 93–6.
Ramphele, Mamphela (1993), *A Bed Called Home: Life in the Migrant Labour Hostels of Cape Town*, Cape Town: David Philip Publishers.
Roye, Susmita (2012), "Toni Morrison's Disrupted Girls and Their Disturbed Girlhoods: *The Bluest Eye* and *A Mercy*," *Callaloo*, 35 (1): 212–27.
Scott, Lynn Orilla (2006), "Revising the Incest Story: Toni Morrison's *The Bluest Eye* and James Baldwin's *Above My Head*," in Lovalerie King and Lynn Orilla Scott (eds.), *James Baldwin and Toni Morrison: Comparative Critical and Theoretical Essays*, New York: Palgrave Macmillan.
Tlhabi, Redi (2017), *The Remarkable Story of Fezekile Ntsukela Kuzwayo*, Johannesburg: Jonathan Bell Publishers.

13

The Other Men of #MeToo:
Male Rape in Hanya Yanagihara's *A Little Life*, Sapphire's *The Kid*, and Amber Tamblyn's *Any Man*

Robin E. Field

American literature abounds in depictions of raped women. Yet rape novels in the twentieth century imagined men only as rapists, not victims, despite the prevalence of male rape—one in ten rape victims is male; one in thirty-three men have been raped ("Scope"). Indeed, the collective American understanding of male rape follows a similar trajectory to that of our evolving comprehension of female rape. Male rape victims are laughed at, scorned, derided; their experiences are dismissed and labeled as their own fault. Boys and young men sexually abused by trusted adults, such as priests or coaches, are disbelieved or accused of seeking attention or financial benefit from a more credible male figure.

Stories of male rape have followed the pattern established by early stories about women victims, portraying male rape as nonexistent, inconsequential, or the fault of the victim.[1] Depictions of male rape in American literature have been infrequent, and many that do portray it, such as James Dickey's *Deliverance* (1970), use rape as a trope for race, class, sexual orientation, or other concerns, largely eliding the physical and psychological harm inflicted upon the violated male body. However, twenty-first-century writers change this silencing pattern by challenging degrading stereotypes about male survivors, shifting the communal understanding of male rape, and creating new narrative perspectives for male survivors. Following the trajectory of rape novels that depict female victim-survivors, the male rape novel first educates readers by demonstrating the physical and psychological damage wrought upon male victims through explicit depictions of violence on the page. They also use narrative ambiguity and a lack of closure to challenge readers to explore the complicated responses of male victim-survivors as they navigate their recoveries and the afterlives of rape.

Three novels from the 2010s illustrate the pain suffered by male rape victims and demand the community take responsibility for the pervasive sexual abuse of children, including boys. Hanya Yanagihara's *A Little Life* (2015) portrays how sexual abuse destroys the victim, while Sapphire's novel *The Kid* (2011) reveals how victims may turn into perpetrators of sexual abuse themselves. Both Yanagihara and Sapphire depict the ramifications of rape and sexual abuse when the perpetrators never face the consequences—the victims do instead. While *A Little Life* and *The Kid* break new ground in their portrayals of boys as victims of rape, the #MeToo movement of 2017 underscores the importance of confronting perpetrators of rape and sexual abuse, empowering female *and* male victim-survivors to name their abusers and demand consequences. In *Any Man* (2018), Amber Tamblyn challenges the long-standing stereotype that only men are rapists by depicting a female rapist. These three novels demand readers understand and empathize with the men and boys who have suffered the physical and psychological trauma so rarely discussed in American culture.

Telling Trauma: Hanya Yanagihara's *A Little Life*

Hanya Yanagihara's *A Little Life* explores the physical and psychological pain of Jude St. Francis, who is horrifically abused as a young child and teenager. *A Little Life* begins by utilizing the silence surrounding sexual violence against men as a narrative device to build a rapport with Jude. Yanagihara introduces Jude as suffering great pain from his severely injured legs and spine, the result of "a car injury" when he was fifteen (2015: 111). Only his best friend Willem understands that a "car injury" differs from a "car accident," although Jude does not reveal that he was deliberately run down. Jude also cuts himself to manage his mental anguish. His traumatic past is explained fleetingly in the first half of the novel, as when he imagines that the pleasures of college will include no one "try[ing] to hurt him or make him do anything he didn't want to do" (113). In Part Two, readers learn that Jude was abandoned at birth and raised in a monastery by Catholic brothers. He is sexually abused nightly by the brothers from age five; Brother Luke absconds with him and prostitutes him for years; he is sexually abused by counselors in the boys home as a teenager; and he is kidnapped, tortured, and run down by a car driven by Doctor Traylor—all in his first fifteen years. Readers concur with Jude's social worker Ana, who believes Jude's experiences prove that "there's a hell and those men need to be in it" (117). While Brother Luke and Doctor Traylor offer specific examples of violent perpetrators, Yanagihara reminds readers that "those men" comprise the hundreds of anonymous men who rape the boy. Jude's body is a persistent physical reminder of the abuse, as he contracts incurable sexually transmitted diseases as well as permanent spinal damage from the car injury. Readers soon understand why Jude loathes his body and cannot ever enjoy sex.

Yanagihara's exploration of Jude's physical torment echoes the narrative strategies of early rape novels that stress the physical injuries derived from rape and sexual abuse to emphasize the pain that women and girls experience. Just as early rape novels tried to combat the voyeurism inherent in witnessing sexual violence, given the initial positioning of rape as pornographic titillation rather than a crime in American fiction, male rape novels have had to carefully depict scenes of rape to explain its inherent violence and pain. Following this formula, Yanagihara decouples erotic voyeurism from scenes of sexual violence by stressing the suffering of the abused child instead of the sexual pleasure of the perpetrator. After detailing Jude's physical injuries, Yanagihara explores his mental distress. Heartbreakingly, Jude believes he is responsible for being abused. This belief begins in the monastery, where the brothers tell him he was "born bad" and thus abandoned (167). They underscore

Jude's belief in his inherent unworthiness by punishing him harshly for minor infractions; and once he begins wetting his bed, several brothers begin "examinations" of his body, a euphemism for molestation and sexual assault (171). Such explanations—both the words and the actions—root the brothers' violence in Jude himself, in his behavior, and ultimately in his very existence. As an adult, Jude resists talking about his childhood even to those who love him. However, he cannot heal his psychological wounds without help, and therefore he cannot move out of the victim position toward survivor or victim-survivor status. Indeed, his past abuse makes him susceptible to being harmed again by his lover Caleb, who nearly kills him. Jude "decided that Caleb was right, that he was disgusting, that he had, somehow, deserved what had happened to him" (418). Yanagihara illustrates Jude's physical and psychological pain in minute detail to combat any readerly tendency to view the sexual violence inflicted by Caleb as erotic or pornographic. The details of Caleb's violence are horrifying and overwhelming—just as Jude experiences it himself—in order to make sure that readers understand and sympathize with Jude's physical pain.

The intimate partner violence in Jude's present segues to the depiction of his traumatic past. In the first half of the book, Yanagihara alludes to the sexual abuse without delineating specific details; however, she abruptly ends the oblique references, so that readers are confronted by the graphic details of physical and psychological torture inflicted by Caleb, just as Jude is surprised by Caleb's first punch. Why Jude remains silent about this abuse until Caleb nearly kills him unfolds in the pages delineating Brother Luke's sex trafficking and Doctor Traylor's sadism. At the monastery, Brother Luke carefully manipulates Jude into believing he is the only person who cares for the eight-year-old child. He even feigns distress that Jude does not love him so the boy promises "that he would do whatever he needed" in order to build a life with the man (428). This promise traps him; Brother Luke brings men to their hotel room to have sex with him, in addition to having sex with Jude himself. Jude's belief that he is inherently disgusting and unworthy is reinforced by the insults of the men who rape him—"garbage, trash, dirty, worthless, a nothing" (476)—but also from Brother Luke's praise: "*You were born for this*" (455, emphasis in original). Brother Luke's sexual and psychological abuse permanently alters Jude's self-image. Decades later, Jude cannot stop blaming himself for being "seduced" and falling "in love" with the pedophile (480).

As an adult, Jude cannot believe that people feel affection for him without concomitantly demanding sex and perpetrating violence upon him. When Caleb begins abusing him, Jude believes he deserves it: "they are the damaged and the damager, the sliding heap of garbage and the jackal sniffing through it" (370). Yanagihara solidifies the reasons for Jude's self-loathing by revealing Doctor Traylor's abuse: he imprisons the teenager, rapes him for three months, and runs him down with a car, which permanently damages Jude's spine and legs. Even if Jude could recover psychologically from the trauma wrought by his abusers, his body persistently reminds him of his past. The love of his friends and family cannot overcome Jude's physical and psychological pain, and ultimately, in his fifties, he ends his life. In this respect, *A Little Life* is not unlike the first rape novels in the 1970s, whose female victims died or disappeared from the texts after being raped (Field 2020: 108). While Yanagihara depicts life after rape for Jude, something that did not happen in the first rape novels, her character remains a victim and cannot experience the recovery process that psychologists such as Judith Herman in *Trauma and Recovery* delineate. In an interview, the author comments that Jude is "just too damaged to recover, that he is, in a fundamental sense, irreparable" ("Hanya Yanagihara"). In emphasizing the trauma that male victims endure from sexual violence, *A Little Life* seems to underscore the difficulty or even impossibility of recovering from rape. Certainly Jude's name suggests such a reading, as St. Jude is the patron saint of lost causes. Yet St. Francis—Jude's surname—has been recognized as the patron saint of activism for peace and justice. *A Little Life* beautifully balances this narrative tension of despair and hope in depicting a protagonist who loses his battle against his painful past but also inspires readers to think deeply about their culpability in a society where children are so often sexually abused.

Perpetuating Sexual Violence: Sapphire's *The Kid*

Just as *A Little Life* portrays the sexual abuse of Jude in graphic detail, *The Kid* (2011) reveals the traumatic childhood of a young victim. Abdul Jones is the beloved son of Precious Jones, the heroine of *Push* (1996) who is raped by her father, bears his children at twelve and sixteen, and tests positive for HIV at the end of the novel. In this sequel, Precious dies when Abdul is nine years old; and he is placed into foster care, where he is violently beaten and raped by another foster child. Once released from the hospital, he lives at St. Ailanthus School for Boys. Here again Abdul is raped: by Brother John, who claims to express his love for the boy through sex, and by Brother Samuel, who punishes any misbehavior with rape. In Book Two, thirteen-year-old Abdul becomes a rapist himself as he sexually assaults his friend Jaime and five-year-old Richie. *The Kid* asks readers to maintain sympathy and empathy for Abdul as both victim and perpetrator of sexual violence, a challenge that some readers may find difficult because of the novel's explicit portrayal of child rape.

Sapphire depicts Abdul as unaware that he is a perpetrator, although his narration demonstrates his friend's lack of consent. Jaime cries out when Abdul sodomizes him and sobs when Abdul demands fellatio. Yet Abdul interprets Jaime's response differently: "He's shivering with excitement ... He squeal, I slam his face in the pillow, kill that" (Sapphire 2011: 53). When Abdul returns to his own bed, he notes his fearfulness: "Why I'm so stink panicked I don't know. Ain' nobody gonna hear that stupid little motherfucker. Shit, nobody heard me ... Huh? What happened? ... Nothin' happened" (54). Abdul's note that no one heard him leads readers to wonder what there was to hear: His crying as he is raped? His moans as he has sex? Both? Abdul truly believes that "nothin' happened"— that he did not rape Jaime. Just as his reality of being raped by the brothers and possibly other boys is never acknowledged, Abdul himself suppresses any admission of himself as a perpetrator.

Indeed, calling male rape "nothin'" denies its very existence, just as Abdul similarly imagines his abusive actions as a dream. When he leaves his bed in the night to rape Richie, he thinks, "Maybe I am in my dreams. Maybe this is not real. It is a dream" (74). These versions exist simultaneously for Abdul: he does "nothin'" wrong; he has consensual sex with Jaime and Richie; he does something (i.e., the opposite of "nothin'") wrong to Jaime and Richie; he is himself raped by the brothers and other boys. Before Abdul leaves St. Ailanthus, he thinks, "I know I'm a good boy... ask Brother John" (86). Just as Brother John "knows" that Jaime's accusation is a lie, Abdul "knows" he is a good person—that is, if he asserts it, it must be true, especially if Brother John agrees.

Reality for Abdul is what he "knows," rather than an objective truth. Such a disconnection from reality underscores the trauma Abdul experiences, while also allowing him to perpetrate abuse upon others without acknowledging his actions as violent.

Is it possible to feel sympathy for Abdul? The rape novel as a genre asks readers to sympathize with the physical and emotional trauma suffered by rape victim-survivors. As a survivor of repeated assaults by multiple perpetrators, Abdul deserves compassion. In Book One, after empathizing with Abdul's sorrow during his mother's funeral, readers are horrified when he is violently raped in foster care. Yet Sapphire immediately challenges readers to maintain sympathy for Abdul by beginning Book Two with Abdul's rape of Jaime. Readers struggling with the graphic depictions of pain and violence in Book One are doubly challenged to witness Abdul's crimes against other boys, let alone to maintain empathy for his suffering throughout another 300 pages, even though he continues to be assaulted by trusted adults. As Erica D. Galioto notes, "If identifying with Precious and Abdul in their moments of trauma is repellent, identifying with Abdul as he traumatizes other children is unthinkable" (2014: 138). *The Kid* forces readers to confront the difficult reality lived by some survivors of sexual violence, asking whether they deserve sympathy and compassion when they inflict pain upon others. Herman argues, "It is morally impossible to remain neutral in this conflict [between victim and perpetrator]. The bystander is forced to take sides" (1992: 7). This position is deeply complicated when the victim and perpetrator are one and the same. In *The Kid*, Sapphire underscores how male rape victims may become sexual offenders themselves, a cycle of violence that compounds the initial tragedy and complicates the community's reaction to these victims. Whether readers can sympathize—and empathize—with the pain of these victim-perpetrators will be an ongoing challenge for the male rape novel.

The Other Men of #MeToo: Amber Tamblyn's *Any Man*

In 2017, the #MeToo movement reinvigorated conversations about rape and accountability in the United States and worldwide.

Significantly, men joined the conversation by identifying as victims of rape and sexual violence, and Amber Tamblyn's *Any Man* explores the experiences of both cisgender and transgender male victim-survivors. Largely eschewing the female rapist's perspective, Tamblyn focuses upon the victim-survivors of traumatic violence and their journey toward physical and psychological healing, as rape novels in the 1980s and 1990s demonstrated for female victim-survivors.

Tamblyn challenges stereotypes about male rape victim-survivors from the beginning of the novel. Her characters range from a married father of two, a thrice-divorced man in his sixties, and a mixed-race twenty-something power lifter, to a gay Libertarian polemicist, a transgender man, and a ten-year-old boy—showing that any man or boy can be raped. The married father Donald has GBH slipped into his drink at a bar, the power lifter Jamar invites the rapist Maude into his home after an online chat, and the ten-year-old Ezra is assaulted at a friend's house—showing that victims can be raped anywhere and anytime. Tamblyn also illustrates the devastating physical and psychological injuries suffered by male survivors. Donald is unconscious when Maude assaults him, and he wakes up to find that his penis has been destroyed. Jamar is psychologically tormented after Maude forces him to perform sex acts with a cat. Contrary to stereotypes that males always enjoy sex—and that a boy is privileged to be "initiated" by an older woman—Ezra is devastated by Maude's assault and his life completely changes. After dabbling in petty crime, he goes to prison at nineteen; once released, his anger leads him to rape and murder a woman during a home invasion. He never tells anyone about his own rape until he realizes his assailant was Maude, who raped five men in the ensuing years—more, in all likelihood, as men are especially unlikely to report rape. By portraying a diverse group of men as victims of rape, Tamblyn demonstrates the pervasiveness of this crime within a population that has been understood as immune from sexual violence until their stories began to be told at the end of the twentieth century.

Alongside the details of terrible violence, Tamblyn also reveals the persistence of particular rape myths. While these myths about the culpability of victims were used to blame female victims decades ago, Tamblyn demonstrates how they are applicable today and how male victims are shamed for being raped. In the chapter depicting a transcript of The Melissa Hope Show, three women debate the details of Maude's assaults. The criminal defense attorney doubts whether the men were in fact raped, arguing that Donald should have been at home with his family rather than drinking at a bar and that Jamar showed "poor judgment" by inviting an unknown woman into his home. She asks, "shouldn't people engage in commonsense behavior ... so as not to put themselves in a vulnerable position"? (Tamblyn 2018: 160). It is notable that a woman blames the victims, though Tamblyn emphasizes that such attitudes about rape survivors persist across contemporary American culture. For instance, as the host of a radio show focused upon catching sexual predators, Donald details how the aftermath of his rape was as psychologically damaging as the attack itself:

> As if the shame and the guilt and the scraps of my broken body weren't constant reminders, my wife and I received hateful letters—death threats, even—from people all across the country, for months. I had "asked for it," they wrote. I was a piece of shit. [...] The bullying ... It was a cruelty I would not wish on anyone. [...] It ripped me apart.
>
> (193)

Donald then reminds listeners (and readers) that they likely know a male survivor, given the pervasiveness of rape regardless of gender. Tamblyn cultivates empathy for Donald by demonstrating that the community's reaction to sexual violence may be as traumatic as the crime itself. Such a move places responsibility upon all readers to offer support and compassion, rather than blame, shame, and further abuse, to survivors of rape.

While Tamblyn's novel is graphic and horrifying, as is appropriate for its subject, it also explores the afterlives of male rape survivors and their possibilities for recovery, should the community actively work to challenge rape culture. For the transgender man Michael Parker, the stigma of being trans compounds the blame he endures for being raped. Tamblyn depicts this assault obliquely through a series of tweets to critique contemporary social media—its speed, its callousness, its commodification of a person's pain. The tweets show Michael's rape as breaking news, then skepticism about whether he is one of Maude's victims, then criticism about his gender identity (inspiring the hashtag #IStandWithMichael and merchandise that "supports" him), and then the news of his suicide (170–6). For Michael, there is no life after rape. Sebastian, the Libertarian polemicist, writes a book, gives speeches, and "used [his] anger as a way to create action" (235). Yet he admits on Donald's radio show that these actions did not help him to heal. Other victims do move on, albeit slowly and painfully. While Jamar is so traumatized that he attempts suicide, he recovers with the help of a support group and ultimately marries and becomes a father. Even Ezra, serving life in prison without parole, finally reconnects with his estranged father once he tells what happened to him. In addition, only Ezra has seen Maude's face, so the authorities might finally identify her. While the novel ends ominously with a brief chapter depicting Maude scouting for a new victim, Ezra's evidence offers the possibility that Maude will be stopped. Exactly when, and by whom, is left up to readers' imagination. This "refus[al]" of "narrative closure positions readers as active producers of knowledge, rather than as passive consumers of readily consumable stories" (Romero 2012: 44). Just as in *A Little Life* and *The Kid*, *Any Man* demands that readers engage deeply with, and reflect upon, the stories of male rape survivors, instead of voyeuristically consuming them for pornographic titillation, as in earlier depictions of male rape in the twentieth century.

The rapist Maude is the lacuna of *Any Man*. Tamblyn allows no motivation to temper the horror of Maude's violence; she says that Maude is not seeking revenge on "a father, a husband, or a john … It was rooted in power" ("Amber Tamblyn"). Consider Ezra: Readers understand where his murderous rage comes from, even as they cannot condone his own act of rape and murder. Tamblyn disallows readers the same understanding of Maude through the opacity of this character. As Shannon Carlin (2018) writes, "Tamblyn didn't want to give Maude an excuse for her actions that would lead readers to sympathize with her and turn her into an anti-hero." Instead, Maude becomes representative of the larger culture in America that has allowed sexual violence to flourish. By underscoring how anybody can be a victim-survivor of rape, Tamblyn's novel encourages an inclusive conversation about sexual violence and its effects upon any woman, any man—any person.

By 2020, the male rape novel had begun to educate readers, shatter stereotypes, and urge empathy for victim-survivors— thus joining the rape novels featuring female victim-survivors in presenting accurate and honest portrayals of sexual violence. In *Any Man*, Donald says on his radio show, "the work we do here matters" (194), and the same may be said for rape novels. In telling the stories of victim-survivors of all genders, rape novels demand an end to rape culture and a safer world for everyone.

Note

1 The rape novel emerged in the 1970s to portray rape *as* rape and make the victim-survivor the central figure, rather than the perpetrator or bystanders. See *Writing the Survivor: The Rape Novel in Late Twentieth-Century American Fiction* (Field 2020). I am grateful to reprint portions of this essay that appear in this book.

Works Cited

Carlin, Shannon (2018), "Amber Tamblyn: Inside a #MeToo Advocate's Novel about Male Sexual Assault," *Rolling Stone*, July 13.
Field, Robin F. (2020), *Writing the Survivor: The Rape Novel in Late Twentieth-Century American Fiction*, Clemson, SC: Clemson University Press.
Galioto, Erica D. (2014), "'Shame, Thas a Shame': The Anti-Sentiment of Sapphire's *Push* and *The Kid*," in Jennifer A. Williamson, Jennifer Larson, and Ashley Reed (eds.), *The Sentimental Mode: Essays in Literature, Film, and Television*, 134–50, Jefferson, NC: McFarland & Company, Inc.
"Hanya Yanagihara: About the Author," *Foyles*. Available online: https://www.foyles.co.uk/hanya-yanagihara (accessed June 18, 2019).
Herman, Judith (1992), *Trauma and Recovery*, New York: Basic Books.
Romero, Channette (2012), *Activism and the American Novel: Religion and Resistance in Fiction by Women of Color*, Charlottesville: University of Virginia Press.
Sapphire (2011), *The Kid*, New York: Penguin Books.
"Scope of the Problem: Statistics," RAINN. Available online: https://www.rainn.org/statistics/scope-problem (accessed August 1, 2019).
Tamblyn, Amber (2018), *Any Man*, New York: Harper Perennial.
Yanagihara, Hanya (2015), *A Little Life*, New York: Anchor Books.

14

Reading Junot Díaz after Me Too and #MeToo

Ann Marie Alfonso Short

> *I could have called after her me too me too. I could have said the words: I was also raped.*
>
> —JUNOT DÍAZ, "THE SILENCES"

In many ways, Junot Díaz's devastating account of having been raped as a child is a love letter to the #MeToo movement. "The Silence: The Legacy of Childhood Trauma" was published by *The New Yorker* a few months after the hashtag went viral, and throughout the exploration of trauma accompanying his simple declaration, "Yes, it happened to me," Díaz describes how the experience imprinted itself on his psyche, affecting every single aspect of his life despite his best efforts to forget it (2018). He documents decades of depression, suicide attempts, and missed opportunities for intimacy, interrogating his compulsive silence about the assaults and referring to the way he co-existed with his trauma as "wearing a mask." In telling his story publicly for the first time, Díaz attempts to reclaim the power that fear and shame wielded over him for most of his life.

Just a few weeks later, however, when Díaz himself was accused of sexual harassment and misogynistic verbal abuse by a fellow writer, his profile shifted quickly from survivor to perpetrator. News of the allegations broke in the *New York Times* in early May after writer Zinzi Clemmons confronted Díaz at the Sydney Writers' Festival and, later that day, tweeted about her past experiences with him.[1] Her tweets prompted several additional writers—all women of color—to come forward about their own problematic encounters with Díaz, exposing an alleged pattern of sexist and abusive behaviors. The accusations quickly divided the literary community, and within a few days another group of women—mostly academics and writers of color—co-signed a public letter coming to Díaz's defense (Latino Rebels 2018).

This chapter navigates complex questions about how we might responsibly treat Junot Díaz's work in light of the allegations against him, and the conflicting responses to those allegations: what does it mean to admire an Afro-Latinx author for his depiction of historically underrepresented peoples when he may have participated in oppressive or violent behaviors himself? What are our ethical and intellectual obligations when handling texts by such problematic writers in our teaching and scholarship? If we stop reading and teaching his work, do we also banish all male writers who are known to have been sexual aggressors? Though these questions are not new, how we answer them takes on new urgency after #MeToo, particularly among feminist scholars who "#BelieveSurvivors" as praxis. I argue that the answer is not to ban Díaz from our syllabi and scholarship, but to approach his body of work from a critical feminist perspective, specifically through the lens of toxic masculinity. #MeToo demands that we re-read, not "cancel," books like *Drown* (1996), *The Brief Wondrous Life of Oscar Wao* (2007), and *This Is How You Lose Her* (2012), which provide instructive insight into how toxic masculinity has informed Díaz's literary ethos. Rather than compartmentalize "great writers" and "bad men" as mutually exclusive categories, we must consider how writers like Díaz, in their work if not in real life, have externalized misogynistic values in order to maintain a particular kind of masculine authority. Moreover, given Díaz's position as both survivor and perpetrator, #MeToo implores us to re-read in ways that are attentive to both compassion and accountability.

The Junot Díaz situation demonstrates that in order to be transformative, #MeToo must go beyond exposing the breadth of the problem and condemning perpetrators.[2] The day news of the Díaz allegations broke, Roxane Gay tweeted that "We need to have a more vigorous debate than simply saying 'Junot Díaz is cancelled' because that does not cancel misogyny or how the literary community protects powerful men at the expense of women" (Gilchrist 2018). "Cancelling" is a controversial process by which a public or popular figure is declared irrelevant and devoid of value, usually in response to something they said or did. Cancel culture has gained traction in online social spaces, particularly in the years since #MeToo went viral, as a form of collective punishment. Gay's tweet is an instructive reminder that the objective of exposing Díaz's wrongdoing—or any other perpetrator's—should not be to exercise mob justice, but instead to lay the groundwork for improving institutions that have facilitated and perpetuated sexism. In other words, to stop reading and teaching Díaz's work does very little to challenge the misogyny that is as deeply embedded in literary production as it is across all major cultural institutions.

Perhaps more so than any other male writer, however, Díaz has been forthcoming, blunt, even, about the internalized sexism that informs his work. In an NPR interview about his short story collection, *This Is How You Lose Her*, Díaz admits that growing up he "wasn't really encouraged to imagine women as fully human" (NPR Staff 2012). In a different interview during the same book publicity tour, he is self-conscious about the limited success with which male writers are able to create and sustain complex female characters in their fiction. "The baseline is, you suck," Díaz tells Joe Fassler in *The Atlantic* (2012b). He calls his male privilege a "deficiency" in his writing, noting that while women writers have far greater access to complex representations of male experience to draw from when creating characters, men tend to stereotype women as objects of sexual desire in their writing:

> I think that unless you are actively, consciously working against the gravitational pull of the culture, you will predictably, thematically, create these sort of fucked-up representations. Without fail. The only way not to do them is to admit to yourself [that] you're fucked up, admit to yourself that you're not good at this shit, and to be conscious in the way that you create these characters.
>
> (2012b)

While these comments from Díaz might be understood as enlightened self-awareness, they also reveal a man who admits to harboring internalized misogyny and who is working toward understanding women better for a decidedly self-serving purpose: his craft. And while Díaz's fiction has been almost universally lauded, particularly for its anticolonial, anti-racist commitments and for giving voice to an immigrant Latinx group that remains underrepresented in American literature, his work is (also) almost entirely invested in the representation of Dominican men. More specifically, his fiction is almost obsessively interested in the sexual behavior of straight, cisgender Dominican men.

Given the prevalence of problematic sexual behavior from the men in Díaz's books, not all of his readers, fans, and colleagues were shocked by the allegations against him. As Roxane Gay and others have noted, Díaz's fiction is rife with depictions of male sexual aggression, mostly perpetrated by his protagonists. Women and children, on the other hand, are mostly represented as the objects of this aggression, and they are rarely offered the opportunity to resist or subvert it. Gay writes, "Women are their bodies and what they can offer men. They are pulled apart for [their] sexual amusement" (2012). While not all critics find Díaz's fiction problematic,[3] it is clear about who does and does not have power in the sexual dynamics he portrays. Moreover, Díaz does not simply bestow his male sexual aggressors with power; his fiction equates Dominican masculinity with the power to assert (sexual) dominance. Reading his work post #MeToo—that is, in the wake of both "The Silences" and the allegations against him—offers new opportunities to ask difficult questions about his literary authority and to push back against the way he normalizes problematic constructions of gender.

Despite its skillful triangulation of European colonization in the Caribbean, the devastating regime of Dominican dictator Rafael Trujillo, and the deleterious effects of US interventionism in Latin America, Díaz's first and only novel, *The Brief Wondrous Life of Oscar Wao*, is essentially the story of a lonely young man who cannot get anyone to have sex with him. The blurb on the back cover describes Oscar as "a sweet but disastrously overweight ghetto nerd" and a "romantic who dreams of becoming the Dominican J.R.R. Tolkien and, most of all, of finding love." This sketch introduces readers to a sympathetic protagonist who falls victim to the toxic masculinity he seems unable to conform to and whose Dominicanness is therefore constantly in question. He is taught at a young age that real Dominican men take what they want from women, from respect ("Dale un galletazo ... then see if the little puta respects you," his mom instructs him when he is seven years old) to sex ("Listen palomo: you have to grab a muchacha, y metéselo") (Díaz 2007: 14, 24).[4] Oscar does not follow his family's directives; instead, he gets dumped, rejected, or flat-out ignored by the women he desires. In its portrayal of Oscar's repeated failures, the novel suggests that it is his lack of aggression, which translates into inability or unwillingness to assert masculine authority over women, that prevents Oscar from having sex and excludes him from Dominican masculinity.

However, Díaz's complicated position as both survivor and perpetrator opens up new ways of understanding Oscar post #MeToo. Although some scholars have interpreted Oscar's shortcomings as a subversion of masculine norms and made interesting connections between his failure to embody Dominican masculinity and the novel's political projects, and while Oscar is frequently understood as a victim of these repressive expectations, he also behaves in toxic ways toward women throughout the novel.[5] For instance, after learning that Jenny, a classmate he spends time with hoping that they might sleep together, is actually sleeping with someone else, Oscar lashes out at her violently. Calling her a whore while destroying her dorm room, Oscar releases a repressed fury reminiscent of the virulent male entitlement found online in "incel" chat rooms.[6] Oscar is, in fact, involuntarily celibate, not unlike the young men who connect on websites like Reddit to vilify women who will not sleep with them. He has internalized a toxic ideology in which heteronormative sexual relationships are determined by reductive masculine and feminine power dynamics. Indeed, when he finally loses his virginity by consummating his relationship with the much older, married Ybón at the end of the novel, it is only because he had finally "gotten some power of his own" (Díaz 2007: 319). This power helps him win over Ybón through a combination of persistent stalking and promising to save her from another abusive relationship. In his violence toward Jenny, his obsessive insistence that Ybón give him a chance, and his heroic fantasies, Oscar's power negates the full subjectivity of the women he desires. As is the case with most cis-het men who hurt women (and others) to claim power to which they feel entitled, the line between desire and hatred is dangerously blurred.

While Yunior, the recurring protagonist in both of Díaz's short story collections, has internalized the same toxic masculinity as Oscar, he externalizes it in more predictable ways. As the narrator in *Oscar Wao*, Yunior de Las Casas provides a foil for Oscar. He is, in many ways, everything Oscar is not: physically fit, sexually desirable, unemotional, aggressive, and thus a "real Dominican man."[7] In *Drown*, Díaz's first book, and *This Is How You Lose Her*, published five years after *Oscar Wao*, he introduces and fleshes out his central character, the one whom Díaz has described as his own "alter ego" (Okie 2008). Like Oscar, though certainly more successfully, young Yunior is forced to repress parts of himself in order to conform to the oppressive expectations of masculinity. Readers see this in the opening story of *Drown*, when nine-year-old Yunior is sexually assaulted by a man he sits next to on a bus. When Yunior begins to cry after he and his older brother, Rafa (who did not notice the assault), get off the bus at the next stop, Rafa does not ask what is wrong or comfort him, but uses the opportunity to initiate Yunior into manhood: "You ... are a pussy ... If you can't stop crying, I'll leave you" (Díaz 1996: 13). This imperative to be invulnerable to fear and pain pressures Yunior to repress difficult— ostensibly feminine—emotions: the fear and powerlessness of being sexually overpowered. It transforms them into something hard and protective, much like the mask that Díaz has alluded to in interviews when discussing both Yunior and himself (Okie 2008), and which reappears as a central trope in his *New Yorker* essay in which he describes his own assault.

Throughout the stories in *Drown*, readers re-encounter Yunior at different stages of this dehumanizing process: when he is an adolescent in "Fiesta, 1980," his father physically and emotionally abuses him for not being able to control his motion sickness in the new family car. In "How to Date a Browngirl, Blackgirl, Whitegirl, or Halfie," we learn that growing up, Yunior never spoke up about the aunt who squeezed his testicles every time she saw him. It is not surprising, then, that he becomes the kind of man who sexually objectifies women, the serial cheater of *This Is How You Lose Her* who describes himself as "a sucio, an asshole" (Díaz 2012: 3).[8] In both collections, Yunior understands successful masculinity as power over whatever is considered feminine, and he recognizes failed masculinity in the admission of powerlessness. Yet what Díaz repeatedly shows readers is that the men who exert power over women in dehumanizing ways are acting under the same system that has dehumanized them. As Roxane Gay puts it, "*this is how we all lose*" (2012).

What Díaz's fiction ends up doing, especially in failing to develop its women characters, is indulging and perpetuating a masculinist imagination. The women in *Drown* are jilted wives, desperate mistresses, addicts who have sex for money, and girls Yunior wants to sleep with. The women in *This Is How You Lose Her* are not rendered with much more complexity, and both books provide frequent crass descriptions of women's bodies that focus almost exclusively on their weight, breasts, and backsides without paying much attention at all to what goes on inside their minds. They are almost exclusively objects of either pity or desire. And while Yunior loses the love of his life because of his problematic behavior, if he experiences any growth it happens at the expense of the women he has slept with. To be clear, Díaz does not create a world that treats women so casually, violently, and with so little nuance; that world already exists. But he fails to use his artistic authority to imagine men or women who successfully resist simplistic gender constructions. In fact, his fiction—successful as it may be by certain metrics—relies entirely upon those constructions for its success. However, for both Díaz the survivor and Díaz the perpetrator, these constructions are central to a literary ethos that #MeToo challenges us to expose and repair.

In the wake of #MeToo, Díaz's comments about agency and bodies, made in the aftermath of the 2016 US presidential election, feel more poignant than ever:

> Coming from a reality where our oppression was ineluctably linked to our bodies—that we had, for centuries, no rights to our bodies and that all of the traditional pleasures and all of the traditional freedoms of human agency were forbidden to those of us of African descent in the New World, for a long period of time—the body, in such a murderous regime, under such nightmarish conditions, becomes chapel, cathedral, dogma.
>
> (Tippet 2017)

The destructive masculinity that shaped Díaz and his work was inherited from various oppressive systems, as patriarchy rarely functions in a vacuum. Racism, colonization, and capitalism are all implicated, as is the Trujillo regime, which materialized these intersections in particularly violent ways.[9] In addition to stripping people of embodied self-determination, Díaz tells Tippet, these oppressive systems thrive on silence—as imposed on the oppressed and as strategically used by the oppressed in their own "counterstrategy."

What is #MeToo if not a similar counterstrategy against the systemic silencing of sexual assault survivors? What is Díaz's essay "The Silences" if not a way of coming forward about his own place on the spectrum between perpetrator and victim? Its pervasive thematic dependence on masking, silence, and hiding truths indicates there is more to Díaz's story, and the essay functions as a kind of confession. Acknowledging his own problematic behavior in sexual relationships, Díaz not only calls Yunior his "perfect cover story" but also notes that "since us Afro-Latinx brothers are viewed by society as always already sexual perils, very few people ever noticed what was written between the lines in my fiction—that Afro-Latinx brothers are often sexually *imperilled*" (2018). He suggests more than once that in facing his past he is also making amends for the harm that he has caused others, and he draws a straight line between those injuries and the violence done to his own body and psyche. And though much has been made about the timing of Díaz's going public about the experience of having been raped as a child and whether he meant to inoculate himself against future allegations by positioning himself in the role of survivor, any such calculation is not cause to dismiss the messy connection between compassion and accountability that the essay and the allegations demand from his readers.

Díaz rescinded the apology he had extended in the immediate aftermath of the Clemmons tweets, and maintains that the accusations against him are false. Restorative justice provides a framework for perpetrators to be compassionately rehabilitated and held accountable for their actions, but that requires them to face their actions rather than double down on their innocence as Díaz has done. However, his case still provides a pathway to redemption, if not for him then for all of us who have read, written about, or taught his work. Rather than focusing on the individual perpetrator, Schulman and others argue that we can more effectively direct our energy toward dismantling systems of abuse, a framework that resonates with Tarana Burke's vision of empathy (2016). This combination of compassion and accountability for men like Díaz requires us to do difficult work in literary studies, which has for so long encouraged readers to overlook the writer in deference to the art. We should not cancel Díaz unless we are also willing to cancel Byron, Hemingway, Poe, and Wallace, let alone Thomas Jefferson. But because #MeToo insists on accountability in a way that has not been demanded of us before, we should not be reading Díaz the way we did before. Re-reading Díaz in the ways I am suggesting, not to condemn or excuse but to re-contextualize, resists a different kind of silencing. It forces us to lay bare his complex participation in rape culture, giving a pass to neither the author nor his readers, but instead forcing everyone to reckon with the work that still needs to be done.

Notes

1. Díaz's list of accusers includes writers Carmen Maria Machado, Monica Byrne, Alisa Rivera, Alisa Valdes, Marianelle Belliard, and Karina Marina Cabreja.
2. Tarana Burke's concern that the movement has become salacious and obsessed with perpetrators (Rowley 2018) echoes what Sarah Schulman argues in her book *Conflict Is Not Abuse*, that society's desire to escalate conflict at the expense of building community prevents resolution on serious systems of abuse (2016: 17).
3. In a different *Atlantic* article about Díaz published the same week as the interview cited above, Joe Fassler—a man—determined that while Díaz may write sexist characters, that does not make his books sexist (2012a).
4. "Dale un galletazo" means "smack her" in Spanish; "puta" means "bitch." In telling teenaged Oscar to "grab a muchacha, y méteselo" ("grab a girl and stick it in"), Oscar's uncle is essentially suggesting rape as an alternative to remaining a virgin (Díaz 2007).
5. See Machado-Saez (2011), Weese (2014), Wilks (2019), and Ahn (2020).
6. "Incels" or involuntary celibates have become the subject of scrutiny over the past decade as their online spaces have become explicitly violent; self-proclaimed "incels" have committed several of the most high-profile mass killings in North America over the past five years. See Bosmon, Taylor, and Arango (2019); Maxwell et al. (2020).

7   This term appears in various ways throughout writings by and about Díaz, including his *New Yorker* essay about his own sexual assault.
8   "Sucio," meaning "dirty" in Spanish, is used idiomatically to suggest sexual deviance.
9   Trujillo's sexual violence is a well-documented facet of his regime's brutality. In *Oscar Wao*, this historical detail is central to the plot, as Oscar's grandfather is said to have set the family's misfortune in motion by refusing to bring his most beautiful daughter to Trujillo's mansion at the dictator's invitation.

Works Cited

Ahn, Hakyoung (2020), "Masculine Failure: Rape Culture and Intergenerational Trauma in Junot Díaz's *The Brief Wondrous Life of Oscar Wao*," in K. Rose (ed.), *Displaced: Literature of Indigeneity, Migration, and Trauma*, 214–28, New York: Routledge.
Bosman, Julie, Kate Taylor, and Tim Arango (2019), "A Common Trait among Mass Killers: Hatred toward Women," *The New York Times*, August 10. Available online: https://www.nytimes.com/2019/08/10/us/mass-shootings-misogyny-dayton.html (accessed July 15, 2020).
Díaz, Junot (1996), *Drown*, New York: Riverhead Books.
Díaz, Junot (2007), *The Brief Wondrous Life of Oscar Wao*, New York: Riverhead Books.
Díaz, Junot (2012), *This Is How You Lose Her*, New York: Riverhead Books.
Díaz, Junot (2018), "The Silence: The Legacy of Childhood Trauma," *The New Yorker*, April 9. Available online: https://www.newyorker.com/magazine/2018/04/16/the-silence-the-legacy-of-childhood-trauma (accessed October 10, 2019).
Fassler, Joe (2012a), "How Junot Díaz Wrote a Sexist Character, but Not a Sexist Book," *The Atlantic*, September 11. Available online: https://www.theatlantic.com/entertainment/archive/2012/09/how-junot-diaz-wrote-a-sexist-character-but-not-a-sexist-book/262169/ (accessed October 14, 2019).
Fassler, Joe (2012b), "The Baseline Is, You Suck: Junot Díaz on Men Who Write about Women," *The Atlantic*, September 12. Available online: https://www.theatlantic.com/entertainment/archive/2012/09/the-baseline-is-you-suck-junot-diaz-on-men-who-write-about-women/262163/ (accessed October 14, 2019).
Gay, Roxane (2012), "How We All Lose," *The Rumpus*, October 26. Available online: https://therumpus.net/2012/10/how-we-all-lose/ (accessed June 15, 2020).

Gilchrist, Tracy E. (2018), "Roxane Gay Explains Why Junot Díaz's Explanations Don't Excuse Him," *The Advocate*, May 4. Available online: https://www.advocate.com/books/2018/5/04/roxane-gay-explains-why-junot-diazs-explanations-dont-excuse-him (accessed June 15, 2020).

Latino Rebels (2018), "Open Letter Written by 26 Women Academics about Junot Díaz Says Media and Tweets Are to Blame," May 14. Available online: https://www.latinorebels.com/2018/05/14/open-letter-written-by-26-women-academics-about-junot-diaz-says-media-and-tweets-are-to-blame/ (accessed June 15, 2020).

Machado-Saez, Elena (2011), "Dictating Desire, Dictating Diaspora: Junot Díaz's *The Brief Wondrous Life of Oscar Wao* as Foundational Romance," *Contemporary Literature*, 52 (3): 522–55.

Maxwell, December, Sarah R. Robinson, Jessica R. Williams, and Craig Keaton (2020), "A Short Story of a Lonely Guy: A Qualitative Thematic Analysis of Involuntary Celibacy Using Reddit," *Sexuality & Culture*, March 25. Available online: https://doi.org/10.1007/s12119-020-09724-6 (accessed August 1, 2020).

NPR Staff (2012), "Fidelity in Fiction: Junot Díaz Deconstructs a Cheater," *NPR*, September 11. Available online: https://www.npr.org/2012/09/11/160252399/fidelity-in-fiction-junot-diaz-deconstructs-a-cheater (accessed June 15, 2020).

Okie, Matt (2008), "*Mil Máscaras*: An Interview with Pulitzer-Winner Junot Díaz (*The Brief Wondrous Life of Oscar Wao*)," *Identity Theory*, September 2. Available online: http://www.identitytheory.com/interview-pulitzer-winner-junot-diaz-wondrous-life-oscar-wao/ (accessed June 15, 2020).

Rowley, Liz (2018), "The Architect of #MeToo Says the Movement Has Lost Its Way," *The Cut*, October 23. Available online: https://www.thecut.com/2018/10/tarana-burke-me-too-founder-movement-has-lost-its-way.html.

Schulman, Sarah (2016), *Conflict Is Not Abuse*, Vancouver: Arsenal Pulp Press.

Tippet, Krista (2017), "Junot Díaz: Radical Hope Is Our Best Weapon," *On Being*, September 14. Available online: https://onbeing.org/programs/junot-diaz-radical-hope-is-our-best-weapon-sep2017/ (accessed June 15, 2020).

Weese, Katherine (2014), "'Tu No Eres Nada De Dominicano': Unnatural Narration and De-Naturalizing Gender Constructs in Junot Díaz's *The Brief Wondrous Life of Oscar Wao*," *The Journal of Men's Studies*, 22 (2): 89–104.

Wilks, Jennifer M. (2019), "Dominican *Décalage*: Comparative Negotiations of Race and Gender in Junot Díaz's *The Brief Wondrous Life of Oscar Wao*," *Comparative Literature Studies*, 56 (2): 348–73.

PART III

Pedagogy: Practices and Methods

15

Beyond Safe Spaces:
Working toward Access and Accountability Using Trauma-Informed Pedagogy

Maureen McDonnell

Women's Studies as a field insists on connections between classrooms and everyday experiences. Public conversations about "trigger warnings" and the #MeToo movement may prompt people in classrooms to request transparency about charged content and harm. Rather than succumbing to moral panic at the prospect that students may request accommodation or accountability, the authors in this book offer a sustained dialogue about who is in classrooms, how we learn together, and how we might be responsible to each other. My contribution focuses on my facilitation of trauma-informed pedagogy, which includes pedagogical tools that introduce students to argumentation and controlling images, pedagogical practice that responds to student experience, and student contributions to classroom content. I explicitly ask students in both my literature and Women's Studies classes to consider issues of harm. These conversations are not neutral ones: their challenges are heightened by cultural discourse that deems public discussion about the negative effects of racist, misogynistic, and transphobic language and violence as "cancel culture" that negates free speech. Yet those dialogues are necessary for thinking through how inclusion and equity might be enacted in our classrooms.

Trauma-informed pedagogy is appropriate not only because most college classrooms contain survivors of interpersonal violence but also because of the ways that individual, collective, and intergenerational trauma construct and constrain humans and the communities in which we reside. The impacts of historical and recent trauma may manifest in a range of ways linked to our intersectional identities of race, gender, citizenship, ability, neurodiversity, sexuality, language, nationality, and other factors. Such practices are important as a means of accommodating educational challenges, and thus serve as an appropriate part of universal design for learning. Universal design frameworks offer students multiple ways of navigating our classes, irrespective of documented disabilities—a designation only available to those with the financial and cultural wherewithal to secure that paperwork—and help establish a more coherent pedagogical environment for learners who do not fit into designated accommodation categories. Such pedagogical practices resist ahistorical notions about who enrolls in college and how they learn.

It is an uncomfortable fact that some universities exist today because of endowments generated by past institutional violence that imagined people of color to be commodities rather than human. Anti-Black bias and misogyny also colluded in university-sanctioned segregation, so that colleges have never represented the general public. Past events are not inert ones, as suggested by the mission of the Georgetown Memory Project (funded by alum Richard Cellini) to share the historical record of Georgetown's 1838 sale of 272 slaves with their descendants (Swarns 2016). As institutions that trafficked people of color grapple with what restitution they owe, such reckonings could more broadly inform campuses' support of their students. Where I teach, students of color have become increasingly vocal about the ways in which their experience at a PWI (Predominantly White Institution) includes microaggressions, hate speech, and threatened and actual violence. I find their disclosures courageous and disquieting. News reports of college activists airing these past and ongoing harms sometimes present these adults as over-sensitive. Such depictions compel me to return to Sara Ahmed's (2015) formulation: "over-sensitive can be translated as: sensitive to that which is not over." To dismiss conversation about such legacies is itself a type of violence.

Exposing these ongoing efforts to exclude and intimidate might prompt conversations among students, alums, teachers, staff, and administrators about reparative actions. Those participants would likely begin (or avoid) that restorative process for a range of reasons that would also shape the collective conversation about the "appropriateness" of possible interventions for that campus and those who use it.

Pedagogical Tools: Argumentation and Controlling Images

Early in the term, I typically introduce my students in all of my classes to a streamlined version of Stephen Toulmin's argumentation (1958), which highlights three components: the claim (the position being maintained), the evidence (the information being used), and the warrant (the assumptions that allow for connections between the other features). So for instance, in this chapter, I make a policy claim: that instructors' classroom practice should be culturally competent and trauma-informed. My evidence draws on qualitative information (including conversations with students and colleagues) as well as quantitative research. One of my warrants is that those regularly in the classroom should shape the practices of what happens there, and should interrogate their desires about what happens in those spaces and how. When I provide this argumentation overview (claim, evidence, and warrant) to students, they are typically more familiar with the first two components. I discuss the warrant at greater length, one of my many strategies for "teaching the other" content (Keating 2007: 104–21) historically absent from syllabuses. In doing so, I emphasize the ways in which personal experiences, values, and beliefs shape individual premises about what is credible. This vocabulary allows for clarity—and, sometimes, efficiency—as the class continues.

When we search for writers' warrants, we excavate others' assumptions. As an example, when discussing university policies about trigger warnings, I share Greg Lukianoff and Jonathan Haidt's "The Coddling of the American Mind" (2015) in an early printed iteration. They are explicit about the warrant that drives their efforts to ban trigger warnings: "[the current movement] presumes an extraordinary fragility of the collegiate psyche, and therefore elevates the goal of protecting students from psychological harm." Their clarity is useful for me, illustrating how antithetical to theirs my own premise is. Students have given me ample evidence of their physical and psychological resilience, testimonies that lead me to discount as inaccurate and dismissive Lukianoff and Haidt's characterization of their fragility. Two factors shape my perspective: the number of people at my workplace who have told me of their experiences with violence, and my responsibility as a mandated reporter to relay students' disclosure to other, designated professionals at my university (a process that requires considerable resources from all involved, especially the person reporting the trauma). I defer to other adults' expertise about their experiences, what they can handle on a given day, and under what circumstances they might decide to report. Lukianoff and Haidt might posit my voicing trigger warnings as "coddling"; however, my approach is driven by students' demonstrated capacities.

Attentiveness to warrants can also help us decode visual rhetoric like the picture that accompanies the Lukianoff and Haidt article. The image features a blue-eyed child wearing a vacant expression. He sits on a booster seat. A Mac laptop rests nearby. Affluent, with commercial resources conspicuously on display, the student is literally infantilized. Although this picture mocks students, it also reveals a fantasy: a White, male student who is the singular focus of educational enterprise. Students often quickly fact-check this invented figure, an image that belies college students' demographics. As we discuss the image and its construction, I introduce the term "controlling images," which Patricia Hill Collins (2002: 69) defines as raced, gendered, and classed depictions in the media that shape stereotypes. I announce my claim: this visual advances a controlling image of college students as too developmentally immature to engage in academic rigor.

Focusing on controlling images allows us to both identify and sidestep familiar cultural narratives. For instance, my recent Lesbian Literature class raised productive questions not only about collaboration in the published works of Michael Field (a pseudonym for two British writers), but also about consent. They noted that writer Edith Emma Cooper was not only fifteen years younger than her co-author, Katherine Harris Bradley, but was also her niece and ward. Students' speculation about how those factors might have affected Cooper's agency evaded heteronormative scripts, compared historical contexts, and centered a nuanced, productive discussion.

Practice: Responding to Student Experience

Throughout the term, I solicit student input on what work should be underway, and how we should undertake it. We generate this data in two modes. Bi-weekly, students undertake anonymous check-ins about classroom dynamics, letting me know of "pluses, minuses, and questions" (+, –, ?) that they have. Mid-term, I circulate a more extensive questionnaire about classroom activities and students' preparation for our time together. Reporting their collective feedback to them allows us to view the multiple—sometimes competing— perspectives on best practices in the room. Consensus is not always possible. Even if students in a class fervently share an overarching goal for our time together, this hypothetical coalition would not function as a place of safety and ease for all who contribute to its maintenance (a scenario Sasaki [2002] thoughtfully considers). Still, student reports offer me information about how we might adjust practices that may not be working for that constellation of students. More importantly, making my own ongoing learning visible helps me resist the temptation to smooth over instructive conflicts and the "invitation to collude" (Sasaki 2002: 47) with larger university practices.

Student collaboration guides their extended work and my assessment of it. Students in my upper-level classes (in literature and in Women's Studies) work together in designing any essay exams, building upon templates that I provide them with examples of interpretive, evaluative, critical, and comparative questions.[1] Within a single class period, students generate a range of prompts that I document and then circulate. Individual writers can then choose which question(s) they see as best for their intellectual and creative work.

Although that exercise showcases the boons of collaboration, positive outcomes are not guaranteed. Whenever peer editing or other activities ask that students work together, they fill in preference sheets to confidentially inform me of their priorities and whether there are persons or topics that they feel they cannot work with professionally. Given that they are more familiar with their individual histories than I am and that their campus networks are often out of my view, this input allows me to avoid some of the pitfalls of group work, and hopefully minimize the prospective harm that classmates might inflict upon each other. (Typically, fewer than 5 percent of students make specific requests to avoid a peer.) In Women's Studies classes, at the introductory and intermediate levels, students investigate our individual campus's policies, resources, and self-regulatory procedures. Sharing Whitley and Page's "Sexism at the Centre: Locating the Problem of Sexual Harassment" (2015) allows us to discuss harassment between academic staff and students, and the ways in which universities' efforts to diminish their liability can enable perpetrators. Such discussions allow us to study our varied locations within our classes, campus, and communities, and our shifting relationships to power as we move among those settings. Drawing on their investigative and academic work, I volunteer another claim: that it is necessary to hold institutions accountable, and to compel them to revise policies that limit student agency and well-being.

In addition to calculated acts of harm, we also take into account cultural and bureaucratic norms that cause lapses in students' educational access or amplify trauma. Although over 65 percent of students who receive counseling center services in the United States and internationally indicate that these resources helped them stay admitted (AAUCCD 2018: 40; Gallagher 2014: 7), stigma about and underfunding of those services jeopardize their efficacy. Some students' subject positions make reporting health concerns risky on multiple fronts. Resident assistants who disclose suicidal ideation, for instance, may risk losing their jobs and housing. Students accessing university health services may learn that their medical records are "owned" by their institution, rather than covered by HIPAA. Survivors of crimes handled by university public safety offices may find their assaults electronically circulated to hundreds of other students, or be charged copying fees to acquire a copy of that agency's paperwork. Such bureaucratic practices are not quirks.

They resurrect longer debates about property and personhood on campus. In my classrooms, my efforts to affirm my students' humanity include asking people to introduce themselves and their pronouns to our class, rather than relying on rosters that can include students' deadnames or not reflect changes in marital status. I frequently assign content that introduces disability as a rhetorical/political system rather than a biological, consistent truth. These relationship practices matter to me, even as my larger questions remain unanswered. Do students own their experiences, or are they university property? Is physical autonomy supported or suspended in campus spaces?

I admire people brave enough to ask for support. Sometimes the request is a form of disclosure. Melanie Yergeau notes that despite "impulses that emblemize minoritized activism as inherently threatening and apocalyptic," such apocalypses are not new (2016: 16). She states that recent alarms about "the rhetoric of trigger warnings ... can help us uncover ableism engrained deep within our cultural spaces" (2016: 7), noting the contemporary debate's similarities with public (and higher education's) outcry about the Americans for Disabilities Act three decades ago. Disability rights work, like anti-racist and anti-misogynist efforts, creates a range of tactics for making our classes more equitable. Students often have specific recommendations about how to further the knowledge-making of our class, how we might transform the spaces and structures that we share—and how people can, and do, sustain themselves.

Student Contributions

Student insight into what we need to learn centers our classwork in the last part of the term. Students in intro and upper-level classes convey their extended research on academic topics and related activism through teach-ins. I also request that they share their resources for survival, self-care, and joy. This move often follows a discussion of Bernice Johnson Reagon (1983), who notes the demands and difficulty of coalition work. I present as a model Sara Ahmed's "A Killjoy Survival Kit" (2017: 235–50), which lists her categories for survival and self-care, and ask that students create their own survival kit and share one of those items with our class. This invitation to publicly express a specifically individual aspect of interiority is not simply show-and-tell; rather, this activity offers glimpses at the potential of literary scholar Kevin Quashie's claim that inner lives are "not apolitical or without social value, but neither [are they] determined entirely by publicness. In fact, the interior—dynamic and ravishing—is a stay against the dominance of the social world; it has its own sovereignty" (2012: 6). We sometimes leave the room with new playlists, a list of books for post-term rejuvenation, or a new way to approach mindfulness, or we experience some ease in our bodies after watching a video clip of a dog frolicking in the snow. The students' offerings challenge me to sit and consider vulnerability, tenderness, what a human might want, what we might need.

A superficial reading of this undertaking might seem to conform to Lukianoff and Haidt's ending mandate that "students should also be taught how to live in a world full of potential offenses." Certainly, self-care might extend our endurance. Yet, instead of teaching subjugation, I hope that attentive reflection might facilitate self-advocacy. Why not resistance or rebellion? My optimism is heavily indebted to Audre Lorde's assertion that "caring for one's self is not self-indulgence, it is self-preservation, and that is an act of political warfare" (1988: 131). The "survival kit" enterprise asks students to be accountable to their own particular quirks, expertise, and humanity. That interiority offers us windows to our bodyminds, Margaret Price's term (2015) to counter the artificial separation of our mental and physical experiences. This holistic perspective might help people follow the lead of Kathleen Ann Livingston (2014), who recommends that would-be allies "deal with disclosures of trauma histories by students in [two] ways: 1. Believe them; 2. Ask, *what do you need?*" Learning what a specific moment requires is not a discrete task, as a colleague reminded me (Flood 2016). As we talked about the contested phrase of "safe spaces," he posited that "maybe some students don't give a damn about safe spaces. Maybe some students will settle for safe moments and stringing them together." His reminder to me of the ephemeral, evolving, shifting nature of what we might need to sustain ourselves still resonates. Those conversations and the people I share them with help me re-commit to our finding new creative, challenging ways to engage with the painful process of being fully human, of practicing freedom.

Note

1
- **Interpretative questions** (How does the idea X apply to Y)?
- **Evaluative questions** (Which of these texts better contributes to our understanding of X?)
- **Critical questions** (X states Y. Under what conditions might that not be true?)
- **Comparative questions** (How might theory/text X or Y relate to each other?)

Works Cited

Ahmed, Sara (2015), "Against Students," *The New Inquiry*, June 29. Available online: https://thenewinquiry.com/against-students/ (accessed August 9, 2015).

Ahmed, Sara (2017), *Living a Feminist Life*, Durham: Duke University Press.

Association for University and College Counseling Center Directors Annual Survey—Public Version (2018). Available online: https://www.aucccd.org/director-surveys-public (accessed July 15, 2020).

Collins, Patricia Hill (2002), *Black Feminist Thought: Knowledge, Consciousness, and the Politics of Empowerment*, New York: Routledge.

Flood, Reginald L. (2016), Conversation, May 5.

Gallagher, Robert P. (2014), *National Survey of College Counseling Centers*, Alexandria, VA: The International Association of Counseling Services, Inc.

Keating, AnaLouise (2007), *Teaching Transformation: Transcultural Classroom Dialogues*, New York: Palgrave.

Livingston, Kathleen Ann (2014), "On Rage, Shame, 'Realness,' and Accountability to Survivors," *Harlot of the Arts*, 12. Available online: http://harlotofthearts.org/index.php/harlot/article/view/237 (accessed April 25, 2016).

Lorde, Audre (1988), *A Burst of Light: Essays*, London: Sheba Feminist Publishers.

Lukianoff, Greg and Jonathan Haidt (2015), "The Coddling of the American Mind," *The Atlantic*, September 15. Available online: https://www.theatlantic.com/magazine/archive/2015/09/the-coddling-of-the-american-mind/399356/ (accessed September 1, 2015).

Price, Margaret (2015), "The Bodymind Problem and the Possibilities of Pain," *Hypatia*, 30 (1): 268–84.

Quashie, Kevin (2012), *The Sovereignty of Quiet: Beyond Resistance in Black Culture*, New Brunswick: Rutgers University Press.

Reagon, Bernice Johnson (1983), "Coalition Politics: Turning the Century," in Barbara Smith (ed.), *Home Girls: A Black Feminist Anthology*, 356–68, New York: Kitchen Table—Women of Color Press.

Sasaki, Betty (2002), "Toward a Pedagogy of Coalition," in Amie A. Macdonald and Susan Sánchez-Casal (eds.), *Twenty-First-Century Feminist Classrooms: Pedagogies of Identity and Difference*, 31–58, New York: Palgrave.

Swarns, Rachel L. (2016), "272 Slaves Were Sold to Save Georgetown. What Does It Owe Their Descendants?" *New York Times*, April 16. Available online: https://www.nytimes.com/2016/04/17/us/georgetown-university-search-for-slave-descendants.html (accessed April 21, 2016).

Toulmin, Stephen E. (1958), *The Uses of Argument*, Cambridge: Cambridge University Press.

Whitley, Leila and Tiffany Page (2015), "Sexism at the Centre: Locating the Problem of Sexual Harassment," *New Formations: A Journal of Culture/Theory/Politics* 86: 34–53.

Yergeau, Melanie (2010), *Disable All the Things: On Affect, Metadata, and Audience*. Available online: http://kuiama.net/portfolio/wp-content/uploads/2010/08/LARGE-PRINT-of-Disable-all-the-things_-FINAL-Google-Docs.pdf (accessed April 14, 2016).

16

Trigger Warnings:
An Ethics for Tutoring #MeToo Content and Rape Narratives in Writing Centers

Beth Walker

In the wake of the 2017 #MeToo movement, writers are sharing their stories of sexual trauma online, in writing groups, and in the classroom. Websites, forums, and online magazines, such as *Persephone's Daughters, Entropy,* and *The Rumpus,* to name a few outstanding publishing ventures, offer safe spaces where writers can publish #MeToo content. But providing feedback to prepare #MeToo content for a larger audience can be tricky—indeed, even risky. Teachers and editors have long recognized the difficulties in responding to writing about severe trauma. What do you say, for example, to someone who has chosen to write about rape for the common freshman composition narrative assignment, "your scariest moment"? How do you even suggest revision? After all, "it really happened that way." What grade, if any, would you dare place on such a piece?

In her 1995 award-winning essay for the national Conference on College Composition and Communication, "Responding When a Life Depends on It: What to Write in the Margins When

Students Self-Disclose," Marilyn Valentino outlines the most common ways of responding to highly personal controversial material such as drug use, PTSD, and rape, and declares that instructors "have an ethical and legal responsibility to *effectively* respond and refer if necessary" (1995: 5, original italics). Her suggestions have become a touchstone for instructors looking for guidance on compassionate critique. Little attention, however, has been paid to the special considerations of rape narratives in academic settings.[1] The role of writing centers in this process in particular needs more clarification. Virtually nothing has been written about how tutors should handle conferences about sexual trauma, yet tutors usually are "first responders," the first to see a draft and guide revision. Our training aims to ensure that writers retain ownership of their work not just by requesting that they make their own corrections but more importantly by asking questions that encourage the writers to make the best choices to improve their work. These are positive, time-tested ways to build rapport and help writers establish productive writing habits and develop transferable skills. Ironically though, much of what writing centers do can intimidate the very people we are trying to help, for, as Julie Bokser argues, "With only a slight shift in perspective, what appears to be help … might be understood as the violence of imposition" (2001: 23). In particular, how do first responders invite writers to revise when the act of questioning, a standard tutoring technique, seems like a deliberate and confrontational expression of doubt? This chapter outlines an ethics of responding to #MeToo content; first responders can adapt its advice beyond the writing center for workshops, student-teacher conferences, and the classroom.

Knowing When to Report

First things first: Your writing center should complete its mandatory reporting training and federal privacy training regularly. Describing when and how to report criminal activity is beyond the scope of this chapter. For this discussion, let us assume that the writers we will be helping have already taken all the legal and mental health steps that they need to take and that they are ready to share their #MeToo writing. Now what?

Creating Safe Spaces

Regrettably, both first responders and writers can be triggered by reading and discussing sexual trauma, especially in unfamiliar settings with strangers. Despite our training, first responders are not clinical counselors, so many focus on writing skills rather than content, for fear of saying the wrong thing. Ignoring the obvious may come across as cold-hearted, but writers generally are not asking for personal help.[2] At the end of the session, you can always add, "You know, counseling services on campus are free if you're interested. You want their phone number?" However, offering "Thank you for sharing this" or "I know this piece is important to you. Please come back. Our door is open" may be better than offering to fish out a phone number.

Indeed, our door is always open. Writers walk right in, sometimes just to sit on our couch. Unfortunately, if your writing center is like ours, having an open floor plan with several tutoring tables and a wall of computers also means that several strangers could be listening in on very private material. Alas, there are no guaranteed solutions for creating safe spaces: in fact, intimate settings with first responders might come across as intimidating. For example, Jennifer Fox dramatizes a small-group setting in her 2018 autobiographical movie *The Tale*: her thirteen-year-old self is reading aloud the story of her sexual grooming by a much older couple, and the camera circles to the disgust and disbelief on the students' faces and the worry on the teacher's brow. At the end, Jennifer quickly surveys the room, realizes that she must lie, and smirks: "I made it up." Relieved, the teacher responds, "That's what I thought." That lie cements the fiction that Fox tells herself for thirty years. To protect writers' privacy, some first responders' instinct might be to retreat into an office, door closed; yet isolated spaces can come across as even more confining than being encircled by a group, especially when discussing details of sexual trauma. For everyone's peace of mind, I invite first responders to rethink shutting the door on writers.

In any case, first responders must be mindful of their surroundings. Then, of course, plan *how* the writing will be shared: In the writing center? Around a conference table? In an office? Online? Zoom? Discussion board? Email? Who is listening in and who has access? For groups, establish ground rules, get permission to distribute, and establish guidelines for acceptable feedback *ahead of time*. Writers can fold and staple parts of paper drafts they do not wish others to read. Then model a practice session. Having guidelines not only helps first responders maintain decorum in difficult group sessions but more importantly helps writers keep control over their own work.

Overcoming the Rhetoric of Trauma

Thirteen-year-old Jennifer Fox loved to write and, after reading aloud, looked hopefully to her circle of peers for praise, but she was met with scorn for her content and doubt and questions about its details from her teacher. No wonder writers walk into writing centers, shaking, full of shame about the stories of their lives, apologizing for their hard work: "I know I'm a bad writer. I know this is wrong. I'm sorry." Indeed, writers' perception of verbal and written feedback historically echoes the rhetoric of trauma: "My teacher *bled* all over my paper. My teacher *butchered* my paper. My teacher *killed* my grade. My teacher is *out to get me*. I only got a B, so my teacher must be *punishing me*, because it really happened that way!"

Even attempts at building rapport and using positive language can backfire. Comments praising craft, for example, can come across as insensitive. For example, "I like the part about _____," a favorite strategy to discuss details that are working, suddenly becomes an awkward moment about liking a particular detail of a rape. Even praising the writer's courage can, with Bokser's "slight shift in perspective," become twisted out of context, which is what (I hope) happened with the tone-deaf comment I found on one writer's paper: "You must think very highly of yourself." How many times have we heard someone say, "I'm glad you told so that no one else has to get hurt"? I invite first responders, however, to reconsider saying such a thing. True, many people feel the need to come forward for this very reason, but many do not; in fact, it implies that a person's value lies only in her or his ability to prevent harm. The person in front of you has worth: stick to that. Even spouting the cliché "You're so brave" may fly in the face of the terror you have just read. Try this instead: "I bet writing this was scary, but it was also a pretty brave thing to do. I hope it helps. Now what do you need this draft to do? And what do you need from me?" This language strikes a nice balance between the person and the writing, and it keeps the discussion focused on the task, revision.

Understanding the Responsibility of Revision

Your responsibility as a first responder is twofold: what, in your professional expertise, are the two or three suggestions that will make the most difference in the draft? And more importantly, how can you help the writer shape the draft so that she or he cannot possibly be misunderstood? Usually, writers will mention a couple of things that worry them, so you can take your cues accordingly. Then again, you may feel obligated to address something else, such as following the assignment, or you may need to help the writer find alternate, difficult solutions. One woman said to me, "Pardon my French," about her explicit language. I said, "That's okay. You said what you said, but who is the primary audience? Will your instructor appreciate what you are trying to do here?" Although we both agreed she should not substitute childish slang or clinical vocabulary for actual dialogue, neither of us thought her instructor would approve of curse words, so we settled on simple, indirect discourse.

Helping writers keep track of the *current* audience is essential, for #MeToo content has many versions, many audiences. Chances are, the person sitting next to you has told this story before: how many times has Christine Blasey Ford told her story, and in how many forms? She told her husband and her counselor; her story exists in her therapy records, as letters to her state representatives and to her senator, and as her opening statement and verbal testimony before the United States Senate (Ford 2018). In each case, she chose her words carefully for that particular audience. In the 2018 movie, Jennifer Fox's thirteen-year-old self stresses that both her fictionalized essay and her adult-self's autobiographical movie script are two "version[s] of what happened," with their own truths to tell. You may wonder why the writer is making much over a detail, only to discover that an earlier audience, such as the police or an attorney, kept asking about it. Help writers stay focused on the current audience and assignment by asking: "What do you want these readers to know? What do you want these readers to understand? Do your readers need this detail? Will your readers ever miss this?" Otherwise, #MeToo content will lose its focus and suffer from length issues.

Revision as Listening

I often joke that our writing center is called the Listening Center. I learned this workshopping technique from my long-time writing guru, Natalie Goldberg, author of the 1986 bestseller *Writing Down the Bones*. In Goldberg's workshops, a participant reads aloud, then the rest of the room does a "recall."[3] Someone offers, "I heard ... " then repeats some striking word, phrase, or sentence from the writing. No pressure exists to say something is "good" or "bad"; instead, first responders listen, then reaffirm. Writers get heard. In small groups, my students embrace this technique readily; everyone feels more comfortable sharing.

Revising, however, is different from sharing. Start "listening" by asking an open-ended question, anything from "So, what's the assignment?" or "What would be helpful at this point in the process?" and then repeat some version of the writer's answer to show you are on the same page, literally and figuratively. Asking questions that do not *question* is especially important with #MeToo writers. Use their answers to fill in the gaps and clarify details. Matters of content usually involve who is doing or saying what, where, when, and why. For example, instead of asking, "So why did you go back into that scary house?" which sounds accusatory, try "Where are you in this paragraph? Okay. Is it important for us to know that? Oh, so maybe you should put that down. That's why you went back into the house, right?"

Revision as Choice

Equally tricky are matters of craft and style; bombarding writers with lots of sentence-level errors can silence writers by implying that they are too incompetent to tell their own stories. Assume competency, even that artistry is at work—even if the story itself reads incoherently. "Can I ask you some questions about the artistic choices you made?" particularly evokes a smile, for I am willing to posit that their writing is becoming more than a victim statement: it is evolving into a work of art. Here are some open-ended questions about the nuts and bolts, anything from punctuation and grammar to structure and style: "What can you tell me about _____? Why did you choose to _____? Did you mean to _____? Is _____ intentional? Are you going for _____ here?" Notice that the last three templates ask for clarity, but all of these employ the rhetoric of choice, allowing #MeToo writers to be artists who control the decisions about their words and their meaning. In sum, in an effort to capture the horror on the page, these writers are willing to break the rules. It does no good to point out a bunch of fragments. Try something like this instead: "Can I ask about these short sentences? What's the effect you're going for here?" Then help them achieve that effect.

Revision as Subversion

#MeToo material characteristically subverts the rules of content, structure, style, and mechanics as a way of artistically exerting resistance, control, agency, and choice. The genre is filled with fragmentation and experimental techniques.[4] First responders will be befuddled by gaps in detail in some scenes, and an overabundance of detail in others. Likewise, gaps or unusual treatment of time signals that not all time is equal, nor is it linear; there is much flashing forward and backward to show cause and effect and, above all, trauma. These stylistic choices help give writers voice, even when it is breaking.

It is *their* voice, not ours. You may find some of their choices odd, but work with the text rather than against it. For example, in 2018 when Ford was asked before the Senate what she remembered most about her attack thirty years earlier, she famously responded: "Indelible in the hippocampus is the laughter." Such an odd way of putting it, but that phrase was likely the detail that converted doubters. Indeed, Ford's off-the-cuff comment reveals several of the key stylistic characteristics of #MeToo content. For one, #MeToo writers use the vocabulary that they know. Who else but Ford, a clinical psychologist, would have said it that way? Second, #MeToo writers use parts to represent the whole experience—an example of how fragmentation, often a target for revision, gets used to great effect in these narratives. In this case, the hippocampus stands in for the whole person (a *synecdoche*), and the laughter represents Ford's shame (a *metonym*). Third, #MeToo writers repeat key phrases and images, in Ford's case, "I remember" and "laughter."

Revision as Empowerment

First responders should encourage writers to see the act of revision as an act of empowerment. #MeToo writers even choose margins, fonts, and other decorative ways to symbolize in writing what is happening to them psychologically. For example, in her untitled poem re-posted on a #MeToo movement Facebook page, Chloe Frayne demonstrates that revision is in progress:

~~I hope that~~
one day
a mirror
will not be a battleground.

In her Facebook post, Frayne notes: "After I wrote this poem, I stopped and crossed out the first line and it felt like the strongest thing I had done in a long time" (January 22, 2019). She kept the strikethrough to represent how the act of revision—a simple matter of editing tentative language—created a huge change in her thinking.

Some of these writers will come into your writing center or workshop having already made that cognitive leap; others will be asking how to make it. As first responders, your responsibility is not just to help them get a better grade or a publishable piece—even though, yes, those are important—but to listen well and deeply and to respond ethically. You are witnessing a transformation, both on paper and in the person before you, so I invite you to end every session as I end this chapter by saying, "Thank you. I'm honored."

Notes

1 Jeffrey Berman's excellent *Risky Writing* (2001) addresses various sub-genres of life writing in the classroom, while Miriam Kalman Harris' *Rape Incest Battery* (2000) focuses on editing trauma narratives for publication. Jen Cross has written a detailed writing guide for rape survivors called *Writing Ourselves Whole* (2017).
2 Berman points out that his students are adults; "those who write about being victims of sexual crimes seek neither legal advice nor psychological counsel from me" (2001: 46). He concludes that to discourage students from sharing their stories in academic settings "as inappropriate ... is to deny life as it occurs in high schools and colleges throughout the country" (2001: 270).
3 I have attended Goldberg's workshops where we practiced this technique, and she explains it in almost all of her books and audio workshops, but her first description of it appears in the chapter called "Listening" in *Writing Down the Bones* (1986: 52–4).
4 *Persephone's Daughters*, an online magazine for survivors of abuse, offers an impressive selection of genre-defying poetry and prose, especially in its "Sunday Stories" section.

Works Cited

Berman, Jeffrey (2001), *Risky Writing: Self-Disclosure and Self-Transformation in the Classroom*, Amherst: University of Massachusetts Press.

Bokser, Julie A. (2001), "Peer Tutoring and Gorgias: Acknowledging Aggression in the Writing Center," *The Writing Center Journal*, 21 (2): 21–34. Available online: http://www.jstor.org/stable/43442122 (accessed August 18, 2020).

Cross, Jen (2017), *Writing Ourselves Whole: Using the Power of Your Own Creativity to Recover and Heal from Sexual Trauma*, Coral Gables, FL: Mango Publishing.

Ford, Christine Blasey (2018), "Kavanaugh Hearing: Transcript: Senate Judiciary Committee Hearing on the Nomination of Brett M.

Kavanaugh to Be an Associate Justice of the Supreme Court, Day 5, Focusing on Allegations of Sexual Assault," *The Washington Post*, September 27. Available online: https://www.washingtonpost.com/news/national/wp/2018/09/27/kavanaugh-hearing-transcript/ (accessed August 17, 2020).

Frayne, Chloe (2019), "Untitled Poem," *Sisters of Indigo Light*, Facebook home page. Available online: http://facebook.com/sistersofindigolight (accessed January 22, 2019).

Goldberg, Natalie (1986), *Writing Down the Bones: Freeing the Writer Within*, Boston: Shambhala.

Harris, Miriam Kalman, ed. (2000), *Rape Incest Battery: Women Writing Out the Pain*, Fort Worth: TCU Press.

Persephone's Daughters. Available online: http://persephonesdaughters.tk (accessed August 18, 2020).

The Tale (2018), [Film] Dir. Jennifer Fox, USA: HBO.

Valentino, Marilyn J. (1995), "Responding When a Life Depends on It: What to Write in the Margins When Students Self-Disclose," Paper presented at the 46th Annual Meeting of the Conference on College Composition and Communication, 23–5 March, Washington, DC. Available Online: http://pdfs.semanticsscholar.org (accessed August 17, 2020).

17

From Sympathy to Detoxification:

Pedagogical Approaches for Dismantling Rape Culture

Jeremy Posadas

For the past decade, I have taught a multi-week unit on preventing sexual violence in a course that analyzes and critiques dominant sexual culture in the United States from feminist, queer, and anti-racist perspectives. In this essay, I will highlight the most important pedagogical practices that shape the unit and describe a simple typology I've devised to think about and engage students' different positionalities within structures of sexual violence, concluding with questions useful for (re-)designing such a unit. Although I am by training a social ethicist rather than a literary scholar, the concepts I focus on here apply to both fields (and many others).[1]

The course I teach is an intermediate general education course with no prerequisites. Of the thirty students who enroll every year, White cis women usually comprise 35–50 percent, women of color and trans/non-binary students comprise 25–40 percent, and cis men (mostly but never exclusively White) comprise 20–30 percent. Typically about 50–60 percent of the students have middle-class backgrounds and 40–50 percent have working-class backgrounds.

Anywhere from 30 to 50 percent grew up in rural towns in Texas and Oklahoma (the college is located on the rural border of the two states), with about half the remainder coming from affluent suburbs/urban neighborhoods and the other half from poorer urban neighborhoods.

Making "Brave Space" for the Topic[2]

To create the most emotionally supportive learning experience I can, I follow four general procedures in building the unit and course. First, I schedule the unit for halfway into the semester to ensure that the class has had time to become familiar with one another through discussion as well as to practice talking about topics that students are invested in but often have not had much prior opportunity to examine critically. As I do in all my courses, I include several ongoing group practices that foster a sense of community and mutuality among the students; these are especially important for laying emotionally supportive foundations for this unit.

Second, I allow any student to opt out of attending class on any day in the unit, without penalty, if they think doing so would re-traumatize them; they are required to notify me that they will be opting out but *not* required to give any details, though I explain that I'm happy to talk one-on-one and, as appropriate and desired, connect them to further support and resources. Absent students are still required to complete the readings and written reflections for the unit—I indicate which readings contain descriptions of sexual violence and in how much detail (though at this point none of the assigned readings includes a highly detailed or graphic description)—and if a student were to approach me to request alternative readings, I would not hesitate to individualize a plan.

Third, I intentionally check in with the class at several points throughout the unit to see how the experience is going. I acknowledge that it can be challenging, for different reasons, to engage the topics in the unit. I invite them to talk about what it's like to read the materials we're reading and have the conversations we're having. I want students to be heard as they name whatever they're experiencing and to hear one another. These check-ins give me a sense of how the unit is working with *this* particular group of students and whether some real-time adjustments are necessary. They also provide an additional way to see if individual students might be experiencing distress from the unit, so that I can follow up with them one-on-one. I conclude the check-in by affirming that the unit is not emotionally easy, but that by doing it we are moving ourselves toward a more gender-equitable world.

Fourth, I find as many opportunities as I can to discuss (or at least acknowledge) the intersectional dynamics of sexual violence and the diverse identities of people who are victimized by it. Often this means adding simple, overt reminders that women of color, queer and trans/non-binary people, and working-class people face heightened targeting for sexual violence as well as how cis men can be targets as well. This is not only a matter of accurately portraying the reality of sexual violence and its pervasiveness across many demographics; it's also one way to communicate to any survivors in the class—particularly those who belong to groups that aren't stereotypically portrayed as targets—as well as those who've offered survivors care that their diverse identities matter and that I, as the instructor, want to create space where diverse experiences of sexual violence are heard and taken seriously.

Recognizing Multiple Structural Positions within Rape Culture

Honoring my students' diverse identities requires attention to my greatest challenge in this unit: the fact that among the students there are different groups who have vastly different relationships with, and stakes in addressing, sexual violence and its eradication. In my ongoing planning and reflection for the unit, I have come to find it useful to think about three major structural positions within rape culture, of which each student occupies at least one (and sometimes more): *survivors, potentially targeted students,* and *perpetrator-adjacent students.* These functionally defined structural positions are more pedagogically useful than demographic categories based on gender, race, and class because demography alone does not determine the pedagogical needs of different groups of students in this unit, even though we can certainly recognize demographic patterns and disproportions among students holding each position. I do not use the positions to individually classify actual students; rather, they offer an alternative way to identify the main *groups* represented among my students and think carefully about these groups' distinct learning needs.

By "potentially targeted," I mean those students who have not been victimized by sexual violence but belong to groups that are disparately victimized by it, especially women (cis and trans), other trans/non-binary people, queer people, and, within each of these groups, working-class people and people of color; by not conceptualizing this structural position strictly in demographic terms, I'm acknowledging that members of all demographic groups are and can be targeted by perpetrators of sexual violence. Identifying the "perpetrator-adjacent" position acknowledges how peers can reinforce or disrupt pro-violence dynamics. Although most cis men in the course occupy this position—since most perpetrators of sexual violence are cis men—intersectionality reminds us that Black and Latino cis men are often stereotyped as greater threats for violence. Thus, not every student who is in a perpetrator-adjacent position stands equally adjacent.

Because students may occupy more than one of these structural positions, the instructor must design learning activities that offer something relevant to each one. An overall goal of the unit is for students to better recognize the role(s) they can play within rape culture, so that they can perform them more conscientiously. In the next section, I describe three approaches to realizing this goal. These approaches are not mutually exclusive; currently I blend all three. Nor do I claim that these three approaches are the only or best ones for this unit. Some readers will find that their own approach fits more closely with one of the three I describe; I'd like to invite such readers to imagine the possibilities of blending in aspects of the other two approaches. Other readers will find that their approach is quite different from any of the ones I discuss below; I hope they will add their respective approaches to the palette I've begun to assemble here and share their approaches in other publications or conferences. This will offer the community of educators against sexual violence the widest range of options for finding the combination that best works for a particular institution, student body, and instructor background.

Getting to the Root Cause: From Sympathy and Structural Analysis to Detoxification

When I first started teaching the course, my approach centered on reading a first-person account by a sexual assault survivor. For two weeks (four 80-minute sessions), we read and discussed a rape memoir, seeking to understand not just the experience and aftermath of the assault, but the totality of the narrator's life and how she re-crafted her own sense of her life as she healed.[3] I refer to this first approach as the "sympathy" approach: when handled conscientiously, it can allow potentially targeted and perpetrator-adjacent students to gain fuller insight into what it is like to experience and survive sexual assault, hearing across the chasm though not bridging it. Being able to learn from a survivor's perspective over multiple sessions and across a longer life-trajectory before and after the assault often creates a visceral sense of the real-ness of assault and, ideally, allows readers to share the author's outrage against sexual violence, which can begin forging a commitment to eradicating it.

Over the several semesters when I used this first approach exclusively, most of the perpetrator-adjacent cis men in the class said that this was the first time they'd ever really been told in-depth what the experience and aftermath of sexual assault were like for the survivor. The potentially targeted students recognized how similar their family members' and friends' recounted experiences were to that of the writer yet also realized aspects of sexual assault they hadn't been familiar with. Only a handful of students identified themselves as survivors (mostly to me only, though some disclosed to the class), and they described how reading the memoir was at times difficult but allowed them to reflect further on their experience. A few survivors said that it felt encouraging to discuss an assault and the topic of sexual violence in a space that was explicitly committed to believing survivors and disrupting sexual violence.

Of the three approaches I've used, this one poses by far the greatest risk for doing more pedagogical harm than good, if one is not constantly vigilant. Focusing on an individual story allows some perpetrator-adjacent students who do not have a developed anti-violence consciousness to disbelieve or blame the survivor and minimize the societal prevalence of sexual assault. This, in turn, can re-traumatize survivors and make potentially targeted students feel again devalued. Moreover, it can be difficult to connect the individual story with macrosocial patterns of sexual violence and its root causes.

That risk led me to develop a second major approach, which I call "structural analysis." Genre-wise, it was a shift to anchoring the unit in the statistics of the Centers for Disease Control and Prevention's (CDC) comprehensive 2010 *National Intimate Partner and Sexual Violence Survey* (NISVS) report and the spirit of the groundbreaking collection *Transforming a Rape Culture*, edited by Emilie Buchwald, Pamela Fletcher, and Martha Roth (2005). The goal here is for students to comprehend the sheer scale of sexual violence and its pervasiveness in every dimension of US society and culture. I use the NISVS report as the statistical foundation for the unit because it is methodologically sound, examines not only rape but also stalking and non-sexual intimate-partner violence, and incorporates at least a basic intersectional perspective. I selected chapters from *Transforming a Rape Culture* (as well as scholarly and popular articles, such as Desmond-Harris 2014) that explain the concept of rape culture and discuss its roots and effects in gendered child-raising practices, media representations (including porn), sports, and religious communities, along with chapters that present feminist movements to dismantle rape culture. Eventually I also added research (Lind 2015) demonstrating that nearly all rape allegations are true, to challenge many perpetrator-adjacent cis men's widely inaccurate estimates of false allegations. More recently, I've incorporated Grigoriadis (2017) and Keehan et al. (2015), excellent resources for students to use in analyzing rape culture specifically in the college context.

What can this approach achieve? First, it encourages perpetrator-adjacent students to move beyond trying to "prove" whether any particular incident was "really" a sexual assault, because it confronts them with the vast number of assaults taking place all the time in our society. I'm able to point out that "even if one-third of these were false allegations" (which nearly all students agree is absurd), the number and rate of assaults would be unacceptable to all students, enabling perpetrator-adjacent students to see sexual violence as a serious problem that must be addressed. This approach also offers survivors a different mental space for thinking about sexual violence, by connecting their experience to that of many other survivors. While the course is not intended as a survivor support group, a number of survivors have commented in their written reflections that this approach allowed them to feel part of a movement to fight back against sexual violence.

The structural analysis approach also allows all students to understand that sexual violence is not an isolated incident, but that each instance emerges from a larger systemic phenomenon. We discuss how multiple social and cultural forces and mechanisms promote and legitimize sexual violence and delegitimize people victimized by it. And we explore how various intersectionally targeted groups—women of color, queer and trans/non-binary people, and working-class people within all targeted groups—are made more vulnerable to sexual violence. The NISVS report and several selections from *Transforming a Rape Culture* also address male-identified victims of sexual violence, which allows us to recognize how sexual violence is inflicted on many cis boys and men as well, complicating our understanding of cis men's relationships to and roles within rape culture: some as victims, some as perpetrators, and some as both.

As this unit kept delving into such complexities, however, I realized that neither the sympathy nor the structural analysis approach brought us to the root cause of sexual violence: dominant constructions of masculinity that intrinsically ground it in a violent relationship with self and others, for which I still find the term "toxic masculinity" effectively evocative.[4] The scholarship on and activism against rape culture already recognized its rootedness in toxic masculinity, but I had focused the unit on the violence that results from toxic masculinity rather than toxic masculinity as its root cause. So I again re-designed the unit, foregrounding toxic masculinity as the core problem while not abandoning the sympathy and structural analysis approaches; presently, the unit covers seven 80-minute sessions, with approximately 20 percent utilizing each of the first two approaches and 60 percent utilizing this third approach. Whereas the sympathy approach focuses on understanding the experiences of specific victims of sexual violence and the structural analysis approach focuses on the experiences of victims in the aggregate and at intersections, the third approach—perhaps best named the "detoxification" approach—asks students to consider what leads cis men to perpetrate most sexual violence in the first place.[5]

We read a number of chapters from Jackson Katz's *The Macho Paradox* (re-issued in 2019 in an expanded edition). This book certainly has its limitations: I especially wish it engaged more substantially with intersectionality throughout, particularly with how class supports male entitlement; and, in its commitment to reforming masculinity rather than queering beyond gender binaries, it does not go far enough. But I have found no book that more directly and accessibly lays it out for undergraduates: eradicating sexual violence means redefining manhood away from toxic masculinity and toward an ethic of care and mutuality. We also read articles that define toxic masculinity (as well as some alternative framings of the concept) and critique how boys are raised in emotionally stunting ways (Bell 2018; Kimmel and Wade 2017; Marcotte 2016; O'Malley 2018). I ask students of all gender identities to reflect on ways they have witnessed others (or themselves experienced) being inculcated in toxic masculinity; we also trace the myriad social incitements to and celebrations of toxic masculinity that face us at every phase of life in our society.

One significant challenge of this approach is finding effective strategies to help students recognize the largely invisible ways in which they can participate in or enable toxic masculinity. For instance, most of the straight cis women in the course are close friends or potential sexual partners with straight cis men and actively share a college social life with them.[6] Within that social world, they have capacities to uphold (or at least not contest) the value of toxic masculinity or, alternatively, to encourage a different kind of masculinity. To make this complex opportunity apparent, at one point I ask everyone in the course to anonymously write down three qualities they look for in a man they want to be sexual partners (or close friends, as appropriate) with. I gather the slips of paper and write all the qualities on the board. Then I ask the class to identify which qualities are directly linked with toxic masculinity, which ones have resonances with it, and which ones directly challenge or undermine it. Each time I've done this activity, the vast majority of qualities are either directly linked or have resonances with toxic masculinity, which leads us to discuss ways people of all genders can be drawn into tacitly enabling toxic masculinity without intending to. A concomitant challenge, however, is to be absolutely clear that the primary responsibility for holding cis men accountable to counter-toxic standards of masculinity lies with other cis men, while also mobilizing the impact cis women can have as accomplices in this project. To that end, the unit involves a number of activities through which students of all gender identities imagine together how they can encourage a transformation of masculinity in their lives and in society as a whole. For example, the preparatory assignment for several days in the unit asks students to identify facts, concepts, and perspectives in the readings that they would want all the men at our school to reflect on. This exercise encourages students to treat the readings as resources for engaging their peers and to imagine what kinds of conversations would be constructive. We watch a widely shared YouTube video about consent (May 2015) and imagine how it could be used in freshman seminar to educate students on this topic. And the unit's concluding activity involves collectively designing a week-long camp for middle school boys that fosters healthy masculinity. We discuss how we think "healthy masculinity" is best defined and then divide into small groups, each focused on a different element of our definition. Groups brainstorm different ideas for camp activities that would allow participants to practice each element of healthy masculinity and reflect on how that element differs from socially prevalent ideas about masculinity. All of these activities ask students to think of themselves as sharing in the power to re-shape masculinity away from its present toxicity toward respect and care for others' bodily integrity and emotional wellness—as well as their own.

Reflecting on One's Pedagogical Context

In conclusion, I offer questions that instructors may find useful for reflecting on their goals for a unit on dismantling rape culture. The first three apply to any approach one might use for the unit, while the last two are particularly apt if one makes countering toxic masculinity a main theme of the unit.

1. *What is the typical mix of students in your course?*
   Remembering that demographics alone do not determine the learning needs of students for a unit on dismantling sexual violence, instructors should be aware of the proportions of students in the three structural positions I've

highlighted, while recognizing any additional pedagogically relevant (and possibly overlapping) positions their students may hold within rape culture.

2. *What kind of work is your institution doing (or not doing) to disrupt and prevent sexual violence?* How widely is this issue even discussed on campus (among students and in programs involving students and faculty/staff)? Among potentially targeted groups, what are perceptions regarding the prevalence of sexual violence and the institution's effectiveness in disrupting and preventing it? Where do students perceive that the institution is concretely addressing (or failing to address) the issue? Have there been any incidents in recent years that shape ongoing discussions within the student body about sexual violence? Such questions allow an instructor to understand the primary social world in which students encounter sexual violence and its sustaining culture, which shapes the interests and questions students bring to the unit and often implicitly constrains how students are able to think about sexual violence at the start of the unit.

3. *What kinds of conversations do you want your students to be able to have with their peers as a result of the unit?* Students who complete the unit will have thought more intentionally and critically about sexual violence than the majority of their peers and social circles, allowing them to play different roles in future conversations with their peers. Thus, an instructor should think carefully about what kinds of role(s) they want to prepare their students for in these conversations: rememberer of survivors, poser of previously unconsidered questions, summoner to re-imagination, awakener of conscience for those in similar structural positions, inciter of coalitions across structural positions, and many others. Each of these roles requires a distinct set of not only intellectual skills but also interpersonal ones, and the unit should provide activities that allow students to practice them, even if only in miniature.

4. *By what methods do you want your students to be able to "call in" the cis men in their lives to reflect on the toxic masculinity in which they were formed?* Cis men can't choose not to be born into and shaped by toxic masculinity,

nor can they determine the child-rearing strategies of the adults who raised them. So if cis men are to become active agents in undoing toxic masculinity both within themselves and among their peers, they will need mental pathways that invite them to reconsider things they've always taken for granted about who they're supposed to be and why. Our students need to know how to ask open-ended questions that get cis men talking about the messages they received growing up concerning what makes a "real man," how those messages feel constraining, and the differences between, to use Michael Kimmel's distinction, what makes a "real man" and what makes a "good man."

5. *What strategies do you want your students to be able to use to incentivize the cis men in their lives to become agents of transforming masculinity?* Those of us who have struggled against the power of cis men's toxic masculinity for all our lives are tired of it, and the idea that we must do yet more work to try to get cis men to *want* to undo toxic masculinity can very justifiably induce resentment. But de-programming oneself from any cultural formation inculcated through childhood and culture is extremely difficult, time-consuming, and often painful, and shame is not an effective way to encourage people to do it. Instead, people must feel supported, allowed to make and grow from mistakes, and enticed with the excitement of a more meaningful and freer way of living. Because most sexual violence is committed by cis men steeped in toxic masculinity, to palpably decrease sexual violence requires a massive number of cis men recognizing that another masculinity is livable, more liberated, and more fulfilling. Thus, we must cultivate in our students the proficiency to both help their cis men friends come to this recognition and encourage their experimentation with counter-toxic masculinities.

Notes

1 With love and ever-abiding admiration, I dedicate this essay to feminist practical theologian Dr. Mary Elizabeth Moore, who taught me so much of what I strive for in feminist-liberationist pedagogy.

2   I apply the concept of "brave space" rather than "safe space"; see Arao and Klemens (2013).
3   At the time, we read Alice Sebold's *Lucky* (1999), which I'd chosen because it explored these aspects effectively and accessibly. Yet it is also the story of a middle-class White woman assaulted by a working-class Black man previously unknown to her, which risked reinforcing both the misconception of sexual assault as mostly committed by strangers and racist tropes of Black men as aggressors (myths that I worked to debunk in the classroom while honoring the truth of Sebold's survivor story). If this approach were still the primary organization of the unit, I would now assign Chanel Miller's *Know My Name* (2019). Currently I assign the chapter on sexual violence (chap. 9) in Wade (2017) and selections from several chapters in Grigoriadis (2017).
4   Michael Kimmel, a preeminent scholar of masculinity, has moved away from using the term (Kimmel and Wade 2017). For an examination of using "toxic masculinity" when teaching African texts, see Hewett's essay in this volume.
5   This approach could just as accurately (plus alliteratively) be called the "sissification" approach, because the kind of rebuilt masculinity we imagine in the unit requires taking on qualities that, in my students' gender-traditionalist Southern childhoods, were associated with "sissies" or similar masculinity-policing terms. Although using that term in class would cost me too much credibility, the challenge remains to create pathways that encourage students to queer the gendered world they make with their peers, even if they don't identify as queer (see Jakobsen 1998).
6   I emphasize cis women here not to exclude trans women, but to acknowledge that, due to patriarchy and heteronormativity, cis women have much greater influence on cis men in the social-sexual worlds they share.

Works Cited

Arao, Brian, and Kristi Clemens (2013), "From Safe Spaces to Brave Spaces: A New Way to Frame Dialogue around Diversity and Social Justice," in Lisa M. Landreman (ed.), *The Art of Effective Facilitation: Reflections from Social Justice Educators*, 135–50, Sterling, VA: Stylus.

Bell, Laura (2018), "Guys Tell Us about Their Struggles with Toxic Masculinity," *Vice* website. Available online: https://www.vice.com/en_us/article/gympmx/guys-tell-us-about-their-struggles-with-toxic-masculinity.

Buchwald, Emilie, Pamela Fletcher, and Martha Roth (2005), *Transforming a Rape Culture*, rev. edn., Minneapolis, MN: Milkweed Editions.
Centers for Disease Control and Prevention (2010), *The National Intimate Partner and Sexual Violence Survey (NISVS)*, Atlanta, GA: Centers for Disease Control. Available online: https://www.cdc.gov/violenceprevention/datasources/nisvs/index.html.
Desmond-Harris, Jenée (2014), "9 Myths about Sexual Assault," *Vox* website. Available online: http://www.vox.com/2014/12/6/7342971/rape-myths-sexual-assault.
Grigoriadis, Vanessa (2017), *Blurred Lines: Rethinking Sex, Power & Consent on Campus*, New York: Houghton Mifflin Harcourt.
Jakobsen, Janet R. (1998), "Queer Is? Queer Does? Normativity and the Problem of Resistance," *Gay and Lesbian Quarterly* 4 (4): 511–36.
Katz, Jackson (2019), *The Macho Paradox: Why Some Men Hurt Women and How All Men Can Help*, rev. edn., Naperville, IL: Sourcebooks.
Keehan, Alyssa, Emily Caputo, Hillary Pettegrew, and Melanie Bennett (2015), *Confronting Campus Sexual Assault: An Examination of Higher Education Claims*, Bethesda, MD: EduRisk Solutions. Available online: http://www.ncdsv.org/ERS_Confronting-Campus-Sexual-Assault_2015.pdf.
Kimmel, Michael and Lisa Wade (2017), "Ask a Feminist: Michael Kimmel and Lisa Wade Discuss Toxic Masculinity," *Signs* journal blog. Available online: http://signsjournal.org/kimmel-wade-toxic-masculinity.
Lind, Dara (2015), "What We Know about False Rape Allegations," *Vox* website. Available online: http://www.vox.com/2015/6/1/8687479/lie-rape-statistics.
Marcotte, Amanda (2016), "Overcompensation Nation: It's Time to Admit That Toxic Masculinity Drives Gun Violence," *Salon* website. Available online: http://www.salon.com/2016/06/13/overcompensation_nation_its_time_to_admit_that_toxic_masculinity_drives_gun_violence.
May, Emmeline (2015), "Tea Consent." Available online: http://www.youtube.com/watch?v=oQbei5JGiT8.
Miller, Chanel (2019), *Know My Name: A Memoir*, New York: Viking.
O'Malley, Harris (2018), "What Is Toxic Masculinity?" Available online: https://www.youtube.com/watch?v=z_fgOibd6U0.
Sebold, Alice (1999), *Lucky*, New York: Scribner.
Wade, Lisa (2017), *American Hookup: The New Culture of Sex on Campus*, New York: Norton.

18

Theorizing "Toxic" Masculinity across Cultures and Nations:

The Case of Achebe's *Things Fall Apart*

Heather Hewett

Published in 1958 and with more than 20 million copies sold, *Things Fall Apart* frequently appears on syllabi in English departments around the world. Indeed, as Simon Gikandi argues, it is "the one work of postcolonial literature that almost every student of English is bound to encounter at one time or another, often in high school, and most certainly in college and university" (2009: 297). I first taught the novel to high school students in 1993, and as a college professor I have taught it multiple times—initially in a course on postcolonial literature, and more recently in a "transnational literature" class focusing on African literatures in English. In fall 2019, the first time I had taught the novel since Alyssa Milano's reignition of the #MeToo movement, I was struck by my students' immediate and ubiquitous assessment of the main character, Okonkwo, as suffering from "toxic" masculinity. Quite a few students were vocal about the troubling nature of Okonkwo's physical violence—he beats his wives (Achebe 1994: 29, 38), his son (151–2), and shoots at (though misses) one of his wives (39); he participates in the killing of an adopted son (61); he beheads a colonial messenger (204); and at the end, he commits an unthinkable crime by killing himself. (Another violent act, the shooting of a fellow clan member, occurs accidentally [124].) Although the novel focuses on Okonkwo's rejection of everything "feminine" in his construction of his own masculine identity, I'd never before considered the diagnosis of toxic masculinity. While it felt accurate, it also seemed not quite right—how could a term that gained popularity in the twenty-first-century United States be applied to a novel set in late nineteenth-century Igboland and written by an African author on the eve of Nigerian independence?

My students' reaction felt like a palpable shift, one that created an opening for conversations about gendered and interpersonal violence. But while I'd had similar conversations in other classrooms about violence in different texts, I found myself hesitating. I realized that in my years of teaching the novel, I had shied away from talking about these violent incidents. In my courses that included the novel, students had spent time learning about and dismantling racist stereotypes about Africa, both during colonialism and in the present, and I had not wanted to reanimate these stereotypes, particularly given how many readers tend to approach the novel as historically and ethnographically accurate. But in so doing, might I have shut down important conversations? And what messages about violence and silence had I unwittingly sent to my students, some of whom may well have experienced or witnessed domestic and interpersonal violence themselves?

This essay interrogates whether "toxic" masculinity is a proper diagnosis for Okonkwo and lays out strategies for teachers to situate *Things Fall Apart* in discussions about gendered violence and masculinity across the borders of time, nation, and culture.[1] I draw from literary critical and pedagogical scholarship on gender in Chinua Achebe's work, as well as interdisciplinary scholarship on African masculinities. Given how few critics have written about how to approach discussions about Okonkwo's violent masculinity in the classroom, I hope this perspective will contribute to scholarly conversations about the "great African novel" (Franklin 2008).

Existing Approaches to Teaching *Things Fall Apart*

Like many instructors, I teach Achebe's novel using a mixture of historical, postcolonial, textual, and feminist approaches. As a college instructor in the United States, I am aware that many if not most of my students have never read a novel authored by an African writer (or studied African history), so I spend some time on basic information (the geography of the continent; the names of its nations; its diverse range of cultures and languages). We reflect on the impact of imperialism, colonialism, slavery, and racism on the production of knowledge about Africa and, similar to Bernth Lindfors's approach (2011), unpack racist Western stereotypes. This sets up Achebe's writing of *Things Fall Apart* and his own attacks on the misrepresentations of the colonial novel and "colonialist criticism," as he called it.[2]

In situating the novel in a postcolonial framework, my teaching takes what has been the dominant critical approach to the novel since the 1980s (Okunoye 2010: 51). However, like many other instructors, I also highlight how readings of the novel have changed over time, how Achebe draws from both Western literary and Igbo oral traditions, and how his style (such as his use of short sentences without subordinating clauses) represents the experience of living in an oral society.[3] Most pertinent to this essay, I conduct class discussions on Okonkwo and gender in the novel. To support our discussions, I often assign several critical essays in the Norton edition. Because only two selections directly address gender, and one of these, an essay by Rhonda Cobham, is more easily accessible to students, I tend to assign her piece.

Cobham helps students think about the particularity of Okonkwo's character. She distinguishes between Okonkwo's "limited personal understanding of physical ascendancy as courage and his equation of courage with masculinity" and the "much richer and more complex set of values available to his clan as a whole" (2009: 514). Cobham further argues that Achebe's portrayal of Igbo women is "selective" (519): women at the time would have had more access to political power than they have in the novel, and this "omission from the narrative leaves us with no example of female authority within the Igbo social structure that is not compatible with traditional Western ideals of femininity as nurturing, ornamental or in need of protection" (519). This misrepresentation is only an issue, she argues, if "his representation of the past" becomes a "substitute for the reality which, inevitably, is far more complex than one novel could hope to make it" (520). While Cobham's point—that the narrative is constructed—is made by other critics as well,[4] most students understand Cobham's clear argument, and the danger of ethnographic readings more broadly, after reading her essay.

If Cobham's essay invites a more nuanced understanding of Achebe's representation of gender, it simultaneously shuts down opportunities to talk with students about their visceral, affective reactions to the novel. In order to make her point about how readers often conflate "lived and imagined realities" (512), she begins with two anecdotes illustrating different misreadings: the first, a moment when a white female student declares that *Things Fall Apart* is "sexist," and the second when a Nigerian female student declares that another novel (Buchi Emecheta's *The Joys of Motherhood*) is inauthentic because it does not represent Igbo women in the same way as *Things Fall Apart* (510–12). While very different reactions, Cobham argues that both share an assumption: writers have a "duty" to represent a "truly objective, unbiased version of traditional life" without considering the imaginative "preoccupations and perspectives" of the writer himself (512). But this argument fails to take seriously the legitimate experiences of readers, and for my purposes here, the charge of sexism.

While Cobham accurately points out that the charge of "sexism" usually means that "Western student readers [...] find Okonkwo misogynist" (511–2), she goes on to dismiss this claim. She observes that this student finds the character's "viciousness" to be a "more vivid travesty of human rights than the action of the District Commissioner in the novel, when he enjoins the [jailers] to treat with dignity the elders whom he has just tricked, humiliated and imprisoned" (immediately after which the jailers proceed to humiliate and physically abuse the elders [512]). Cobham accurately points out that focusing on Okonkwo's violent masculinity to the exclusion of the violence of colonialism misses the point of the novel; and yet, I am not so sure that my students actually view these two scenes in the "human rights" hierarchy she describes. Furthermore, her dismissive characterization of Okonkwo's domestic violence as "a *petty* viciousness" (my emphasis), and her argument that the violence of colonialism trumps Okonkwo's violence, forecloses a serious, intersectional discussion about interpersonal violence.

The existing pedagogical literature reveals a similar inattention to the relationship between gender and violence in *Things Fall Apart*.[5] In six edited collections that include essays on teaching or were designed with teachers and students in mind, plus the Norton Critical Edition, only four authors focus their analysis on gender, and of these only Cobham's essay engages pedagogy.[6] Literary journals offer little more. The main article on this topic, authored by the renowned historian Nwando Achebe, describes an "African-centered and female-centered" reading of the novel grounded in history (2002: 122). Achebe draws attention to elements of the text that we might miss—such as the important role of "the female principle" seen in deities such as Ani, the earth goddess—which helps to ground the reader's understanding of gender in Igbo spirituality and shows how the novel provides a "cautionary narrative" about "the dangers of excess, of disregarding the female principle" (139). Like Cobham, Achebe was part of a larger wave of African and African diasporic feminist scholarship beginning in the 1980s that "established that African women were powerful and autonomous historical subjects, and that gender was separate from biological sex, was best understood in the light of other analytic categories such as age/seniority, and wealth, and derived its meaning from geo-cultural and sociopolitical contexts" (Mbah 2019).[7] Eileen Boris explains that this group of scholars provided a much-needed corrective to Western feminist scholarship, particularly in their "questioning of the privileging of gender over other social attributes, especially age, lineage, kinship, and wealth, thus complicating understandings of 'intersectionality'" (2007: 192). Achebe's and Cobham's essays both provide these correctives, but neither focuses on how readers should understand acts of violence in the novel. Picking up where they left off, this chapter suggests methods of helping students talk about masculinity and violence in *Things Fall Apart*.

Theorizing Gender and Violence in the Classroom

I always begin by asking my students to define the term "gender," and I then share with them a definition from the field of gender studies: a social category that one is given by society, usually at birth. While Western societies have historically conceptualized gender as being organized in a dual sex-gender system (which equates sex with gender and sexuality), this is not always the case across Africa, and certainly not for the Igbo. Despite the rigid sex-gender-sexuality system in the novel, scholarly research beginning with Ifi Amadiume's *Male Daughters, Female Husbands* (1987) has shown that the Igbo culture had a more flexible system of gender.

Given the ways in which masculinity and femininity are intertwined in *Things Fall Apart*, I usually begin our discussion of the novel by posing the following questions to students. This can be done in short writing assignments outside of class or during in-class discussion:

- What does the text show us about masculinity? How do different characters define, enact, and perform their masculinity? (This occurs in both positive and negative ways—that is, what qualities and actions constitute masculinity, and what qualities and actions are set in opposition to masculinity?)
- What does the text show us about femininity? How do different characters define, enact, and perform their femininity?
- Pick a relationship. How is it inflected or defined by gender? What other elements define it?
- What does the text show us about the interactions between gender and power?

While the discussion usually begins with Okonkwo, other male characters are also important to consider, such as Okonkwo's father, Unoka, and their relationship; his son, Nwoye, and their relationship; his friend, Obierika, and their relationship; the ancestral spirits, the *egwugwu*; and the District Commissioner. So, too, with female characters: students should consider not only Ekwefi and her relationship with her husband, Okonkwo, but also her relationship with his other wives; their daughter, Ezinma, and her relationship with both parents; and the priestess, Agbala. It is also important to prod students to come up with examples of how various characters are gendered female as a way of designating them as weak, a concept brought up by the term *agbala* (meaning "women and untitled men," and used for Unoka); this feminizing would also include the missionary Mr. Brown, and the Umuofians at the end, when they refuse to fight the British colonizers.

After finishing the novel, I would ask a more open-ended question: how does *Things Fall Apart* produce gender outside of the text? Cobham's anecdote about the Nigerian female student's reaction provides one example of how the novel can inform images of precolonial African femininity. How else might *Things Fall Apart* produce understandings of gender in its readers worldwide?

In my experience, several issues may come up during these discussions:

1. **Cultural relativism.** While students tend to be quite willing to critique Okonkwo, they may shy away from judgments about cultural practices among the Igbo, despite the fact that they are talking about a novel. If this hesitation comes up, it is worth naming this reluctance as "cultural relativism" and asking: where is the line between cultural respect and silence about harmful practices? Clearly we should steer clear of cultural condescension and the "imperial feminism" that has characterized Western feminism for several centuries (Hawkesworth 2018: 56–7), yet feminists and womanists throughout Africa, and in Nigeria specifically, have long worked to end violence and other injustices in their communities. What might solidarity with their efforts look like? (It is also worth noting that Achebe himself most likely experienced complex feelings about the Igbo; as Gikandi puts it, his novel presents an "African perspective […] without romanticizing the African past" [2009: 299]).

2. **Colonial and interpersonal violence.** While these two kinds of violence occur on very different scales, a feminist reading of the text invites us to see them as connected.[8] Both require that individuals in positions of dominance refuse to care for others and inflict harm—bodily, psychologically, culturally, spiritually, and structurally. Here, I find Tom Digby's philosophical exploration of "warrior" masculinity helpful. Digby provides a comparative view of "militaristic" societies

that helps to explain not only Okonkwo's masculinity but also the District Commissioner's (2014: 7). For a man to be an effective warrior, Digby writes, "he must be able to focus selectively, and sometimes suspend altogether, the capacity to care about the suffering of others, but also his own suffering. In short, he must be emotionally tough" (54). He later observes that the "pursuit of the ideal of warrior masculinity radically individualizes a man" (72), precisely what happens to Okonkwo. Posing questions about how warrior masculinity functions in the text can also be expanded to a discussion of contemporary warrior masculinities, including their manifestation in the United States,[9] although it is essential to identify the distinct differences between these societies and the radically different scale and degree of harm their masculinities can inflict.

3. **Is *Things Fall Apart* sexist? Is Achebe?** Students may question how the text views various characters—for example, how it sees Okonkwo's violence—and the Igbo more generally. Literary scholars have debated this point for decades. Ato Quayson, for example, finds a "richly ambivalent" stance in the narrative (1994: 133). He argues that while *Things Fall Apart* has "foregrounded the masculine in the male-female hierarchy inscribed at the level of the description of events," it has "also opened up the hierarchy to a subtle interrogation of its values, even if ultimately leaving it intact" (131). In this way, he argues, the text reveals that "its own realism is a construction traversed by both sensitivity and ambivalence" (133).

Others disagree. Florence Stratton finds no such ambivalence: she argues that while the novel may critique colonialism, it fails to critique patriarchy: "what he [Achebe] advocates is not a dismantling of the structures of male domination but the incorporation into the male personality of qualities conventionally associated with the feminine" (1994: 37). Achebe may have been motivated to debunk the racism in the work of colonial writers such as Joseph Conrad, but he fails to bring full humanity to African women. Ultimately, she charges, "the representation of pre-colonial society as governed entirely by men" legitimizes the process "whereby women were excluded from post-colonial politics and public affairs" (27). Needless to say, several scholars have disagreed with Stratton's perspective, including a wide-ranging critique by Obioma Nnaemeka (2003). Instructors can highlight these contrasting critical perspectives by providing students with relevant quotations on a handout and assigning some of these articles, including Achebe's own compelling analysis of racism in his essay about *Heart of Darkness* (1990). Those students who find evidence of sexism in *Things Fall Apart* may ask, should we not apply Achebe's logic, which leads him to argue against reading Conrad's racist novel, to his own sexist one? I would ask these students to consider what anti-racist and anti-sexist actions in relation to Achebe's novel we might take: should we foreground these conflicts, as I am suggesting in this essay, or cease reading these texts altogether? What might be the risks and benefits of each approach?

Textual pairings can provide another way to address this question. Many writers have responded to *Things Fall Apart* in their own work, including several contemporary Nigerian authors, and pairing these texts with Achebe's novel suggests alternative narratives about gender and violence. Several texts have directly "written back" to Achebe's novel—for example, Chimamanda Ngozi Adichie's *Purple Hibiscus* (2004) and "The Headstrong Historian" (2008)—whereas others imagine contemporary characters with "complex, alternative masculinities," such as Chris Abani's *Graceland* (2004) (Etter-Lewis 2010: 168). These textual pairings provide rich juxtapositions of gender representations as well as new questions and insights in their own right about identity, violence, and power.

Understanding African Masculinities

Contextualizing Okonkwo's masculinity in contemporary research on African masculinities, as Gwendolyn Etter-Lewis (2010) does, adds another important dimension to students' frameworks for understanding how the novel conceptualizes gender and violence.

Over the last few decades, the growth of masculinity studies has led to better understanding of the "evolution and devolution of women's and men's sociopolitical power as synchronous and mutually constitutive historical processes" (Mbah 2019). Using concepts from this field can equip students with a more specific vocabulary with which to approach the text and model interdisciplinary modes of engaging with literature.

An overview of some of the relevant research on precolonial and colonial Igbo masculinities can deepen and complicate discussions about *Things Fall Apart*. Some of the following points could be made in a brief lecture or handout for students, providing alternative concepts for talking about masculinity in *Things Fall Apart*:

1. Among the seventeenth-century Igbo, there were two dominant masculinities: "martial" and "agrarian" (Mbah 2019). Both were "hegemonic" masculinities—masculinities that were "dominant in society, established the cultural ideal for what it was to be a man, silenced other masculinities, and combated alternative visions of masculinity" (Morrell and Ouzgane 2005: 4)—and both were linked to wealth and social standing. These qualities were in turn measured by "the number of yams" a man possessed; and because "yam ownership was the privilege of warriors, and *ufiem* [hegemonic masculinity] was an insurance against dispossession, martial and agrarian masculinities became mutually constitutive" (Mbah).

2. Colonization led to a "bolstering of African patriarchy" (Mbah). Between the eighteenth and nineteenth centuries, wealth became masculinized as a result of African slavery, colonialism, the Atlantic slave trade, and missionary evangelism (Mbah). As a result, the emergence of "Big Man Masculinity," with a new emphasis on "wealth-based sociopolitical differentiation" and the control of people and resources, became a new form of hegemonic masculinity (Mbah). Although some women participated in this form of masculinity, these changes "largely empower[ed] men, and marginaliz[ed] women" (Mbah).

3. Age is also an important vector of identity, and some scholars use the concept of "senior masculinity," which also

changed with European influence. Boris observes that "[c]olonialism particularly exacerbated generational struggles, as between 'senior men,' considered social fathers, and 'junior' men" (2007: 199). Miescher and Lindsay go so far as to use this concept to explain Okonkwo's death: he "kills himself because his masculinity, based on his identity as a senior man, has been challenged by new structures of authority and power" (2003: 1).
4. Additional changes came in the late nineteenth and early twentieth centuries. Western education, colonial wage labor, and Christian leadership led to some African men achieving "Big Man Masculinity" through working in the colonial enterprise (Mbah). This in turn produced more male privilege, as women did not have the same access to these institutions.

In presenting this information, I would frame it as follows: these concepts may help us explore how the novel represents "divergent, conflicting constructions of 'maleness'" in the novel (Jeyifo 1993: 855). We should use these ideas about masculinity as literary critics, not as sociologists; they are not a "diagnosis," but rather tools with which to open up the text and our relationship to it.

I would then pose the following questions for class discussion: how are the concepts of "martial" and "agrarian" masculinities, and "Big Man" and "senior" masculinities, helpful for understanding what Okonkwo does and thinks? What is the relationship of these forms of masculinity to physical harm and war? to the accumulation of wealth and the acquisition of social status? How do these terms describe other titled men in the clan? other men (such as the jailers at the end)? Whom do they not describe?

Research also shows that masculinity is marked by multiplicity— that is, in addition to hegemonic masculinity, there are "complicit, marginal, and subordinate" masculinities (Morrell and Ouzgane 2005: 16). In the case of Africa, the existence of both colonial and indigenous systems of gender has resulted in more than one hegemonic masculinity (Miescher and Lindsay 2003: 3). These insights can help frame questions about other characters: how can we describe the masculinity of Obierika, Nwoye, and Unoka? How does Okonkwo view and treat these forms of masculinity? Whose masculinity is silenced? Whose masculinity is more resilient or powerful?

What about Toxic Masculinity?

At the time of this writing, toxic masculinity possesses a particular explanatory power. Its meaning in current usage conveys the "poisonous" and "harmful" nature of a masculinity that engages in violence, dominance, and misogyny, and whose expression is harmful not only to others but also to the one who embodies it. With roots in the US mythopoetic men's movement in the 1980s and 1990s, the wider adoption of the term in the media and in feminist circles has come as a result of its intersections with the growing field of masculinity studies and the #MeToo movement (Boise 2019; Salter 2019). As such, it is not tied to any particular sociological, anthropological, historical, or political study. Not surprisingly, the term has its critics. Michael Salter observes that toxic masculinity provides "an appealingly simple diagnosis" because it assumes that "the causes of male violence and other social problems are the same everywhere, and therefore, that the solutions are the same as well" (2019). Similarly, Sam de Boise argues against "falling too easily into ready-made typologies which provide reductive answers to wider problems" (2019: 150). Boise makes the further case that "toxic masculinity" is racialized:

> At worst, however, much like the concept of "hypermasculinity," toxic masculinity risks racialising a concept with its roots already deeply founded in colonialism. Evaluative accusations of being "too" masculine are more commonly directed toward men of colour, resting as they do on assumptions that the "ideal" is the attributes most commonly discursively linked to white, cisgendered, heterosexual, bourgeois and able-bodied men in the West. Men of colour, by contrast, are frequently judged as "too masculine" or "not masculine enough."
> (Boise 2019: 149)

Such critiques of toxic masculinity should give those of us teaching African literature pause. If a student uses this term again, I will provide its history—as I have done with African masculinities—and then pose the question: do you think this is a useful concept for reading this novel, or not? I can think of no better exercise than examining the politics of knowledge production as a class when discussing a novel that asks us to think about who gets to tell whose story. As we grapple with understanding expressions of violence in the text and their relationship to culture and gender, we must think about our own language, lest we commit a secondary violence in the names we attach to the worlds others have created for us to experience.

Notes

1 Also see Jeremy Posadas's chapter on toxic masculinity in this volume.
2 "Colonialist Criticism" was first delivered as a speech in 1974 and subsequently collected in *Hopes and Impediments* (Achebe 1990). See also "An Image of Africa: Racism in Conrad's *Heart of Darkness*" in the same volume.
3 See JanMohammed (2009) and Achebe (1975).
4 See, for example, Quayson (1994), Stratton (1994), Gikandi (2009), and Snyder (2008).
5 Although outside the scope of this essay, high school teaching materials are equally unhelpful in advising teachers about how to enable students to grapple with violence and masculinity in the novel.
6 Cobham's essay (like several others) is reprinted multiple times. I examined four collections focused on *Things Fall Apart*: *Chinua Achebe's Things Fall Apart: 1958–2008* (Whittaker 2011), *Chinua Achebe's Things Fall Apart* (Whittaker and Msiska 2007), *Chinua Achebe's Things Fall Apart: A Casebook* (Okpewho 2003), and *Approaches to Teaching Achebe's Things Fall Apart* (Lindfors 1991). I also examined two collections on teaching African literature, each with one essay about *Things Fall Apart*: *Teaching the African Novel* (Desai 2009) and *African Novels in the Classroom* (Hay 2000).
7 Also see Morrell and Ouzgane (2005).
8 This is particularly true for Global South feminisms; see Hall (2014) for an overview, pp. 396–99, and Bennett (2010) for some of ways that African feminists theorize the relationship between colonialism and gendered violence.
9 See Candice Pipes's chapter in this volume, on sexual violence and masculinity in the US military.

Works Cited

Achebe, Chinua (1975), *Morning Yet on Creation Day: Essays*, New York: Anchor Books/Doubleday.

Achebe, Chinua (1990), *Hopes and Impediments: Selected Essays*, New York: Anchor Books.

Achebe, Chinua (1994), *Things Fall Apart*, New York: Anchor Books.

Achebe, Nwando (2002), "Balancing Male and Female Principles: Teaching about Gender in Chinua Achebe's *Things Fall Apart*," *Ufahamu: African Studies Journal* 29 (1): 121–43.

Amadiume, Ifi (1987), *Male Daughters, Female Husbands: Gender and Sex in an African Society*, London: Bloomsbury.

Bennett, Jane (2010), "'Circles and Circles': Notes on African Feminist Debates around Gender and Violence in the c21," *Feminist Africa* 14, *Rethinking Gender and Violence*: 21–47. Available online: http://www.agi.ac.za/sites/default/files/image_tool/images/429/feminist_africa_journals/archive/14/fa14__entire_journal.pdf (accessed September 11, 2020).

Boise, Sam de (2019), "Editorial: Is Masculinity Toxic?," *NORMA: International Journal for Masculinity Studies*, 14 (3): 147–51. Available online: https://doi.org/10.1080/18902138.2019.1654742 (accessed October 11, 2020).

Boris, Eileen (2007), "Gender after Africa!" in Stephan Miescher, Takyiwaa Manuh, and Catherine M. Cole (eds.), *Africa after Gender?*, 191–204, Bloomington: Indiana University Press.

Cobham, Rhonda (2009), "Problems of Gender and History in the Teaching of *Things Fall Apart*," in Francis Abiola Irele (ed.), *Things Fall Apart: Authoritative Text, Contexts and Criticism*, 510–21, New York: W. W. Norton & Company.

Desai, Gaurav, ed. (2009), *Teaching the African Novel*, New York: The Modern Language Association of America.

Digby, Tom (2014), *Love and War: How Militarism Shapes Sexuality and Romance*, New York: Columbia University Press.

Etter-Lewis, Gwendolyn (2010), "Dark Bodies/White Masks: African Masculinities and Visual Culture in *Graceland*, *The Joys of Motherhood* and *Things Fall Apart*," in Tuzyline J. Allan and Helen N. Mugambi (eds.), *Masculinities in African Literary and Cultural Texts*, 160–77, Banbury, UK and Boulder: Ayebia Clarke Publishing.

Franklin, Ruth (2008), "Chinua Achebe and the Great African Novel," *The New Yorker*, May 26. Available online: https://www.newyorker.com/magazine/2008/05/26/after-empire (accessed September 11, 2020).

Gikandi, Simon (2009), "Chinua Achebe and the Invention of African Literature," in Francis Abiola Irele (ed.), *Things Fall Apart: Authoritative*

Text, Contexts and Criticism, 297–303, New York: W. W. Norton & Company.
Hall, Rebecca Jane (2014), "Feminist Strategies to End Violence against Women," in Rawwida Baksh and Wendy Harcourt (eds.), The Oxford Handbook of Transnational Feminist Movements, 396–418, New York: Oxford University Press. Available online: doi: 10.1093/oxfordhb/9780199943494.013.005 (accessed June 16, 2020).
Hawkesworth, Mary E. (2018), Globalization and Feminist Activism, 2nd edn., Lanham, MD: Rowman & Littlefield Publishers.
Hay, Margaret Jean, ed. (2000), African Novels in the Classroom, Boulder: Lynne Rienner Publishers.
JanMohamed, Abdul ([1984] 2009), "Sophisticated Primitivism: The Syncretism of Oral and Literate Modes in Achebe's Things Fall Apart," in Francis Abiola Irele (ed.), Things Fall Apart: Authoritative Text, Contexts and Criticism, 571–86, New York: W. W. Norton & Company.
Jeyifo, Biodun (1993), "Okonkwo and His Mother: Things Fall Apart and Issues of Gender in the Constitution of African Postcolonial Discourse," Callaloo, 16 (4): 847–58. Available online: https://www.jstor.org/stable/2932213 (accessed October 12, 2020).
Lindfors, Bernth, ed. (1991), Approaches to Teaching Achebe's Things Fall Apart, New York: Modern Language Association of America.
Lindfors, Bernth (2011), "Teaching Things Fall Apart in Texas," in David Whittaker (ed.), Chinua Achebe's Things Fall Apart: 1958–2008, 141–8, Amsterdam: Brill/Rodopi.
Mbah, Ndubueze L. (2019), "African Masculinities," in Thomas Spear et al. (eds.), Oxford Research Encyclopedia of African History, Oxford: Oxford University Press. Available online: https://doi.org/10.1093/acrefore/9780190277734.013.270 (accessed July 21, 2020).
Miescher, Stephan F., and Lisa A. Lindsay (2003), "Introduction: Men and Masculinities in Modern African History," in Lisa A. Lindsay and Stephan F. Miescher (eds.), Men and Masculinities in Modern Africa, 1–29, Portsmouth, NH: Heinemann.
Morrell, Robert, and Lahoucine Ouzgane (2005), "African Masculinities: An Introduction," in Lahoucine Ouzgane and Robert Morrell (eds.), African Masculinities: Men in Africa from the Late Nineteenth Century to the Present, 1–20, New York: Palgrave Macmillan.
Nnaemeka, Obioma (2003), "Nego-Feminism: Theorizing, Practicing, and Pruning Africa's Way," Signs: Journal of Women in Culture and Society, 29 (2): 357–85. Available online: https://doi.org/10.1086/378553 (accessed September 9, 2020).
Okpewho, Isidore, ed. (2003), Chinua Achebe's Things Fall Apart: A Casebook, Oxford: Oxford University Press.

Okunoye, Oyeniyi (2010), "Half a Century of Reading Chinua Achebe's *Things Fall Apart*," *English Studies*, 91 (1): 42–57. Available online: https://doi.org/10.1080/00138380903355189 (accessed September 30, 2020).

Quayson, Ato (1994), "Realism, Criticism, and the Disguises of Both: A Reading of Chinua Achebe's *Things Fall Apart* with an Evaluation of the Criticism Relating to It," *Research in African Literatures*, 25 (4): 117–36.

Salter, Michael (2019), "The Problem with the Term 'Toxic Masculinity,'" *The Atlantic*, February 2. Available online: https://www.theatlantic.com/health/archive/2019/02/toxic-masculinity-history/583411/ (accessed September 11, 2020).

Snyder, Carey (2008), "The Possibilities and Pitfalls of Ethnographic Readings: Narrative Complexity in *Things Fall Apart*," *College Literature*, 35 (2): 154–74.

Stratton, Florence (1994), *Contemporary African Literature and the Politics of Gender*, London and New York: Routledge.

Whittaker, David, ed. (2011), *Chinua Achebe's Things Fall Apart: 1958–2008*. Amsterdam: Brill/Rodopi.

Whittaker, David and Mpalive-Hangson Msiska, eds. (2007), *Chinua Achebe's Things Fall Apart*, London and New York: Routledge.

19

"I said nothing":
Teaching *Corregidora* and Black Women's Relationship to Consent

Carlyn Ferrari

Introduction: Black Women's Bodies as Unconsentable Terrain

In her gripping *New York Times* Op-Ed, poet Caroline Randall Williams writes, "I have rape-colored skin. My light-brown-blackness is a living testament to the rules, the practices, the causes of the Old South. ... I am more than half white, and none of it was consensual" (Williams 2020). Arguing that her body is a living monument of the legacy of enslavement, Williams deftly notes that the origin of her Black womanhood—and Black womanhood in general—is inextricably linked to sexual violence.

Current conversations about consent are indeed urgent and long overdue. However, Black women's lived experiences are often erased because, historically, their bodies have been deemed unconsentable terrain. In order to understand Black women's relationship to consent and sexual assault, their bodies must be situated within the context of enslavement because like colonized territories, Black women's bodies were seen as an exploitable resource.¹ Thus, because Black women's relationship to ideologies of womanhood has always been contested, consent, in reality, is often an unattainable privilege, not a right. In this essay, I position Gayl Jones's 1975 novel, *Corregidora*, as a much-needed entry point into a historicized conversation about Black women's relationship to consent and present strategies for teaching the novel.

Corregidora is fraught with the cyclical nature of sexual assault, domestic violence, and trauma. The novel follows the journey of Ursa Corregidora, a Blues singer who struggles to come to terms with her identity after becoming infertile. Drawing upon the tradition of the neo-slave narrative, Jones grounds Ursa's story in enslavement, so the voices of her maternal female ancestors are present and remind her of her gendered obligation to "make generations" (10). As she narrates her story of trauma and abuse, Ursa reveals that she was often rendered speechless, saying: "I said nothing" (5). What is particularly instructive about this text is that it situates Black womanhood and the Black female body within the context of colonialism and slavery and juxtaposes these histories with Ursa's present in the twentieth century. Ursa's ancestral past haunts her in the present, which Jones represents formally through flashbacks of her maternal ancestors' stories of sexual assault. That Ursa's contemporary lived experiences are nearly identical to her enslaved ancestors' experiences is both striking and telling, as the similarities reveal how Black womanhood is inextricably linked to the aftermath and traumas of slavery and how little has changed for contemporary Black women since the period of enslavement.

Intellectual Well-Being: Brief Notes on Pedagogy

My pedagogy is grounded in a Black feminist framework, so I adhere to bell hooks's advice in *Teaching to Transgress*: "To teach in a manner that respects and cares for the souls of our students is essential if we are to provide the necessary conditions where learning can most deeply and intimately begin" (1994: 13). I heed hooks's imperative by caring for the intellectual well-being of my students. I preface all of my courses by reminding students that learning is an uncomfortable process, noting there is a difference between feeling uncomfortable and feeling unsafe. My goal then is for them to become comfortable with the discomfort that is learning. I realize that this approach raises questions and concerns about trigger warnings, a topic too fraught and varied for me to discuss here. After much trial and error, I have opted to include a statement on my syllabus that serves as the sole trigger warning for the semester, one that I adapt each semester for each class. I also invite students to communicate with me about their specific needs.

I am a Black, cisgender, heterosexual, able-bodied woman who has only taught in predominantly white classrooms and institutions (in Gender Studies and English departments). I name my positionality and institutional contexts to signal that I am acutely aware that my teaching philosophy and the teaching of this text, more specifically, are inextricably linked to the body I occupy and how it is read in the classroom. My approach will not work for everyone and *should* be adapted to meet the specific needs of the instructor and students. However, my aim is to facilitate (1) critical engagement with Black women's lived experiences; (2) a historical understanding of Black women's relationship to consent, one that creates a bridge between the past and the present and helps students to identify the past in the present; (3) a heightened awareness of the relationship between consent and one's positionality/standpoint; and (4) an environment that cares for the intellectual well-being of students and treats Black womanhood and consent with the reverence they deserve.

Historical Context: (Mis)conceptions of Black Womanhood

Our historical context focuses on understanding the myths and stereotypes about Black womanhood that stem from enslavement. Because of this attention to enslavement, I begin with texts that explain how enslaved Black women's bodies were gendered and assign Jennifer Morgan's (1997) article "'Some Could Suckle Over Their Shoulder': Male Travelers, Female Bodies and the Gendering of Racial Ideology, 1500–1700" and Dorothy Roberts's chapter "Reproduction in Bondage" (from *Killing the Black Body: Race, Reproduction, and the Meaning of Liberty*, 1999) before we begin reading the novel.[2] The texts give students the necessary historical understanding of Ursa and her family's obligation to "make generations" (10). Morgan's essay delineates how Black women's bodies were mythologized and deemed grotesque and bestial during the early modern period. Roberts's essay reveals how enslaved Black women were valued and governed by their reproductive abilities while simultaneously denied reproductive agency. Together, these texts contextualize and historicize *Corregidora* because they explain how slavery inscribed meaning into and gendered Black women's bodies. Morgan's and Roberts's texts represent the fields of history and sociology, respectively, so this context is historical and interdisciplinary. Moreover, they illustrate how the very notion of Black womanhood was predicated on a denial of humanity, which rendered Black women both deviantly sexualized and beyond the realm of consent.

The charge to "make generations" (10) is juxtaposed with Ursa's infertility, a fact Ursa shares with the reader just a few paragraphs into the novel. She leads the reader to believe an accidental fall led to her hysterectomy (we later learn her then-husband, Mutt, pushed her down the staircase), with a brevity that is both chilling and suspicious: "The doctors in the hospital said my womb would have to come out" (4). To help students understand how Ursa is still bound by historical notions of Black womanhood, I call their attention to the ambiguity surrounding her hysterectomy. I ask students what they perceive to be a trick question: *why does Ursa have a hysterectomy?* Indeed, Ursa does fall and suffers a miscarriage, so I am in no way questioning whether she sustained an injury. I am, however, questioning whether she was given the option not to have one. My intention with this line of questioning is to suggest to students that Ursa's brevity might reveal that she does not know why she had to have a hysterectomy. I then direct students to additional passages that raise questions about Black women's reproductive agency.

Ursa's brusqueness becomes increasingly profound when we learn that medical visits have always been fraught for her. Following her post-operative doctor's appointment, Ursa shares what medical visits are like for her as well as an anecdote about her friend, Cat:

"He had me up on the table so he could look at the scar. Every time you go to the doctor they say 'Get up on the table' or 'Take your clothes off and get up on the table.' Somebody ought to say Naw."
"That's what Cat did once. She said the man told her 'Get up on the table.' So she said, 'I told the bastard, Naw, I wasn't getting up on the table. And he didn't make me neither.'"
(21)

It is important to point out to students that Ursa is talking about what *routine* visits are like "every time" for her—and Black women in her community—and the discomfort, frustration, and anger they generate. Ursa's anecdotes cast doubt on whether she consented to her hysterectomy because what we see here is a pattern of Black women's objectification. This pattern is further corroborated when Lurene, a neighbor and community member, quips, "I know womens that's had it out been up by now" (36). What is an attempt to shame Ursa's seemingly slow recovery is actually a revelation of the ubiquity of hysterectomies within this small Black community.[3] In other words, Ursa's case is not exceptional. This discussion of Ursa's reproductive autonomy invites connections to Morgan and Roberts because Ursa's probable ignorance and her disdain for medical appointments are directly related to the gendering of Black women's bodies during enslavement.

The act of bearing children was rooted in perpetuating the institution of slavery, not enslaved Black women's autonomous choices. In other words, enslaved Black women were breeding chattel and "[r]acism created for white slaveowners the possibility of unrestrained reproductive control" (Roberts 1999: 23). The refrain "make generations"—as opposed to "bearing children"—is also indicative of this gendering process that reduced Black women's bodies to vessels of biological reproduction indefinitely. Slavery set the terms through which Black women's reproduction would be (mis)read and (mis)understood. Though enslaved Black women birthed children, they were not mothers; their ability to reproduce was valued only because it guaranteed a replenished workforce. What Ursa and the Black women in her community experience is a continuation of this "unrestrained reproductive control" (Roberts 1999: 23) because her anecdotes signal how contemporary Black women are not viewed as individuals with the right to reproductive autonomy and motherhood. The presence of hysterectomies in Ursa's community also points to the utilitarian motives attached to enslaved Black women's reproduction. In other words, since post-emancipation Black women's children are not valuable, they do not need to be born and Black women do not need to reproduce.

With the foundational, historical context established, I turn to a discussion of why Ursa literally says "nothing."

Saying "Nothing": Critically Analyzing Silence

Our critical analysis focuses on the fact that Ursa reveals that she was often rendered speechless, saying, "I said nothing" (5). The first time Ursa says nothing is shortly after her fall while she is recovering in the home of her boss-turned-love-interest, Tadpole McCormick, and trying to thwart his flirtation (5). That Ursa says "nothing" not only urges us, as readers, to bear witness to her silence and the discomfort it carries but also compels us to say *something* and interrogate the silence to which she and other Black women are bound because their bodies do not matter. Those three words are rife with ambiguity and deeply troubling, especially since Ursa asserts the centrality of her voice by introducing herself as a singer on the first page of the novel: "I sang because it was something I had to do" (3). Ursa's silence reveals a profound vulnerability as a Black woman, a vulnerability, Jones illustrates, that white male capitalist patriarchy has exploited for centuries.

To facilitate a critical discussion that interrogates the relationship between Ursa's silence and Black womanhood, I frame class discussions around such questions as *Why does Ursa say "nothing"? What does saying "nothing" reveal about her positionality as a Black woman and her relationship to consent? How and where do we see misogynoir in Ursa's life?*[4] *Who or what is rendering her speechless?* Through this line of questioning, I want to help students see that Ursa's silence is more than merely willful restraint. Her silence is as systemic as it is personal. We should not interpret her silence as resignation or acceptance, and it is certainly not consent. Rather, it is Ursa's acknowledgment of her marginalized position. Looking back to Morgan's and Roberts's texts, I remind students of how the devaluation of Black women is embedded in the fabric of society. I also point to such current events as the #SayHerName campaign and #MeToo movement founder Tarana Burke's erasure as contemporary examples of how Black Women's voices are both silenced and negated. I want students to question whether Ursa *can* say something and question whether her speech would be valued. In other words, what Ursa might be saying is *I said nothing because I know that nobody will listen to me.*

Forms of Meaning(s): Formal Analysis

Our formal analysis interrogates how the novel demonstrates connections between form and theme. One of the central themes of the novel is the tension between the individual and the generational stories. I direct attention to Jones's multivocal narration that includes Ursa's, her mother's, her grandmother's, and her great-grandmother's voices, which can be difficult to differentiate at times. I ask students, *Is this novel about Ursa or her family? Or both?* I facilitate a discussion of Jones's formal choices and highlight that she draws upon the bildungsroman, Künstlerroman, neo-slave narrative, and Blues novel genres.[5]

To help students understand the genres used, I do interactive board work. After I write a term on the board and provide a definition, I ask students for textual evidence. For example, with "neo-slave narrative," I ask, *Where do we see depictions of slavery in the text?* These questions help students to understand the genre and also identify key aspects of the novel's form. I repeat the same activity with the narration, and I begin by writing Jones's name on the board in parentheses to signal that she is the authorial voice. Rather than tell students who is speaking, I ask, *Who is our narrator? In addition to Ursa, whose voices do we hear? Is it always clear who is speaking?* After each name, I insert a downward-pointing arrow (↓) to illustrate that these voices are embedded in Ursa's narrative. This exercise helps students identify the multiple voices in the text and also visualize how Ursa is both a narrator and her family's historiographer. I explain to students that in addition to telling her own story, Ursa is also telling a Black women's history because her narrative gives insight into what enslavement was like from a Black woman's perspective.

I call attention to Jones's formal ingenuity and also acknowledge the rich legacy of Black women's theoretical savviness and creativity, a legacy that Barbara Christian argues in "The Race for Theory" is a hallmark of writings from people of color:

> For people of color have always theorized—but in forms quite different from the Western form of abstract logic. And I am inclined to say that our theorizing (and I intentionally use the verb rather than the noun) is often in narrative forms, in the stories we create, in riddles and proverbs, in the play with language, because dynamic rather than fixed ideas seem more to our liking. How else have we managed to survive with such spiritedness the assault on our bodies, social institutions, countries, our very humanity?
>
> (1988: 68)

I do not always have time to teach this entire article, so I excerpt this quote to explain that Jones's techniques are a part of a longstanding tradition. I invite students to think about how the aforementioned genres represent the multiple facets of Ursa's Black womanhood and the multiplicity of Black womanhood, more generally. Therefore, the formal structure of the novel mirrors intersectionality. In other words, just as Black women cannot separate their Blackness from their gender, this novel does not easily fit into a single category and is not the narrative of only one Black woman. But just as intersectionality is more than simply identifying and naming the particulars of one's identity, I ask students, *How does Jones's multivocal, multi-generic aesthetic choice create meaning(s)?* Through this question, I invite students to analyze how Jones formally and thematically illustrates that Ursa's past is her present. Just as her ancestors' narratives are inextricably linked to hers and take up literal space in the novel, the (mis)conceptions and narratives of Black womanhood have a material impact and occupy space in Ursa's contemporary life.

Saying Something: Personal Reflection

Throughout the class, I invite various forms of personal reflection, and I often begin each class discussion by asking such questions as *What is your gut reaction today? What passage(s) stood out to you and why?* Corregidora centers Black women's trauma and pain, so it can be a challenging text to read. I incorporate reflective writing into my teaching of this text as a way to create space for students to share their experiences *confidentially*.⁶ I also want them to be mindful, self-aware readers, so I ask students to keep a reading journal in which they share their experience with the text. (While my bias is for these journals to be handwritten, I have had far more success and consistency when they are managed through an online course management system.) These journals are only accessible to me, and they enable me to gauge students' individual engagement with the text and identify broader issues and themes to discuss with the class as a whole. Students are also more inclined to be candid when the performative environment of the classroom is removed, so these journals have been important ways for me, as an instructor, to check in individually with students and learn such vital details as the kind of trigger warnings that a student needs. For Morgan's and Robert's texts, I ask students to respond to the following prompt(s): *Discuss your response to the material. Had you previously heard of these narrative origins around Black bodies? How did you digest the accounts (both visual and narrative) of Morgan's male travelers and the forced breeding that Roberts discusses? What, if anything, stuck out to you in your reading of Morgan's and Roberts's texts? How do you imagine African American women writers might approach these (mis)conceptions of Black womanhood in their fiction?*

I conclude our study of *Corregidora* by assigning a culminating critical reading response. I ask students to craft responses to several guiding questions that synthesize the historical, formal, critical, and personal categories. These questions include: *what does the novel tell us about Black women's lived experiences? How does the novel help us understand Black women's lived experiences in our present day? How has it shaped your understanding? How did Gayl Jones's telling of Ursa's story contribute to your understanding of Black women's experiences? What questions about the text and/or Black feminism do you still have now that you have analyzed it? Why do you think these questions still linger? Did you have any expectations about the journaling assignment? What did you learn about yourself—as a reader, writer, thinker, learner, and etc.— through the journaling assignment?*

A Story to Pass On

While working as an editor for Random House, Toni Morrison selected *Corregidora* for publication, saying, "no novel about any Black woman could ever be the same after this. This girl had changed the terms, the definitions of the whole enterprise" (2008: 109–10). And to extend Morrison's appraisal, conversations about consent cannot be the same after this. Yet *Corregidora* remains curiously understudied.

I was inspired to write this chapter after a powerful class discussion. I noticed one of my students growing visibly frustrated. I invited him to share his thoughts and he said, "Ursa is always saying 'nothing!' I'm not comfortable with that!" I teach literature because it enables us to bear witness to perspectives that are different from our own, perspectives that can—and probably will—make us uncomfortable. The act of bearing witness can be transformative because it compels us to step outside of ourselves and think about whole human experiences that we otherwise would have negated. I insist upon teaching *Corregidora* because it is a text that invites one to think not only about Ursa as a singular character but also about Black women as a whole and the reasons why they say "nothing." It is an essential text for Black women's literary studies and for understanding Black women's relationship to consent. Though I have presented my teaching strategies here, this essay is also an attempt to (re)introduce *Corregidora* into extant critical conversations, especially the ones that take place in the classroom. As educators, this is a story for us to pass on to our students to ensure that Black women's voices are not excluded from such urgent conversations.

Notes

1 For a history of rape during enslavement, see Rachel A. Feinstein (2018), *When Rape Was Legal: The Untold History of Sexual Violence during Slavery*.
2 I have experimented with assigning these texts after the novel, and I have found that discussions are richer and more nuanced when students are given the appropriate context beforehand.

3   For additional readings on medical racism and Black women's reproductive agency, I recommend Chapter 3 of *Killing the Black Body*, "From Norplant to the Contraceptive Vaccine: The New Frontier of Population Control"; Harriet A. Washington (2006), *Medical Apartheid: The Dark History of Medical Experimentation on Black Americans from Colonial Times to the Present*, especially Chapter 8: "The Black Stork: The Eugenic Control of African American Reproduction"; and Linda Villarosa (2018), "Why America's Black Mothers and Babies Are in a Life-or-Death Crisis," *The New York Times*.
4   Dr. Moya Bailey coined the term "misogynoir" in 2010 to describe the specific kind of misogyny that Black women experience because of their race and gender. It is a combination of the words "misogyny" and "noir," the French word for "black." Please see "On Misogynoir: Citation, Erasure, and Plagiarism" by Moya Bailey and Trudy (2018) for a full definition of "misogynoir."
5   For a definition of a "neo-slave narrative," see Valerie Smith (2007), "Neo-Slave Narratives," in *The Cambridge Companion to the African American Slave Narrative*, 168–86. For a definition of a "Blues novel," see Steven C. Tracy (2004), "The Blues Novel," in *The Cambridge Companion to the African American Novel*, 122–38.
6   This type of "confessional writing" places students at ease, so I am careful to note what I am required to report by law and university policy. I also include the appropriate links to campus mental health resources and for reporting misconduct and discrimination.

Works Cited

Bailey, Moya and Trudy (2018), "On Misogynoir: Citation, Erasure, and Plagiarism," *Feminist Media Studies*, 18 (4): 762–8. Available online: https://doi.org/10.1080/14680777.2018.1447395 (accessed January 17, 2020).

Christian, Barbara (1988), "The Race for Theory," *Feminist Studies*, 14 (1): 66–79. Available online: https://doi.org/10.2307/3177999 https://www.jstor.org/stable/3177999 (accessed May 1, 2015).

Feinstein, Rachel A. (2018), *When Rape Was Legal: The Untold History of Sexual Violence during Slavery*, New York: Routledge.

hooks, bell (1994), *Teaching to Transgress: Education as the Practice of Freedom*, New York: Routledge Press.

Hubbard, Shanita (2017), "Russell Simmons, R. Kelly, and Why Black Women Can't Say #MeToo," *New York Times*, December 15. Available online: https://www.nytimes.com/2017/12/15/opinion/russell-simmons-black-women-metoo.html?smid=url-share (accessed July 17, 2020).

Jones, Gayl (1975), *Corregidora*, Boston: Beacon Press.

Morgan, Jennifer (1997), "'Some Could Suckle over Their Shoulder': Male Travelers, Female Bodies, and the Gendering of Racial Ideology, 1500–1700," *The William and Mary Quarterly*, 54 (1): 167–92. Available online: http://www.jstor.org/stable/2953316?origin=JSTOR-pdf (accessed January 15, 2014).

Morrison, Toni (2008), "Toni Morrison on a Book She Loves: Gayl Jones's *Corregidora*," in Toni Morrison and Carolyn C. Denard (eds.), *What Moves at the Margin: Selected Nonfiction*, 108–10, Jackson: University of Mississippi Press.

Roberts, Dorothy (1999), *Killing the Black Body: Race, Reproduction, and the Meaning of Liberty*, 1st edn, New York: Vintage Press.

Smith, Valerie (2007), "Neo-Slave Narratives," in Audrey Fisch (ed.), *The Cambridge Companion to the African American Slave Narrative*, 168–86, Cambridge: Cambridge University Press. Available online: doi:https://doi.org/10.1017/CCOL0521850193.011 (accessed August 8, 2020).

Tracy, Steven C. (2004), "The Blues Novel," in Maryemma Graham (ed.), *The Cambridge Companion to the African American Novel*, 122–38, Cambridge: Cambridge University Press. Available online: doi:10.1017/CCOL0521815746.008 (accessed August 6, 2020).

Washington, Harriet A. (2006), *Medical Apartheid: The Dark History of Medical Experimentation on Black Americans from Colonial Times to the Present*, New York: Harlem Moon Press.

Williams, Caroline Randall (2020), "You Want a Confederate Monument? My Body Is a Confederate Monument," *New York Times*, June 26. Available online: https://www.nytimes.com/2020/06/26/opinion/confederate-monuments-racism.html (accessed July 2, 2020).

Villarosa, Linda (2018), "Why America's Black Mothers and Babies Are in a Life-or-Death Crisis," *New York Times*, April 11. Available online: https://www.nytimes.com/2018/04/11/magazine/black-mothers-babies-death-maternal-mortality.html (accessed July 30, 2020).

20

"Teach as if you aren't afraid of getting fired":
A Queer Survivor's Use of Restorative Justice Circles to Embrace Vulnerability in the Classroom

Sarah Goldbort

I'm struggling really bad with my mental health right now. Before this craziness, I made the choice to wean off all my psych medication. The withdrawals are rough then the stress of the situation just makes it worse. I'm trying desperately to keep up with my students. I guess I'm wondering if it's professional to update my students on my wellbeing as I'm asking them to keep me updated on theirs.
—APRIL 4, 2020: "PANDEMIC PEDAGOGY" *FACEBOOK* GROUP

Concerned with being "professional," this teacher seeks advice about whether to be authentic with her students or keep the personal private. Zaretta Hammond (2015) underscores that teacher-student relationships built on trust and authenticity are central to successful teaching practices. However, what happens when one's authenticity clashes with what it means to be professional? The responses to the above post ranged from "No. Vent here" to "You do not have to give them details. However, you can let them know you are human and that this is a hard transition for you too." Others expressed fear of retaliation from disgruntled students, which could adversely affect job security because of mental health stigmas. Some recognized that students may not have the "right training (and possibly not the right level of maturity) to know how to respond." While it is prudent to consider the *how*, *when*, and *what* in terms of sharing personal information, teachers risk erasing authenticity when we conflate professionalism with adhering to straight, white, male, able-bodied standards.

Brené Brown (2012) asks two questions that are at the heart of my inquiry: "How can you talk about the importance of vulnerability in an honest and meaningful way without being vulnerable? On the other hand, how can you be vulnerable without sacrificing your legitimacy as a researcher?" (12). Fetishizing objectivity reinforces the "personal" as a credibility issue, which "malign[s] embodied, land-based, and spiritual ways of knowing and is wrapped up in the project of white supremacist heteropatriarchal domination" (Edwards and Esposito 2020: 27). In contrast, mindfulness practices can help us "pause, discern, and disrupt" dominant ideologies, which is significant for marginalized groups as "self-healing and wellness is never just an individual thing because WHAT they need to heal from includes structural oppression that targets their whole group" (Berila 2016: 8). Recognizing vulnerability as something "we all share" is particularly important for teaching rape culture because it allows us to reimagine victims[1] as "people whose vulnerability to others has been abused rather than people who [...] let themselves fall prey to a condition (vulnerability) to which the rest of us are supposedly impermeable" (Mardorossian 2014: 15). As a queer survivor of sexual assault, I prioritize creating a safe space to acknowledge our whole selves by utilizing restorative justice circles as a valid form of knowledge production and potential liberation.

As a future high school teacher, I am particularly concerned about the ability to teach without fear of repercussions. Delane

Bender-Slack (2010) found that eighteen of twenty-two social justice secondary education teachers from a midwestern metropolis "reported being oppressed by fear" (192). Fear leads many teachers to address controversial topics behind closed doors or not at all, which may send a message to marginalized students that we value systems of oppression more than those who are oppressed. LGBTQ+ students and trauma survivors are acutely aware of whether or not an environment is safe, so when we openly challenge these systems, we increase the potential for our students to live more fully. In 2012, I realized the value of queer visibility when one of my students revealed in class that he was gay; I knew the risk he was taking, and I supported his vulnerability by replying: "me too." This was the first time I had disclosed my sexuality to anyone, and I saw it as an opportunity to heed hooks's (1994) warning: "Professors who expect students to share confessional narratives but who are themselves unwilling to share are exercising power in a manner that could be coercive" (21). Having never had an "out" teacher myself, I was determined to be visible. Encouragingly, Daniel DellaPosta (2018) found that people who had "at least one gay or lesbian acquaintance" were more likely to exhibit attitude changes toward homosexuality (1). My fear of retribution was lessened because the department chair encouraged us to teach as if we weren't "afraid of getting fired." As a fixed term instructor, I appreciated this institutional support because it allowed me to see vulnerability and fear linked in a way that produces courageous teaching practices rather than hinders them. Depending on one's identity and job security, there are widely different levels of risk and institutional support. I choose to be transparent in order to create a liberating environment for my students: whether instructors are "out" about being a survivor, a feminist, pansexual, depressed, gay, or differently abled—we cannot ignore the power of counternarratives to foster empathy.

In spring of 2020, I used circles in a literature course focused on women writers' representations of sexual assault. This course introduced intersectional feminist theories and history, focusing on the changing definitions of rape and their legal ramifications (or lack thereof). We explored historical accounts of rape in Danielle L. McGuire's history of the civil rights movement, *At the Dark End of the Street: Black Women, Rape, and Resistance* (2010), and fictional accounts in Edwidge Danticat's *Breath, Eyes, Memory* (1994) to make sense of how we use storytelling to understand or escape our environments. There were fifteen students in the class, two of which identified as men. Students ranged from freshmen to seniors and included eight white students, two Chinese students, two Indian students, and three African American students. I implemented restorative justice circles to create a safe place to explore issues related to campus safety that might arise due to the nature of our last text: Chanel Miller's 2019 memoir *Know My Name*, which traces her experience of sexual assault and the trial against her assailant, Brock Turner.

Restorative justice circles are based on indigenous traditions that emphasize the interconnectivity of all living creatures by gathering in a circle to share and heal. Non-indigenous communities have used circles as alternatives to punitive welfare, education, and criminal law systems. Robert Yazzie, a retired chief justice of the Navajo Nation Supreme Court, explains that respect or "k'e" is central to the peacemaking process: "K'e means to restore my dignity, to restore my worthiness" (as qtd. in Mirsky). In adopting this tradition of respect, we used a talking piece to pass around during our first circle: I used my pocketknife, perhaps a jarring choice, to represent the course theme of violence and vulnerability. Since we had already explored readings that encourage self-defense, I explained that even though I felt safer with a knife, I do not believe the onus to combat rape should be on the victim's ability to use violence. One student enthusiastically pulled out her pocket knife, which led to a discussion of "the things we carry." In an attempt to see students holistically, we answered a check-in question: "What is your level of stress today, on a scale from 1–10?" Most students shared their number with an explanation of their current stressors, which is one way to acknowledge our present environments and state of mind.

This circle was dedicated to answering questions, such as who has the right to speak up, who will listen, and when is the right time? I shared with my students how I was twenty-three when I first heard a fellow graduate student state, "I was raped." Her bravery helped me realize the pervasiveness of sexual violence and the value of talking to other survivors to combat self-blame and widen the circle of solidarity. Pennebaker found that keeping trauma a secret "could be more damaging than the actual event," whereas sharing stories has documented healing results (Brown 2012: 72, 84). The use of "secret" here indicates that it is a choice to hide trauma, when the reality is that society expects it to remain "private." In the classroom context, silence may exacerbate trauma:

> [A]s a result of the failure to acknowledge that survivors might inhabit the same classroom, students may logically assume that they are not likely to encounter victims in other contexts. Thus, the presentation of sexual violence as unusual suggests that victims themselves are unusual and unlike other "normal" women.[2] These messages are also being absorbed by survivors in the room, reinforcing their invisibility and making them less likely to reveal themselves as survivors.
>
> (Betram and Crowley 2012: 66)

A trauma-informed pedagogy advocates for survivors through attempts to "minimize the possibilities for inadvertent retraumatization, secondary traumatization, or wholly new traumatizations" (Carello and Butler 2013: 156). While I recognize that sharing could be triggering (for students *and* faculty), there are ways to minimize potential (re)traumatization through content warnings posted in advance and opt-out assignments, though these have their limitations. Students should be directed to resources for their mental, physical, sexual, and spiritual health. Integrating mindfulness practices can also provide space for students and teachers to share, reflect, and self-author.

To model to my students that our lives are not linear and the way we process experiences can change, I traced my shifting understandings of consent. I shared how, after drinking alcohol for the first time, I was molested at age fourteen by my sister's thirty-year-old fiancé. Because of a lack of understanding of consent, I blamed myself because I thought he "cheated" on my sister, so I did not tell anyone. Twenty years later, when I had the courage to speak out, my sister revealed that she was the one who had pulled him off me. She feared saying anything in case I was traumatized or unaware from blacking out from alcohol. Not having the language to define consent meant that later in college, I excused my boyfriend for raping me because we were dating, so it did not count. It meant that when my neighbor "helped" me get my key in my door after

I drank too much, only to follow me inside and assault me, I did not call it rape because it was forced oral sex, not penetrative violence. When we define intercourse as "penis-in-vagina," this translates to heterosexual sex as "real" sex, discounting other queer sexual encounters and other forms of sexual violence. By understanding that sexual violence occurs on a spectrum—a lesson I learned from the police officer who took my victim report—I was able to understand and define my experiences. It was not until graduate school that I came to understand myself as a "'patch-work survivor'—one who has experienced different kinds of sexual abuse at different times in his or her life" (Maltz 2012: xvi).

My students then examined their own definitions: for example, one student revealed that rather than using "rape"—a term she felt was too violent or extreme—"coercion" felt more accurate because she was pressured into eventually saying "yes." We collectively concluded that victims may take time to process, name, and understand their experiences. This conversation fostered a more transparent analysis of our readings on victim blaming, college alcohol consumption, and definitions of consent, revealing the common pressure to fit into heteronormative scripts for sexual encounters (men pursue, women are pursued). We thus considered how queer and non-normative sexual communities, such as the BDSM community, provide diverse models of affirmative consent. For example, we discussed negotiation worksheets, such as how a "yes, no, maybe" checklist can help partners articulate their needs, desires, and limits.[3] Thomas Millar's (2008) "performance model of sex" also provides a useful understanding of collaborative consent to move beyond a "hetero paradigm": rather than seeing sex as a woman trading a commodity of value to a man, this model does not limit the number or gender of the participants, but rather describes sex as a collaboration using communication to create positive, respectful, and creative sexual experiences. Some students asserted that their generation challenges the gender binary and is more accepting of polyamorous relationships. We considered how empowering it can be to take control of our own narratives and envision new futures. For example, I shared how at first, I thought identifying as bisexual upheld the gender binary, but I also worried that I was contributing to bi-invisibility by preferring "pansexual." Yet, "pansexual" did not speak to my desire to buck the whole system. While I originally thought I was too "femme" to earn being "queer," I now embrace this term as a personal political rebuttal against heteronormative values. Queering the classroom by openly discussing such issues allows us to dismantle the belief that the more "domineering" partner initiates sex, that intimacy is only for monogamous and romantic relationships, and that marriage and children are the key to happiness.

Afterward, my students conversed in an online forum about how the circles allowed them to see me and be seen *by* me as complex beings beyond the identities typically allowed by teacher-student dynamics.[4] All students elected to continue the circles, especially the mindfulness check-ins. One student emphasized the "reality check" that rape culture is not just something we read about but rather something people experience daily. Other students argued that concealing personal stories means "some students may never be exposed to certain experiences that are very real." One student noticed that the erasure of the barrier between students and teacher meant that we could "discuss our work on a deeper level and reach conclusions or interpretations that we might not have had before." Another stressed how this experience encouraged her to be "open and honest and share things that make me uncomfortable and that I normally repress." Using circles can create the "feeling of being recognized, heard, respected, and valued" which is "itself a form of healing" (Pranis and Boyes-Watson 2015: 7). In a course focused on rape culture, it is important to consider this type of positive outcome; as hooks (1994) argues: "While it is utterly unreasonable for students to expect classrooms to be therapy sessions, it is appropriate for them to hope that the knowledge received in these settings will enrich and enhance them" (19). Throughout the remainder of the course, we traced stereotypes of victims without the barrier of distancing ourselves from the material.

My goal with the circles is to normalize talking about sexual violence. On the first day of class, rather than watering down my feminist ethics, I was transparent about the difficulties of teaching controversial content without appearing politically biased. This encouraged a classroom culture that allowed for openness, and the small class size contributed to the success of creating an intimate and safe space. Yet, sharing personal trauma may not always be the best or only way to effectively teach controversial topics because doing so could exacerbate trauma or burden students. The content of this particular course—narratives of sexual assault—invited these intimate discussions, but I might handle disclosure differently in classes focused on other topics. Reevaluating our teacher identities to include the personal can enable us to move beyond necessary curriculum changes and show how tending to our mental, physical, and emotional selves is key to combating the dominant systems that support rape culture. This is especially important at the time of my writing during a pandemic, when multiple layers of trauma—national, institutional, and personal—are converging. Ultimately, I strive to institute a trauma-informed pedagogy that celebrates the positive potentials of vulnerability: as Brown (2012) argues, "vulnerability is the birthplace of love, belonging, joy, courage, empathy, and creativity. [...] If we want greater clarity in our purpose or deeper and more meaningful spiritual lives, vulnerability is the path" (34). If we teach without fear, we can model to our students that resistance also includes creating space for pleasure and worthiness, rather than centering on oppression and repression.

Notes

1. I use "victim" and "survivor" interchangeably to recognize both as valid.
2. While women are referenced here as victims, I recognize that anyone can be a victim of sexual assault. I also acknowledge that cis and trans women, especially transwomen of color, are disproportionately targets of sexual violence.
3. An example can be found here: http://www.bextalkssex.com/wp-content/uploads/2016/10/BexCaputoYesNoMaybe.pdf.
4. Students might conceal negative responses because they fear appearing unsupportive of the instructor.

Works Cited

Bender-Slack, Delane (2010), "'Texts, Talk ... and Fear'?: English Language Arts Teachers Negotiate Social Justice Teaching," *English Education*, 42 (2): 181–203.
Berila, Beth (2016), "Mindfulness as a Healing, Liberatory Practice in Queer Anti-Oppression Pedagogy," *Social Alternatives*, 35 (3): 1–10.

Bertram, Corrine and M. Sue Crowley (2012), "Teaching about Sexual Violence in Higher Education: Moving from Concern to Conscious Resistance," *A Journal of Women Studies*, 33 (1): 63–82.

Brown, Brené (2012), *Daring Greatly: How the Courage to Be Vulnerable Transforms the Way We Live, Love, Parent, and Lead*, New York: Penguin Random House.

Carello, Janice and Lisa Butler (2013), "Potentially Perilous Pedagogies: Teaching Trauma Is Not the Same as Trauma-Informed Teaching," *Journal of Trauma & Dissociation*, 15 (2): 153–68.

DellaPosta, Daniel (2018), "Gay Acquaintanceship and Attitudes toward Homosexuality: A Conservative Test," *Socius: Sociological Research for a Dynamic World*, 4: 1–12.

Edwards, Erica and Jennifer Esposito (2020), *Intersectional Analysis as a Method to Analyze Popular Culture: Clarity in the Matrix*, London and New York: Routledge.

Hammond, Zaretta (2015), *Culturally Responsive Teaching and the Brain: Promoting Authentic Engagement and Rigor among Culturally and Linguistically Diverse Students*, Thousand Oaks, CA: Corwin, a SAGE Company.

hooks, bell (1994), *Teaching to Transgress: Education as the Practice of Freedom*, New York: Routledge.

Maltz, Wendy (2012), *The Sexual Healing Journey: A Guide for Survivors of Sexual Abuse*, New York: William Morrow.

Mardorossian, Carine (2014), *Framing the Rape Victim: Gender and Agency Reconsidered*, New Brunswick and London: Rutgers University Press.

Millar, Thomas (2008), "Toward a Performance Model of Sex," in Joclyn Friedman and Jessica Valenti (eds.), *Yes Means Yes!: Visions of Female Sexual Power & A World Without Rape*, 29–41, Berkeley: Seal Press.

Mirsky, Laura (2004), "Restorative Justice Practices of Native American, First Nation and Other Indigenous People of North America: Part One," *Restorative Practices e-Forum*, April 27, International Institute of Restorative Practices.

Pranis, Kay and Carolyn Boyes-Watson (2015), *Circle Forward: Building a Restorative School Community*, St. Paul, MN: Living Justice Press.

21

Praxis of Empowerment:

Latina Decolonial Feminist Pedagogy and Jaquira Díaz's *Ordinary Girls*

Roberta Hurtado

In 2020, more than a decade after the #MeToo movement began, one thing is painfully clear: many of the women I know have experienced sexually motivated violence. Women who are writers and artists, home- and public-professionals, mothers and aunts and cousins and daughters.[1] Ordinary women going about their lives. Ordinary women circulating in worlds where they are taught to survive sexual violation as if it is normal. Not ordinary in the sense of mundane, or inconsequential; ordinary in the sense of being girls and women in a world that naturalizes violations that should be treated as abnormal. It leads me to think of the ways that survival, itself, can be an act of resistance and lead to all types of action—whether direct or indirect—that can have long-lasting impacts in our different communities.

As I write these words, Vanessa Guillén's face hovers on my computer screen. Page after internet page details the final moments of yet another ordinary woman's life. So far, only one—LULAC's "Predator Alert" (2020), which warns families to discourage daughters from enlisting because they "cannot be protected"—seems to acknowledge that, in the United States, Latina bodies are routinely dehumanized into sexual objects available for the kind of violation suffered by Vanessa Guillén in her short life. I shift the pages of my screen. Thoughts of Guillén's experiences bring me back to what it means to teach about such people and their realities in my classrooms: how can I craft a syllabus that recognizes their humanity while also maintaining awareness of the intricacies of teaching literature as a cultural artifact governed by aesthetic sensibilities and culturally attuned epistemologies? I question what sorts of books will attend to these needs, and also the ways that I will work with students to move through these texts and the kinds of artistic visions that they afford. And, most importantly, to what end am I doing all of this?

The decisions I make as an educator crafting such a syllabus are guided by Latina decolonial feminisms. This framework leads to me to view my classroom as a space for developing a praxis of empowerment, which is a carefully crafted method of working with students to explore Latina/e/o/x literature in a manner that allows for complexities while encouraging student critical social-consciousness. I believe that the literary classroom—and Women's Studies and Latino Studies classrooms where Latina/e/o/x texts can also be taught—is vital for creating space where students move into the path of *conocimento*, Gloria Anzaldúa's concept of critical social-consciousness as an ever-shifting journey rather than an end goal (2001). This approach also encourages students to re-angle their perspectives to embrace alternative narratives of history from those they were taught in school, in recollection of work by Boricua feminists Lisa Sánchez-González (2015) and Iris López (2010/11). Engaging this path enables students to shift their thinking about themselves, their lives, and the communities in which they circulate. Indeed, this movement requires students to think through the worlds they want to live in and inhabit, and their own roles in creating them.

The decision to frame my pedagogy within Latina decolonial feminisms is borne from its potential to not only challenge oppressive social structures but also imagine shifts in consciousness beyond them. It means that, as the instructor, I must be aware of the subject positions of individuals within the books we read in my classes, of the authors, and of the students who enter and exit the room, and I must ground this knowledge in historical understandings of how power has manifested within the United States as a result of colonial endeavors that mark specific people and communities as available for exploitation and violation. It means moving through the layers of how students have been taught in their own communities to read and perceive Latina/e/o/x "bodies" and cultures. It means finding books with the craft and quality to aid in this movement.

In this chapter, I provide a case study of teaching Jaquira Díaz's *Ordinary Girls* (2019) by engaging Latina decolonial feminisms to create a praxis of empowerment within the classroom. This memoir details Díaz's experiences growing up in Puerto Rico and Miami Beach, Florida, the different forms of abuse she endured, and her journey to become a writer. In it, she details poverty, colonial migration, and bureaucratic negligence. She describes family experiences of drug use; intergenerational child abuse; racialization and colorism; mental health issues; homophobia; and physical, sexual, and verbal abuse. Díaz also depicts matrilineal love, feminine strength, and the need for compassion to understand individual circumstances as reflecting the impact of different social structures in order to avoid pathologizing people's lives. Integral to this memoir is an understanding of the author, herself, as an "ordinary girl." Her experiences of violence and violation as a Puerto Rican woman are, sadly, unique to neither her nor members of her community. The commonness of violence—sexual and otherwise—might appear to make it mundane, but I believe the classroom can be a space in which to disrupt that notion. In what follows, I describe how a praxis of empowerment, using specific pedagogical techniques, can identify and delineate colonial impositions impacting the author and the classroom and enable a subversion of coloniality in order to promote social justice.

Latina Decolonial Feminist Pedagogy

Díaz's memoir requires the reader to be conscious of what happens to ordinary Latinas in the United States.[2] As an educator, I must consider how to work with students as they explore a memoir that places a human face in contexts that media outlets gloss over or gorify, knowing that students will enter the course already familiar with media representations of Latina experience. My courses have as their foundation my belief that the literary classroom can be more than a space where students regurgitate facts; rather, it can be a site for critical engagement with literature as an artifact of the world around them. I believe the classroom can be a location of cultural activism, as described by Aurora Levins Morales (1998: 4), in which we consider why artistic expression is important for resisting oppression and formulating visions of social justice and equity.

In the United States, we are impacted by what Aníbal Quijano (2000) describes as coloniality of power: structures of power fall along two main axes, labor and race, that have been functioning for centuries. Integral to it, and at the core of coloniality, is gender (Lugones 2010). Anglo-US feminist scholars such as Ann Cahill have identified Eurocentric patriarchal framings of gender specifically in regard to sexual violation, such as Michel Foucault's attempt to historically situate understandings of sexuality (2000). This insight is vital for unpacking the intricacies of Anglo-US/Eurocentric experiences of gender oppression. It also creates a vibrant need to understand the intersections of race and ethnicity, as Levins Morales suggests (1998: 122) by pointing out how gendered experiences—including rape and sexual violence—emerge as a result of coloniality's machinations and are experienced in culturally nuanced ways.

Exploring historical and sociopolitical contexts provides insight into the intersections of gender, coloniality, and race. Indeed, approaching Latina experiences such as Guillén's, a Chicana from the US Southwest, and Díaz's, a Boricua born on the island and raised in Florida, *requires* attention to the intricacies of their communities. Lisa Sánchez-González's "Teaching Boricua Literature" emphasizes the need for educators' fluency with Puerto Rican history when teaching Boricua literature. She describes the importance of teaching this literature on its own merits rather than lapsing into Anglo-US/Eurocentric grapplings with subjectivity. To do so, educators must know Puerto Rican island and diasporic literary genealogies, the political histories of these communities, and also the socio-spatial realities of both the island and its diaspora because of the communal ruptures that exist as a result of Spanish and then US colonialism.

With this information, it is possible to understand Puerto Ricans, and specifically Puerto Rican women, as more than victims of a colonial apparatus even as they suffer from it. López, for instance, has written of the need to engage what she describes as an "integral approach" (2010/11), which enables exploration of historical and/or social experiences of Puerto Rican women within Anglo-US coloniality without flattening them to singular images of people with no agency. As López's work shows, while it is important to understand US interventions in Puerto Rican women's reproductive experiences, it is just as essential to understand how Puerto Rican women have fought for reproductive justice. Further, this approach demonstrates that it is possible to shift perspective on how historical and cultural events are narrated and, in that way, challenge the manner in which we engage the world around us.

Subversive Empowered Learning

I begin my class by constructing an environment conducive to engaging Latina/e/o/x literature utilizing Latina decolonial feminisms. My first task is to shift power dynamics so that students can understand our class as a safe space for discussing difficult questions, as well as for assault survivors in our class. I begin with a statement that falls along these lines:

> *These texts contain representations of different forms of violence, including domestic abuse, verbal violence, and sexual assault. The reality is that some of us in here have experiences with these. I encourage you, if you decide to stay in this class, to reach out to your network of support while reading these books to ensure that you have the necessary support to be safe while reading. This network does not have to be only your friends. It can be the counselling services on campus, your doctors, or even faculty members whom you trust. While we are reading these texts, if we are discussing a scene that is too much for you, you are not required to be in the class. Please know that you can step out, center yourself, reach out to your network, and rejoin us when you are ready. I know these moments can be painful. Part of our task in here will be to consider why these authors choose to*

create artwork that gives us these representations, and the kind of integrity and emotional labor it takes to do so.

I believe that these words, stated at the outset of the semester, are vital for a number of reasons. Paramount among them is that students will be all too familiar with how US media treats survivors of sexual assault, and the tactics of dehumanization that are levied against them. Thus, one major task is to guide students away from these damaging tactics and to instead create a space where we can trust one another to promote emotional safety even if we become uncomfortable.

Identifying Coloniality

This disruption of interacting with and responding to experiences of assault sets the classroom up to also shift how students perceive the larger social tapestry in which the author's experiences of sociosexual geo-racialization manifest. Teaching at a non-Hispanic-Serving Institution in the US Northeast, I am all too familiar with the fact that mainland US high school curriculum does not provide the majority of students adequate entry points into Latino history, or require traction with Puerto Rican experience. Thus, when teaching Díaz's memoir, I must ensure that students gain accurate working knowledge to contextualize this text as a means of identifying the impact of coloniality as distinct from Puerto Rican identity, even as it impacts it. However, I have found that explaining Puerto Rico's geographic space and providing basic dates for major events can create a passive environment that is not conducive to student engagement. As such, while I do provide a map of the island(s) so students can see its geography, this map alone is not where they will begin.

Instead, I implement group projects that require students to research, synthesize, and share scholarly information about Puerto Rico and its diaspora, historically and currently. Group projects, unfortunately, often stray from the vision many faculty have of collaborative research where students develop learning skills together, and instead can become data dumps of individually found information in awkwardly connected slides. To avoid this possibility, and encourage students to decolonize their knowledge and how they engage with this assignment, I ask them to begin by finding major events connected to Puerto Ricans and their different geopolitical spaces: students will need to research the history of different diasporic communities as well as the island. Next, I provide students an article that speaks to themes in the texts but not the texts themselves. For instance, in a course on borders I have used Mary Pat Brady's "The Fungibility of Borders," because *Ordinary Girls* can and should be placed in dialogue with scholarly conversations about ideological and concrete borders. Students read the article and, with their research content, create coherent statements regarding how all of this information can frame our class discussions for the book, such as how conceptual boundaries contribute to oppressive structures. They share their work with me for review and, lastly, present their findings to the class on the first scheduled day for the book.

This group project creates important grounding for reading Díaz's memoir. First, it provides students an active historical understanding of the contexts from which a book such as Díaz's emerges. This information is necessary because, in the twenty-first century, over 500 years after the dawn of Western European colonization in the Americas, Puerto Ricans remain a colonialized people who are subject to the US federal government. This assignment also encourages students to be cognizant of Puerto Ricans as more than narratives of trauma. I know that for every instance of oppression they will also find examples of resistance, and images of Puerto Rican women beyond the scope of colonization. These research encounters, in combination with the article, expose and disrupt colonial narratives of Puerto Ricans as a dependent people, while also decentering Anglo-US/Eurocentric judgments of who or what is worthy or unworthy of classroom discussion. Further, this assignment requires students to question why texts are labeled "academically rigorous," and the kinds of "standards" that must be critiqued because they are based in oppressive posturing.

Delineating Oppression

This group project also positions our class to engage *Ordinary Girls* honestly, openly, and on its own terms. Díaz's memoir is a raw depiction of a real-life person's experiences with Anglo-US coloniality and the outcomes of its machinations. Delineating the difference between colonial imposition and the person being imposed upon builds a learning environment in which we can shift how we discuss the memoir.

I begin each class session with a question based on that day's reading that specifies a quote, character/person, plot device, or theme. These questions are designed to foster an environment where we engage the "path of *conocimiento*" (Anzaldúa 2001). I will not know beforehand how students will respond, or what a question will bring up for them. Thus, the questions must allow/encourage students to safely acknowledge painful truths in the texts, self-reflect, and explore their responses in a self-reflexive manner. For instance, I might ask, "On page 100, Díaz provides an exploration of motherhood—why? What insights does this page provide us about the dynamics of her own life, and her fears? Do you think these fears are valid? Include quotes in your answer." Such a question can help students more directly explore their thoughts about a text and how their thinking is manifesting at any given point in a way that also requires them to be *present* by referencing the book.

The presentation and daily prompting questions give an entryway for the class to collaboratively discuss questions specifically tailored to the text, particularly moments related to sexual violence. For instance, in one section, the author describes a sexual assault while she is an adolescent (Díaz 2019: 137–9). The man who enacts this violation is an older male friend named Chris. I set up discussion of this scene by asking, in the previous class, "What is the nature of Chris and Jaquira's friendship? What does it mean for these two individuals to be Puerto Ricans living in Miami Beach, Florida? What are their experiences of poverty?" So, as we begin to discuss this assault, we see both individuals for what they are: ordinary people.

In recognizing the narrator and Chris as such, rather than viewing them as victim and rapist, I am not arguing for removing responsibility from the perpetrator of violence. Instead, I am asking students to consider what social mores, norms, and procedures have made it so that this man, in his early twenties, believes that it is acceptable to have sex with an adolescent girl, and to force her to do so, while not perceiving the act as rape.

In making this turn away from the victim/rapist narrative, I engage Levins Morales's discussion of the ways that oppression attempts to rob us of our ability to humanize one another (1998: 111–14) by preventing us from seeing the humanity of those who hurt us, thus making it easier to violate each another. And this reality raises the urgent question: what do we do with those who harm us if we are to create a real revolution? Someone like Chris must always be understood as responsible for his actions, but I believe that for a shift to occur that can lead to social justice we must hold the context accountable as well. The reality is that Anglo-US coloniality instills the lesson that female/feminine bodies—especially those of color—are to be dominated, and more importantly that being dominated is part of these bodies' nature. I do not seek for students to acknowledge the implications of these structures in a passive manner. As a class we must work together to unpack how these deeply entrenched lessons of power manifest in the lives of ordinary people, influencing their range of behaviors from within their subject positions, and thus question whether coloniality is the only reality or future available to us.

Subversive Empowerment

The colonial structures that we live and circulate in are about domination. They create and promote behavior that is, to put it bluntly, unhealthy. *Ordinary Girls* depicts scenes in which Díaz gets into physical altercations, and others where she uses drugs as a coping mechanism (171–2, 207–9). It also details the court-ordered counseling Díaz undergoes as an adolescent, and the counselor's statement that some things are beyond Díaz's control but "some things are not" (131–4, 134). These scenes create opportunities to ask students whether Díaz's experiences represent how members of our communities have internalized the lessons with which they have been disciplined over the course of their lives. First, we must consider if some of her behaviors are problematic. I then ask students to share their interpretations of Díaz's actions and whether they see Díaz as a girl in need of help or as only a stereotypical juvenile delinquent. We also need to assess how the counselor responds to Díaz. With these insights, I ask them to consider how the counselor, or anyone in her position, could have responded more conscientiously to what Díaz's behavior suggested in terms of her experiences. And, just as importantly, they can reflect on what accountability looks like when it is not designed to be solely punitive: can it be, or contribute to, social justice?

Such considerations allow the class to witness the moments of hope and love within the text even as we explore Díaz's pain. We witness her challenge to homophobia while in the Navy. We learn to appreciate complicated people, such as Díaz's Abuela, who struggles with machista culture while also teaching Díaz about self-love and resisting anti-blackness; her friends, who throw down for her in fights; and her love for and from her ex-husband. These moments help students understand that, while violence and violations do exist in Puerto Rican communities, there is more to these communities than *only* criminals or narratives of trauma. And, reading in this way, we shift toward an empowered critical social-consciousness that can subvert colonial imposition through informed engagement with creative expression.

Notes

1   "Woman"/"female"/"feminine" are used to identify specific social identities and experiences within Anglo-US patriarchal coloniality.
2   I do not intend to collapse the differences among communities. However, the term "Latina" can offer solidarity, while also necessitating heightened awareness to each community's unique distinctions when formulating assignments.

Works Cited

Anzaldúa, Gloria (2001), "Now Let Us Shift: The Path to *Conocimiento*," in AnaLouise Keating and Gloria Anzaldúa (eds.), *This Bridge We Call Home*, 540–79, New York: Routledge.
Cahill, Ann (2000), "Foucault, Rape, and the Construction of the Feminine Body," *Hypatia*, 15 (1): 43–63.
Díaz, Jaquíra (2019), *Ordinary Girls: A Memoir*, Chapel Hill, NC: Algonquin.

Levins Morales, Aurora (1998), *Medicine Stories*, Boston, MA: South End.

López, Iris (2010/11), "Sterilization and the Ethics of Reproductive Technology: An Integral Approach," *S & F Online*, 9 (1–2): 1–5.

Lugones, María (2010), "Toward a Decolonial Feminism," *Hypatia*, 25 (4): 743–59.

LULAC (2020), "LULAC Joins Mother's Pleas for Zero Enlistment of Latinas into Military," LULAC.ORG.

Quijano, Aníbal (2000), "Coloniality and Power, Eurocentrism, and Latin America," *Nepantla*, 1 (3): 533–80.

Sánchez-González, Lisa (2015), "Teaching Boricua Literature," in Frederick Aldama (ed.), *Latina/o Literature in the Classroom*, 111–18, New York: Routledge.

PART IV

Pedagogy: Classroom Contexts

22

Teaching the #MeToo Memoir:

Creating Empathy in the First-Year College Classroom

Elif S. Armbruster

In the fall of 2019, I offered a First Year Seminar on writing in the #MeToo era which focused on memoirs written by women with a variety of racial and ethnic identities that sought to engage first-year college students in important conversations regarding sexual consent and abuse. Using works by Roxane Gay, Janet Mock, Grace Talusan, and Jessica Valenti, I was able to create a classroom environment where students connected with the authors we read as well as each other and grew confident about sharing their own stories. Ultimately, only women enrolled in the course, and the students both supported and felt supported by a community of women who would remain their cohort throughout their undergraduate years, precisely the point of the First Year Seminar that my university requires of all incoming students and of the global #MeToo movement as a whole.

One of the greatest satisfactions of teaching this course and the #MeToo memoir specifically was witnessing the self-articulation, group identification, and community building that transpired in the classroom throughout the semester. Particularly moving was the degree of empathy that the women evinced for each other as they both read and shared their own #MeToo stories and the ensuant empowerment they felt. As feminist theorist Leigh Gilmore has written, "In response to the invitation to join a collective intersectional witness of survivors by sharing the #MeToo hashtag, survivors [see] themselves in relation to each other, primarily, rather than as victims of specific perpetrators" (2019a: 619). While literature increasingly is recognized for its power to open people's eyes to the struggles of others and to develop empathy in readers, the #MeToo memoir—a genre that is expanding every day as the abundance of new titles since 2017 indicates (see, for example, Miller 2019 and Crawford 2020)—has the added ability to reach potential victims of sexual abuse and to offer them, often for the first time, a safe space in which to face their trauma and share their stories with others. Gilmore notes, "The memoir boom provides an important context for reading these new [#MeToo] narratives. Life writing has proven to be an especially compelling form of testimonial empowerment for those who are marginalized" (2019b: 162). As I saw in my classroom, reading the memoirs, connecting with each other, and sharing our own stories lightened the emotional burden imposed by shame and/or secrets, typical feelings for victims. This is precisely the power of the #MeToo movement and the memoir genre that sprang from it, as Gilmore highlights: "#MeToo underscores the importance of an emergent culture of witness in hailing survivors into testimonial agency, rather than shaming and silencing them" (2019b: 162).

In addition, reading the #MeToo memoir can foster in some students a sense of moral outrage concerning sexual abuse against women and can drive them to action, both of which I saw in my course. Reading sensitive material together, combined with reflective writing, critical thinking, and group discussion, engendered a change in perspective for many of my students. In fact, students were so transformed by the knowledge they gained and the community we created that they decided to form a #MeToo campus support group, illustrating how academic work can extend beyond the classroom.

Getting Started: Background, Context, and Terms

On the first day of class, I gave students a trigger warning by providing brief synopses of each of the assigned books and asked them to supply information about what they already knew about the #MeToo movement, terms associated with it such as "sexual harassment" and "sexual assault," the memoir genre, and their own experiences with sexual abuse. Students wrote for a timed ten minutes during class and placed their folded paper in a hat, without their names. I passed around the hat and each student took a piece of paper to read aloud what was written. This exercise protects anonymity and reveals the depth and breadth of student knowledge on and experience with the subject (or lack thereof). Not surprisingly, sixteen out of my twenty students acknowledged that they had suffered some sort of sexual harassment or assault, with at least a quarter sharing that that experience had taken place during their first two weeks at the university—knowledge that later contributed to the students' desire to form a #MeToo group on campus.

Once I am aware of students' background knowledge, I am better prepared both to be respectful of where they are coming from and to fill in the blanks with respect to their awareness of human, and in particular, women's rights. Since students seemed to be working with a wide variety of ideas around what exactly constitutes "sexual harassment," "sexual misconduct," and "sexual assault," for example, I reviewed accepted definitions such as those used by the Equal Employment Opportunity Commission and the *New York Times*. The *Times*'s 2018 resource entitled "The Reckoning: Teaching About the #MeToo Moment and Sexual Harassment with Resources from the *New York Times*" proved helpful in all aspects of my course, from supplying links to articles on #MeToo to suggestions for class assignments. Another resource that was launched while I was teaching my course, and that I highly recommend, is Harvard University's Schlesinger Library's #MeToo Digital Media Collection, which documents the digital footprint of #MeToo since 2017. Comprising millions of tweets, newspaper articles, web-forum discussions, and more, the archive is invaluable for all readers of #MeToo literature.

In order to provide students with some perspective on women's fight for equality, students and I constructed a timeline of key moments and players in women's history on a whiteboard, beginning in 1848 with the first women's rights convention held in Seneca Falls. Because few students knew of Elizabeth Cady Stanton or the "Declaration of Sentiments" (1848), among other crucial events and people, I assigned a student or two to look up these topics on their phones in order to add details to the timeline. When students came up blank, I prompted them with questions such as "Does anyone know who founded *Ms.* Magazine and when?" "Does anyone know what Roe vs. Wade refers to?" As we worked together to fill in events up to the present day, other questions organically arose such as "Why is sexual harassment getting so much attention now?" and "Do you think we are living through a watershed moment and why or why not?"

Diving In: Readings and Discussions

When I taught this course for the first time, I sought as diverse a syllabus as possible (something I do for all my classes) so that students could view the topic from a variety of perspectives. I assigned the following four memoirs: *Sex Object* (2016) by Jessica Valenti, *Hunger* (2017) by Roxane Gay, *The Body Papers* (2019) by Grace Talusan, and *Redefining Realness* (2014) by Janet Mock.[1] I supplemented the memoirs with historical, critical, and contemporary writings, including (to name just a few) Elizabeth Stanton's "Solitude of Self" (1892), Charlotte Perkins Gilman's "What Is Feminism?" (1916), excerpts from Roxane Gay's *Not That Bad: Dispatches from Rape Culture* (2018), and Leigh Gilmore's essays, "Frames of Witness: The Kavanaugh Hearings, Survivor Testimony, and #MeToo" (2019) and "#MeToo and the Memoir Boom: The Year in the US" (2019).

I began the course with Jessica Valenti's memoir for the simple reason that of the four authors she has the highest internet presence and the widest social media following, so I expected that some students were likely to be familiar with her and her work (which they were). Not unlike the #MeToo movement, Valenti has gained prominence through her online use of hashtags, posts, and reposts, and her writing style, like the medium itself, is accessible, chatty, and direct. We spent only one week on her book because students read it and were able to respond to its honesty and accessibility rather quickly. Thus, beginning with *Sex Object* allowed students to put aside any hesitations they may have had about discussing sexual harassment or assault.

Valenti details harassment at work, on the subway, in comments via her website, on Twitter and other social media, and describes suffering assault from strangers and boyfriends alike. When I taught *Sex Object*, I learned how many of my students had experienced a similar level of sexual objectification, harassment, and violence as Valenti, and most identified with her depiction of how such negative attention alters one's sense of reality. Valenti writes, "Living in a place that has given up on the expectation of your safety means walking around in a permanently dissociative state" (16). I witnessed students suddenly understanding what "state" they were in, particularly when traveling in Boston at night alone. For many, reading Valenti's memoir proved to be the first time they either identified with someone else's story and/or shared their own stories publicly. This was a true case of "empowering through empathy," which, according to many, is the cornerstone of the #MeToo movement (Rodino-Colocino 2018: 96). For example, some of my students were compelled to share stories about being cat-called, followed, and even stalked as they regularly traveled across the Boston Common (which is adjacent to our campus) or returned home to the same dorm every night. Some students realized they were being harassed by the same perpetrators and began swapping stories in class about how to avoid particular people and places. They exchanged cell phone numbers so that they could walk with each other in the city, especially at night.

Following our reading of Valenti, we moved to Roxane Gay's memoir *Hunger,* a work distinct from Valenti's because rather than describing a lifetime of abuses, Gay focuses on one crucial assault that happened when she was twelve years old—she was raped by a group of boys from her school, one of whom she had considered her best friend—and how her life changed afterward. Unlike Valenti, for example, Gay turned to food to fill the emotional trauma at her core, a trauma that she did not disclose to her family, friends, or schoolteachers. Instead she began to eat and grew increasingly disassociated from her environment: "I ate and ate and ate and I became more and more lost [...] I didn't know who I was. Mostly, I was numb [...] I was trying to forget what happened to me" (64). For my students, reading Gay was especially fraught; they could identify with eating to avoid feeling and they empathized with her pain. Realizing how significant the aspect of controlling (or not controlling) food was in my students' lives, as it became for Gay, led me to give an impromptu assignment that asked my students to keep a food journal for a full week. They moaned and groaned—I could tell this was an especially touchy subject for most of them—but they kept their journals and we spent a class period dissecting their eating patterns. Many confided that they too either stuffed or starved themselves when they didn't want to deal with their home life, relationships, or schoolwork. All agreed that facing the reality of their food consumption was an "awakening" for them, and to help each other, I asked every student to share suggestions for either an affordable healthy restaurant, a healthy food choice they could buy at the grocery store, or a recipe. I compiled this information, entitled it "Healthy (and Cheap) Food Choices for First Year College Students," and gave a copy to each student.

Grace Talusan's memoir *The Body Papers* offered an effective segue from Gay's in that Talusan also focuses on the aftermath of sexual abuse and the ways in which it continues to affect her life today. She presents a story of immigration, cancer, and family trauma—in her case, the crimes of her paternal grandfather who came to live with the family when Grace was seven years old. Talusan documents the many years her grandfather came to her bedroom each night and sexually assaulted her while her parents and siblings slept nearby, and the aftereffects of his transgressions: "For most of my life I believed I was a bad person because something bad had happened to me. I had to learn that I was not bad" (145)—a sentiment that resonated with my entire classroom. Talusan also underscores the importance of victims' testimony: "I tell my story now in the hope that it will do the same for others, create an opening for their own stories and alleviate those feelings of aloneness" (145)—precisely the reason why both #MeToo and memoir work so effectively in creating community.

Because Talusan lives in the same geographic area as my university (Boston, MA), I invited her to our classroom to discuss her memoir and to lead a creative writing workshop. This firsthand experience with a notable writer further connected students to the author and to the reading and resulted in a marked degree of empathy for both the author and each other. When Talusan visited our class and read from her memoir, my students were moved spontaneously to share their own experiences. One student told the class about the sexual abuse her father had inflicted upon her when she was young—a story she had never shared publicly before. While it was difficult to see the student cry as she recounted her story, the response of her classmates was powerful: everyone applauded her, offering words of love and support. My student, along with others who also shared their stories, told the class in the following weeks of the semester that reading Talusan's memoir and discussing it with the author had been a transformative moment for her: she felt newly liberated and empowered by sharing her "secret."

Reading Janet Mock's memoir *Redefining Realness* was an excellent way to end the semester because my students were so captivated by her story. Students were deeply moved by Mock's courage to determine her identity and then write about it forthrightly and unselfconsciously. They were empowered by Mock's story because of the success she attained despite facing enormous challenges while growing up, including being transgender, coming from a family without a lot of money, and suffering a great deal of sexual harassment and abuse when she worked as a prostitute—which she did in order to earn money for gender-reassignment surgery when she was eighteen. That Mock persevered in her pursuit of happiness and became a nationally known writer and speaker inspired my students, especially those who had felt trapped or misunderstood in their own lives. A common sentiment in the class while reading Mock was astonishment that she had made it so far, which gave my students a boost of confidence in themselves. Many were so captivated by Mock's story that they purchased her follow-up memoir, *Surpassing Certainty: What My Twenties Taught Me* (2017), and wrote reflective essays on the book for extra credit.

Working Things Out: Assignments and Projects

Because my course was a first-year seminar open to all majors, I stressed the importance of regular, short (two pages) writing responses rather than longer papers so that the students had practice reflecting and expressing themselves in writing. At times, I required the students to write by hand rather than typing, and I asked that they write their responses in the form of letters to me. These two approaches brought immediacy and intimacy to the assignments and generated more pages from the students than required. Many of my students, most of whom were eighteen years old when I met them, had suffered their own forms of sexual abuse and had never been given the opportunity to write about them. Their weekly writing responses indicated that they were feeling more and more empowered after each week—their writing became forthright, revealing, and voluminous—leading them to open up about their own stories as they read the memoirs of other survivors. Typically, I gave open-ended prompts, focusing either on a discussion point that came up in class or something I wanted to learn from them and that I thought would benefit them to answer. Some of my questions included: "Which passage in the book did you feel was the most difficult to read and why?" "If you had been this person what do you think you would you have done differently in their situation?" and "What do you *wish* the author had done differently and why?"

At the end of the semester, I adopted an assignment that I myself had been given thirty years earlier in an undergraduate course in Women's Studies at Bryn Mawr College. The parameters were that the students had to engage all four of the assigned memoirs plus any additional readings they chose, use a minimum of two quotes from each memoir, and include a two-to-four page typed "Project Rationale." Beyond this, the options were wide-ranging and included the following choices (this is taken from my assignment sheet): "A long poem (four or more pages) or a coherent group of two or more poems; a performance piece such as a monologue or play (if students wish to work together); a personal essay on, for example, the 'Autobiography of a Feminist' or 'Autobiography of a Class'; a short film, video, PowerPoint, blog, podcast, website, or other type of presentation; a piece of visual art such as a collage, painting, poster board, scrapbook, photographic essay, or short graphic novel; or anything else [they could] think of," provided they ran their idea by me first. My students did not disappoint. Some standout projects included creating a wardrobe for a "#MeToo

Thriver" (not "survivor"), designing a dress with words from the memoirs stitched into the fabric, creating book jackets for each memoir, designing *Time* magazine's "Woman of the Year" covers for each author, and writing and performing a one-woman show entitled "I'm a Survivor: Hear Me Roar!" During the last week of the course, each student came to the front of the classroom to present their project to the class. It was clear from the applause that everyone in the class was inspired and impressed, if not rendered speechless or teary-eyed, by what their classmates produced.

My students did not want the semester to end, a sentiment I shared with them. Together we had learned so much about the #MeToo memoir, ourselves, each other, and navigating the tricky world of being a first-year female college student on a densely populated urban campus. My students found a home inside the classroom and gave each other the voices they had been looking for, voices that I am confident they will use for the rest of their college careers and their lives.[2]

Notes

1   While Mock's and Valenti's memoirs were published before the hashtag #MeToo went viral in 2017, they were published after Tarana Burke first used the two words together in 2006 to symbolize solidarity among survivors of sexual abuse. Today, Mock's and Valenti's work, like the other two memoirs treated here, forms part of the genre of the trauma memoir that emerged in the last fifteen years.

2   I would like to thank the incredible women—all twenty of them—who took my First Year Seminar, "Rebel Girls and Nasty Women: Writing in the #MeToo Era," in the fall of 2019 at Suffolk University in Boston. These students—brave, compassionate, hardworking, and honest—are the kind who make my job not only meaningful and thought-provoking but immensely rewarding. I would also like to thank Lori Harrison-Kahan and Kimberly Chabot Davis for their thoughtful comments on early drafts of this essay. Finally, my deepest gratitude to the editors of this collection, Mary Holland and Heather Hewett, who had the courage to pursue a most important topic at a crucial time in women's history.

Works Cited

Crawford, Lacy (2020), *Notes on a Silencing: A Memoir*, New York: Little Brown.

Gay, Roxane (2017), *Hunger: A Memoir of (My) Body*, New York: HarperCollins.

Gay, Roxane (2018), *Not That Bad: Dispatches from Rape Culture*, New York: HarperPerennial.

Gilman, Charlotte Perkins (1916), "What is Feminism?" *The Atlanta Constitution Magazine* Section. Available online: https://www.newspapers.com/clip/39281446/what-is-feminism-by-charlotte/(accessed July 23, 2020).

Gilmore, Leigh (2019), "Frames of Witness: The Kavanaugh Hearings, Survivor Testimony, and #MeToo," *Biography*, 42 (3): 610–23.

Gilmore, Leigh (2019), "#MeToo and the Memoir Boom: The Year in the US," *Biography*, 42 (1): 162–7.

Miller, Chanel (2019), *Know My Name: A Memoir*, New York: Random House.

Mock, Janet (2017), *Surpassing Certainty: What My Twenties Taught Me*, New York: Atria.

Mock, Janet (2014), *Redefining Realness: My Path to Womanhood, Identity, Love, and So Much More*, New York: Atria.

Proulx, Natalie, Christopher Pepper, and Katherine Schulten (2018), "The Reckoning: Teaching About the #MeToo Moment and Sexual Harassment with Resources from *The New York Times*," *The New York Times*, January 25. Available online: https://www.nytimes.com/2018/01/25/learning/lesson-plans/the-reckoning-teaching-about-the-metoo-moment-and-sexual-harassment-with-resources-from-the-new-york-times.html#:~:text=the%20main%20story-,The%20Reckoning%3A%20Teaching%20About%20the%20%23MeToo%20Moment%20and%20Sexual%20Harassment,From%20The%20New%20York%20Times&text=The%20%23MeToo%20movement%20has%20inspired,believe%2C%20a%20watershed%20cultural%20moment (accessed July 23, 2020).

Report of the Woman's Rights Convention, held at Seneca Falls, New York, July 19th and 20th (1848), "Proceedings and Declaration of Sentiments," John Dick at the North Star Office, Rochester, New York. Online Text. Retrieved from the Library of Congress, www.loc.gov/item/rbcmiller001106/ (accessed July 23, 2020).

Rodino-Colocino, Michelle (2018), "Me Too, #MeToo: Countering Cruelty with Empathy," *Communication and Critical/Cultural Studies*, 15 (1): 96–100.

Stanton, Elizabeth Cady, et al. (1892), "Solitude of Self." Washington, D.C.: Government Printing Office, 1915s. Retrieved from the Library of Congress, www.loc.gov/item/93838358/ (accessed July 23, 2020).

Talusan, Grace (2019), *The Body Papers: A Memoir*, Brooklyn, NY: Restless Books.

U.S. Equal Employment Opportunity Commission (2020), https://www.eeoc.gov/sexualharassment (accessed August 10, 2020).

Valenti, Jessica (2016), *Sex Object: A Memoir*, New York: HarperCollins.

23

Teaching Courtly Love in the Medieval Literature Classroom:

Desire, Consent, and the #MeToo Movement

Sara V. Torres and Rebecca F. McNamara

Rape is pervasive in several late medieval vernacular genres, including hagiography, dream visions, lyric, and romance. Literary representations of sexual violence in the Middle Ages drew on a classical legacy that depicted rape and its afterlives (Edwards 2016); at the same time, medieval accounts of rape are inextricable from contemporary legal and institutional cultures that regulated sexual behavior and moral codes. Indeed, late antique and medieval writers developed a sophisticated theological and cultural body of responses to rape. Recent feminist scholars have traced the semantics of rape and ravishment in medieval texts and documents (Edwards 2016; Gravdal 1991; Harris 2018; Robertson and Rose 2001; Saunders 2001; Wofthal 2000). In particular, Carissa Harris's work (2018) shows how lyric forms can both reproduce conventional discourses of misogyny and serve as sites of resistance for voicing women's agency—and how such forms function pedagogically within and beyond their medieval contexts.

This #MeToo moment offers us an opportunity to equip students to understand the cultural histories of rape in ways that enrich their understanding of medieval literature and the intellectual history surrounding legal and social contexts of sexual violence. Our readings concentrate on the cultural discourse of *fin' amor*, noble or courtly love, as it appears in late medieval English and French texts frequently taught in medieval literature courses. We aim to explore the imaginative and social power of courtly love and provide strategies for learning that promote contextualized, historicized readings even as they bring the medieval past into conversation with #MeToo's concerns to voice stories that promote healing and empathy and make systemic changes to end sexual violence (Rodino-Colocino 2018; Walsh 2020). This approach responds to a call by scholars (Alcoff 2018: 122) to historicize the discourse of rape and address the cultural constructedness of attitudes toward sexual violence. It simultaneously foregrounds the urgent concerns of our own institutional spaces and their relationships with dynamics of power and consent.

After briefly reviewing the critical tradition on courtly love, our first section draws on scholarly insights from the history of emotions to explore coercive male desire and equivocal female consent in Geoffrey Chaucer's *Troilus and Criseyde*. A second section addresses desire and violence in late medieval dream visions, including the *Romance of the Rose*, Christine de Pizan's *Book of the City of Ladies*, and Chaucer's *The Legend of Good Women*. The third section discusses teaching approaches that address power and sexual violence in Chaucer's *The Wife of Bath's Tale*. The goal of our pedagogical interventions is to identify the pre-modern literary studies classroom as a site where the social issues raised by #MeToo can help students better understand discursive practices in the past and recognize the long histories of sexual violence and consent.

Love and Coercion in Romance

Fictive codes of desire and power underlie medieval romances' gendered subjectivities and relationships, and such codes are malleable—pressed into service but also resisted by writers. In literature from the twelfth through the fifteenth centuries, conventions of *fin' amor* characterized courtship as a game or a battle that was founded on the suspension of pleasure (Gravdal 1991; Saunders 2001). Feminist readings have illuminated *fin' amor*'s power imbalances and limiting masculine and feminine roles as well as ways that writers resist such conventions (Harris 2018). By exploring desire in these texts and considering ways that emotion is historicized and embodied, we trace how medieval literature manufactures love, desire, hope, shame, and bliss in the context of its time and place, and to what effects it does so (Burger 2019; Flannery 2019; Saunders 2015).

Romance and lyric frequently feature the lovesick male, whose suffering and potential bliss depend on the "mercy" of the female beloved, even as his anguish spurs him to realize noble ideals such as honor and martial prowess. Such male lovesickness can often be read as coercive, exercising language, bodies, and social pressure to pursue the lady's love. Critically reading male lovesickness in Chaucer's *Troilus and Criseyde* provides pedagogical opportunities for examining the frameworks of power that underscore romance's scenes of love lament, consent, and the construction of gendered subjectivities. Such an approach makes visible the disconcerting continuities between the medieval past and present regarding medieval amatory literature's authorization of oppressive masculinity and sexual violence (Harris 2018).

We foreground coercion and consent in *Troilus and Criseyde* by teaching Chaucer's poem with a translation of its source, Boccaccio's *Il Filostrato*. We analyze Chaucer's dilation of the lovers' first sexual encounter, focusing on the amplification of Pandarus and Troilus's manipulation of Criseyde and Chaucer's narratorial interventions. Chaucer adds, for example, the troubling metaphor of a lark caught by a sparrowhawk as Troilus seizes Criseyde (3.1191–92) and the simile of Criseyde shaking "as an aspes leef" (3.1200) while Troilus is "al hool of cares colde" (3.1202). These stanzas presage the negotiation of consent, where Troilus exclaims, "Now be ye kaught; now is ther but we tweyne!/ Now yeldeth yow, for other bote is non!" (3.1207–08): she must yield because she has no other choice. But Criseyde's reply, "Ne hadde I er now, my swete herte deere,/ Ben yolde [yielded], ywis, I were now nought heere!" (3.1210–11), raises questions for students about how Troilus and Criseyde understand her consent differently, and whether it was coerced.

Vocality and Violence in Medieval Dream Visions

The metatextual genre of dream visions and the intellectual debates it generated offer students a context to explore medieval affect, sexuality, and women's vocality. Even though the structure and tropes of dream visions are conventional, the effect of these texts, which deploy a first-person narrative voice and subjectivity, can be deeply personal. This genre, with its focus on personal experience and interiority, shares some of the tonal impact of #MeToo's confessional mode. The voyeuristic ethos of dream visions thematizes the boundaries of the self and other in their explorations of intersubjectivity, cognition, and textual authority (Spearing 1993). Some dream visions even incorporate a confessional mode (however stylized or performative) that provides instructors an opportunity to bring in the #MeToo movement's dialectic of personal and communal vocality.

The Romance of the Rose, a dream-vision allegory written by Guillaume de Lorris and continued by Jean de Meun, was one of the most popular and controversial vernacular texts in the later Middle Ages. The text featured a large cast of allegorical characters who sought to aid or prevent the Lover from reaching his desired Rose. The Lover's final conquest of the Rose—figured as a violent penetration of her intimate chambers—serves as a culmination of the poem's misogynist rhetoric, which is voiced by characters such as La Vieille (Old Woman) (Desmond 2006: 115; Gravdal 1991: 68; Hult 2006: 186). Students are often shocked by this scene: the Rose itself, which is silent and thus never able to express desire, consent, or outward resistance, is reduced to a botanical symbol, and mutuality is rendered irrelevant. The ambiguous presence of Bel Accueil ("Fair Welcome") further complicates the poem's representation of the Rose's will; in light of the conventional misogynist stereotype that a women's refusal belies unspoken desire, some readers might even see the Rose as complicit in the breaching of the fortress walls. This assault echoes not only the *paraclausithyron* (complaint of the lover at his beloved's door) of Ovid's *Amores* (I.6; Hanning 2010: 110) and medieval lyric, but also the language of siege warfare and the tradition of *psychomachia*, where the body is sometimes represented as a walled enclosure.

The ethos of erotic violence (Desmond 2006; Saunders 2001: 188–95) and the specter of rape (Gravdal 1991) pervade the text. The misogyny of the *Rose* is steeped in both patristic and classical sources; the text owes a particular debt to "seduction manuals" such as Andreas Capellanus's *De Amore* and Ovid's *Ars Amatoria* that advise a male reader on how to manipulate women into reciprocating his desire—how to deceive and ultimately abandon them in the name of love (Desmond 2006: 35–54; Hult 2006: 185). Selections from these works make useful intertexts for discussions of the *Rose*, especially because they provide the *Rose* with its fundamental analogy between love and war, which turns on an acknowledgment of the implicit violence (rhetorical and sexual) of the "art of love" (Desmond 2006: 37–54). These were, moreover, pedagogical texts, read at court or in universities, and functioned as part of a wider culture of instruction and exegesis (Desmond 2006: 51–4; Harris 2018: 23–5). Despite the poem's popularity, it was not without its detractors, as the debate about the poem known as *la querelle de la Rose* shows (Desmond 2006: 144–64; Margolis 2011: 47–68). Christine de Pizan's criticism of the *Rose* focused on its obscenity, its use of universalizing, misogynist tropes, and its ambiguity, which required exegetical practices and interpretive capacities that would not be available to all its readers—some of whom might uncritically accept or, worse, reproduce its violent portrayals of gendered relations (Hult 2006: 186).

Christine's *Book of the City of Ladies* (hereafter *BCL*) serves as an imaginative extension of her earlier participation in the intellectual debate about the *Rose*. The *BCL* combines the dream-vision form and the humanist catalogue of illustrious women, and its author occupies the literary spaces drawn from Boethius' *Consolation of Philosophy* and Boccaccio's *De Mulieribus Claris* (although she markedly shifts Boccaccio's tonal register in her act of textual remediation). When teaching the *BCL*, we ask students: "What does it feel like to be excluded from a literary tradition? And what are the strategies to write your way back in?"[1] Christine's defense of women's intellect and character shows that women were foundational in the creation of language and texts themselves (Nicostrata, Carmentis), including through their artisan craft of weaving textiles (Minerva, Arachne). She links these ancient examples to more contemporary female artisanship, such as that of Anastasia, in a deft act of product placement that calls to mind the materiality of Christine's own writerly labor (I.41.4; 85). By featuring women as agents in the civilizing process, she creates a new canon of female exempla to serve as a defensive "structure" against verbal attacks of hostile men. We invite students to create their own list of "exemplary women" to encourage them to experiment with the rhetoric and aesthetics of the list as a form, allowing them to explore modes of exemplarity and representation and consider issues of exclusion and formal constraint.

Christine's insights in the *BCL* suggest that discursive violence produces physical violence and reveal the linguistic determinants of sexual assault (Amsler 2011: 234). In their discussion of Lucretia, Lady Rectitude tells the Christine-dreamer, "Rest assured, dear friend, chaste ladies who live honestly take absolutely no pleasure in being raped. Indeed, rape is the greatest possible sorrow for them" (II.44.1; 161). In addition to the iconic story of Lucretia's suicide, which patristic writers such as Augustine and Jerome glossed differently (Edwards 2016: 1–10), Christine provides several stories of rape or attempted rape to model a variety of situations, outcomes, and responses to violent encounters, including that of the queen of the Galatians who, when faced with a rape attempt, killed the assailant for "vengeance" (II.45.1; 163). Other stories include Hyppo's suicide through drowning; the Sicambrian wives taking up arms against the Romans; the death of Virginia; and the Lombard lord's daughters, who "took raw chicken meat and placed it on their breasts" to deter the invading army from raping them (II.46.1–4; 163–4). Christine's narratives of rape prevention and retribution revise the social rape "scripts" that focus on women's essential vulnerability (Marcus 1992: 387). The *BCL*'s accounts of rape draw on "discourses of survival [that] elaborate how sexual violence reconfigures a victim's understanding of corporeality, the will, temporality, and community … [and] emphasize life after rape as both desirable and ethically important" (Edwards 2016: 2).

Chaucer's *The Legend of Good Women* (hereafter *LGW*) showcases many of the exemplary figures in Christine's *BCL* who experience sexual violence and gendered power imbalances. The framing of the *LGW* as atonement by the poet for trespass against Cupid differs from the *BCL*'s goals of transformatively redressing male authors' mischaracterizations of women. In the *LGW*'s prologue, the narrator dreams that he is admonished by Cupid and defended by legendary faithful wife Alceste for his literary mistreatments of women in love, including his portrayal of Criseyde (332–4). Alceste's defense and the narrator's response foreground male poets' complicity in the mistreatment of women, regardless of good intentions (462–74). The narrator agrees to Alceste's charge that he write new versions of legendary good women (485). We ask students: can this storyteller be trusted to change the narrative by re-telling stories he knows from his "bookes alle" (556); how might these retellings perpetuate male authors' mistreatment of women? Moreover, we attend to the ways in which Chaucer and the poem's narrator amplify, elide, and suppress women's voices in order to foreground for students the representational possibilities of female storytelling.

Crises of power and representation turn on the issue of voice in *LGW*, where the lyrical voice is identified as the poet and the narrator repeatedly draws attention to ways he edits his sources, especially Ovid's *Heroides* (Lawton 2017; Pugh 2018). Whereas in Ovid the women write first-person letters about being wronged in love, Chaucer abridges their voices, with the narrator referring readers to Ovid for more of the women's laments (*LGW* 1366–7, 1564–5, 1678–9, 2218–21). The stories exemplify the discursive nature of sexual assault accounts by foregrounding who speaks, who is silenced, what is said and omitted, and how readers are directed to interpret the story. We ask students to examine how sexual violence, like the rapes of Philomela and Lucrece, and manipulated sexual negotiations, like the male peer-supported coercive behavior of Jason in his pursuit of Hypsipyle, play a part in creating feminine "good" subjects and "false" male subjects (Burger 2017). And we prompt students to attend to the women's strategies of survival, which include vocality and its absence to express their experiences—from tongue-silenced Philomela's tapestry weaving to share with her sister her rape and the sorrow and fury it has engendered (Harris 2019), to Lucrece's narration of her rape and its seemingly inescapable shame before her death by suicide (Flannery 2019: 122–59).

As Tarana Burke's Me Too movement and #MeToo emphasize the collective power of women's voices in creating empathy that leads to healing and activism (Rodino-Colocino 2018), the stories in the *LGW* provide opportunities to examine vocality and its moderation. However, whereas these movements seek to expose and upend systems that foster sexual violence, Chaucer's *LGW* does not dismantle the systems in which it operates (Dumitrescu 2017). Alceste's defense of Chaucer indicates that the poet may be aware of his complicity in translating a long line of "olde clerkes" (370) who have mistreated women and love, but he did not invent this "malice" (371), suggesting that he should not be held culpable for his works' effects. We ask students, then, whether the *LGW* might prompt us to echo the exasperated cry raised in the *Wife of Bath's Prologue* about who gets to voice women's stories in order to overturn systematically misogynistic narratives: "Who peyntede the leon, tel me who" (III.692)?

Women's conspicuous silence and marginalization in these dream visions offer opportunities for pedagogical explorations of medieval women's vocality and agency. Classroom discussions can explore the literary forms that constitute narratives of assault and agency, as well as modes of critical exegesis. They can also put contemporary texts and issues into dialogue with medieval ones. Boccaccio, Chaucer, and Christine de Pizan leveraged the rhetorical force of a list to explore the relations of gender, power, and narrative. This "list" form can be reimagined as a thread (to use the predominant textile image of the *BCL,* and the jargon of Twitter), in which individual voices accrete and interact. #MeToo depends upon a community of activists amplifying their social impact (and confessional declarations) through media. Tanya Serisier emphasizes that "feminist anti-rape politics is founded on the belief that producing and disseminating a genre of personal experiential narratives can end sexual violence" (2018: 4), and Alcoff writes, "voices of victims [...] need to remain at the center of the fight for cultural change" (2018: 2). Personal testimony can serve as an important form for individual and collective self-articulation, whether in the form of "collective storytelling of hasthtag activism" (Serisier 2018: 17) or essay collections.

Violence and Pedagogy in *The Wife of Bath's Tale*

Despite *The Canterbury Tales*'s initial (if fraught) vision of social accord, the ideal of consent is complicated by the recurrent *lack* of consent afforded to women. The *Canterbury Tales*, like its antecedent, Boccaccio's *Decameron*, is also concerned with the problem of rape and its relationship with sovereignty, gendered language, class, and law. The political stakes of these issues are raised in the first story, *The Knight's Tale*, in which the largely silenced Amazonian sisters Hypolita and Emelye are forced into marriages reflecting their conquered status (Crane 1994: 162, 170–85; Fowler 1987). Students' readings of *The Knight's Tale* serve as a fascinating litmus of current events, and in creative projects where students "rewrite" one of the tales to reflect contemporary concerns, we have seen students use the tale to address institutionalized violence or gender inequality.

Later, in Fragment III, *The Wife of Bath's Prologue* often gives readers a sense that the status quo of gendered power dynamics in *The Canterbury Tales* has been reversed, as Dame Alisoun asserts a refreshingly fearless brand of feminine experience and desire in the face of clerkly, patriarchal authority. But *The Wife of Bath's Tale* can be startling or disappointing to students in that its narrative centers on a rapist knight (Gulley 2018). By contextualizing the story's genre as an English Arthurian romance, we think about how intersectionality provides insight into the ways in which rape is portrayed and adjudicated in the *Tale*, and we consider the possibilities opened by the *Tale*'s ending. We first draw students' attention to the nostalgia evoked and quickly problematized in the *Tale*'s opening. The narrator describes a past Arthurian fairy-world and her present as occupying the same geographical space and posing similar threats of rape to women (though by different perpetrators: incubi in Arthur's time, friars in the narrator's present), creating an uncanny immediacy in the tale (Edwards 2016: 96; Harris 2017). We ask students how this coincidental narratorial perspective helps to assess relationships between the historical and mythological past and the present, suggesting that this opening points to sexual violence against women as a systemic problem (Lipton 2019). We then turn our attention to the rape perpetrated by Arthur's knight and the questions it raises about justice for rape, while listening carefully to the voices in the *Tale*. Students notice that the maiden who is raped is unnamed and never speaks and that the process of justice is quickly taken over by the Queen and her council of ladies. We contextualize these moments of silence and vocality using an intersectional framework, asking students to consider how gender and class participate in the ways in which the maiden and the knight differently experience sexual violence and its judicial effects (Crenshaw 1991; Harris 2017, 2018). We extend this intersectional framing to the wedding night at the tale's end to contextualize the rapist knight's treatment of the old woman. Her ugliness, age, and low-born status so disgust the knight that he does not want to consummate their marriage (III.1100–1). In a move similar to other female wisdom figures (like Christine's Reason, Rectitude, and Justice), the woman schools the knight on his mischaracterizations, thus teaching the audience, too, about the pitfalls of socialized identity markers. Character is more deeply situated, she maintains, and the knight must do better in recognizing people's worth—a lesson he should have learned following his quest to discern what women most desire. From the position of being expected to have sex when he does not want to, the knight is forced to contemplate this woman's subjectivity and to reassess his own power, reflective practices that might have prevented him from raping the maiden at the tale's start. With newfound discernment, he surrenders "maistrie" to the woman (III.1230–7) and finds himself happily married to a transformed "fair and good" wife (III.1241).

The story's ending presents an alternative to retributive justice in the form of education for rapists (Harris 2017; Lipton 2019: 348), and it generates questions that resonate with #MeToo: whose experiences are centered and marginalized in the telling of rape, what judicial and educational possibilities exist to address rape, how can a subjectivity that is empathetic of others help the self and others to flourish, and how might power be surrendered or shared in order to develop more ethical sociopolitical and interpersonal relationships? (Rodino-Colocino 2018; Walsh 2020). Alisoun's *Prologue* and *Tale* make clear that consent and power are still contested, but they also narrate possibilities for challenging systems that elide women's desires and condone violence against women (Burger 2019; Harris 2017; Lipton 2019).

In teaching sexual violence in Chaucer, instructors must also grapple with Chaucer's legal entanglements with Cecily Chaumpaigne, who accused and then exonerated him of rape (Cannon 1993; Prendergast and Trigg 2020: 65–70; Waymack 2020). The act in the surviving legal documents remains inscrutable (Cannon 2001; Dinshaw 1998), but the legal records nonetheless indicate that *de raptu meo* ("to my rape") was an "inflammatory" phrase (Cannon 1993: 93). Confronting Chaucer's act of rape provides historical and social context for reading his literature and also brings into conversation ways in which literary representations of rape are in relationship with the realities of sexual violence (Dinshaw 1989: 11). We follow Tison Pugh in acknowledging with students the challenges we face in reading literature alongside authorial malfeasance and also the growth as ethical and empathetic critical readers that such reading develops (2005).

Conclusion

The medieval literature classroom provides a venue to explore representations of sexual violence, to historicize languages of consent and coercion, and to support student dialogue on issues of gendered violence. Our pedagogical efforts underscore the timeliness of these texts in our society and also the ways that medieval representations of sexual violence served as sites of intellectual, social, and aesthetic debate in their own historical moment. Restoring the historical contexts of rape narratives in medieval literature, and recognizing these as central to discourses of gender and violence in premodern culture and our own, supports a critical pedagogy that recognizes the classroom as a consensual space and ultimately supports anti-rape activism in our universities.

Stories matter, and the prominent status within the literary tradition accorded to the medieval texts we have discussed underscores the importance of contextualizing their representations of rape as sites of cultural inquiry. As Elissa Bassist shows in "Why I Didn't Say No," cultural narratives and scripts shape desire and expectation and constitute the linguistic texture of embodied sexual experience (see also Marcus 1992: 388–98). Our literature classrooms must be aware of these negotiations, sensitive to the migration and reproduction of such scripts beyond the canon and classroom, their movement from textual to social *corpa*. Teaching medieval texts that represent rape and thematize consent requires an "unquiet pedagogy" (Kutz and Roskelly 1991) committed to exploring the range of exegetical practices they model, sustain, or resist—even if such reading practices decenter the literary canon. At the same time, this approach offers an opportunity to critically assess the institutional languages of consent that address (whether effectively or not) rape prevention and response—especially on campuses like the University of Virginia, where rape culture (sensationalized several years ago during the *Rolling Stone* magazine controversy) has been described as persistent, and sexual assault prevention and survivor support programs are in need of more resources in order to be more effectual ("Not on Our Grounds"; Coronel 2015; Entzminger 2019; Strike 2020). Our medieval literature classrooms can serve as a space to both examine and produce new bodies of knowledge, new narratives, and new canons that transform authoritative texts and received traditions into sites of inquiry or reform.[2]

Notes

1 This approach was developed in part through conversations with Bridget Whearty, whom we thank.
2 We thank Abigail Watson for her bibliographic assistance in preparing this essay.

Works Cited

Alcoff, Linda Martín (2018), *Rape and Resistance: Understanding the Complexities of Sexual Violation*, Cambridge: Polity Press.
Amsler, Mark (2011), *Affective Literacies: Writing and Multilingualism in the Later Middle Ages*, Turnhout, Belgium: Brepols.
Bassist, Elissa (2018), "Why I Didn't Say No," in Roxane Gay (ed.), *Not That Bad: Dispatches from Rape Culture*, 323–39, New York: Harper Perennial.
Burger, Glenn D. (2019), "Becoming One Flesh, Inhabiting Two Genders: Ugly Feelings and Blocked Emotion in the *Wife of Bath's Prologue and*

Tale," in Glenn D. Burger and Holly A. Crocker (eds.), *Medieval Affect, Feeling, and Emotion*, 90–117, Cambridge: Cambridge University Press.

Burger, Glenn D (2017), "'Pite rennet soone in gentil herte': Ugly Feelings and Gendered Conduct in Chaucer's *Legend of Good Women*," *Chaucer Review* 52 (1): 66–84.

Cannon, Christopher (1993), "*Raptus* in the Chaumpiegne Release and a Newly Discovered Document Concerning the Life of Geoffrey Chaucer," *Speculum* 68: 79–94.

Cannon, Christopher (2001), "Chaucer and Rape: Uncertainty's Certainties," in Elizabeth Robertson and Christine M. Rose (eds.), *Representing Rape in Medieval and Early Modern Literature*, 225–79, New York: Palgrave.

Chaucer, Geoffrey (1987), *The Riverside Chaucer*, ed. Larry D. Benson, Boston: Houghton Mifflin.

Coronel, Sheila, Steve Coll, and Derek Kravitz (2015), "Rolling Stone and UVA: The Columbia University Graduate School of Journalism Report," *Rolling Stone*, April 5. Available online: https://www.rollingstone.com/culture/culture-news/rolling-stone-and-uva-the-columbia-university-graduate-school-of-journalism-report-44930/.

Crane, Susan (1994), *Gender and Romance in Chaucer's Canterbury Tales*, Princeton: Princeton University Press.

Crenshaw, Kimberlé (1991), "Mapping the Margins: Intersectionality, Identity Politics, and Violence against Women of Color," *Stanford Law Review* 43 (6): 1241–99.

de Lorris, Guillaume and Jean de Meun (2008), *The Romance of the Rose*, trans. Frances Horgan, Oxford: Oxford University Press.

Desmond, Marilynn (2006), *Ovid's Art and the Wife of Bath: The Ethics of Erotic Violence*, Ithaca: Cornell University Press.

Dinshaw, Carolyn (1989), *Chaucer's Sexual Poetics*, Madison: University of Wisconsin Press.

Dinshaw, Carolyn (1998), "Rivalry, Rape, and Manhood: Gower and Chaucer," in Anna Roberts (ed.), *Violence against Women in Medieval Texts*, 137–60, Gainesville: University of Florida Press.

Dumitrescu, Irina (2017), "Beautiful Suffering and the Culpable Narrator in Chaucer's *Legend of Good Women*," *Chaucer Review* 52 (1): 106–23.

Edwards, Suzanne (2016), *The Afterlives of Rape in Medieval English Literature*, New York: Palgrave.

Entzminger, Brielle (2019), "Five Years Later: What Has (or Hasn't) Changed at UVA since Rolling Stone?" *C-Ville Weekly*, December 4. Available online: https://www.c-ville.com/five-years-later-what-has-or-hasnt-changed-at-uva-since-rolling-stone/.

Flannery, Mary C. (2019), *Practising Shame: Female Honour in Late Medieval England*, Manchester: Manchester University Press.
Fowler, Elizabeth (1987), "The Afterlife of the Civil Dead: Conquest in the Knight's Tale," in Thomas C. Stillinger (ed.), *Critical Essays on Geoffrey Chaucer*, 59–81, New York: G. K. Hall.
Gravdal, Kathryn (1991), *Ravishing Maidens: Writing Rape in Medieval French Literature and Law*, Philadelphia: University of Pennsylvania Press.
Gulley, Alison, ed. (2018), *Teaching Rape in the Medieval Literature Classroom: Approaches to Difficult Texts*, Leeds: Arc Humanities Press.
Hanning, R.W. (2010), "Always Hopeless, Never Serious: Wit and Wordplay in Ovid's *Amores*," in Barbara Weiden Boyd and Cora Fox (eds.), *Approaches to Teaching the Works of Ovid and the Ovidian Tradition, Approaches to Teaching World Literature 113*, 109–16, New York: Modern Language Association of America.
Harris, Carissa M. (2017), "Rape and Justice in the Wife of Bath's Tale," in *The Open Access Companion to the Canterbury Tales*, https://opencanterburytales.dsl.lsu.edu/wobt1/.
Harris, Carissa M. (2018), *Obscene Pedagogies: Transgressive Talk and Sexual Education in Late Medieval Britain*, Ithaca: Cornell University Press.
Harris, Carissa M. (2019), "'For Rage': Rape Survival, Women's Anger, and Sisterhood in Chaucer's *Legend of Philomela*," *Chaucer Review* 54 (3): 253–69.
Hult, David F. (2006), "The *Roman de la Rose*, Christine de Pizan, and the *querelle des femmes*," in Carolyn Dinshaw and David Wallace (eds.), *The Cambridge Companion to Medieval Women's Writing*, 184–94, Cambridge: Cambridge UP.
Kutz, Eleanor and Hephzibah Roskelly, with a foreword by Paulo Freire (1991), *An Unquiet Pedagogy: Transforming Practice in the English Classroom*, Portsmouth, NH: Boynton/Cook.
Lawton, David (2017), *Voice in Later Medieval English Literature: Public Interiorities*, Oxford: Oxford University Press.
Lipton, Emma (2019), "Contracts, Activist Feminism, and the *Wife of Bath's Tale*," *Chaucer Review* 54 (3): 335–51.
Marcus, Sharon (1992), "Fighting Bodies, Fighting Words: A Theory and Politics of Rape Prevention," in Judith Butler and Joan W. Scott (eds.), *Feminists Theorize the Political*, 385–403, New York: Routledge.
Margolis, Nadia (2011), *An Introduction to Christine de Pizan*, Gainesville: University of Florida Press.
"Not on Our Grounds—Responsible Employee Training," (2020), [Online Title IX Training Module] *University of Virginia* (accessed March 2020).

Pizan, Christine de ([1982] 1998), *The Book of the City of Ladies*, trans. Earl Jeffrey Richards, foreword by Natalie Zeemon Davis, rev. edn, New York: Persea.

Prendergast, Thomas A. and Stephanie Trigg (2020), *30 Great Myths About Chaucer*, Hoboken, NJ: Wiley.

Pugh, Tison (2005), "Chaucer's Rape, Southern Racism, and the Pedagogical Ethics of Authorial Malfeasance," *College English* 67 (6): 569–86.

Pugh, Tison (2018), "Speech, Silence, and Teaching Chaucer's Rapes," in Alison Gulley (ed.), *Teaching Rape in the Medieval Literature Classroom: Approaches to Difficult Texts*, 77–90, Amsterdam: Arc Humanities Press.

Robertson, Elizabeth and Christine M. Rose, eds. (2001), *Representing Rape in Medieval and Early Modern Literature*, New York: Palgrave.

Rodino-Colocino, Michelle (2018), "Me Too, #MeToo: Countering Cruelty with Empathy," *Communication and Critical/Cultural Studies* 15 (1): 96–100.

Saunders, Corinne (2001), *Rape and Ravishment in the Literature of Medieval England*, Woodbridge, Suffolk: D. S. Brewer.

Saunders, Corrine (2015), "Mind, Body, and Affect in Medieval English Arthurian Romance," in Frank Brandsma, Carolyne Larrington and Corinne Saunders (eds.), *Emotions in Medieval Arthurian Literature: Body, Mind, Voice*, 31–46, Cambridge: D.S. Brewer.

Serisier, Tanya (2018), *Speaking Out: Feminism, Rape and Narrative Politics*, New York: Palgrave.

Spearing, A. C. (1993), *The Medieval Poet as Voyeur: Looking and Listening in Medieval Love-Narratives*, Cambridge: Cambridge University Press.

Strike, Noah (2020), "What's Changed since Rolling Stone? Not Enough," op. ed., *The Cavalier Daily*, February 5. Available online: https://www.cavalierdaily.com/article/2020/02/strike-whats-changed-since-rolling-stone-not-enough.

Walsh, Colleen (2020), "Me Too Founder Discusses Where We Go from Here," *The Harvard Gazette*, February 21. Available online: https://news.harvard.edu/gazette/story/2020/02/me-too-founder-tarana-burke-discusses-where-we-go-from-here/.

Waymack, Anna Fore (2020), *De Raptu Meo*, http://chaumpaigne.org.

Wofthal, Diane (1998), "'Douleur sur toutes autres': Revisualizing the Rape Script in the *Epistre Othea* and the *Cité des dames*," in Marilynn Desmond (ed.), *Christine de Pizan and the Categories of Difference*, 41–70, Minneapolis: University of Minnesota Press.

Wofthal, Diane (2000), *Images of Rape: The "Heroic" Tradition and Its Alternatives*, Cambridge: Cambridge University Press.

24

Centering Black Women in the Classroom:

Teaching Harriet Jacobs's *Incidents in the Life of a Slave Girl* after #MeToo

Linda Chavers

> *I don't understand. How can they be black?*
> *They are women!*
> *I think they might be both.*
> *[screaming] Both? No!*
> – "THE DAY BEYONCÉ TURNED BLACK" (2016)

This essay addresses an urgent need to discover, unpack, and correct the dangerously misleading and inaccurate historical narratives about white supremacy and civil rights in the United States. If we are to understand how we got here today—"here" being a place where Black mothers are still dying at a disproportionally high rate after childbirth and where Black girls are punished more severely than their white peers in daycare and secondary school—then there needs to be a radical shifting of the center. When we talk about women, we must talk about Black women. Such a fundamental shift can help uncover our path to today and support our way to better solutions.

In my teaching, I focus on the historical and continuing silencing of Black women with a pedagogical goal of pushing students to critically interrogate the popular and ruling discourses on sexual violence, racism, and white supremacy. I have found that Harriet Jacobs, an enslaved and then freed Black woman from nineteenth-century North Carolina, provides a compelling point of entry for this conversation. Jacobs's biography and written narrative, *Incidents in the Life of a Slave Girl* (1861), foregrounds the potent intersections of racism and sexism. With the advent of the #MeToo movement in the twenty-first century, I found an opportunity to help students further examine this history and make vivid connections to ongoing sexual violence and racism as well as their iterations in health and medicine (specifically the Covid-19 global pandemic). In this essay, I describe a class I created that places the stories of Black women at the center and the pedagogy I developed that radically shifts students' understanding of American slavery as it relates to our current world.

#MeToo and Correcting History

As a teacher of Black literature, I find that there is a general gap in students' understanding of Black history in the United States. The history that students learn prior to college is an incomplete if not inaccurate one. After one painfully slow session on Du Bois's *Souls of Black Folk*, I paused and asked the class about the "nadir of black history" (Gilmore 1993). Blank faces stared back at me. After asking pointedly about the *lowest point* in Black history, I saw quickly raised hands from students eager to show off their well-informed understanding of Black history. "Slavery!" they'd shout. Surely, the lowest and worst point in Black history had to be slavery.

And, surely, they were absolutely wrong. I found that I had to build in an extra week of lesson planning just on this point: the nadir of black history was *after* Reconstruction, *following* the Civil War, from 1910 to the mid-1950s or 1960s. "I knew it, I just knew it!" one angry student said, "It just didn't make any sense." "What didn't?" I asked. She, a statistics concentrator, explained, "*This* is how we learned Black history in middle school: slavery, Lincoln, Martin Luther King, *Obama. The* end." This truncated and inaccurate version of history is what our nation touts domestically and abroad.

Black women in particular are left out and misrepresented in this history. It is the norm to cite Rosa Parks as a figure of the Civil Rights Movement, but the story we commonly teach is incomplete. Parks was already a human rights activist at the time of the Montgomery Bus Boycott and had been doing extensive investigative and advocacy work for the Black women targeted by white men using sexual violence as a tool of white supremacy. In the twenty-first century, Tarana Burke advocated for Black girls and women victimized by sexual violence years before the 2017 #MeToo movement as reignited by Alyssa Milano, and Anita Hill testified against Clarence Thomas decades before Dr. Ford testified in the 2018 Kavanaugh confirmation hearings. When I heard Dr. Ford's testimony about being groped and held down at a party, and when I read the many first-person essays from well-known actresses detailing experiences of severe harassment and assault in Hollywood, I was sent back to yet another place: nineteenth-century Edenton, North Carolina, where Harriet Jacobs wrote her story of survival as an enslaved Black woman in the United States ([1861] 2000). Jacobs belongs in the stories we tell about sexual violence, and yet we don't often start with her.

In 2018, I went to my department chair and proposed a course that placed Black American women in the center of the current popular conversations around sexual oppression. I wanted to focus primarily on the structural and intersectional analysis embedded in Harriet Jacobs's narrative, long before intersectionality became an analytical norm in feminist theory. I crafted my course to get students to understand that Black women have been speaking these stories of resistance and agency in the face of sexual oppression for centuries. By showing students the historic roots of our contemporary critique, and by teaching and showing how racism and misogyny permeate every single facet of American life, I hoped to embolden students to bring anti-racist and anti-sexist practices into their future personal and professional journeys.

The Conversation in the Classroom

I have offered "Black Women and #MeToo: A Conversation" for three semesters. The explicit inclusion of the term "Conversation" mattered because I continue to see a problem in language and popular culture that lends itself to parallel issues in law and public policy regarding the marginalization and oppression of Black girls and women. For example, we have the celebration and coopting of Black hair styles by white celebrities in the space of social media and the punishing and expelling of Black girls and women for the same hairstyles in schools and the military. A conversation, an informed and authentic discussion about the history of Black women in this country, would help my students, I hoped, to examine their positionality in society and their capacity to change it.

I focus the course on *Incidents*, written by a Black American woman who was born enslaved, resisted violence to her race and her gender, and died a free woman. Jacobs's story—and her written story (one that was treated as fiction for well into the twentieth century)—is the embodiment of resistance and intersectionality. She employed her gender to escape slavery and employed her enslavement and race to escape sexual oppression. Looking at the details of her life and her actions toward her own freedom, we see a surprising level of bodily autonomy for *any* woman to achieve. Facing sexual harassment in the form of grooming from her owner Dr. Flint and knowing that any sex would result in pregnancy, Jacobs engages in consensual sex with a white man (their neighbor, Mr. Sands) in order to exert control over the inevitable pregnancies to come.[1] By choosing the father of her children (and, therefore, their potential value in the market), we see a woman with absolutely no agency *control her births*. Furthermore, when she escapes she does not flee the state; she goes a mere few yards away to live in a tiny, cramped crawl-space (she could not stand up) where, for the next seven years, she watches over the bodies of her children and intervenes in their movements and Mr. Sands's decisions about whether to sell them.

By creating her own version of *family planning*, Jacobs had more control in her children's lives than did most enslaved Black women. In our discussion of the theme of creating and refining what control looks like to an enslaved Black woman facing sexual oppression, we perform close readings of her text, particularly her use of the second person and its effects.[2]

In doing so we, her readers, insert ourselves into her situation and are forced to regard her on her own terms. For example, we witness how she claims agency when she informs her reader of her decision to engage in an affair with her white neighbor, Mr. Sands, in order to avoid rape by her owner. Jacobs writes: "I know what I did, and I did it with deliberate calculation" (Jacobs 2000: 83). The "I" is incredibly impactful: it provides a rare instance of deliberate calculation and strategy not traditionally highlighted or even discussed when teaching the history of slavery in the United States. Students are tasked with finding more instances of Jacobs's agency and they find plenty: her description of choosing a lover ("It seems less degrading to give one's self, than to submit to compulsion," 55) and the subtle yet direct ways in which she indicts slavery by discussing her limited options as a mother ("Of a man who was not my master I could ask to have my children well supported," 55). Students express excitement in locating agency and resistance in an antebellum text authored by a Black woman, and they are primed to start tracing examples of agency through history to the present day.

In order to chart similar themes, the reading list pairs primary texts from the past (nineteenth to twentieth centuries) with secondary texts from the current moment (smaller readings or articles and videos from the twenty-first century). The students experience the words and writings of Harriet Jacobs and Sojourner Truth with the voices of various named and unnamed women (of all identities) sharing their stories of sexual harassment and assault today. They come to see the radical feminist content of Jacobs and trace it into our current popular language and discourse. The texts below are a sampling:

- *Incidents* is paired with Drs. Salamishah and Scheherazade Tillet's op-ed on the #MeToo movement's connections with Black girls (Tillet and Tillet 2019) and Allyson Hobbs's article on the legacy of #MeToo and Black women's testimonies (2018).

All three texts harness the power of testimony, and all four authors reclaim a narrative that they have been systematically robbed of.

- *The Narrative of Sojourner Truth* by Sojourner Truth (1850) is positioned next to Nell Irvin Painter's biography of Truth (1998). When students read Truth's words next to Painter's, I ask them to read and discuss what it means that the "Sojourner Truth" we know as a nation is far from who the woman actually was, particularly in that her entire life took place in New York and not the Deep South. What does it mean to know and celebrate what is not factual? And what role—if any—does cultural appropriation play here?
- Octavia Butler's novel *Kindred* (1974) is placed next to Emily Nussbaum's *New Yorker* article on television's reckoning with #MeToo (2019). Students discuss the consequences and effects of fictionalizing a slave narrative and the symbolism of time travel with trauma.
- Gayl Jones's *Corregidora* (1975) is about the legacy of intergenerational trauma borne from the systemic rape of enslaved Black women.[3] We watch scenes from Spike Lee's *She's Gotta Have It* (1986) and excerpts from the documentary *Surviving R. Kelly* (2019), and we discuss the jury's inability to convict Kelly in 2008 due in part to their perception of a black teenager as an adult (dream Hampton et al. 2019). These moments also connect with the current disparities in punishments of Black girls and their non-Black peers in schools.

We read everything with these overarching questions: "How have women of color made sense of and resisted the nation's prevailing structures of patriarchal capitalist white nationalism? What are the epistemic threads of connection between nineteenth-century abolition and early twenty-first century Black feminist resistance to anti-Black violence and neoliberal carcerality?"

In order to show how much of our present is connected to our past, I start every class with a popular culture artifact that points to a significant historical (or present-day) problem. I prepare the students to do this work by starting the term with a "coda"—something to be experienced at the beginning and again at the end of the academic term that will inevitably read differently over time. I use the artistic productions of Beyoncé, but the coda could be any number of cultural productions that point to deeply rooted challenges in society. For example, at the start of the first class I play Beyoncé's video "Formation" (2016), a work that has been lauded for all of its nods to Black history and culture. I ask the students to watch the video and to listen to the lyrics as if it were a book of clues—to pick up on anything that resonates, even and especially if they cannot fully articulate why something resonates. I ask that they write it all down, every single thing, no matter how trivial it may seem. Then we open up to share what they observed and after ten minutes, I explain that we will watch the same video again at the end of the term to see how much has or has not changed in reception and understanding. At the end of the term, after re-viewing the video, the students find at least twice as much symbolism and signposts to Black culture as they did four and half months earlier.

In the past year I have opened class with a range of cultural moments: a Pepsi-Cola ad aired during the 2017 Superbowl featuring Kendall Jenner handing a can to a line of police meant to address the Black Lives Matter movement; a digital short from *Saturday Night Live*, "The Day Beyoncé Turned Black," parodying the national response to Beyoncé's "Formation"; a *New York Times* Opinion digital video featuring Niecy Nash advertising a hotline for white people to use instead of calling the police on Black people. (After playing this clip, I ask students to think about chapter 12 in Jacobs's *Incidents*, "Fear of Insurrection," which covers the period following Nat Turner's rebellion.) Sometimes, I will begin simply with a passage from the text we're reading and draw an explicit parallel to a recent moment. Following the aforementioned rebellion, Jacobs writes about how poor whites were commissioned to raid Black homes and slave quarters. She describes their violence and how they would bring and then sprinkle gunshot onto the dirt floors in order to arrest, harm, or kill Black people ([1861] 2000: 63–8). I'll open class with the national headlines around Susan Smith or Charles Stuart or a clip from the Black comedian Dave Chappelle's *Killin' Them Softly*. In the clip, Chappelle jokingly describes how policemen will "sprinkle a little crack on" the Black people they have shot and killed in order to justify their actions (Lathan 2000). Or, when addressing cultural appropriation, we'll discuss the moment when Jacobs approached literary celebrity Harriet Beecher Stowe about promoting her book with an introduction. Stowe not only snubbed her but also offered to adapt Jacobs's story into her own fictional work (Yellin 2000: xxi).

Jacobs works as our earliest model of radicalism vis-à-vis centering oneself and one's body as the source of agency and power, a countercharge to the mistrust and dismantling of the Black body that remains codified in our nation's laws. I employ Jacobs as a model for students not only to read and study but also to model regarding this radical trusting of the self as the expert on bodily experience. In this way, students start to re-examine common and popular narratives about sexual assault, particularly around modalities of power, and make direct ties to the institution of slavery. Jacobs's text expands our thinking on the gender and sexual implications of racial capitalism in three fundamental ways:

1. By revealing how she calculated her own passage into motherhood, Jacobs writes in resistance to the Black female body as white property;
2. In calculating not only her own modes of resistance but also planning her own motherhood, she reclaims how her body will become a site of extraction for white patriarchal wealth and power: "I knew that as soon as a new fancy took [Dr. Flint], his victims were sold far off to get rid of them; especially if they had children ... Of a man *who was not my master* I could ask to have my children well supported ... " (55, emphasis added);
3. By exposing the tensions of maintaining a feminine ideal ("I wanted to keep myself pure; and, under the most adverse circumstances, I tried hard to preserve my self-respect; but I was struggling alone in the powerful grasp of the demon Slavery," 54), she exposes a web of structural injustice that racializes gender, thus revealing the hypocrisy of white capitalist patriarchy.

The class itself works as a radical act of trust and forgiveness. Undergraduates are appropriately righteous when it comes to right and wrong. We talk about the role of the law, the courts specifically, in regards to sexual assault, with the goal of reaching a nuanced understanding that something can be immoral while still legal (or, rather, not designated illegal). This nuance is better understood when we look at the narratives of Jacobs and Truth, which both discuss immoral acts that were allowed by, if not codified into, existing law at the time. I lead the class by saying, "we must stop equating justice with right and wrong when justice itself is situated within larger oppressive structures," providing students with a better understanding of how someone who commits sexual assault may not be legally convicted of doing so—but that doesn't mean it didn't happen. I stress that obviating this distinction is critical to understanding the role of law in a white supremacist structure. Jacobs uses the term "forgiveness" (1861: 89). I ask my students to imagine what it looks like to co-exist with those who have committed harm but were not convicted of doing so, just as Jacobs and countless other Black Americans have had to do for centuries. Only then do students start to see how resistance is a way of being.

The anger and frustration about the teaching of history expressed by my former student come up repeatedly. When we read Truth's *Narrative* with Painter's biography, we question and discuss the implications of revering a Black woman and a speech so inaccurately rendered into history. We look at the history and honoring of J. Marion Sims, the documented founder of Western gynecology and his groundbreaking research performed on enslaved Black women, who were unable to give any sort of consent, and connect these examples with the ongoing lethal disparities in the treatment and care of pregnant Black women today.

Ongoing Conversations: From Sexual Assault to Covid-19

This class became a consciousness-raising group that discussed individual and systemic issues surrounding grooming and coercion, workplace sexual harassment, sexual assault, and consent. Students have occasionally shared their own experiences of sexual harassment and assault. Many of our discussions centered on the grey zone that impacts them (and their peers) personally. Our discussions often focused on the disconnect between students' actual lived experiences and administrative policy of colleges or the law and court outcomes. Our class shifted into a space of #MeToo—empowered education where a collective activism occurred. Many students said that they discussed these issues with their parents, peers, siblings, and partners. One student told me that the class helped her bridge an old divide between herself and her mother;

her mother was a survivor of sexual assault as was the student, but neither knew about the other's assault. Others said that our class discussions surrounding consent and coercion compelled them to have important discussions with partners regarding boundaries and consent. More than one student expressed an increased interest in medicine and midwifery, citing this class as raising awareness in the discrepancies for Black women in prenatal and maternal healthcare.

When I began writing this essay, a global pandemic changed the lives of my students and provided new material for our conversations about the intersections of sexism and racism. In mid-March of 2020, the Covid-19 pandemic hit, and we all transitioned to online teaching. I incorporated topics of race and medicine and, particularly, the current disparities we continue to see in Covid-19 treatment and outcomes in Black and brown communities. Again, the history of slavery matters: Black communities are among those suffering the most, and Black women make up large portions of service and health care workers. We discussed other ways that the legacy of slavery manifests in our current pandemic, such as when a Black person goes to the emergency room describing their pain and is not believed, only to die later (CBS News 2020). We also observed the inverse, when Black people do not trust the government when it comes to health care, not out of an unfounded paranoia but due to a real history, such as the gynecological research performed without consent by Dr. Sims.

At the time of this writing, my inbox is flooded with urgent emails from former students expressing outrage over this moment. Some of them have created listening circles for their non-Black peers, and others who are headed into education make pledges to incorporate what they've learned into their own practices. It is my hope that classes such as mine ignite a flame—an eternal one—where all conversations about survival place the history of Black women at their center.

Notes

1   I use *consensual* generously here, as Jacobs was not considered a full citizen or human being at the time, and it is a well-founded argument that no enslaved persons could consent to anything given the condition of their enslavement.

2   For a different reading of agency in a similar context, see Ethan Madarieta's chapter in this volume.
3   See Carlyn Ferrari's chapter in this volume for a detailed plan for teaching Jones's *Corregidora*.

Works Cited

Butler, Octavia E. (2003), *Kindred*, Boston, MA: Beacon Press.

CBS News Interactive (2020), "Detroit Man with Virus Symptoms Dies after 3 ERs Turn Him Away, Family Says: 'He Was Begging for His Life,'" *CBS News*, April 22. Available online: https://www.cbsnews.com/news/coronavirus-detroit-man-dead-turned-away-from-er/ (accessed September 25, 2020).

Crenshaw, Kimberlé (1989), "Demarginalizing the Intersection of Race and Sex: A Black Feminist Critique of Antidiscrimination Doctrine, Feminist Theory and Antiracist Politics," *University of Chicago Legal Forum*, 8 (1). Available online: https://chicagounbound.uchicago.edu/uclf/vol1989/iss1/8.

Formation (2016), [Film], Contrib. Beyoncé Knowles, Rae et al., USA: Parkwood Entertainment. Available online: https://www.youtube.com/watch?v=WDZJPJV__bQ.

Hobbs, Allyson (2018), "One Year of #MeToo: The Legacy of Black Women's Testimonies." *The New Yorker*, October 10. Available online: https://www.newyorker.com/culture/personal-history/one-year-of-metoo-the-legacy-of-black-womens-testimonies.

Gilmore, Glenda Elizabeth (1993), "'Somewhere' in the Nadir of African American History, 1890–1920," Freedom's Story, TeacherServe©. National Humanities Center. http://nationalhumanitiescenter.org/tserve/freedom/1865-1917/essays/nadir.htm.

Jacobs, Harriet ([1861] 2000), *Incidents in the Life of a Slave Girl, Written By Herself*, ed. Jean Fagan Yellin, Cambridge: Harvard University Press.

Jones, Gayl (1998), *Corregidora*, Boston, MA: Beacon Press.

Lathan, Stan, dir. (2000), *Killin' Them Softly*, USA: Home Box Office (HBO), YouTube. https://www.youtube.com/watch?v=FclScfPoKes.

Lee, Spike, dir. (1986), *She's Gotta Have It*, Brooklyn, NY: 40 Acres & A Mule/Island Pictures.

Nussbaum, Emily (2019), "TV's Reckoning with #MeToo," *The New Yorker*, May 27. Available online: https://www.newyorker.com/magazine/2019/06/03/tvs-reckoning-with-metoo (accessed September 25, 2020).

Painter, Nell Irvin (1996), *Sojourner Truth: A Life*, New York: W. W. Norton & Company.

Surviving R. Kelly (2019), Produced by Tamra Simmons, Dream Hampton, Nigel Bellis, Astral Finnie, Jesse Daniels, Joel Karsberg, Jessica Everleth, and Maria Pepin, United States: Bunim/Murray Productions.

The Day Beyoncé Turned Black (2016), *Saturday Night Live*, NBC, February 14. Available online: https://www.youtube.com/watch?v=ociMBfkDG1w&list=FLfLpEZMVPVsDuqWn6VVcFYw&index=43.

Tillet, Salamishah, and Scheherazade Tillet (2019), "After the 'Surviving R. Kelly' Documentary, #MeToo Has Finally Returned to Black Girls," *The New York Times*, January 10. Available online: https://www.nytimes.com/2019/01/10/opinion/r-kelly-documentary-metoo.html.

Truth, Sojourner, Olive Gilbert, and Nell Irvin Painter ([1884] 1998), *Narrative of Sojourner Truth: A Bondswoman of Olden Time, with a History of Her Labors and Correspondence Drawn from Her Book of Life; Also, A Memorial Chapter*, New York: Penguin Books.

Yellin, Jean Fagan (2000), "Introduction," in Jean Fagan Yellin (ed.), *Incidents in the Life of a Slave Girl, Written by Herself*, xiii–xliii, Cambridge: Harvard University Press.

25

Lessons in Credibility and Complicity in Two Modern Dramas

Amy B. Hagenrater-Gooding

Setting the Scene

Class was winding down after a productive discussion on characterization, specifically the animal imagery used to portray Stanley Kowalski and the use of lighting and water references to depict Blanche DuBois in Tennessee Williams's *A Streetcar Named Desire* (1947). Stopping with the end of scene ten seemed logical, as I felt students needed to sit with the shocking violence and obvious rape to process it before our next class. But surprisingly, a tentative hand shot up right before dismissal. This student rarely spoke in class. She was a good student and I always enjoyed reading her insightful papers, so I was stunned when she proffered this observation: "But didn't Blanche, in some ways, deserve what she got?" In twenty years of teaching, I have rarely been rendered mute. Yet here I was, watching heads nod as young, seemingly progressive women had a hard time finding Blanche's claim of rape credible; like many readers, like her own sister, some students were complicit in sending her off to her doom.

I left class that day rattled and thought about this course—Modern Drama, a required, upper-division class for all English majors—and other potholes of understanding that had occurred in my time teaching the course. At that moment in the 2015 semester, we were rapidly approaching David Mamet's *Oleanna*. I routinely screened a portion of the film after students had read the play, and it never failed to shock me how students responded to John's violence toward Carol. They literally jumped from their seats, clapped, laughed, and cheered, as John raised a chair above Carol's head spewing "you vicious little bitch" (Mamet 1992: 45). I had watched such responses escalate every semester, and as I walked back to my office that day, I realized I needed to thematically adjust my approach to this class and zero in on gender, violence, and trauma. By focusing on contemporary issues and inviting students to share their own connections with the dramatic works, the course enabled students to understand not only the theoretical elements of drama and how they apply to non-literary texts, but also the complex problems of complicity and abuse.

The Course

One of my main goals for the class was showing how literature, drama specifically, is a site for exploring social issues. The class begins in earnest with Henrik Ibsen and his contribution to modern drama with the problem play. We often jump in with *A Doll's House*, where we talk about feminist themes and power. While most students don't fault Nora for leaving Torvald, they do feel a bit conflicted about her leaving her children. Students often repeatedly assume Nora is wrong to choose self-understanding and betterment over her family, even though we have been privy to her perspective from the onset of the play. Because Nora "goes along" with Torvald's imagining of her, students often feel she plays a role as the weak and submissive wife, casting herself in a part and duping him in the end. Her decision ultimately to stand up to him leads many students to feel for Torvald, negating her experience and ignoring his, and society's, power. Students recognize that she has been verbally diminished by Torvald and objectified, but again, within the confines of marriage, students often read these abuses as old-fashioned or not worth examination. This conversation is a relatively safe space in which to begin our discussion of female agency.

The first half of the semester is devoted to exploring issues related to gender, specifically how men silence women by "authoring" their narratives. After reading Ibsen, we move to Susan Glaspell's *Trifles*, a brief play that discusses separate spheres and the value and worth ascribed to the people and labor contained in those spheres. Then we move to a conversation about who writes the story that is told. Is it based on evidence or supposition? We ask similar questions about *Mud*, by Maria Irene Fornes, which also focuses on women who are isolated and trapped by domesticity and, like Glaspell's main character, have been subjected to emotional violence and implicit physical abuse. For example, in *Trifles* Mr. Wright is described as like "a raw wind that gets to the bone" (Glaspell [1916] 2004). And the force with which Mr. Wright breaks the neck of his wife's canary—which had previously symbolized her pre-isolation freedom and voice—presages the revenge she exacts on him after enduring his abuse for years. Mae of *Mud* is not so lucky. Likened to a starfish, she is also portrayed as rooted to her home and is killed by her husband when she tries to leave. Both women try to control their own lives, but find the violence that pervades them inescapable. This violence and lack of agency connect back to Williams's play and create a clear thematic foundation for discussing complicity and credibility during the second half of the semester.

Revisions and Additions to the Course

In past semesters, the second half of the course has used contemporary drama to consider issues of race. But my experiences teaching this class in 2015, coupled with my students' discussions about believability and consent in the context of conversations begun in 2017 by #MeToo, led me to retool the course to focus on consent. I added two new plays that would allow us to discuss the role of complicity and believability within the context of the "problem play" as a site for exploring societal problems. But I also intended the plays to require students to question *their* complicity as readers in judging these women, specifically in relation to the problem of rape and assault.

Before reading each play, students write responses to general questions about consent and complicity, such as the following: can verbal consent be withdrawn? Can one assume lowered inhibitions and alcohol remove the need for consent? Can consent be implicit? They return to these questions after we have completed our class discussion of the literary texts and of contemporary news stories about consent, complicity, and assault. This approach allows students to scaffold their learning so that these "case studies," fictional and real, allow them to develop a greater understanding of these fictional characters, whose stories often mirror those of real women.

Paula Vogel's *How I Learned to Drive* (1997)

Vogel's play tells the story of Li'l Bit and her abuse at the hands of her doting Uncle Peck. Through various encounters whereby he teaches her how to drive, introduces her to alcohol, and manipulates her perception of events, readers see a clear-cut portrayal of sexual abuse. What I like to focus on in the play, however, is how her family and the community create an atmosphere in which this abuse is not only tolerated, but seemingly encouraged. Although Uncle Peck is the primary abuser, abuse is normalized within the family by entrenched attitudes of debasement and sexual servitude.

The play uses a Greek Chorus to establish the characters of her family members and reveal misogyny as an inherited system of oppression. Her grandfather dismisses her desire to attend college when he asserts, "What does she need a college degree for? She's got all the credentials she'll need on her chest" (Vogel 1998: 17). Her aunt, casting her husband as a "good man," paints her niece as the "sly one" who "knows exactly what she's doing; she's twisted Peck around her little finger and thinks it's all a big secret" (66–7). Aunt Mary expresses her support for Peck early in the play: "Peck's so good with them when they get to be this age" (19). Although these characters are presented individually, their words are attributed to either the male or female chorus. This overlap between individual characters and communal chorus establishes the family legacy of submission passed down through the maternal line and echoed repeatedly by the chorus of societal voices. The play's use of the chorus offers a clear opportunity for students to consider both the theme of how society judges individuals' behavior and establishes rules for abuse victims' believability, and the formal mechanism by which the play communicates that theme.

Li'l Bit is defined by her body; she states, "In my family, folks tend to get nicknamed for their genitalia" (13). Her nickname in fact sexualizes her from infancy, as her mother describes how she, in her need to establish her baby's gender, parted her legs to discover "Just a little bit" (14). Both the Greek chorus and Peck use this phrase, with Peck naming and sexualizing her from the start. The double entendre of his claim "I held you, one day old, right in this hand" (14) pervades the drama and establishes the seemingly innocent complicity that allows this abuse to occur. He holds her, innocently, as an uncle would a child, yet grooms her to hold her innocence in his hand through manipulation and abused trust. Juxtaposed with such scenarios are more overt scenes of her objectification. Her grandfather, again as the male Greek chorus, observes: "If Li'l Bit gets any bigger, we're gonna haveta buy her a wheelbarrow to carry in front of her" (15). Her peers reduce her to a sexualized body as well, as we see when she recalls girls in middle school mocking her body in the showers after gym class and forcing her to avoid dancing for fear of the attention her jiggling breasts would receive (54, 57). Her body is a "walking Mary Jane joke," and she feels that she is " ... being looked at all the time" (57). Tellingly, women and girls participate in her objectification and abuse.

Vogel uses the metaphor of driving to illustrate the cumulative effect of everyone's complicity in the abuse. As Uncle Peck teaches Li'l Bit to drive, sexual imagery linking cars and women provides a powerful touchpoint for discussing abuse and consent. The action of the play begins with "Idling in the Neutral Gear" and goes through "Shifting Forward from First to Second Gear" to "Implied Consent," where we are presented with the vehicular laws in the state of Maryland asserting that "As an individual operating a motor vehicle ..., you must abide by 'Implied Consent'" (66). These rules for driving set the tenor for the drama. When Li'l Bit asks why a car is described as a "she," Peck suggests that she " ... think of someone who responds to your touch—someone who performs just for you and gives you want you ask for—I guess I always see a 'she'" (51). Considering the misogynistic environment in which she has been raised and lives, it isn't surprising that when Peck asserts that nothing is going to happen between them until she wants it, and asks if she understands, she affirms that she does. He casts her as complicit to ameliorate his responsibility.

Peck also uses alcohol to prevent her from perceiving that he is using his power and relational status to exert control over her, which he obtains for her with another man's assistance. Upon obtaining her license, Peck takes her out for a celebratory dinner where the waiter serves her alcohol despite her age because he anticipates a large tip. When she gets a little sloppy and drunk, Peck tells her she has had her last drink, yet signals for the waiter to bring her more: "The Waiter looks at Li'l Bit and shakes his head no. Peck raises his eyebrow, raises his finger to indicate one more, and then rubs his fingers together. It looks like a secret code" (28). This conspiracy between men to incapacitate her, much like the family's complicity in objectifying her, creates a culture that offers her as victim for his whims.

As students work through this play, I push them to see it as more than just a drama about familial abuse, but rather as an opportunity to reflect on their own experiences with abuses of power. We focus on the role of agency and power and the use of jokes to undermine one's self-worth and self-confidence, the role of alcohol in aiding abuse, and the dubiousness of consent which can be, as we see with Li'l Bit, exacted under duress. Most of my students are familiar with the 2017 Netflix series *13 Reasons Why*, which allows us to discuss many of the issues that have shaped our discussions of the plays: the events leading up to the sexual assault, which include the complicity of the victim's female friends in rape culture and in diminishing the victim's sense of herself, the role of alcohol in the assault, and its repercussions for the main character. Much as the women in *Trifles* piece together the clues in the play to decipher what really occurred to Mr. Wright, I encourage students to reflect on each of the tapes presented by the main character of *13 Reasons*, explaining what ultimately led her to take her own life. How did the environment facilitate her assault? In what ways beyond the assault itself was she victimized? While I don't have class time to show the series, this is a great opportunity to allow avid viewers of the show (of which I always have many), to take over and lead the discussion through clips and examples.[1]

Arlene Hutton's *I Dream before I Take the Stand* (2003)

Hutton's brief play consists of only a lawyer and a young, nameless woman who recounts events leading up to her sexual assault. The two-character drama neatly showcases the binary of he said/she said (especially as the characters are delineated as "he" and "she"), while also presenting the idea of narrative authorship: how can someone else's counter-reading of one's experiences diminish and discount the incident of abuse? At this point, we return to Blanche in Williams's play. Her sister tells her neighbour, Eunice, that "I couldn't believe her story and go on living with Stanley" (Williams [1947], 1951: 133). Instead of contradicting Stella, instead of believing Blanche, Eunice tells Stella, "Don't ever believe it. Life has got to go on. No matter what happens, you've got to keep going" (133). While Eunice's reaction might initially seem like optimistic support of a friend forced to endure the trials of marriage, it also reveals how both women are equally complicit in victimizing her and sealing her fate by choosing self-preservation over the truth.

By pairing Hutton's and Williams's plays, students see how they, too, often judge and victim-blame. In Hutton's play, the female victim must give a linear account of the assault on the stand, but the male lawyer is free to digress from factual recounting to interrogate her about her appearance and choice of clothing. The questions are designed not to paint a picture of the event but to paint a picture of a woman who " ... walked quickly through the park wearing sexy clothes with [her] breasts bouncing and [her] thighs damp and [she] smiled and nodded at a stranger" (Hutton 2003: 31), implying that she asked for the assault by being a woman moving through the world.

Although the process of trial is supposed to yield justice and ultimately punish the criminal, here the lawyer attacks the victim, in another format, again and again. The "he" of the drama continues to ask leading questions to which the "she" repeatedly responds "no"; her no is ignored and the side note in the play reveals "(he verbally rapes her) ... Your body was scented. You were wearing a revealing outfit ... you were shaking your breasts and rolling your hips at this man" (32). This obvious illustration of victim-blaming connects straight back to Blanche, also a victim who is derided for her dress, her speech, and her presence. Once they have made this connection, students must examine their own preconceived notions about how a woman's choices in her appearance or behavior relate to her "culpability" in her own assault.

To round out our discussion of gender, abuse, and complicity, I like to call on Netflix's *Unbelievable*, a series that dramatizes a real-life serial rape case while focusing primarily on the discrediting and public shaming of one disbelieved victim whose credibility can only be reclaimed through the advocacy of two female detectives who refused to dismiss her allegation as just a story. First, I show in class a scene in which a young woman is belittled and discredited by two male police officers until she recants her claim of assault. As homework, students then complete a reflective response via Flipgrid (a short-form video recording application where students share their recorded responses) in which they consider their own reactions to and questions about this viewing. By assigning written responses both before and after textual readings and video response discussions that seem more informal than our face-to-face discussion, I repeatedly and variously call on students to interrogate their own assumptions as well as apply the literary lessons to their own understanding.

Connections and Wrapping Up

At the end of Vogel's play, readers see Li'l Bit adjusting her mirrors while watching Peck recede in her rear-view mirror as she floors the car, moving forward into her own story, devoid of the chorus. Hearkening to an earlier observation from Peck that "When you are driving, your life is in your own two hands," we see her regain agency at play's end (Vogel 1998, 50). In Hutton's play, "she," at the man's prompting, begins her story again, repeating it in the hopes of somehow, someway, getting it "right" for the "he" and the audience who doubt her veracity. I ask students to consider whether we read this forced repetition as re-victimizing her or as her chance to revisit the narrative, having seen the systemic bias pervading the judgment leveled against her. Does this repetition cause us to reform our own verdict? As the course ends and students look in the rear-view mirror at the previous fifteen weeks, it is my hope that they begin to make connections to their own biases and their own complicity in damning these women and enabling the misogyny and rape culture that victimize them both within and outside of the page.

Note

1 Michaela Coel's *I May Destroy You*, a contemporary British TV show dealing with rape and consent, is one I hope to use the next time I teach this course.

Works Cited

13 Reasons Why (2017), [TV Program], Netflix, 17 March.
Fornes, Maria Irene (1983), "*Mud*," in J. Gainoi and M. Puchner (eds.), *The Norton Anthology of Drama* Vol. 2, 1234–52, New York: W. W. Norton & Company.
Glaspell, Susan ([1916] 2004), *Trifles*, Project Gutenberg. Available online: https://www.gutenberg.org/files/10623/10623-h/10623-h.htm (accessed July 13, 2020).
Hutton, Arlene (2003), *I Dream Before I Take the Stand*, New York: Playscripts, Inc.
Ibsen, Henrik ([1879] 2008), *A Doll's House*, Project Gutenberg. Available online: https://www.gutenberg.org/files/2542/2542-h/2542-h.htm (accessed July 13, 2020).
I May Destroy You (2020), [TV Program], HBO, 29 June.
Mamet, David (1992), *Oleanna*, New York: Dramatists Play Service.
Unbelievable (2019), [TV Program], Netflix, September 13.
Vogel, Paula (1998), *How I Learned to Drive*, *The Mammary Plays*, 7–92, New York: Theatre Communications Group.
Williams, Tennessee ([1947] 1951), *A Streetcar Named Desire*, New York: Signet.

26

An Impulse toward Agency:
Teaching Scenes of Sexual Violence
in Afro-Latina/o/x Literature

Ethan Madarieta

When teaching Latina/o/x[1] literature, I find that students are compelled to read agency into scenes of violence against Black, Indigenous, and Latina/o/x bodies, particularly in scenes of sexual violence. This is a well-intentioned impulse that seems to emerge from the desire to imbue Latina/o/x subjects with an agency that subverts the force of intersectional oppressions. But this impulse often causes one to overlook how agency is also a condition of subjugation and therefore always predetermined and restricted. In order to unpack this (mis)understanding of agency, I work with students in the first weeks of class to better understand the processes of subject formation and subjugation involved in becoming a subject—a prerequisite to identity formation. This essay will present how I teach these complex theoretical ideas through scenes of sexual violence using examples from two Afro-Latina/o/x novels: the canonical novelized memoir *Down These Mean Streets* (1967) by Piri Thomas and the often-overlooked *Daughters of the Stone* (2009) by Dahlma Llanos-Figueroa. In *Down These Mean Streets,* I will attend to the pressures on normative Black masculinities and sexualities, as well as complicate the prescriptive and proscriptive sexualities of Latinx trans women in order to think about agency and consent. To set the foundations for reading Thomas's novel, I will begin by interrogating students' interpretations of enslaved Black women's agency in encounters of sexual violence in *Daughters of the Stone*.

Teaching scenes of sexual violence in Afro-Latina/o/x literature requires an attention to the complex conditions of race and processes of racialization that attend specifically to the Black body, which is why I begin my course "Afro-Latina/o/x Literature: Race, Genealogy, and the Decolonial Imagination" with three weeks of readings in critical race theory specifically concerning Latinas/os/xs and Afro-Latinas/os/xs. I propose to the students that in addition to the racial preconstitution of the subject based on (mis)recognition of phenotypic difference, we must also understand that race is informed by language, cultural practice, geography, religion, climate, and political organization (Hesse 2007; Roberts 2011). In addition, we must attend to this primacy of blackness as the Afro-Latina/o/x ontological condition read in its relation to capture and enslavement, and to the afterlives of slavery, as these, in many ways, determine the always already racialized Black body *over* Latina/o/x ethnic or racial identity. Particularly within the binary US black-white racial regime, a prior significance adheres to the Black body through the accrual of racialized narratives about the body that emerge with slavery and morph according to its afterlives. As I tell my students, the meanings of our body precede the existence of our body. Our identities as raced, gendered, sexed, classed, and so on, all await us when we are born.

Intersectionality and Subjectivation

Some students push against the idea of intersectionality because of a fundamental misunderstanding of it as hierarchical and divisive. This misunderstanding usually results from only conceptualizing the simultaneous and overlapping oppressions tied to frames of identity: gender, sexuality, race, ethnicity, culture, ability, and so on. We can clarify this misunderstanding by discussing the constitution of the subject as also always intersectional, a condition of living what Black feminist scholar Kathryn T. Gines writes are "multiplicitous, intersectional, interconnected, and interdependent existences" (2011: 275). Gines locates these existences at the site of the body as identities which "often [operate] in complex power relations with others" (275). Thus, our multiple existential identities are also primarily tied to how those identities are uniquely and simultaneously formed through subjugation. Judith Butler, expanding on Althusser and Foucault, offers a concept of subject formation through subjugation—subjectivation—that allows us to extend this concept of intersectionality to the complex agency of the racialized body. In subjectivation, subjectivity is produced when one responds to a "hail" and enters into a set of social relations *by which one acquires agency,* but that subjectivity is coerced and requires the acceptance of the subjugation that determines it (Althusser 2020: 56; Butler 1997: 5; Foucault 1982: 781). Therefore, to become a subject is to be (mis)recognized within a certain set of social relations that always predetermine the limits of that subjectivity. Any identity that lies outside or beyond the intersections, interconnections, and interdependence of subjectivity is denied the subject.

The importance of this nuancing intersectional analysis becomes intensified when interpreting scenes of sexual violence against the Afro-Latina/o/x body, which is primarily read as the Black body. Hortense Spillers describes both the enslaved Black male and female body as understood to be a "vulnerable, supine body" that "might be invaded/raided by another *woman* or man" (77 emphasis in original). This particular condition is due to the subjugation of the enslaved as "slave" rather than human, and thus without recognized access to the characteristics of human subjectivity such as a proper gendered identity, which is to say, a gendered identity which is recognized as human rather than animal. Within this context, sexual violence against the enslaved Black woman is not understood to be the same as the sexual violence against a white woman. In fact, this ontological difference ensures that the white woman also does not see the rape of an enslaved Black woman *as* rape.

Slavery, Rape, and Agency in *Daughters of the Stone*

Daughters of the Stone spans five generations of women, defined by their relationships with their mothers across two continents and a century. The novel portrays the women's many experiences of gendered and sexual violence as an inheritance of the trauma of slavery. The primary matriarch, Fela, is captured from her village in an unnamed African region,[2] separated from her husband, Imo, and sold into slavery, arriving in Puerto Rico in the first scene of the novel. We later find out that this "arrival" is her second, after being raped and then resold by her former *patrón* (slave master) on the island, an event we learn of only when Fela decides to have sex with the new patrón, Don Tomás.

In many ways, this decision determines the lives of all subsequent generations who live both in, and then "in the wake of slavery" (Sharp 2016). Fela is standing outside at night staring at the moon, an imagined point of connection to Imo and the ancestors who have passed. She and Imo had enacted a ritual in which a small stone was imbued with the knowledge of the ancestors and the spirit of their unborn child, so that no matter the biological father, Fela's daughter would be theirs.[3] Fela is compelled to bear a child, to fulfill an obligation to the goddess Oshun, before she is allowed to die and rejoin her husband and the ancestors.[4] When she sees the patrón also walking in the moonlight she gets "an idea that had been growing in her mind" to have her child with him (Llanos-Figueroa 2009: 47), in the hope that her daughter might not be subjected to the imminence of death, as Fela had been, and might therefore survive to have a child of her own.

On its surface, the scene presents Fela as acting with agency. The patrón is reported to be concerned with how Fela feels and tentative about forcing himself on one of his slaves as do all the other patrones (42, 47). The narrator writes:

> Fela's resolve never wavered as she felt herself being led toward the river. Her step was sure-footed and determined. Then she felt the moist earth beneath, heard the river as it flowed in the background. She let him do as he chose, focusing on the white shoulder above her.
>
> (49)

Students always interpret this scene as showing Fela's agency; after all, it is her decision to walk with the patrón to the river and have sex with him. But we must attend to Fela's subjugation as slave and the fact that her decision was always already coerced. I ask my students, *would Fela have had to make the same decision if she were not enslaved?*, and the answer is always *no*.

We also have to attend to the narrative context surrounding Fela's decision. When she first has the thought to have a child with the patrón, she immediately remembers "that other *patrón* on that other plantation. The scene flashed through her mind with such vividness that it stopped her for a moment" (47). This memory of her rape by the "other *patrón*" is described in some detail, signaling Fela's reliving of the trauma in the present of her remembering. When she feels the ground beneath her and the patrón's body is atop her own, "unexpectedly, the details of that other night came back to her *like a sudden blow*" (49; emphasis mine). This visceral doubling of the two rapes occurs through Fela's embodied traumatic memory of the first rape during the second, confirming that this current encounter with Don Tomás can only ever be rape. Both rapes are made possible by the originary trauma of capture and enslavement that foreclosed Fela's agency by excluding her from the category of the human. This very much complicates the idea that she has acted with agency or given consent.[5]

This can be a troubling, although very important, "ah ha" moment for students. They often feel ashamed of their initial impulse to read Fela's agency and consent into the scene. It is crucial, here, for us as educators to attend to these feelings of shame for (mis)understanding agency in scenes of sexual violence. Though resulting from a well-meaning desire to imbue the oppressed with power, this (mis)recognition of agency is an effect of the very processes of subjugation that give power to the patrón and exclude Fela from the category of human. Our inability to initially recognize these "complex power relations" (Gines 275) is due to our own interpellation into a set of social relations by which we understand race, gender, sexuality, and so on—always in relation to our "selves." This "self" is the agential "I" of the subject that freely gives into subjugation to access the power to respond to the oppressive power of subjectivation itself. Shame, in this teaching/ learning moment, is recognition of the disjuncture between the self as central subject and the experiences of others. It should thus be praised as the work of critical self and social analysis necessary for social and political change. I am attentive to the signs of shame in my students and make sure to tell them: "Good job! That's how you know you're doing the work! You are no longer the you that did not see the complexity of that relationship."

Llanos-Figueroa's text further complicates our understanding of Fela's ontological position and the possibility of her agency, in terms of her access to a gendered subjectivity. After the patrón "left [Fela] there, as he would an animal that had performed her task," she runs to the slave master's wife, "thinking another woman would surely understand" (47). Instead of seeing Fela as a woman, and therefore seeing her husband's rape *as* rape, the patrona reacts in astonishment that she is speaking to her at all: "The *patrona* would no longer endure this black woman who obviously hadn't been taught her place yet" (47). For this, what the patrona sees as Fela's insistence on ontological equality, she has Fela's tongue cut out before she is sold. These scenes complicate notions of consent and agency and the narrative of Fela's ability to be recognized within the gendered subjectivities afforded those recognized as human—a subjectivity foreclosed to the slave.

Coerced Masculinities and Trans (Mis)-Recognition in *Down These Mean Streets*

Thomas's novelized memoir is an ideal teaching text. Like Llanos-Figueroa's novel, *Down These Mean Streets* implies that much of the language being spoken in the home is Spanish and that the different geographies and spaces the characters occupy are apprehended through a lens of Latinidades. The focus of the text is the protagonist Piri's struggle with his racial identity. Piri has the darkest skin in his family, second only to his father, Poppa, who claims his brown skin is due to "hav[ing] Indian blood" (153).[6] Piri describes Poppa's own relation to racial identity through his overperformance of Puerto Ricanness as proximity to whiteness, and therefore of "value." His father tells a very young Piri, "I can remember the time when I made my accent heavier, to make me more of a Puerto Rican than the most Puerto Rican there ever was. I wanted a value on me, son" (153). This alignment of Puerto Rican identity with whiteness and Piri's exclusion from being Puerto

Rican because he is always already determined in the binary logics of the US racial regime is the foundation of Piri's identity struggle for the rest of his life. Like his father, "To prove he is Puerto Rican and by default white, [Piri] performs society's Latino stereotype" of a violent, homophobic hypermasculinity to assert a heteronormative masculinity (Sánchez 1998: 122). Teachers must unpack this connection between racial identity and violent hypermasculinity with students before discussing scenes of sexual violence in the text. Examples of the meanings of masculinity in the text, or, more precisely, "becoming *hombre*," occur within the first few pages (15). The very notion of "becoming" is a working-toward rather than a state of being. It is an identity that must always be re-asserted through (re)performance. Piri's examples of "becoming *hombre*" are "wanting to have a beard to shave, a driver's license, a draft card, a 'stoneness' which enabled you to go into a bar *like* a man" (15–16, emphasis mine). Furthermore, becoming a man is the act of not allowing "anyone to tell you what to do," and the knowledge that, if they did, "You'd smack him down like Whiplash ...." (16). Such descriptions of masculinity point toward the unfixed nature of being *hombre*, and the need to enact (or become—a transitive state) *hombre*. For Piri, the negative racialized preconstitution of the categories of masculinity and sexuality is entwined.

This preoccupation with becoming *hombre* and its relation to sexuality is played out in the chapter "If You Ain't Got Heart, You Ain't Got Nada." The chapter begins with Piri and his friends fighting another Latino rival gang. Before the physical fight begins, they realize one of their crew hasn't shown up because he's gone to his sister's birthday party. The boys "took turns sounding his mother for giving birth to a *maricón* like him," meaning they insulted his mother for giving birth to what translates as a "faggot" (52). This positioning of gayness or queerness as in binary opposition to the kind of masculinity that constitutes *un hombre* is repeated upwards of a hundred times throughout the novelized memoir. During the fist fight that ensues we read Piri's internal narrative. He is overjoyed that he gets to fight a leader of the rival gang because "[He'd] been aching to chill that *maricón*" (53). It is important to draw connections with the students between definitions and performances of a particular kind of racialized masculinity and homophobia/homophobic violence in this scene because it directly precedes the first scene of physical sexual violence (as opposed to the anticipating linguistic violence of hate speech) in the text.[7]

To help my students better understand this scene, I introduce the idea that gender and sexuality are performances not determined by biological sex, by drawing their attention to the conversation that follows the fighting scene. Piri and his friends are talking about "faggots and their asses which, swinging from side to side, could make a girl look ridiculous, like she wasn't moving" (54). In this conversation the boys assert that anyone's sexuality can be identified, not by sex acts or sexual desires, but by an underperformance of the kind of masculinity the boys deem *hombre*. One of the boys, Alfredo, whom Piri identifies as a "stud," then says they should "make it up to the faggots' pad and cop some bread" (55). Their derogatory and violent speech against men who sleep with men brings to mind, for Alfredo, a group of trans women who live in the neighborhood— this is the first act of misrecognition. We are told that "None of them looked happy" to go except Alfredo (55). Alfredo says, "Motherfuckers, who's a punk?" to which Piri answers internally for all of them, "Nobody, man"—though *nobody speaks* (55). Piri asks, if none of them wanted to go, "why were we making it up to the *maricones'* pad? Cause we wanted to belong, and belonging meant doing whatever had to be done" (55). This desire to belong above all else suggests that one cannot belong and not go along with whatever the group posits as a heteronormative masculine act, here defined as the opposite of being "a punk." Here we see how peer pressure complicates the idea of agency and consent in this and the following scene. That "nobody speaks" further complicates the boys' consent to the visit.

It is important at this point to discuss the historical origins of the term "punk" as it relates to masculine-identified sexualities.[8] Don Romesburg defines "'Punking,' [as] when a usually masculine-identified boy or younger male would take the receptive role in sex with an older male for cash or some other form of compensation" (2009: 381). This context gives new meaning to Alfredo's taunt to not be a "punk," particularly in light of "all the coins we were going to hustle" but with "no talk about the down payment that had to be made by all of us" (55–6). Regardless of Alfredo's knowledge of the history of the term, it must be understood as a palimpsest where the prior meanings also rise to the surface of current meanings. Implied in the above definition of "punk," to not be a "punk" means the boys will have sex with men for money or other compensation, but not in the "receiving" role.

The idea that the boys were headed to "the faggots' pad" assigns male sex to the people the boys are set to visit. Every time I have taught this text, the students have taken up this assignment of gender, by failing to recognize the trans women as trans rather than as gay men. This misrecognition is important to note because it so distinctly conflicts with the two women's voices that come "from behind the closed door" when they arrive (56). When Antonia opens the door, Piri "saw that the women's voices belonged to men" (56). His assertion that the trans women are men starkly contrasts with the women's understanding of themselves. When one of the women, Concha, tells Antonia about a time when she was raped "by four boys" in one night, Antonia replies, "Don't make eet sound so *importante,* beetch" (57). Concha is hurt and insists that the experience was really bad because "I haf my period an' eet ees all right for some womans to make love like that, but I no one of them. For me eet ees not comfortable" (57–8). These women obviously identify as women and have women's experiences, so much so that Piri says, "If I had my eyes closed, I would have sworn these were real broads talking" (58).[9] The boys' assertions that the women are actually gay men might be read as reflecting on the desires for intimacy among the group of friends. Students astutely point to the male-to-male intimacy enjoyed by the group, both on the streets and in the company of these trans women, which offers an opportunity to discuss the concept of homosociality.[10] The boys are able to share intimacy with each other while maintaining their sense of heteronormative masculinity through both physical and linguistic violence against the women they deem men. This also allows them to contradictorily have sex with the trans women, even as they commit violence upon them as an assertion of their masculinity.

Most students see the boys in this scene as the sole perpetrators of violence. There is, after all, much textual evidence of their violence. But what I find interesting is that students want to read agency only in the boys' linguistic and physical violence against the women, preventing them from recognizing Piri's own sexual violation. In one key scene, Piri becomes the object of sexual violence perpetrated by one of the trans women, raising complex questions about his agency and consent. The boys are all sitting around the apartment smoking weed when Piri hears a "feminine voice" offering him a "king-sized" joint and, without looking up, he takes "the stick from the fingers" (58), not gendering the fingers as male. He tells us he "was gonna get a gone high" and smokes the joint until it is "burnt to a little bit of a roach" (58). After falling into a reverie about how good it feels to fight with friends, Piri is awakened "because somebody was touching [him] where only [he] and a girl should touch" (60).

Piri comes back to himself, "but [his] body was still relaxed" (60–1). One of the women, Concha, is unzipping his pants and "with cold fingers take[s] [his] pee-pee out and begin[s] to pull it up and down" (61). Piri tries to resist the assault, but cannot seem to make his body do what his mind wants:

> I tried to make me get up and move away from those squeezing fingers, but no good; I was like paralyzed. I pushed away at the fingers, but they just held on tighter. I tried to stop my pee-pee's growth, but it grew independently. If I didn't like the scene, my pee-pee did. I couldn't move.
>
> (61)

We don't know if Piri was paralyzed because of the assault or because he was so high, but we do know that the resistance he is able to give is met with a greater force as the fingers "just held tighter." At this point students see emerging in the language a young boy who is being raped, but they simultaneously question the assault since Piri's penis becomes erect and he appears to be acting in kind with his peers, who are also having sex with the trans women.

But we must disentangle the feeling of pleasure from the act of consent. When Piri's "pee-pee disappear[s] into Concha's mouth ... it both scared and pleased [him]" (61). For the entire duration of the oral sex, Piri is "chant[ing]" "*I like broads, I like muchachas, I like girls*" until the "slurping sounds" mark that the rape "was all over" (61). This is the last sentence in the paragraph, leaving a heavy silence that lingers and defies the supposed pleasure of orgasm. The next paragraph starts: "Concha was gone. I was left alone, weak and confused" (61). While the others are still sexually engaged with the women, Piri leaves the apartment feeling "both good and bad" (62).

Students rarely initiate discussion of this scene, which is uncomfortable to read because of its sexual explicitness and anti-trans and homophobic violence. One of the ways students defend against this discomfort is by reading agency into the scene to suppress the multiple registers and layers of sexual violence happening in it. While the boys are undeniably linguistically and physically violent toward the women, we cannot dismiss Piri's own violation.

Reading Scenes of Sexual Violence through Racial Myths

Scenes of sexual violence in Latina/o/x and Afro-Latina/o/x literature are often misinterpreted as evidence that such violence is somehow more common among Afro-Latinas/os/xs and Latinas/os/xs than it is in other ethno-racial groups. Teaching these literary scenes inevitably results in multiple papers about "machismo," a highly contested term that should be understood in relation to other racialized concepts such as the "angry Black man/woman"—as myths that have acquired social validity by the same pathways as other racializing narratives.[11] As educators of Afro-Latina/o/x and Latina/o/x literature, we must teach as context the centuries-long persistence of racist violence enabled by the sexualization of racialized bodies. In particular, the dehumanization and objectification, sexual and otherwise, of Black bodies must be understood as an ongoing context for these scenes. As is surely evidenced by this collection, sexual violence is not endemic to or emergent from any racialized, sexed, or gendered group.

Students' impulse toward assigning agency to the "oppressed" or to blanket demonization of the "oppressor" in scenes of sexual violence should always be considered in concert with understandings of consent and the processes of subjectivation. What is often read as agency, such as the misalignment of consent with the experience of pleasure, is coerced action and therefore cannot be a marker of consent or agency. Furthermore, encouraging a de-centralized understanding of subjectivity offers an empathic approach to reading the experiences of others, understanding an/other's experience as valid even if it cannot be integrated into our own matrix of experiences. We must therefore practice a critical pedagogy that encourages students to be bold in their analysis of the ongoing violent legacies of slavery and colonialism in their many forms, and in relation to themselves. As we demonstrate what this analysis looks like in the classroom through historicizing and interrogating the texts we read, we are able to perform with our students the disentangling of shame, and (mis)understandings of subjectivity, agency, and consent that can help students better understand sexual violence in these texts, the world, and their own lives.

Notes

1. While I believe in the inclusivity of the "x" in its queering of the binary gendered language of Spanish, it should not erase the equally queered identities of the self-identified "Latina lesbian" or "gay Latino" (see Hames-García and Martínez's *Gay Latino Studies*). I include both gendered endings and the ungendered "x" to include and prioritize male-identified, female-identified, butch, femme, trans, and gender non-conforming identities. In addition, in order that form inform content, I mobilize the conventional writing of the pan-ethno-racial category Afro-Latina/o/x not as convention, but to assert the primacy of blackness as the Afro-Latina/o/x ontological condition. Furthermore, part of the project of teaching Afro-Latina/o/x literature is to critique the exclusion of both blackness and indigeneity from the category of Latina/o/x, and to think about the pan-ethno-racial category of Afro-Latina/o/x as multiply entwined with the dynamic ethno-cultural category of Latinidades.
2. Her communication with Oshun suggests she was captured from a Yoruba region in the Kingdom of Benin prior to British colonial rule, what is now southwestern Nigeria.
3. Spillers argues that motherhood is denied the slave, foreclosing Imo and Fela's desire for the future child to be theirs. This becomes even more poignant when Fela lies down and dies directly after giving birth, making the child's only remaining "relative" the patrón.
4. On the Black woman's "obligation to 'make generations'" as a legacy of slavery, see Ferrari's chapter on *Corregidora* in this volume.
5. For a different reading of agency in a similar context, see Linda Chavers's essay in this volume.
6. The trope of replacing blackness with "being Indian" in Latina/o/x literature is rich for explication.

7   For more on linguistic violence and hate speech, see Judith Butler's chapter "On Linguistic Vulnerability" in *Excitable Speech*. I modify "linguistic violence" with "anticipating" to suggest the probability that such language precedes the associative physical act of violence.
8   Also see Cohen (1997) for a queer of color critique of how "punk" performances are (mis)understood without consideration of race, class, and other collective identities.
9   One might also use this scene to discuss other aspects of race and gender in relation to sexual violence. If remarked upon in class, I would discuss the trans women's accents and insertion of Spanish words in speech, a marker of their Latinidad, and would elaborate further on the distinction Piri makes between these women and "real broads." I would also attend to how Antonia's response to Concha's rape shows its quotidian nature in the lives of trans women of color, and think about sexual trauma and associations of affection with sexual abuse when Concha subsequently describes her rape as "mak[ing] love." I'd further attend to the fraught tensions between pleasure and pain when Antonia describes an early sexual experience where from having sex with a "beeg man" she "could not walk for long time without feelin' pain," but "he go away an' I miss what he do to me, so I look for somebody else" (57).
10 For further reading on homosociality and queerness in the novel, see Sifuentes-Jáuregui (2014).
11 Consider Erik Morales's Doctoral dissertation, "Machismo(s): A Cultural History, 1928–1984," where he deftly analyzes and historicizes "the uncritical circulation of the term 'machismo' in scholarly works and American cultural discourse" (2015: 1). On the "bad Black bitch," see Saffold in this volume.

Works Cited

Althusser, Louis (2020), *On Ideology*, New York: Verso.
Butler, Judith (1997), *Excitable Speech: A Politics of the Performative*, New York: Routledge.
Cohen, Cathy (1997), "Punks, Bulldaggers, and Welfare Queens: The Radical Potential of Queer Politics?," *GLQ: A Journal of Lesbian and Gay Studies*, 3 (4): 437–65.
Foucault, Michel (1982), "The Subject and Power," *Critical Inquiry*, 8 (4): 777–95.
Gines, Kathryn T. (2011), "Black Feminism and Intersectional Analyses: A Defense of Intersectionality," *Philosophy Today*, 55: 275–84.

Hames-García, Michael and Ernesto Javier Martínez (2011), *Gay Latino Studies: A Critical Reader*, Durham: Duke University Press.
Hesse, Barnor (2007), "Racialized Modernity: An Analytics of White Mythologies," *Ethnic and Racial Studies*, 30 (4): 643–63.
Llanos-Figueroa, Dahlma (2009), *Daughters of the Stone*, Self-published.
Morales, Erik (2015), "Machismo(s): A Cultural History, 1928–1984," PhD Dissertation, the University of Michigan.
Roberts, Dorothy E. (2011), *Fatal Invention: How Science, Politics, and Big Business Re-Create Race in the Twenty-First Century*, New York: The New Press.
Romesburg, Don (2009), "'Wouldn't a Boy Do?' Placing Early-Twentieth-Century Male Youth Sex Work into Histories of Sexuality," *Journal of the History of Sexuality*, 18 (3): 367–92.
Sánchez, Marta E. (1998), "La Malinche at the Intersection: Race and Gender in *Down These Mean Streets*," *PMLA*, 113 (1): 117–28.
Sharp, Christina (2016), *In the Wake: On Blackness and Being*, Durham: Duke University Press.
Sifuentes-Jáuregui, Ben (2014), *The Avowal of Difference: Queer Latino American Narratives*, Albany: SUNY Press.
Spillers, Hortense (1987), "Mama's Baby, Papa's Maybe: An American Grammar Book," *Diacritics*, 17 (2): 64–81.
Thomas, Piri (1997), *Down These Mean Streets*, New York: Vintage.

27

New Approaches to Short Fiction and Nonfiction in the Classroom:

Challenging Violence from Queer and Straight Perspectives

Zoë Brigley Thompson

The short story and nonfiction essay are on the front line of the #MeToo movement. Take Kristen Roupenian's short story "Cat Person" and Ocean Vuong's "A Letter to My Mother That She Will Never Read," which were published online around the time when the #MeToo movement gained momentum in 2017. Roupenian's story about a disturbing sexual encounter taps issues of consent that began to be talked about in complex ways in light of #MeToo, while Ocean Vuong's essay about domestic violence offers the subjectivity of a Vietnamese American, queer man. These stories counter understandings of #MeToo as highlighting only particular kinds of violence that happen to white, straight, cisgender women (cf. White 2017)—thus returning to the intentions of its originator, social worker Tarana Burke, as a means to find solidarity with Black girls who had experienced violence (cf. Garcia 2017). This essay will offer strategies and models for using nonfiction essays (by

Vuong and Carmen Machado) and short stories (by Roupenian and Eileen Chang) to ask questions about violence as an act impacted by institutions and cultural narratives, while showing how specific literary strategies allow writers to challenge assumptions about how violence works and how it is experienced.

Short stories can be appropriate vehicles for writing about violence, as they offer a window into a specific time and place in a person's life—a concentrated moment—and the form forces us to quickly enter another person's reality. Frank O'Connor suggests that short story writers offer a different view of human beings than novelists because "the short story remains by its very nature remote from the community—romantic, individualistic, and intransigent" (1963: 21). Kristine Somerville and Speer Morgan claim that the short story is about the individual's "struggle with love, work, family, or community" (2019: xii). Perhaps the short story is fitting as a form in which to write about violence, because so often acts of violence are impacted by the way that communities and institutions fail to respond to them or support their victims.

Creative nonfiction is also valuable for studying experiences of violence, and the struggle experienced by harmed individuals or groups. Anita Sinner describes the genre as an emergent form that "renders facts and events (content) with the conventions of fiction writing (form) including narrative voice, persona, authentic characterisation of place and settings, and pursuit of an idea or goal" (2013: 2). In creative nonfiction, "the contexts of everyday stories are not singular events but a form of relational interactivity" (Sinner 2013: 5). The mingling of the personal, the cultural, observations of place and people, and philosophical ideas offers a combination of theory and personal experience that can challenge pervasive stereotypes where victims of violence are blamed for their own experiences (cf. Kabir 2010). As F. W. Renker (1998) puts it, teaching nonfiction can be valuable because "[w]e're surrounded by a culture that promotes lies, evasions, distortions, creating a media-generated miasma" while nonfiction "frees us to attempt truth—maybe not *the* truth but our authentic response to experience." Just as with the short story, short nonfiction sometimes pits the "truth" of the individual against violences enacted by individuals *and* institutions.

In class, I pose this conundrum as a kind of triad (see Figure 27.1), which highlights three factors in how acts of violence are perceived, processes that directly impact responses to violence by individuals and institutions. At the top of the triangle is the act of violence itself, yet responses to that violence—by people and organizations who should help the victim—depend upon two other factors. At the second point of the triad, policies and procedures of institutions are not always set up to support those who have experienced violence (cf. Kabir 2010). Also, the third point of the triangle—cultural representations and stereotypes about violence toward particular groups of people—can enormously influence these behaviors and policies.

So for example, if a white police officer commits an act of violence against a Black woman of a lower socioeconomic group, institutional practices in the police are also at fault (institutional racism, lack of training, and the failure to create an atmosphere where problematic police officers can be reported). Cultural representations come into play, because of racist stereotypes that associate low-income Black people with criminality (cf. Ghandnoosh 2014) as well as the devaluing of Black women's experiences of violence (cf. Lindsey and Johnson 2014). This theoretical example is based on the real case of Daniel Holtzclaw, a police officer who was convicted for repeatedly assaulting low-income Black women in Oklahoma City (cf. Miller 2019). Students need to think about the institutional policies and

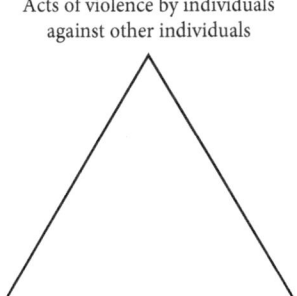

FIGURE 27.1 *Triad of contexts in experiences of violence. Created by Zoë Brigley Thompson, 2020.*

cultural stereotyping that contribute to and compound individual acts of violence in either hypothetical scenarios or real case studies.[1] This model can also be used when teaching short fiction and creative nonfiction as a way of illuminating power structures and dynamics that compound acts of violence against women and minorities.

In teaching the short story and nonfiction essay, I am most often interested in how writing speaks to structures of power. Introducing the volume *Feminism, Literature, and Rape Narratives* in 2010, Sorcha Gunne and I discuss methods of resistance in writing about sexual violence and identify a number of strategies that writers and artists use to combat scripts and assumptions about acts of violence (see Figure 27.2). Ultimately all of these strategies engage with power dynamics.

The first method entails using a "subversive symbology that […] illuminates the use of women's bodies as a kind of currency" in various disputes, sometimes between men (Brigley Thompson and Gunne 2010: 13; cf. Allen 1986: 41; cf. Sedgwick 1985). In showing how the bodies of women and minorities are used as currency in patriarchal and capitalist systems, the writer draws attention to the invisible workings of power. The second and third strategies involve finding overt or oblique ways to speak about violence. Creating a new trope to describe or depict violence seeks to undermine systems of power by reframing those who experience violence as human beings worthy of care. In addition, silence can be a subversive intervention into power dynamics and is a language in its own right. Finally, writers can work to avoid exploitative representations of violence while stories intervene in scripts that frame women and minorities as inevitable victims.

While this list is not exhaustive, offering this model to students can be extremely effective in studying how writers use subversive strategies to challenge the power structures that deny victims agency and compound the violence that happens with frightening regularity to women, Black and Indigenous people, queer folx, and other minorities. The voices of queer survivors and people of color who have experienced violence can help us avoid focusing on white, straight women as the sole survivors of violent acts. Our readings can also be made more nuanced using Figure 27.1, because the contexts of violence remind students that individual acts are influenced by institutional responses and cultural narratives about violence, race, and sexuality.

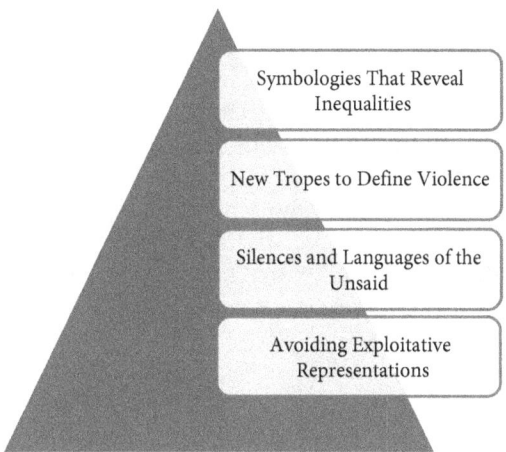

FIGURE 27.2 *Strategies in representing violence. Created by Zoë Brigley Thompson, 2020.*

Short Stories on Sexual Coercion

Eileen Chang's "Lust, Caution" and Kristen Roupenian's "Cat Person" challenge reductive narratives about the purity of virginity, slut-shaming, sexual scripts, passive norms for femininity, and the idea that there can be consent without enthusiasm. As a reading pair, the stories ask questions about how far we have come in terms of rethinking what consent to sexual acts looks like.

"Lust, Caution" (1979) by Chinese American author Eileen Chang (Zhang Ailing 張愛玲) is a long short story set in Shanghai during the Japanese occupation of the city during the Second Sino-Japanese War (1937–45), where the author lived during her early twenties.[2] The story opens as a group of society women playing Mah-jong compare their expensive rings. One woman, Chia-chih, is secretly having an affair with another's husband, Yee Tai-tai, who is intending that day to buy her an expensive ring. Chia-chih, however, is a spy who plans to assassinate Yee Tai-tai for collaborating with the Japanese. In flashbacks, the reader learns that years before, when the plan was concocted, Chia-chih's student friends decided that she would be the seducer, and despite her lack of enthusiastic consent, she was coerced to have sex with one of her student friends to gain experience. In the story's present, Chia-chih feels compelled to go through with the plan so her earlier sacrifice will not be for nothing. However, when the moment comes for Yee Tai-tai to be assassinated at the jewelry store, Chia-chih warns him, he escapes, and she is consequently executed.

To help students think about sex and power in the place and time of the story, I split students into groups and give them each a card with a biographical or historical detail: for example, Shanghai was named by British colonials with a history of being administered by the British, French, and Americans (cf. Rattini 2006); in 1944, the author married Hu Lan-ch'eng, a Japanese sympathizer and serial philanderer (cf. Louie 2012: 8–9); and her deeply conservative, Opium-addict father had a history of committing domestic abuse against his daughter (cf. Louie 2012: 1–5). I ask my students to consider how these settings and contexts might have influenced Chang's ideas about the workings of power and experiences of violence.

Establishing the context of the story is important for understanding the text from a perspective beyond Western assumptions, but it is also necessary to remind students that the story was published in the 1970s by a writer who had lived in the United States for twenty years, giving the story a kind of duality. Deep at the heart of this story—which puts "lust" and "caution" alongside each other—is the question of whether or not women can be autonomous, desiring subjects. Thinking back to Figure 27.1, we see that individual acts in the story have larger contexts. There is one clear individual act of violence when Chia-chih is coerced into having sex with a student friend, and this event also reveals dubious ideas about virginity and sexuality in women, ideas that frame virginity as a valuable commodity but also an obstruction to being sexually confident. Chinese culture, like the West, has a tendency to divide women into pure virgins and promiscuous whores (cf. Xiao Zhou 1989: 279). Institutions and organizations are significant too: the student plan is taken over by a secret operative, Wu, who asks her to continue the seductress/whore role and do her duty for China.

Thinking in terms of Figure 27.2, we see how Eileen Chang shows the exploited nature of Chia-chih through the heroine's currency in patriarchal structures and power games. Subtle uses of symbolism highlight Chia-chih's exploited position. The pink diamond ring that Yee Tai-tai is planning to buy her is an objective correlative for

Chia-chih, a prize used as bait in a contest between men as described by Allen (1986) and Sedgwick (1985). The image of the teapot is also significant in "Lust, Caution," as the lone phallic spout stands in for men's promiscuity, while the many cups represent women, an image that signals double standards for men and women. These symbologies challenge the assumptions of the men in the story and of the reader.

The silences in the story pose unanswered questions: why does Chia-chih warn Yee Tai-tai? Given the spy-ring's treatment of Chia-chih, will the new regime be any better than the old one? Asking students to talk about silences can provoke interesting questions and raise issues about consent, morality, and sex, the objectification of women, and coercion as sexual violence.

Kristen Roupenian's story "Cat Person," which also explores consent, sexual violence, and coercion, went viral when it was published in 2017 (cf. Roupenian 2019). Like "Lust, Caution," "Cat Person" describes doubts about consenting to sexual acts. Flirting by text, Robert tells Margot that he is a "cat person," but his cats are curiously missing when she finally visits his place. The story culminates in a sexual encounter that is unpleasant for Margot, and each of them is dismayed to discover a large age gap: Margot is twenty and Robert is thirty-four. Regretting the encounter, Margot breaks up with Robert by text, and he is amicable: she is a "sweet girl" until he sees her with another man at a bar. His texts become controlling, questioning, and ultimately end with him calling her a "whore." As in "Lust, Caution," women exist in categories defined by cultural narratives, which are weaponized by men.

Kelly Walsh and Terry Murphy (2019) note that "Cat Person" caused controversy about what is not said in the story, as Robert is not explicitly condemned: judgment is left to the reader. What is overlooked in discussions of Robert's guilt or innocence is the story's critique of structures beyond individuals. A key strategy in Figure 27.2 is using silence to speak, and this silence pinpoints problems of masculinity itself rather than Robert as an individual. Students could think about Figure 27.1 too, especially in light of Margot's observation that Robert's approach to sex seems based on pornography. Might Roupenian be critiquing the lack of sex and relationship education for Robert—who fails to gain Margot's enthusiastic consent for sex, makes Margot feel trapped into sleeping with him, and treats her in bed like "a doll made of rubber" (2017)?

Interestingly, this short story—despite being written in the third person—was taken by many readers to be creative nonfiction rather than a short story, and like creative nonfiction, the narrative voice speaks truth convincingly to structures of power that police the bourgeois bedrooms of modern couples. The mistaking of fiction for nonfiction reminds us of the context of #MeToo, during which testimonies of coercion have become commonplace, and in harnessing the power of testimony, stories like "Cat Person" open up knowledge that can be applied beyond fictional worlds.[3]

Queer Nonfiction Essays on Domestic Violence

Alongside fictional stories, it is also worth studying how the nonfiction essay form explores complex, personal experiences beyond reductive narratives about domestic violence. I pair the nonfiction essays "Letter to My Mother That She Will Never Read" by Ocean Vuong and "The Moon over the River Lethe" by Carmen Maria Machado (2019). Both essays speak powerfully to how institutions support and foster violence, revealing this through innovative uses of form. Vuong's epistolary essay intertwines memories of the author's immigrant mother with comments about the survival and migration of the monarch butterfly. Machado also uses the form of vignettes (about being awake at night) to show that she is not defined merely by the violence that is described among a range of experiences. Placing these essays in conversation enables students to consider a broad range of experiences of violence in the family and between intimate partners, and gives two examples where the narrators refuse to condemn the abusive loved one, while the silences—like those in "Lust, Caution" and "Cat Person"—pose questions.

The title of "Letter to My Mother That She Will Never Read" signals paradox as it doubles back on itself: the addressee will never read it. The letter is not so much an address to an abuser as a way of working through experiences of violence. It does not condemn the mother, but simply presents her behaviors—hitting the narrator (her son), throwing things at him, and threatening him with a knife. The silence about guilt or innocence is made more complex by other evidence, deftly woven into the essay, which gestures to the complexity of Figure 27.1. Without relieving his mother of responsibility, Vuong points out the complicated context that gives rise to his mother's behavior as an immigrant survivor of conflicts in Vietnam, probably suffering from PTSD. He also notes that his mother is a victim of poverty and racism. An illustrative example occurs when Vuong's mother, working at a nail salon, hears her customer complaining about "Julie" dying of cancer, and uncharacteristically, the mother shares that her own mother died of cancer, too. Eventually, it emerges that the privileged white woman customer is talking about her horse; she sees her horse's death as equivalent to the loss of the mother. Vuong creates a complex portrait, pondering to what extent conflicts in Vietnam in which the United States was complicit have created his mother's PTSD and violent behaviors. The monarch butterfly is an objective correlative for his feelings about his mother, who is capable of incredible feats—a long migration—but is extremely fragile. Vuong reminds us that abusers are not simply "bad" people who emerged in a vacuum, but people damaged by systems around them.

Machado's "The Moon over the River Lethe" also creates a portrait of a violent individual situated in a complex world. The essay focuses on Machado's "all-nighters": the first when, at fifteen, she stayed up all night for a dance-a-thon; the second when she stayed up writing essays as a student; and the third when her partner dangerously and threateningly insisted on driving cross-country overnight. Night is represented in these three anecdotes as a refuge when the author is alone, but strange and unsettling when she is with other people. The first hint of strangeness occurs in the dance-a-thon anecdote when Machado finds herself taking a rest break with another girl who was once a friend, though they are now estranged. The girl confides in Machado that it is very important when giving oral sex to men to "swallow," unless you are in a hot tub and then you can spit the semen out. At fifteen, Machado's reaction is confusion and embarrassment, which she covers up by agreeing with the girl.

The form of Machado's essay is complex, because it offers a range of experiences beyond the intimate partner violence at the end. One question to ask students is, why include these other anecdotes in the essay? Why not only focus on the intimate partner abuse of the final story? What do these other anecdotes add? Potential discussion might consider how the dance-a-thon frames our character's lack of knowledge about sexual and relationship matters, which is then filled in by the other girl's oppressive narrative about fulfilling men's sexual needs. Another topic for discussion might be the joy Machado experiences at the dance-a-thon, and her serene enjoyment of essay writing in the second anecdote.

The final anecdote is a terrifying account of her partner's refusal to let her drive, and the consequent ordeal as her partner drives recklessly, dangerously, falling asleep at the wheel and defiantly putting Machado's life at risk, while also insulting, belittling, and verbally abusing her. Like Vuong, however, Machado does not condemn her partner, but she does portray a moment of silence as strength: after the drive, she remains outside the house contemplating the abusive nature of the relationship, telling us that by the next summer she will have left this woman. Machado's ordering of the vignettes provides us with a deeper understanding of this final moment. Her narrator is not simply a victim, but a complex human being negotiating various challenges with little education about sex and relationships.

Teaching the short story and creative nonfiction with queer and straight perspectives of violence can draw attention to the complex circumstances surrounding acts of violence (Figure 27.1), priming students by making them aware of the subtle strategies writers use to represent violence (Figure 27.2). If students are able to situate acts of violence within their contexts, bearing in mind the crucial nature of institutional responses and policies as well as cultural narratives that foster certain kinds of violence, then they might be able to see beyond the narrative that frames acts of violence as simply created by individual monsters. Ocean Vuong recognizes this when he qualifies his description of his abusive mother as a monster, noting that he too is defined as a "monster […] freak, fairy" by kids at school, when a schoolfriend catches sight of him wearing a dress in the front yard (2017). Vuong is not denying his mother's culpability here, but he is pointing out how the narrative of "monster" is used to obscure the circumstances and contexts around his mother, while the kids use it to ostracize and shame his queer identity. Readings of narratives of violence ultimately need to be sensitive to the circumstances and systems surrounding an individual act, while also celebrating the subversive techniques that writers use to reveal the experience's complexity. As Vuong puts it, "the end of the sentence is where we might begin" (2017).

Notes

1. As with all such sensitive material, it is worth being extremely careful in minimizing details that are triggering in presenting real cases. I always give my students a week or so to read such materials beforehand with a content warning, so it does not come as a surprise when they come into the classroom, hopefully mitigating triggering effects.
2. I would not advise using the film adaption *Lust, Caution* (2007) directed by Ang Lee, which makes the heroine of the story Chia-chih complicit with her own abuse. Chang's story gives very clear reasons for what the heroine decides to do (cf. Brigley Thompson 2016).
3. For how "Cat Person" allows doubt about sexual desire in ways that are discouraged by #MeToo, see Namrata Mitra and Katherine Conner's essay in this volume.

Works Cited

Allen, Jeffner (1986), *Lesbian Philosophy: Explorations*, Palo Alto, CA: Institute of Lesbian Studies.

Brigley Thompson, Zoë (2016), "Beyond Symbolic Rape: The Insidious Trauma of Conquest in Marguerite Duras's *The Lover* and Eileen Chang's 'Lust, Caution'," *Feminist Formations*, 28 (3): 1–26.

Brigley Thompson, Zoë and Sorcha Gunne (2010), "Introduction," in Sorcha Gunne and Zoë Brigley Thompson (eds.), *Feminism, Literature and Rape Narratives: Violence and Violation*, 1–22, London and New York: Routledge.

Chang, Eileen (2007), "Lust, Caution," in Eileen Chang, Wang Hui Ling, and James Schamus (eds.), *Lust Caution: The Story, the Screenplay, and the Making of the Film*, 1–48, New York: Pantheon.

Garcia, Sandra (2017), "The Woman Who Created #MeToo Long before Hashtags," *The New York Times*, October 20. Available online: https://www.nytimes.com/2017/10/20/us/me-too-movement-tarana-burke.html.

Ghandnoosh, Nazgol (2014), "Race and Punishment: Racial Perception of Crime and Support for punitive Policies," *The Sentencing Project*. Available online: https://www.sentencingproject.org/publications/race-and-punishment-racial-perceptions-of-crime-and-support-for-punitive-policies/.

Kabir, Ananya Jahanara (2010), "Double Violation? (Not) Talking about Sexual Violence in Contemporary South Asia," in Sorcha Gunne and Zoë Brigley Thompson (eds.), *Feminism, Literature and Rape Narratives: Violence and Violation*, 146–63, London and New York: Routledge.

Lindsey, Treva B. and Jessica Marie Johnson (2014), "Searching for Climax: Black Erotic Lives in Slavery and Freedom," *Meridians* 12 (2): 169–95.

Louie, Kam (2012), *Eileen Chang: Romancing Languages, Cultures and Genres*, Hong Kong: Hong Kong University Press.

Machado, Carmen (2016), "The Moon over the River Lethe," *Catapult*. February 9. Available online: https://catapult.co/stories/the-moon-over-the-river-lethe.

Miller, Ken (2019), "Oklahoma Court Upholds Sentence for Ex-cop Accused of Rape," *Associated Press*, August 1. Available online: https://apnews.com/38abab5e04ce42c5a6d5897d38bf4e04.

O'Connor, Frank (1963), *The Lonely Voice: A Study of the Short Story*, Cleveland: World Publishing Company.

Rattini, Kristin Baird (2006), "A Short History of Shanghai," *The New York Times Archive*. Available online: https://archive.nytimes.com/www.nytimes.com/fodors/top/features/travel/destinations/asia/china/shanghai/fdrs_feat_145_5.html?n=Top/Features/Travel/Destinations/Asia/China/Shanghai.

Renker, F. W. (1998), "Authority and Imagined Truth: Notes on Teaching Creative Nonfiction," Eric Institute of Education Science, No. ED422574. Available online: https://files-eric-ed-gov.proxy.lib.ohio-state.edu/fulltext/ED422574.pdf.

Roupenian, Kristen (2017), "Cat Person," *The New Yorker*, December 11. Available online: https://www.newyorker.com/magazine/2017/12/11/cat-person.

Roupenian, Kristen (2019), "What It Felt Like When 'Cat Person' Went Viral," *The New Yorker*, January 10. Available online: https://www.newyorker.com/books/page-turner/what-it-felt-like-when-cat-person-went-viral.

Sedgwick, Eve Kosofsky (1985), *Between Men: English Literature and Male Homosocial Desire*, New York: Columbia University Press.

Shaw, Valerie (1983), *The Short Story, A Critical Introduction*, London: Longman.

Sinner, Anita (2013), *Unfolding the Unexpectedness of Uncertainty*, Rotterdam: Sense Publishers.

Somerville, Kristine and Speer Morgan (2018), "Foreword," in Kristine Somerville (ed.), *Trouble in Mind: The Short Story and Conflict*, viii–xi, Columbia, MO: Missouri Review Books.

Vuong, Ocean (2017), "A Letter to My Mother She Will Never Read," *The New Yorker*, May 13. Available online: https://www.newyorker.

com/culture/personal-history/a-letter-to-my-mother-that-she-will-never-read.

Walsh, Kelly and Terry Murphy (2019), "Irresolute Endings and Rhetorical Poetics," *Style*, 53 (1): 88–104.

White, Gillian B (2017), "The Glaring Blind Spot of the 'Me Too' Movement," *The Atlantic*, November 22. Available online: https://www.theatlantic.com/entertainment/archive/2017/11/the-glaring-blind-spot-of-the-me-too-movement/546458/.

Zhou, Xiao (1989), "Virginity and Premarital Sex in Contemporary China," *Feminist Studies*, 15 (2): 279–88.

28

Recruiting Warriors:
Using Literature in College Classrooms to Fight and Win "The Longest War"

Candice L. Pipes

INSIGNIA

> *One in three female soldiers will experience*
> *sexual assault while serving in the military.*

She hides under a deuce n' half this time—sleeping
on a roll of foam, draped in mosquito netting. Sandflies

hover throughout the night. She sleeps under vehicle exhaust
and heat, dreaming of mortars buried beside her, three stripes

painted on each cold tube, a rocker of yellow hung below.
It's you she's dreaming of, Sergeant—she'll dream of you

for years to come. If she makes it out of this country alive,
which she probably will. You will be the fire and the hovering

breath. Not the sniper. Not the bomber in the streets. You.
So I'm here to ask this one night's reprieve.

Let her sleep tonight. Let her sleep. Pause a moment
under the gibbous moon. Smoke. The gin your wife sent

from New Jersey, colored mint green with food dye
disguised in a bottle of mouthwash: take a long swig of it.

Take the edge out of your knuckles. Let it blur your vision
into a tremor of lights. The explosions in the distance

are not your own. In these long hours before dawn,
on the banks of the Tigris river, let her sleep.

In her dream, your eyes are pools of rifle oil.
You unsheathe the bayonet from its scabbard

while she waits. On a mattress of sand and foam, there
in the motor pool, she waits to kiss bullets into your mouth.

—BRIAN TURNER

When I taught the required senior-level war literature course at the United States Air Force Academy, one of the first assignments I gave cadets was to memorize a war poem and recite it in front of the class. The delivered poems ranged from Wilfred Owen's "Dulce et Decorum Est" to Yusef Komunyakaa's "Facing It," but almost to a cadet, the women chose to recite Brian Turner's "Insignia." Some of these recitations were done quietly, almost in a whisper, as if cautiously sharing a secret. Others were performed in tears, with sadness, anger, or both. One cadet screamed the last lines and seemed to purge something long trapped inside her self.

Turner took the poem's epigraph, "One in three female soldiers will experience sexual assault while serving in the military," from Katie Couric's March 17, 2009, CBS Evening News report entitled, "Sexual Assault Permeates U.S. Armed Forces." In that story, Couric talks to a survivor, Jessica, who at twenty-four enlisted in the Army and was assigned to a unit with only three other women. If the math holds up, she represented the one in three women in her unit to be sexually assaulted. However, she was assaulted more than once. The fact that many sexual assault survivors suffer multiple assaults by different perpetrators at different times is a nuance often overlooked in sexual assault data. In Jessica's case, her squad leader sexually harassed her and then tried to force himself on her, and then she was later raped by someone she knew from another base. So no, the math doesn't hold up, and it was clear to me in my war literature classroom that whether we are survivors of sexual assault or not, Turner's poem breaks open a festering wound in all of us potential warriors. Truth be told, there is no "one in three"— all women, in and outside of the military, experience some level of sexual harassment or assault. Reckoning with this realization is what led me to create a course focused on representations of violence against women in literature. I recognized that I had to become a recruiter of warriors for a different war, the one Rebecca Solnit calls "the longest war." Thus, the classroom became our battlefield and literature our weapon as my students and I began to fight.

I believe we can use literature in the college classroom to bear witness to the pervasive violence women suffer globally, on college campuses, and in our militaries. Literature provides testimonies for us to use to recruit warriors who are willing to confront the reality of sexual assault in our ranks, and it inspires cultural change in the future. Literature— both fiction and nonfiction—offers an accounting of sexual assault and gender-based violence (suppression, control, threats, coercion) and reveals how this violence quietly seeps into the fabric of military culture. Studying such literature requires students to (1) confront the ordinary pervasiveness of sexual assault, (2) question how gender-based violence takes shape and takes hold, and (3) acknowledge the strength of those warriors who have broken through the battle lines of silence and fear to fight hard. Ultimately, using literature to expose the pandemic of sexual assault in our military ranks serves students as both a metaphor and a warning of how stealthily and destructively sexual assault works in all organizations, and how we must fight against it.

In her essay, Rebecca Solnit decries "the pandemic of violence by men against women, both intimate violence and stranger violence" (2013: 21) as "The Longest War" fought by humanity. As is well documented, our country's military quietly triages a host of victims, casualties of this war. Yet, with them marches a small army of dedicated warriors fighting on their behalf—survivors who refuse to be silenced and insist on being counted. The "Fiscal Year 2019 Annual Report on Sexual Assault in the Military," published in April 2020, reveals a 3 percent increase of sexual assault cases in fiscal year 2019, to 6,236 Service-member reported incidents across the Services. But the report also estimates that sexual assault reporting only accounted for about 30 percent of victims in 2018, making the number of active duty Service members who have experienced sexual assault closer to 20,500 Service members, about two-thirds of them women. In addition to sexual assault, in a 2018 survey, an estimated 24.2 percent of active duty women indicated experiencing sexual harassment, a notable increase from 21.4 percent in 2016. Even more than active duty units, military service academies are also not free from sexual violence against women. In 2019, 130 reports of sexual assault were made by and/or against actively enrolled cadets or midshipmen at United States military service academies, up from 103 the year before. The "Annual Report on Sexual Harassment and Violence at the Military Service Academies for Academic Program Year 2018–2019" estimates that this number accounts for only 12 percent of cadet and midshipman victim reports—meaning cadet and midshipman victim numbers are closer to 1,100 each year. These numbers attest to the truth that every year, thousands of military service women can raise their hands and say, "Me, Too."

"Me, Too" is what each of my female cadets said implicitly in their recitations of Turner's poem, which allowed them to connect the woman sleeping under the Humvee to the cadet checking around the corners of her dorm room hallway to escape an unwanted encounter. The power of this analogous process emphasizes the necessity of providing students a safe space to acquire the tools needed to recognize how violence against women plays out in all aspects of their lives, and is what the college literature classroom most usefully provides. These were the goals of a course I designed, "Violence against Women in Literature," in which we started by defining "violence." Does violence have to be physical? Can it be emotional? Implied? Is control a form of violence? Silencing? We spend time working to expose rape myths and explore problematic terms including "forcible rape" and "sex" when discussing rape and sexual assault. We interrogate the engrained psychology of rape exposed by asking one simple question, "What do you do daily to protect yourself from sexual violence?" We read Sharon Allard, Pamela Barnett, Susan Brownmiller, David Brion Davis, Teresa de Lauretis, Estelle Freedman, Judith Herman, Joclyn Friedman and Jessica Valenti, Kate Millett, Rebecca Solnit, Laura Tanner, Karen Tatum, and others who study the effects of violence on victims, communities, economies, and politics for context and, for some, validation. We examine our popular culture and provide close readings of song lyrics, magazine articles, and sitcoms that can't help but reveal the pervasiveness of violent language directed at women in our daily lives.

We read *Jane Eyre* and attempt to answer Karen Tatum's question in her book, *Explaining the Depiction of Violence against Women in Victorian Literature*: "Why was a female body so threatening in nineteenth-century fiction?" (2005: 1). Of course, another question is: why is the female body so threatened in nineteenth-century fiction? We consider the role of colonialism, class, and race in perpetuating acts of violence against women and consider the ways in which the remnants of Victorian literature impact our present culture in a way that perpetuates domestic violence. We read Sherley Anne Williams's *Dessa Rose*, a neo-slave narrative that centers the abused Black female body at the core of the novel. Continuing our discussion of colonialism, we consider the violence inflicted not just on American slaves, but as part of the global institution of slavery. We consider how rape is sewn into the fabric of our American culture and how the common practice of white masters raping Black slaves has created a racial and gender pathology that continues to inform how interracial sexual violence and intimate partner sexual and physical violence are perceived and excused within certain frameworks, contributing to the foundation for our current rape culture.

We read Zora Neale Hurston's *Their Eyes Were Watching God* and must reconcile the novel's condemnation of Janie's first two husbands' abuse with its worship of Tea Cake, who is revealed to be yet another abusive partner in Janie's life. We consider what allows Janie to excuse Tea Cake's violent behavior while reproving that of the others. We review Lenore Walker's ideas about the cycle of abuse and the continuum of harm and engage sociological and psychological research, including Cathy Caruth's work on how trauma is experienced, to more fully understand how violence seeps into the dark corners of relationships. We note that Hurston makes clear that even if Tea Cake had not been bitten by a mad dog, he would continue to act out in violent rage against Janie. Hurston uses the trope of the mad dog to signify the true threat Tea Cake and all batterers pose to their victims. Tea Cake as rabid beast symbolizes the worst-case scenario of abuse and illuminates the madness inherent to all abuse and sexual violence—the always present potential for murder. We read Louise Erdrich's *The Round House* and talk about what it means for rape of women in certain communities to be protected by systems, laws, and institutions; what it means to live as a woman in an environment where rape is committed with impunity. We talk about how rapists are predators and use their protection in these communities to rape with license; about how only 4 percent of reported sexual assaults in the military result in convictions: "The Fiscal Year 2019 Annual Report on Sexual Assault in the Military" reported final outcomes for 5,699 unrestricted reports of sexual assault, but only 264 cases resulting in court martial convictions (DoD 2020: Appendix B, Statistical Data 6, 11). We raise our hands alongside the Indigenous community and say, "Me, Too."

The dedicated study of how sexual violence against women manifests in our communities, cultures, and languages is essential, because the violent treatment of women in military contexts (and college campus contexts and male-dominated workplace contexts) is normalized. It is so pervasive, in fact, that it requires a naming, a calling out of the behaviors as violent, an intentional process of defining the enemy within, if we are even to begin to attack. The cadets I teach are just beginning their military service and most of their lives have been spent encountering and translating violent messaging directed at women outside of the military context. In teaching a course on violence against women at the United States Air Force Academy, a college that, not unlike many others, has been plagued with sexual assault scandals, I quickly recognized the need to foreground for my cadets the reality of sexual assault in military contexts. For those serving and/or preparing to serve, identifying sexual assault as not merely a women's issue or a civilian issue, but as their issue, is critical to stimulating institutional conversations about violence. It is critical that we discuss violence in all its complexity: the dynamics of power, rape culture, cultural/gender programming, patriarchy, objectification, subjugation and subordination of women, war (and sexual violence as a weapon), and trauma, using literature as our point of entry.

If we understand the war against women that Solnit succinctly names as always using the act of sexual violence as a weapon—that sexual violence is weaponized to exert power, to control, to maintain the status quo—then we must further investigate not just how sexual violence functions, but how it is employed as a weapon in war. War literature offers an opportunity to do both. It's important to note that war literature typically doesn't set out to write about sexual assault; instead, it unwittingly writes sexual assault in between the lines, almost in the margins. In doing so, war literature demonstrates how sexual assault is pervasive and whispered even as it functions both as a weapon of war (a means to an end) and as an insubordination (an undermining of that end) in its own right. Once amplified, the insidiousness of sexual assault in one of our most hallowed professions cannot be ignored.

As an entry point to the complex paradox of sex and war, I offer students "Blonde," a vignette from *The Forever War*, Dexter Filkins's nonfiction account of America's post-9/11 wars. A "hot" blonde soldier described by her Captain as a "girl" is used as bait for Iraqi men while the rest of the company raids their houses for weapons. The Captain describes the scene: "So she's standing there on top of the Bradley, blond hair and everything, and we call out on the loudspeaker, 'This woman is for sale. Blonde woman for sale!' And I'll be damned if every Iraqi male in that village wasn't gathered around the Bradley in about two minutes" (Filkins 2008: 135). The soldiers continue to auction off a member of their company as the Iraqis get more "wild." The Captain discloses that they did this in three villages, and it "Worked every time. We got reprimanded. Somebody found out about it. They didn't like it." He continues, "I thought it was brilliant myself. Smartest thing we ever did" (136). The male cadets generally respond like the Captain: "it's brilliant!" But the female cadets challenge this teleological thinking in which the ends justify the means, highlighting the objectification of the female soldier, the threat of violence from the "wild" Iraqi men, the potential threat of violence from her fellow soldiers who show no concern for her safety or psyche, and the always violent act of selling another human being even if done as a prank. This short vignette in a book full of war stories is what my students most remember because it forces them to begin the project of considering how they define violence. They must reconcile who, in this circumstance, is acting violently, and toward whom that violence is directed.

We read Phil Klay's short story "Bodies" in his collection *Redeployment*. In this story, our narrator is one of the "good guys," a newly deployed Marine who chews up the naked pictures his girlfriend sends in the mail rather than share her body with his unit. For this, he is derided and told that "a true Marine wouldn't just share naked photos of his girlfriend with his platoon, but would let them run a train on her as well" (Klay 2014: 58). Although he thinks he "deserves to," he can't bring himself to force himself on his ex-girlfriend upon their reunion post-deployment, even as he reflects on his last sexual experience. In it, an unnamed woman, referred to only by her age, thirty-eight, "had seemed so unwilling. I was almost certain that what happened with her couldn't be called rape" (Klay 2014: 68). He is torn between the clear messaging from his Marine peers that women are objects, bodies to be collected (not unlike those our narrator scrapes off Iraqi streets after suicide bombs explode), and his own internal sense that he knows better. My students and I discuss how, like the narrator, we are constantly forced to sift through hyper-masculine messaging that creates a rape culture in which women are seen as merely bodies.

We read Lynn Nottage's play, *Ruined*, which exposes the crimes against women whose bodies serve as literal battlegrounds in the civil war raging in the Democratic Republic of Congo. The women in Nottage's play are victimized several times over, having been expelled from their villages after surviving rapes perpetrated by greedy, power-hungry soldiers only to have their bodies sold in brothels for profit. My students and I discuss the layers of violence documented in the struggles of these women, and I ask them to consider whether the play itself is an act of violence, an exploitation of these women's stories that works to pacify voyeuristic audiences' need to feel woke, or if it inspires further interrogation of the horror. If the play is, as I've offered in a previous critique, "a desire to represent the complexity of a war-torn country in which the rape of women is used as a weapon against not just the women themselves but their communities and future generations" (2015: para. 7), if we understand that rape is implemented as a policy to disrupt safety and security, an act of terrorism propagated without restraint, then how do we reconcile that desire with the play's all too-satisfying ending? In 2011, the *New York Times* reported a study in the *American Journal of Public Health* estimating that 2 million women and girls have been raped in the Democratic Republic of Congo "with women victimized at a rate of nearly one every minute" (Gettleman). I ask students if it is possible to draw connections between the invisible women Nottage works to make visible in her play and our own "invisible war" documented in a 2012 documentary about sexual assault in the military of the same name. Can we move beyond the inconceivable statistics to recognize human beings calling out, "Me, Too?"

The project of recruiting warriors to fight the longest war against the sexual violation of women through the act of close reading texts achieves two things: (1) it reveals the often-ignored, but ubiquitous language of violence, and (2) it provides students with the tools needed to read closely their own environments and call out the violence women face. Students come to recognize the language of violence as also meaning the language of control, the language of subjugation, the language of silencing, and the language of possession. We turn to Toni Morrison's Nobel Lecture, which reminds us that "Oppressive language does more than represent violence; it is violence," that "It is the language that drinks blood, laps vulnerabilities" and we must recognize this language of violence in the narratives we consume (1993: 104). She calls out sexist, racist, and theistic language as "policing languages of mastery" (104), and students are forced to consider how the language of violence has mastered their own consciousnesses, how the language of violence has, like a parasite or invasive species, threatened to overtake the good that language is meant to do. As Morrison suggests, "Language alone protects us from the scariness of things with no names" (108). Students must become adept at naming the scariness that is the language of violence, language that is hidden as "diplomatic language to countenance rape, torture, assassination" (105). Morrison warns, "There is and will be more seductive, mutant language designed to throttle women, to pack their throats like paté-producing geese with their own unsayable, transgressive words" (105). By reading, recognizing, and naming the violence in texts, we live in Morrison's legacy and can begin the work of making unspeakable things spoken. In literature, students find new language to resist their trained, passive acquiescence to the language of violence that occupies their music, blogs, anonymous comments on social media sites, their basic training cadence calls, the fabric of their, of my nation's history.

I recall when I first became aware of the pervasiveness of the impact of sexual assault amongst my peers at an event I attended as a cadet at the United States Air Force Academy in the late 1990s. A large group of female cadets, maybe all the female cadets, was told to attend a talk in one of the academy's auditoriums. We were confronted with a panel of women, survivors, who shared their stories of sexual abuse. (It must have been Sexual Assault Awareness Month.) I remember sitting in awe of these women, of their bravery, their daring to speak, amazed that they were allowed to tell their truth. We listened and we cried. These women sanctioned our right to name the violence and proved that triumph was possible. The line formed by cadets after the talk, all desperate to connect to the strength of these women, stretched the length of two aisles. We lined up to say, "Me, Too."

Military service women, veterans and active duty, continue to line up and say, "Me, Too." I was recently asked to join a Facebook page for service academy women. The page is filled with stories detailing the violence these women experienced—some of whom have waited decades to share their story in a safe space, others who have battled for decades for justice. Already there are projects in the works (collections of narratives and interviews) led by these women's sisters-in-arms to document and account for the violence enacted on these women. Perhaps the next iteration of a war literature course will bring these women's stories out of the margins, their stories building on the truths a few brave women exposed in *The Invisible War*, their stories in league with Harriet Jacobs and Maya Angelou and Roxane Gay and Chanel Miller—testimonies that span centuries and are still, too often, not heard.

It's not an exaggeration to say that using the college literature classroom to recruit warriors in this battle against weaponized sexual violence against women is a life-or-death mission. I am recruiting warriors to save lives. We need warriors in our ranks, men and women, who could have recognized the potential for violence communicated by Army Specialist Vanessa Guillén's sexual harassment claim, hear her and believe her so that she would not end up burnt, dismembered, and discarded in a shallow grave (Diaz 2020). We need warriors in our ranks, men and women, who will protect Marines like Lance Corporal Maria Lauterbach, eight months pregnant, her skull cracked and her body buried by her accused rapist in his backyard, days after she reported her concerns to military prosecutors (Schoetz 2008). We need warriors who will look critically at the evidence of the suspicious deaths of Private First Class LaVena Johnson (Leonard 2015) and Specialist Kamisha Block (Thayer 2019) and not dismiss them as suicides. We need warriors who will fight to make sure that no soldier finds herself, like the soldier in Turner's poem, sleeping under a truck, hiding. We must rally the troops to protect her. "And, how lovely it will be, this thing we will have done—together" (Morrison 1993: 109).

Works Cited

Couric, Katie (2009), "Sexual Assault Permeates U.S. Armed Forces," CBS News, March 17. Available online: https://www.cbsnews.com/news/sexual-assault-permeates-us-armed-forces/.

Department of Defense (2020), "Annual Report on Sexual Harassment and Violence at the Military Service Academies for Academic Program Year 2018–2019," January 30. Available online: https://www.sapr.mil/sites/default/files/_DoD_Annual_Report_on_Sexual_Harassment_and_Violence_APY18-19.pdf.

Department of Defense (2020), "Fiscal Year 2019 Annual Report on Sexual Assault in the Military," April 28. Available online: https://media.defense.gov/2020/Apr/30/2002291660/1/1/1/1_DEPARTMENT_OF_DEFENSE_FISCAL_YEAR_2019_ANNUAL_REPORT_ON_SEXUAL_ASSAULT_IN_THE_MILITARY.PDF.

Diaz, Johnny, Maria Cramer, and Christina Morales (2020), "What We Know about the Death of Vanessa Guillen," *The New York Times*, July 31. Available online: https://www.nytimes.com/article/vanessa-guillen-fort-hood.html.

Filkins, Dexter (2008), "Blonde," in *The Forever War*, 134–5, New York: Vintage Books.

Gettleman, Jeffrey (2011), "Congo Study Sets Estimates for Rape Much Higher," *The New York Times*, May 11. Available online: https://www.nytimes.com/2011/05/12/world/africa/12congo.html.

Klay, Phil (2014), "Bodies," in *Redeployment*, 53–72, New York: Penguin Press.

Leonard, Mary DeLach (2015), "10 Years Later, a Soldier's Family Still Grieves and Questions the Army's Version of Her Death," St. Louis Public Radio, July 19. Available online: https://news.stlpublicradio.

org/government-politics-issues/2015-07-19/10-years-later-a-soldiers-family-still-grieves-and-questions-the-armys-version-of-her-death.

Morrison, Toni ([1993] 2019), "The Nobel Lecture in Literature," in *The Source of Self-Regard*, 102–9, New York: Alfred A. Knopf.

Pipes, Candice (2015), "Performing War: Making the *Ruined* Visible," *albeit*, August 25.

Tatum, Karen E. (2005), *Explaining the Depiction of Violence against Women in Victorian Literature: Applying Julia Kristeva's Theory of Abjection to Dickens, Bronte, and Braddon*, New York: The Edwin Mellen Press.

Turner, Brian (2010), "Insignia," in *Phantom Noise*, 64–5, Farmington, Maine: Alice James Books.

Schoetz, David (2008), "Scenes from a Pregnant Marine's Murder," *ABC News*, January 22. Available online: https://abcnews.go.com/US/story?id=4170769&page=1.

Solnit, Rebecca ([2013] 2014), "The Longest War," in *Men Explain Things to Me*, 19–36, Chicago: Haymarket Books.

Thayer, Rose L. (2019) "Army Reopens Case of 2007 Murder-Suicide That Was Originally Called 'Friendly Fire,'" *Stars and Stripes*, April 19. Available online: https://www.stripes.com/news/us/army-reopens-case-of-2007-murder-suicide-that-was-originally-called-friendly-fire-1.577635.

The views expressed in this essay are those of the author and do not reflect the views of the Department of Defense or its components.

CONTRIBUTORS

Elif S. Armbruster is Associate Professor of English at Suffolk University in Boston, MA. Her research interests focus on women's writing, women's studies, ethnic literature, and immigrant literature. She is the author of *Domestic Biographies: Stowe, Howells, James, and Wharton at Home* (2011). Recent work includes "Dwelling in American Realism" in Keith Newlin (Ed.), *The Oxford Handbook to American Literary Realism* (2019) and "Ants Become Giants: The Pioneering Perspective of Laura Ingalls in the Little House Books" in Dewey Hall and Jillmarie Murphy (Eds.), *Gendered Ecologies: New Materialist Interpretations of Women Writers in the Long Nineteenth Century* (2020).

Janet Badia is Professor and Director of Women's Studies at Purdue University Fort Wayne. She is the author of *Sylvia Plath and the Mythology of Women Readers* (2011) and co editor of *Reading Women: Literary Figures and Cultural Icons from the Victorian Age to the Present* (2005). Her research interests include the history of women's reading and the reception of American women's writing since the 1950s.

Linda Chavers is Lecturer at Harvard University in the Department of African and African American Studies. Her research interests focus on Black feminisms and literature. She has published in *The Offing*, *The Guardian*, the *Boston Globe* Magazine, *The Rumpus*, *Elle* and *DAME* Magazine. Her most recent book is *Violent Disruptions: American Imaginations of Racial Anxiety in William Faulkner and Richard Wright* (2018).

Katherine Conner is a graduate of Iona College, where she majored in Media and Strategic Communications and English. Her research interests focus on children's literature and the #MeToo movement.

Carlyn Ferrari is Assistant Professor of English at Seattle University. Her research explores the intersection between Black feminist thought and literary ecocriticism. She is currently working on two book projects about poet and civil rights activist Anne Spencer.

Robin E. Field is Professor of English at King's College in Wilkes-Barre, Pennsylvania. Her research focuses on ethnic American literature, women's studies, and South Asian diasporic literature. She has published essays on Jhumpa Lahiri, Sandra Cisneros, Alice Walker, Lynne Sharon Schwartz, and Ayad Akhtar. Her most recent book is *Writing the Survivor: The Rape Novel in Late Twentieth-Century American Fiction* (2020).

Sarah Goldbort is a PhD candidate in the English Department at the University at Buffalo. Her research interests include eighteenth- and nineteenth-century British literature, feminist pedagogy, history of the book studies, and nationalism. She has served as the President of the Women and Gender Studies Caucus of the Northeast Modern Language Association. Having earned a certificate in teaching English Language Arts, grades 7–12, she intends on teaching high school English courses.

Amy B. Hagenrater-Gooding is Associate Professor at the University of Maryland Eastern Shore where she teaches classes on modern drama, the novel, women's literature, and dystopian fiction. Her research interests deal with gender issues and mother-work as seen in her publications "The Impossibility of Male/Female Relationships in Willa Cather's *My Antonia*" (2016) and "Pink Is the New Green: Raising Little Shoppers from Birth" (2013). She has forthcoming chapters featured in *Mothers Who Kill* (2022) and *Seeing the Apocalypse: Essays on Bird Box* (2021).

Hannah Herndon is a PhD candidate in the English Department at Tufts University. Her research interests include girlhood, sound studies, and sexual violence in multiethnic US literature.

Heather Hewett is Associate Professor and Chair of Women's, Gender, and Sexuality Studies and an affiliate of the English Department at SUNY New Paltz. Her research interests include writing, feminism and social change; witness literature; contemporary African women's literature; and motherhood narratives. She has published in scholarly journals such as *WSQ*,

MELUS: Multi-Ethnic Literature of the United States, Atlantis: Critical Studies in Gender, Culture and Social Justice, and *English in Africa* as well as several edited collections. A longtime contributor to the *Women's Review of Books,* she has published essays, articles, and reviews in a variety of mainstream and literary publications.

Mary K. Holland is Professor of English at SUNY New Paltz, where she specializes in contemporary literature and theory. She is the author of *Succeeding Postmodernism: Language and Humanism in Contemporary American Literature* (2013) and *The Moral Worlds of Contemporary Realism* (2020), and co-editor, with Stephen J. Burn, of *Approaches to Teaching the Works of David Foster Wallace* (2019). She has also published articles on gender, power, and communication in literature; mothering and media in film; and intimate partner sexual abuse.

Roberta Hurtado is Assistant Professor of Latina/e/o Literature and Culture at SUNY Oswego. Her research interests focus on Latina Decolonial Feminisms, with an emphasis in Puerto Rican Women's Literature, Epigenetics, and Trauma Studies. She has published in journals such as *Chiricú, Label Me Latina/o,* and *Diálogo.* Her book *Decolonial Puerto Rican Women's Writings: Subversion in the Flesh* was published in 2019 as part of Palgrave Macmillan's "Literature of the Americas" series.

Aditi Joshi, Anushka Srivastava, Katyayani, Mahwash Akhter, Prasanta Bani Ekka, Shivangi Tiwary, Shweta, and **Zahanat** are undergraduate students of English Literature at Miranda House, University of Delhi, India.

Ethan Madarieta is Assistant Professor of English at Syracuse University. His current book manuscript, *People of the Land: Memory, Violence, and the Geographic Imagination,* interrogates state, Indigenous, and diasporic memory, violence, and extranational geographic imaginaries through Latin American and Latina/o/x literature and political performance. He has published and has forthcoming articles in *Latin American Theatre Review, A contracorriente: una revista de estudios latinoamericanos, Critical Times,* and *The Handbook to New Approaches in Cultural Memory Studies.*

Kasey Jones-Matrona is a doctoral candidate and graduate teaching assistant at the University of Oklahoma in Literary and Cultural Studies. Kasey is a settler scholar and her research areas include Native American literature, Indigenous futurisms, and Indigenous feminisms. She is currently working on her dissertation on Indigenous futurisms which places a range of texts from Native American speculative fiction novels, video poems, and cultural center museum exhibits in conversation with one another in order to examine how Indigenous-authored texts and sites create new worlds and audiences, and thus, Indigenous pasts, presents, and futures.

Maureen McDonnell is Professor of English and the Director of Women's and Gender Studies at Eastern Connecticut State University. Her research interests include feminist pedagogy, early modern drama, and bilingual Shakespearean productions performed in English and American Sign Language. Her scholarship appears in *Shakespeare Bulletin, The Journal of American Drama and Theatre,* and *Comparative Drama,* as well as other journals and collections. Recent honors include fellowships in the HERS Leadership Institute and the Mellon School of Theater and Performance Research. Among her awards for service and teaching is the prestigious 2017 Connecticut Board of Regents Teaching Award.

Rebecca F. McNamara is Assistant Professor in the English Department at Westmont College, Santa Barbara, California. Her research interests include the history of emotions related to love, death, and dying as well as political and legal language in medieval English literature. She has published on emotions related to the suicidal impulse in medieval England and teaching strategies for the history of emotions in Middle English literature.

Namrata Mitra is Associate Professor at Iona College in the Department of English. Her research interests focus on feminist philosophy, queer theory, and postcolonial studies. She has published on comparative postcolonial theories, the unrecognizability of routine sexual violence in South Asia, and the problem of unacknowledged contexts in philosophical argumentation.

Douglas Murray is Professor in the Department of English at Belmont University in Nashville, Tennessee. He is editor (with Margaret Anne Doody) of Jane Austen's *Catharine and Other*

Writings (1993). He has written on English hymns, Dryden, Pope, Frances Trollope, and Jane Austen. He is also an organist, with special interest in improvisation.

Nafeesa T. Nichols is Associate Professor of English Literature, Culture and Didactics at Western Norway University of Applied Sciences, Norway. Her research interests focus on contemporary South African literature, Black feminist theory, and popular culture.

Candice L. Pipes is an active duty Air Force Colonel serving in the United States Special Operations Forces Command. Her research interests are African American literature, Black feminist theory, violence in literature, and war literature. She has published on representations of violence in Black women's literature, and teaching Hemingway and race, and has served as managing editor and contributor to the *War, Literature & the Arts* journal.

Jeremy Posadas is Director of Gender Studies and Associate Professor of Religious Studies at Austin College (located on the rural Texas-Oklahoma border) and a co-chair of the American Academy of Religion's Class, Religion, and Theology Unit. He is currently writing an "eco-queer" economic ethics, having recently published essays on reproductive justice and feminist anti-work theory. He is also the creator of the "United Regions of America" map, a county-based scheme of regions that calibrate common perceptions with natural landscapes and major industries.

Jacinta R. Saffold is Assistant Professor of African American Literature at the University of New Orleans. She researches twentieth- and twenty-first-century African American literature, Hip Hop Studies, and the Digital Humanities. Currently, she is working on her first manuscript, *Books & Beats: The Cultural Kinship of Street Lit and Hip Hop*, and the Essence Book Project, a computational collection of popular African American Literature.

Tanya Serisier is Senior Lecturer in the Department of Criminology at Birkbeck College, University of London. Her research focuses on the cultural politics of sexual violence and the treatment of survivors, and the social regulation of sex and sexuality. Her most recent book is *Speaking Out: Feminism, Rape and Narrative Politics* (2018). She is currently working on practices of consent in neoliberal sexual cultures.

Ann Marie Alfonso Short is Associate Professor of English at Saint Mary's College in Notre Dame, Indiana, where she also teaches Gender and Women's Studies and Intercultural Studies courses. Her research interests include global Anglophone literature, US immigrant literature, feminist theory, and motherhood studies. She has published in the *MELUS* (The Society for the Study of Multi-ethnic Literature of the United States) journal and in *Anthurium: A Caribbean Studies Journal*. Her most recent project is an edited collection, *Breastfeeding and Culture: Discourses and Representations* (2018).

Nidhi Shrivastava is a PhD candidate in the Department of English and Writing Studies at the University of Western Ontario in Canada and works as Adjunct Professor in the Department of Languages and Literature at Sacred Heart University. Her research focuses on Hindi film cinema, censorship, sexual and gender-based violence, 1947 Partition, and digital activism. She co-edited the volume of *Bridging the Gaps between Celebrity and Media* and her academic research has also been published in *South Asian Review* and *Graphic Narratives about South Asia and South Asian America* (2019).

Amanda Spallacci is a SSHRC Doctoral Fellow, Killam Laureate, and PhD candidate completing her dissertation, titled *Reading Contemporary Rape Memoirs in the Wake of #MeToo*, in the English and Film Studies Department at the University of Alberta. Her research and publications concern contemporary Hollywood cinema, television, and life writing, through the lenses of memory studies, trauma, affect, and critical race theory. She has published on sexual assault in *A/B Autobiography Studies* (2017), *Studies in Testimony* (2019), and *Arts* (2019). Her most recent work is a forthcoming edited book collection on digital memory cultures in Canada (2021).

Zoë Brigley Thompson is Assistant Professor in English at the Ohio State University. She has research interests in sexuality, trauma, and the body and has edited the Routledge volume *Feminism, Literature, and Rape Narratives* (2010) with Sorcha Gunne. She also has three award-winning collections of poetry—*The Secret* (2007), *Conquest* (2012), and *Hand & Skull* (2019)—and a collection of nonfiction essays, *Notes from a Swing State* (2019).

Sara V. Torres is Visiting Scholar at Converse University. She has published essays on global medieval and early modern studies, pilgrimage allegories, and the literature of the Hundred Years War. Her current book project is entitled *Marvelous Generations: Lancastrian Afterlives in England and Iberia, 1400–1623*.

Beth Walker is a professional Writing Consultant for the Hortense Parrish Writing Center at the University of Tennessee at Martin. Her research interests focus on the imagery and rhetoric of violence in girls' detective fiction, and writing and trauma. Her most recent publications include chapters in *100 Greatest Literary Detectives* (2018), *Fan Phenomena: Game of Thrones* (2017), *New Perspectives on Detective Fiction* (2016), *American Creative Nonfiction* (2015), and *Practical Composition: Exercises for the English Classroom from Working Instructors* (2014).

INDEX

13 Reasons Why 181, 356–7

Abani, Chris, *Graceland* 267
Abrams, Sil Lai, *Black Lotus* 58, 60, 62–6
Achebe, Chinua
   Things Fall Apart 259–71
   Hopes and Impediments 267, 271n.2
   Morning Yet On Creation Day 271n.3
Achebe, Nwando 263
Adichie, Chimamanda Ngozi,
   Purple Hibiscus 267
   "The Headstrong Historian" 267
Ahmed, Sara 227, 231
Airey, Jennifer 160
Alcoff, Linda Martín 6, 45, 66, 324, 330
Allen, Jeffner 378, 381
Althusser, Louis 363
Amadiume, Ifi 264
Amsler, Mark 328
Angelou, Maya, *I Know Why the Caged Bird Sings* 33–6, 39, 398
Anzaldúa, Gloria 298, 304
Arao, Brian and Kristi Clemens 256n.2
Archuleta, Elizabeth 89
Armstrong, Louise 46
Arnold, June 58
Atwood, Margaret, "Nightingale" 139–40

Austen, Jane, *Northanger Abbey* 163–73

Bailey, Moya and Trudy 285n.4
Bassist, Elissa, "Why I Didn't Say No" 333
Beauvoir, Simone de 121
Bender, Jacob and Lydia Maunze-Breese 88
Bender-Slack, Delane 289
Benjamin, Walter 51
Berila, Beth 288
Berman, Jeffrey 243n.1, 243n.2
Betram, Corrine and M. Sue Crowley 291
Beyoncé 344
   "Formation" 345
Bhasin, Kamla 176–7
Biden, Joe 101, 106
Block, Sharon 155, 156
Boccaccio 325, 327, 330, 331
Boise, Sam de 270
Bokser, Julie A. 236, 238
Bontatibus, Donna 152, 153
Boogie Boys, The, "A Fly Girl" 73–4
Boris, Eileen 263, 269
Bowers, Maggie Ann 88
Brady, Mary Pat 303
Brigley Thompson, Zoë 385
Brison, Susan 46, 48, 52
Brown, Brené 288, 291, 294
Brown, Wendy 44
Brownmiller, Susan 4, 393

Buchwald, Emilie, Pamela
    Fletcher, and Martha Roth,
    Transforming a Rape Culture
    6, 250, 251
Bumiller, Elisabeth 179
Burger, Glenn D. 325, 329, 332
Burke, Tarana 1, 9, 31–3, 36, 40,
    44, 50–2, 57–8, 83, 116, 219,
    281, 319n.1, 330, 341, 375
Butalia, Urvashi 176–7
Butler, Judith 363, 373n.7
Butler, Octavia E., *Kindred* 344
Bystrom, Kerry 191

Cahill, Ann 300
Cameron, Debbie 58, 62
Cannon, Christopher 333
Carby, Hazel 5
Carello, Janice and Lisa Butler
    291
Cariou, Warren and Isabelle St-
    Amand 87
Carroll, Hamilton 128n.7
Caruth, Cathy 393
Castle, Terry, *The Professor* 17
CDC, *National Intimate Partner
    and Sexual Violence Survey* 27,
    84, 250, 251
Chang, Eileen, "Lust, Caution"
    376, 379–81, 385n.2
Chappelle, Dave, *Killin' Them
    Softly* 345
Chaucer, Geoffrey 333
    The Knight's Tale 331–2
    The Legend of Good Women
    324, 329–30
    "The Legend of Philomela"
    138–9
    Troilus and Criseyde 324–6
    The Wife of Bath's Tale 324,
    330–1
Cheng, Anne Anlin 65
Christian, Barbara 282

Clinton, Bill 35, 101
Cobham, Rhonda 261–3, 265,
    271n.6
Coel, Michaela, *I May Destroy
    You* 359n.1
Coetzee, J. M., *Disgrace* 187
Cohen, Cathy 373n.8
Collins, Patricia Hill 77, 228
Conrad, Joseph 266–7
Coyle, Dierdre 115
Crane, Susan 331
Crawford, Lacy, *Notes on a
    Silencing* 312
Crenshaw, Kimberlé 50, 58,
    332
Cross, Jen 243n.1

Daiya, Kavita 180
Danticat, Edwidge, *Breath, Eyes,
    Memory* 290
Davidson, Cathy 152, 154, 155,
    158, 159
Deer, Sarah 6, 84, 94
DellaPosta, Daniel 289
Derrida, Jacques 48
Desmond, Marilynn 326–7
Diakoulakis, Christoforos 117–18,
    128n.11
Díaz, Jaquira, *Ordinary Girls*
    299–306
Díaz, Junot 117, 211–19, 220n.7
    *The Brief Wondrous Life of
    Oscar Wao* 212, 214–16,
    219n.4, 220n.9
    Drown 212, 216–17
    This Is How You Lose Her
    212, 213, 216–17
Didur, Jill 180
Digby, Tom 265–6
Dinshaw, Carolyn 333
Dumitrescu, Irina 330
Dumont, Marilyn, "Helen Betty
    Osborne" 88–90

Dunham, Lena, *Not That Kind of Girl* 58, 60, 63–6
Dunn, Stephane 80n.2
Durham, Aisha 66, 79

Edwards, Erica and Jennifer Esposito 288
Edwards, Suzanne 323, 328, 331
Erdrich, Louise, *The Round House* 87–8, 94, 394
Etter-Lewis, Gwendolyn 267

Falak, Uzma 146
Farrow, Ronan 102
Federici, Silvia 157
Feinstein, Rachel A. 18n.11, 284n.1
Felski, Rita 44–5
Field, Robin E. 4, 10, 209n.1
Fileborn, Bianca and Rachel Loney-Howes 7
Flannery, Mary C. 325, 330
Ford, Dr. Christine Blasey 2, 7, 99, 101, 103, 107, 239, 241–2, 341
Forever War, The 395
Fornes, Maria Irene, *Mud* 353
Foster, Hannah Webster, *The Coquette* 151–60
Foucault, Michel 300, 363
Fowler, Elizabeth 331
Fox, Jennifer, *The Tale* 2, 237, 238, 240
Francisco, Patricia Weaver 45
Franklin, M. I. 94
Frayne, Chloe 242
Freitas, Donna, *Consent* 17
Fricker, Miranda, *Epistemic Injustice* 100, 103–5
Friedan, Betty, *The Feminine Mystique* 58

Galioto, Erica D. 205
Garber, Megan 117

Gay, Roxane 212–13, 214, 217, 398
Dispatches from Rape Culture (ed.) 7, 314
Hunger 58–60, 62–3, 65–6, 314, 315–16
Gelfert, Axel 165
Ghandnoosh, Nazgol 377
Ghosh, Shrimoyee Nandini 142
Gikandi, Simon 259, 265
Gilley, Jennifer 60–1
Gilman, Charlotte Perkins, "What is Feminism?" 314
Gilmore, Leigh 3, 7–8, 46, 48, 50, 312, 314
Gines, Kathryn T. 363, 365
Glaspell, Susan, *Trifles* 353, 356
Goldberg, Natalie 240, 243n.3
Gqola, Pumla 187, 188, 189
Gravdal, Kathryn 323, 325, 326, 327
Graves, Robert, "Tereus" 139, 147n.3
Gray-Rosendale, Laura A. 17, 66
Grdešić, Maša 63
Griffin, Susan 53
Griffith, Jessica Greer 86
Grigoriadis, Vanessa 250, 256n.3
Guha, Pallavi 183
Guillén, Vanessa 297–8, 300, 398
Gulley, Alison 331
Gunne, Sorcha 6, 196, 378
Gunne, Sorcha and Zoë Brigley Thompson 6, 7, 378

Hames-García, Michael and Ernesto Javier Martínez 372n.1
Hammond, Zaretta 287
Hammonds, Evelynn 103
Hanisch, Carol 191
Hanning, R.W. 327

Hardt, Michael 156
Hardt, Michael and Antonio Negri 16
Harker, Jaime and Celicia Konchar Farr 59
Harris, Carissa 323, 325, 327, 329, 331, 332
Harris, Charles 127n.2
Harris, Miriam Kalman 243n.1
Harris, Sharon M. 152
Hartman, Saidiya 6, 64
Hayes-Brady, Clare 116–17, 120–1, 122, 126, 128n.6
Heitkamp, Senator Heidi 83
Hering, David 115–16, 126
Herman, Judith 203, 205, 393
Hesse, Barnor 362
Higgins, Lynn and Brenda R. Silver 5, 152
Hill, Anita 101, 106–7, 341
Himmelheber, Rachel 116, 119, 120, 127n.3
Hobbs, Allyson 18n.11, 343
Hogan, Kristen 61
Hogan, Linda 86, 94
hooks, bell 276–7, 289, 293
Horeck, Tanya 47
Hudson, Cory 127n.1
Hult, David 326, 327
Hungerford, Amy 114
Hurston, Zora Neale 34
  Their Eyes Were Watching God 393–4
Hutton, Arlene, *I Dream Before I Take the Stand* 357–9

Ibsen, Henrik, *A Doll's House* 352–3
Invisible War, The 398

Jackson, Edward, *David Foster Wallace's Toxic Masculinity* 122–3

Jacobs, Harriet, *Incidents in the Life of a Slave Girl* 4, 18n.16, 339–48, 398
Jakobsen, Janet 256n.5
Jeyifo, Biodun 269
Jha, Sonora 183
Johnson, Lacy M. 52
Jones, Gayl 4
  Corregidora 276–84, 344
Judd, Ashley 1, 57

Kabir, Ananya Jahanara 376–7
Kantor, Jodi and Megan Twohey, *She Said* 101–2
Karr, Mary 115, 116, 117, 122, 124, 126
  Lit 113–14
Katz, Jackson 252
Katz, Marilyn 147n.2
Kavanaugh, Brett 16, 99, 101, 103, 341
Keating, AnaLouise 227
Keehan, Alyssa, Emily Caputo, Hillary Pettegrew, and Melanie Bennett, *Confronting Campus Sexual Assault: An Examination of Higher Education Claims* 250
Kelly, Adam, "David Foster Wallace and the New Sincerity in American Fiction" 127n.1
Kimball, Whitney 117
Kimmel, Michael and Lisa Wade 252, 255, 256n.4
Klay, Phil, "Bodies" 396
Korobkin, Laura 153
Kutz, Eleanor and Hephzibah Roskelly 334

Lackey, Jennifer 104–5
LaDuke, Winona, *Last Standing Woman* 86
Latifah, Queen, "Fly Girl" 73–4

Lawton, David 329
Lee, Bri, *Eggshell Skull* 7
Lee, Spike, *She's Gotta Have It* 344
Levins Morales, Aurora, *Medicine Stories* 300, 305
Lewinsky, Monica 46
Lewis, C. S., "A Note on Jane Austen" 168
Lewis, Desiree 195, 196
Lindfors, Bernth 261
Lindsey, Treva B. and Jessica Marie Johnson 377
Lipsy, David 122
Lipton, Emma 331–2
Livingstone, Kathleen Ann 232
Llanos-Figueroa, Dahlma, *Daughters of the Stone* 361, 364–6
López, Iris 298, 301
Lorde, Audre 4, 232
Lorris, Guillaume de, and Jean de Meun, *The Romance of the Rose* 324, 326–7
Louie, Kam 380
Lugones, María 300
Lukianoff, Greg and Jonathan Haidt, "The Coddling of the American Mind" 228, 232

Machado, Carmen 219n.1
  In the Dream House 19n.29
  "The Moon over the River Lethe" 376, 382–4
MacKinnon, Catharine A. 100
Mailhot, Terese Marie, *Heart Berries* 7, 94
Maltz, Wendy 292
Mamet, David, *Oleanna* 352
Manne, Kate, *Down Girl* 117
Marcus, Sharon 328, 333
Mardorossian, Carine M. 5, 288
Margolis, Nadia 327
Matlwa, Kopano, *Coconut* 188–96

Max, D. T., *Every Love Story Is a Ghost Story* 114, 115, 117, 122, 126
Mbah, Ndubueze L. 263, 268, 269
McGuire, Danielle L. 18n.11, 49, 58, 289–90
McMillan, Terry 71–2, 74–5
Mehta, Deepa, *Earth* 176–83
Menon, Ritu 176–7
Miescher, Stephan F. and Lisa A. Lindsay 269
Milano, Alyssa 1, 31, 44, 57, 259, 341
Millar, Thomas 292
Miller, Adrienne, *In the Land of Men* 17, 118–19, 126
Miller, Chanel, *Know My Name* 7, 51, 256n.3, 290, 312, 398
Miller, Nancy K., *My Brilliant Friends* 17
Millet, Kate, *Sexual Politics* 5, 393
Mirsky, Laura 290
Mock, Janet, *Redefining Realness* 314, 317, 319n.1
Moele, Kgebetli, *Room 207* 195
Moll, Sorouja, *The Writing Names Project* 89
Morales, Erik 373n.11
Morgan, Jennifer 277–8, 279, 280–1, 283
Morgan, Joan 77
Morrell, Robert and Lahoucine Ouzgane 268, 269
Morrison, Toni 4, 284, 397–8
  The Bluest Eye 33, 36–8, 40, 192–3, 196
  "The Nobel Lecture in Literature" 397, 399
Mudrick, Marvin 163
Murray, Simone 62, 65, 66
Musila, Grace 194, 195

Nagle, Rebecca 85
Ndebele, Njabulo 190, 191

Nnaemeka, Obioma 267
Nobiss, Cherry 85–6
Noire, *G-Spot* 72, 79
Nottage, Lynn, *Ruined* 19n.20, 396–7
O'Connor, Frank 376
Ovid 327, 329
"Philomela" 136–40, 142, 145–6, 147n.1, 147n.2, 329

Page, Ruth 91
Pain, Rachel and Lynn Staeheli 191
Painter, Nell Irvin 344, 347
Parks, Rosa 49, 341
Pember, Mary Annette 90
Pierce-Baker, Charlotte 6
Pizan, Christine de, *The Book of the City of Ladies* 324, 327–9, 330
Plantiga, Carl 181, 184n.4
Pranis, Kay and Carolyn Boyes-Watson 293
Prendergast, Thomas A. and Stephanie Trigg 333
Price, Devon 117, 122, 124
Price, Margaret 232
Pugh, Tison 329, 333
Pulley, Natanya Anna 90
Purkayastha, Sharmila 147

Quashie, Kevin 232
Quayson, Ato 266
Quijano, Aníbal 300

Raditlhalo, Sam 191
Radstone, Susannah and Katharine Hodgkin 61
Rajan, Rajeshwari S. 181
Ramsey, Martha 45
Reade, Tara 101, 106–7
Reagon, Bernice Johnson 231
Reed, T. V. 4
Renker, F. W. 376
Richardson, Samuel, *Clarissa* 170

Roberts, Dorothy 278, 279, 280–1, 283, 285n.3, 362
Robertson, Elizabeth and Christine M. Rose 323
Rodino-Colocino, Michelle 315, 324, 330, 332
Romero, Channette 208
Romesburg, Don 368
Rothfeld, Rebecca 114, 115
Roupenian, Kristen, "Cat Person" 107–9, 375–6, 379, 381–2

Salmon, Marylynn 154
Sánchez-González, Lisa 298, 300
Sánchez, Marta E. 367
Sapphire, *The Kid* 200, 203–5
Push 203
Saunders, Corrine 323, 325, 327
Scanlon, Suzanne, "Final Exam" 114
"The Rape Essay (or Mutilated Pages)" 127n.2
Scherer, Migael 51
Schulman, Sarah 218, 219n.2
Scott, Joan W. 45
Sebold, Alice, *Lucky* 47, 52, 256n.3
Sedgwick, Eve Kosofsky 378, 381
Serisier, Tanya 4, 6–7, 18n.15, 15, 330
Sesaki, Betty 229
Shakespeare, William, *The Tragedy of Titus Andronicus* 139
Shapiro, Mary, *Wallace's Dialects* 123, 125
Sharp, Christina 364
Sidhwa, Bapsi, *Cracking India* 176, 181–3
Sifuentes-Jáuregui, Ben 373n.10
Sims, J. Marion 347–8
Sinner, Anita 376

Smith, Valerie 66, 285n.5
Solnit, Rebecca 46, 152, 391, 393, 395
Somerville, Kristine and Speer Morgan 376
Souljah, Sister (Lisa Williamson), *The Coldest Winter Ever* 71, 76–9
Spallacci, Amanda 181
Spearing, A. C. 326
Spillers, Hortense 363, 372n.3
Stanton, Elizabeth Cady, "Solitude of Self" 314
Stratton, Florence 266–7
Surviving R. Kelly 344
Sweet, Paige L. 166

Talusan, Grace, *The Body Papers* 314, 316–17
Tamblyn, Amber, *Any Man* 200, 206–9
Tatum, Karen 393
Thomas, Clarence 101, 341
Thomas, Piri, *Down These Mean Streets* 361–2, 366–71
Tillet, Salamishah and Scheherazade Tillet 343
Tlali, Miriam 187
Tlhabi, Redi, *Khweze: The Remarkable Story of Fezekile Ntsukela Kuzwayo* 187
Toulmin, Stephen E. 227
Tracy, Steven C. 285n.5
Traister, Rebecca 106
Trujillo, Rafael 214, 220n.9
Trump, Donald 16, 85–6, 101, 106
Trump, Melania 107
Truth, Sojourner, *The Narrative of Sojourner Truth* 343, 344
Turner, Brian, "Insignia" 389–92, 399
Tyree, Omar, *Flyy Girl* 72, 74–5, 79

Udel, Lisa 86
Udwin, Leslee, *India's Daughter* 177
Unbelievable 2, 358
Uraizee, Joya 180, 183

Valenti, Jessica 393
 Sex Object 60, 65–6, 311, 314–15, 319n.1
Valentino, Marilyn 236
Villarosa, Linda 285n.3
Vogel, Paula, *How I Learned to Drive* 354–6, 358
Vuong, Ocean, "A Letter to My Mother She Will Never Read" 375–6, 382–4

Wade, Lisa 256n.3
Waldman, Katy 140
Walker, Lenore 393
Wall, Cheryl 34–5
Wallace, David Foster 113–27
 "Brief Interview #20" 119–21, 128n.11
 Brief Interviews with Hideous Men 114, 116, 118, 119, 126
Walsh, Kelly and Terry Murphy 381
Warshaw, Robin, *I Never Called It Rape* 4, 46
Washington, Harriet A. 285n.3
Waymack, Anna Fore 333
Weinstein, Harvey 1, 2, 31, 99, 101–2, 137
Wessels, Emanuelle 156, 157
Whitley, Leila and Tiffany Page 230
Whitlock, Gillian 60
Williams, Caroline Randall 275
Williams, Sherley Anne, *Dessa Rose* 393

Williams, Tennessee, *A Streetcar Named Desire* 351, 353, 357, 358
Wimsatt, William K. and Monroe C. Beardsley, "The Intentional Fallacy" 115, 122, 127
Winfrey, Oprah 38, 71
Wofthal, Diane 323

Yanagihara, Hanya, *A Little Life* 200–3
Yellin, Jean Fagan 4, 18n.16, 346
Yergeau, Melanie 231

Zane (Kristina Lafrene Roberts), *Addicted* 79
Zhou, Xiao 380